Digital Currency and Consumption

The digitalization of payment modes, combined with the development of Blockchain technology, is shaping the future of digital currency worldwide. Many financial regulators are experimenting with the feasibility of digital currencies nationally in a variety of forms, such as cryptocurrency, virtual currency and central bank digital currency. These digital currencies are just some of those discussed in this book. Each facilitates a transaction efficiently and will likely open an alternative payment system, possibly leading to a global digital currency.

This book will present and highlight a broad view of digital currency in the era of globalization. This book will address the meaning of money in a global world. By going beyond fungible national fiat-based currencies to global cryptocurrency and stablecoins, virtual currencies promise to disintermediate and decentralize money. The digital currencies that are the focus of this book use the internet for transactions and harbor the potential to make a unified digital currency system across the globe. This book explores the role of digital currency in influencing consumer behavior, from spending or saving to gaming, tipping and gambling. It asks what is the future of digital currency and what is its role in facilitating and transforming the future of the metaverse?

Digital Currency and Consumption will be useful reading for a postgraduate audience to understand how digital currencies are shaping the digitalization of transactions and behavior of consumer citizens. It will be of value to researchers interested in a wide variety of disciplines, including international business, finance and consumer behavior.

Jashim Khan is Associate Professor of Marketing and Director of International Business Management at the Surrey International Institute, University of Surrey, UK and Dongbei University of Finance and Economics, China. He earned a doctorate in business marketing from Auckland University of Technology and a Master of Management (with distinction) degree from Massey University in New Zealand. His research is concerned with understanding the influence of emerging technologies on consumer behavior. His work appears in various international journals such as the *Journal of Business Research*, *Journal of Economic Psychology*, *Association for Consumer Research*, *Asia Pacific Journal of Marketing and Logistics*, *International Journal of Non-profit and Voluntary Sector Marketing*, *Journal of Wine Research*, *International Journal of Wine Business Research*, *International Journal of Online Marketing*, *Journal of Product & Brand Management*, *Journal of Marketing for Higher Education*, *Qualitative Market Research*, *Journal of Retailing and Consumer Services*, *Journal of International Consumer Marketing* and *Qualitative Market Research: An International Journal*.

Russell Belk is York University Distinguished Research Professor, Royal Society of Canada Fellow and Kraft Foods Canada Chair in marketing at the Schulich School of Business at York University. His research involves the extended self, meanings of possessions, collecting, gift-giving, sharing, digital consumption and materialism. He co-initiated the Association for Consumer Research (ACR) Film Festival, the Consumer Culture Theory (CCT) Conference and the Consumer Behavior Odyssey. He is the past president and fellow in ACR and has over 750 publications including more than 30 in the *Journal of Consumer Research*. This work is primarily qualitative and is often conceptual, visual and cultural. In 2012, a ten-volume compendium of his work was published in the Sage *Legends in Consumer Behavior* series. In 2023, he received a Doctorate Honoris Causa from Université de Reims Champagne Ardenne with a festschrift and volume in his honor.

Routledge Studies in Marketing

This series welcomes proposals for original research projects that are either single or multi-authored or an edited collection from both established and emerging scholars working on any aspect of marketing theory and practice and provides an outlet for studies dealing with elements of marketing theory, thought, pedagogy and practice.

It aims to reflect the evolving role of marketing and bring together the most innovative work across all aspects of the marketing 'mix'—from product development, consumer behavior, marketing analysis, branding and customer relationships, to sustainability, ethics and the new opportunities and challenges presented by digital and online marketing.

45 **Money and Marketing in the Art World**
Henrik Hagtvedt

46 **Interfaith Marketing**
A Cross-Religious Approach
Frank Cabano, Stefan Müller and Katja Gelbrich

47 **Decolonizing Marketing Theory and Practice**
Beyond Inclusivity and Sustainability Debates
Edited by Hasan Gilani

48 **The Future of Charity Marketing**
Edited by Sarah-Louise Mitchell and Fran Hyde

49 **Digital Currency and Consumption**
The Meaning of Money in an Era of Digital Currency
Jashim Khan and Russell Belk

For more information about this series, please visit: www.routledge.com/Routledge-Studies-in-Marketing/book-series/RMKT

Digital Currency and Consumption

The Meaning of Money in an Era of Digital Currency

Jashim Khan and Russell Belk

Routledge
Taylor & Francis Group
LONDON AND NEW YORK

First published 2025
by Routledge
4 Park Square, Milton Park, Abingdon, Oxon OX14 4RN

and by Routledge
605 Third Avenue, New York, NY 10158

Routledge is an imprint of the Taylor & Francis Group, an informa business

British Library Cataloguing-in-Publication Data
A catalogue record for this book is available from the British Library

Library of Congress Cataloging-in-Publication Data
Names: Khan, Jashim, author. | Belk, Russell W., author.
Title: Digital currency and consumption : the meaning of money in an era of digital currency / Jashim Khan and Russell Belk.
Description: Abingdon, Oxon ; New York, NY : Routledge, 2025. | Series: Routledge studies in marketing | Includes bibliographical references and index. |
Identifiers: LCCN 2024041195 (print) | LCCN 2024041196 (ebook) | ISBN 9781032544618 (hardback) | ISBN 9781032544656 (paperback) | ISBN 9781003425021 (ebook)
Subjects: LCSH: Digital currency. | Money. | Consumer behavior.
Classification: LCC HG1710 .K43 2025 (print) | LCC HG1710 (ebook) | DDC 332.4—dc23/eng/20241107
LC record available at https://lccn.loc.gov/2024041195
LC ebook record available at https://lccn.loc.gov/2024041196

ISBN: 978-1-032-54461-8 (hbk)
ISBN: 978-1-032-54465-6 (pbk)
ISBN: 978-1-003-42502-1 (ebk)

DOI: 10.4324/9781003425021

Typeset in Sabon
by codeMantra

This book is dedicated to some exceptional women: our mothers, our wives, and their children and grandchildren.

Jashim Khan and Russell Belk

Contents

List of Figures *xi*
List of Tables *xiii*
List of Contributors *xv*
Preface *xvii*
JASHIM KHAN AND RUSSELL BELK
Acknowledgments *xix*
List of Abbreviations *xxi*

1 **Money in the Age of Global Digitalization** 1
JASHIM KHAN AND RUSSELL BELK

2 **Money in Digital Assets** 15
JASHIM KHAN AND RUSSELL BELK

3 **Money in Digital Currencies** 42
JASHIM KHAN AND RUSSELL BELK

4 **Psychological Ownership of Digital Currencies** 83
JASHIM KHAN AND RUSSELL BELK

5 **Pushes and Pulls in Switching to Digital Currencies** 105
JASHIM KHAN AND RUSSELL BELK

6 **The Meaning of Money in Cryptocurrency** 130
JASHIM KHAN, RUSSELL BELK AND ANSAR ABBASS

7 **The Meaning of Money in Digital Game Currencies** 143
JASHIM KHAN, RUSSELL BELK, NA ZUO AND ANNE BANIKEMA

8 **The Meaning of Money in Tipping Currencies** 165
JASHIM KHAN AND RUSSELL BELK

9 Generation Z, Digital Currencies and Luxury Purchase 186
JASHIM KHAN, RUSSELL BELK AND GARY RIVERS

10 Generation Z and Irrational Exuberance: Spending in the Present, Speculating and Investing for the Future 204
JASHIM KHAN AND RUSSELL BELK

11 Digital Currency Issues in the Metaverse 219
JASHIM KHAN, RUSSELL BELK, ANSAR ABBASS AND KHALID MEHMOOD

12 Social Currency in the Metaverse 236
JASHIM KHAN AND RUSSELL BELK

Case Study One: Marshall Island's Sovereign Currency 255
JASHIM KHAN AND RUSSELL BELK

Case Study Two: China's e-CNY or Digital RMB 261
JASHIM KHAN AND RUSSELL BELK

Case Study Three: Japan's Digital Currency 270
NA ZUO, JASHIM KHAN AND RUSSELL BELK

Index 277

Figures

2.1	Word Cloud: Digital Assets	26
2.2	Average Likes within Themes	26
3.1	Central Bank Digital Currency Stability	53
3.2	Central Bank Digital Currencies Content Categories	55
3.3	Central Bank Digital Currency Economy	55
3.4	Digital Currency Consumption	56
4.1	Conceptual Model	98
5.1	Proposed Conceptual Model	113
7.1	Microtransaction, Flow State, Impulse Buying Tendency	149
8.1	Word-cloud Representation of Tipping Currency	175
8.2	Likes by Classification of Category	175
8.3	Public Engagement	176
9.1	Research Model	191
9.2	Path Coefficients Results	196
10.1	Word Cloud 1	210
10.2	Word Cloud 2	212
10.3	Word Cloud 3	213
11.1	Personal Data Formation in the Metaverse	220
11.2	Digital Currencies in Metaverse	221
11.3	Blockchain Components in the Metaverse	225

Tables

2.1	Characteristics of Financial Digital Assets	18
2.2	Characteristics of Digital Non-financial Assets	23
3.1	Central Bank Digital Currency	47
4.1	Reliabilities and VIF Values	93
4.2	Discriminant Validity	94
4.3	Path Coefficients Results	95
4.4	Important-Performance Analysis	96
5.1	Respondent Profile	117
5.2	Reliability and Validity	118
5.3	Discriminant Validity	119
5.4	Structural Model Results	120
7.1	Convergent Validity Indexes	152
7.2	Discriminant Validity Indexes	153
7.3	Direct and Indirect Effects	154
8.1	Codes, Category and Themes	178
9.1	Participants Profile	193
9.2	Convergent Validity	194
9.3	Discriminant Validity of Conceptual Model	195
12.1	Metaverse Currencies and Tokens	241

Contributors

Ansar Abbass is a Doctoral Candidate at the School of Business Administration, Dongbei University of Finance and Economics, Dalian, China. His research interests include digital marketing, brand management and metaverse research, with a specific focus on consumer behavior. His research has been published in the *Journal of Management Sciences* and the *International Journal of Business Information Systems*.

Annie Banikema is a Research Professor of Management Science at the University of Évry. Specializing in marketing, her research focuses on the behavior of the consumer and the consumer. It pays particular attention to consumer resistance behavior and alternative consumption strategies.

Khalid Mehmood is a Doctoral Candidate at the Center for Service Intelligence at Ghent University, Belgium. Khalid is passionate about disruptive technologies, interactive marketing and service research, with a specific focus on personalization and customer experiences. His research has been published in the *Journal of Service Marketing* and the *Journal of Service Management*, among other places.

Gary Rivers is the University of Surrey's (UoS) Dean (Operations) posted at the Surrey International Institute (SII), which is located on the partner campus of Dongbei University of Finance and Economics (DUFE) in Dalian City, China. As the senior UoS representative *in situ*, he covers various management and leadership functions at the Surrey International Institute.

Na Zuo is Senior Lecturer in Marketing at the Surrey International Institute, University of Surrey. She has rich industrial experience internationally. Her research interests include consumer behavior, digital currency and higher education studies. Her work has appeared in international journals.

Preface

Jashim Khan and Russell Belk

With the development of Blockchain technology, the digitalization of payment modes defines the future of digital currency (Khan et al., 2015). Many financial regulators worldwide are experimenting with digital currencies nationally, such as cryptocurrency, virtual currency and central bank digital currency. These digital currencies are, among others, discussed in this monograph. Each facilitates transaction efficiency and will likely open an alternative payment system, possibly leading to a global digital currency. This monograph will present and highlight a broad view of digital currency in the era of globalization.

The monograph will address what money is becoming in a global world. By going beyond fungible national fiat-based currencies to global cryptocurrencies and stablecoins, virtual currencies promise to disintermediate and (usually) decentralize money. Virtual currencies of various types (e.g., non-fungible tokens, digital game currency and gambling tokens) and Central Bank Digital Currencies are the topics covered. With the partial exception of digital game currencies, gambling and tipping tokens in livestream commerce aren't currencies because they are non-fungible monies and can't be exchanged for fiat currencies in other contexts. A digital currency is any currency, money or digital asset managed, stored, transferred and exchanged digitally over the Internet (Mullan, 2014). Unlike electronic currency accounts that can be converted to cash (fiat money) from an ATM, it never takes physical form. The digital currencies that are the focus of the volume used on the Internet for transactions and harbor the potential to make a unified digital currency system across the globe are discussed. The globalization of digital currency entails the digital facilitation of payments across borders, competing with the existing payment system.

Within this context, this monograph explores the role of digital currency in influencing digital citizenship and consumer behavior. It will be valuable reading for a postgraduate audience who wants to understand how digital currencies are shaping the digitalization of transactions and payments in the financial sector. Simultaneously, the possibilities of digital currencies will be of interest to researchers interested in fintech (DeFi), finance and international trade.

The motivation for this monograph is interdisciplinary and involves a multimethod approach compilation from different disciplines on the outlook for digital currencies. This necessitates collecting appropriate data from Asia, Europe and North America. One research objective is to determine the methodologies—qualitative and quantitative approaches including historical research, systematic, comprehensive literature reviews, surveys, case studies and ethnographies/netnographies—best suited to understanding the uses, impediments and potential for digital currency in the real world as well as virtual worlds like the currently touted metaverse. The central theme of the monograph is the future of digital currency. What is its role in facilitating and transforming the future of the metaverse? Postgraduate audiences from business, finance, behavioral finance, fintech, consumer finance, international business and sociology disciplines will find the content of this book useful.

This book considers our global future with digital assets and currencies.

Introduction to Digital Currency Consumption

Globalization traces its roots to industrialization, with reducing production costs and increasing economies of scale as the drivers of global trade. In the 20th century, we witnessed the World Wide Web connecting the globe and the digital transformation of electronic payments, containerization and supply chain efficiency. With this understanding, this section addresses an important area of digital currency consumption underpinning the concept of money as a social agreement and the meaning of money in digital currency.

The worldwide fast-tracking of cashless payment adoption became a reality during COVID-19, and the exclusion of Russia from the SWIFT system brought a turbulent period of unified global currency consumption. COVID-19 altered peoples' perceptions of traditional money, so it came to be seen as contaminated and dirty. People thought it was contaminated and would spread COVID. The perceptions of money have far-reaching impacts on behavior such as spending and saving. The digital commodification of payment modes influences spending, saving, speculation, gaming and gambling. One such influence is in lessening the perceived pain of paying (Zellermayer, 1996) through the decoupling effect (Raghubir & Shrivastava, 2008) and tangibility (Khan et al., 2015), which distinguishes digital payment from payments with cash. Thus, intermediated mechanisms like Airbnb that make payments and receipts go through them rather than directly between host and guest.

Next, we draw from classical and current literature to unpack money as a social agreement in the age of digitalization.

Acknowledgments

We are expressing our deepest gratitude and appreciation for the assistance and support we received throughout the completion of this monograph. We want to acknowledge the contributions of all people and institutions that have played a significant role in its completion.

We thank all the co-authors for their contributions to this monograph.

We want to express our heartfelt thanks to our peers and colleagues for their constructive feedback and excellent collaboration, which enriched the intellectual discourse of this monograph project.

Our sincere gratitude for the support provided by the Surrey International Institute, Dongbei University of Finance and Economics, China, and the University of Surrey, UK, providing student research assistant team: Cao Xunmeng, Kong Yangyang, Chen Weixin, Bai Ruiyan, Li Mingxuan, Zhang Jiaxiang, Xia Yiming, Li Xingyu and Li Yuman. Thank you all for participating in research-related activities; all your assistance is unforgettable. These resources were crucial to complete this monograph research successfully.

We acknowledge the editorial team's and reviewers' contributions, strengthening the research project's clarity and consistency.

Heartfelt thanks to family members for being there consistently with us. Thank you.

Once again, we are grateful to all those who have contributed immensely to our academic journey.

Jashim Khan and Russell Belk

Abbreviations

5G	Fifth Generation
AI	Artificial Intelligence
AIDA	Awareness, Interest, Desire and Action
AR	Augmented Realities
AML	Anti-Money Laundering
ATM	Automated Teller Machine
AVE	Average Variance Extracted
BIC	Business Identifier Codes
BIS	Bank for International Settlements
BRICS	Brazil, Russia, India, China and South Africa
BYAC	Bored Apes Yacht Club
CBDC	Central Bank Digital Currency
COVID-19	Coronavirus Disease 2019
CR	Composite Reliability
DAG	Directed Acyclic Graph
DAO	Decentralized Autonomous Organization
dApps	Decentralized Applications
DDoS	Distributed Denial-of-Service
DeFi	Decentralized Finance
DeFi AMMs	Decentralized Finance Automated Market Makers
DEX Protocol	Direct Exchange Protocol
DLT	Distributed Ledger Technology
e-CNY	China's Digital Yuan
ECB	European Central Bank
FL	Factor Loadings
FOMO	Fear-of-Missing-Out
G20	Group of 20
GAN	Generative Adversarial Networks
GDP	Gross Domestic Production
GNN	Graphical Neural Network
GOF	Goodness of Fit
HKMA	Hong Kong Monetary Authority
HTMT ratio	Heterotrait-Monotrait Ratio

ID	Identification
IGD	Internet Gaming Disorder
ILP	Interledger Protocol
ILV	Illuvium
IMF	International Monetary Fund
IMPA	Importance-Performance Analysis
iOS	iPhone Operating System
IoT	Internet of Things
K-anonymity	Re-identifiability of Data
L-diversity	ℓ-diversity/Anonymity
mCBDC	Multiple Central Bank Digital Currency
NFT	Non-Fungible Token
P2P network	Peer-to-Peer Network
PBOC	People's Bank of China
PIN	Personal Identification Number
PLS-SEM	Partial Least Square Structural Equation Modeling
POS	Proof of Stake
POW	Proof of Work
PPM	Push-Pull-Mooring
QR code	Quick-Response Code
RMB	Ren Min Bi (Chinese Currency)
RPG	Role Playing Game
SEM	Structural Equation Model
SNX	Synthetix Network Token
SPOF	Single Point of Failure
SWIFT	Society for Worldwide Interbank Financial Telecommunication
TAM	Technology Acceptance Model
UAE	United Arab Emirates
VIF	Variance Inflation Factor
VR	Virtual Realities
wCBDC	Wholesale CBDC
YOLO	You Only Live Once

References

Khan, J., Belk, R. W., & Craig-Lees, M. (2015). Measuring consumer perceptions of payment mode. *Journal of Economic Psychology*, *47*, 34–49.

Mullan, P. (2014). *The digital currency challenge: Shaping online payment systems through US financial regulations*. Springer.

Raghubir, P., & Srivastava, J. (2008). Monopoly money: The effect of payment coupling and form on spending behavior. *Journal of Experimental Psychology: Applied*, *14*(3), 213.

Zellermayer, O. (1996). *The pain of paying*. Carnegie Mellon University.

1 Money in the Age of Global Digitalization

Jashim Khan and Russell Belk

Philosophy of Money

The Economic Perspective

Mainstream economists agreed in the 18th century that their discipline specialized in studying wealth (Gough, 1936; Parsons, 1937; Baker, 1987; Snelders et al., 1992; Ingham, 1998). Gold is a commodity that was considered wealth (Roy, 2012). Representative money was one possible form of measurement of wealth where value was pegged to precious metals representing the value in use. Adam Smith proposed that money is a measure of the 'wealth of a nation' and that wealth is associated with commodities or advantages that a nation possesses. He regarded wealth as being due to the commodities or natural resources and assets generating comparative advantages of nations. The concern with wealth has since dominated classical economic thought. How is the wealth that money represents derived? Does it arise from natural assets, or could it be trust in the currency? In classical economics, money is a measurement of value, a medium of exchange, a measure of account and a means of storing value (Keynes, 1930; Grierson, 1977; Furnham & Lewis, 1986; Hicks, 1989; Graziani, 2004). Classical economics views money as something that can be stored and circulated because it is essentially tangible. This reflects the dominance of the commodity theory of money in the 18th and 19th centuries (Ingham, 2004). For these classical economics, social agreement existed that gold and silver were scarce materials and thus a valuable store of wealth.

John Stuart Mill (1862, 1871) recognized the need to understand money at the individual rather than the societal level, thus shifting the discussion of money. Within this framework, monetary issues became the subject of a science that dealt with one of many human motives: the desire to maximize wealth. Mills noted that the

> love of money is not only one of the strongest moving forces of human life, but money is, in many cases, desired in and for itself; the desire to possess it is often stronger than the desire to use it and goes on

DOI: 10.4324/9781003425021-1

increasing when all the desires which point to ends beyond it, to be compassed by it.

Classical economics maintains:

- that money is a tangible entity; that the value of precious metals determines the value it contains or represents (Helfferich, 1927),
- that value is determined by the supply and demand of the material constituting the entity and cost of production (Graziani, 2003),
- that the variation in the quantity of money causes price movement and not vice versa (Laughlin, 1924) and
- that the bank's liabilities in the form of notes and bills of exchange were acknowledged as part of the money supply only if they were convertible into gold and/or silver (Petty, 1963).

Marx criticized Mill's economic assumptions. A key characteristic of Mills (and other classical economists) is that they emphasize the interests of the capitalist class, excluding the socialism of money from consideration. In the 19th and 20th centuries, new ideas in economics emerged. There are two dominant theories: marginal utility and general equilibrium. According to marginal utility theory (Jevons, 1879), consumption maximizes the total utility received from goods and services. Despite the criticisms, prominent economists suggest that utility maximization remains a fundamental pillar of economic thought (Friedman, 1953). Assuming that millions of individuals maximize their utility, general equilibrium theory considers both the actions of producers and consumers. Based on this view, money remains a medium of exchange and a store of value. A commodity concept of money implies that the token has intrinsic value and/or represents tangible sources of wealth rather than abstract ones, such as society's trust in the currency (Moor, 2020).

The Sociological Perspective

Social scientists have not studied the social production of money per se. Instead, they focused on understanding the social effects or meanings of money—namely, its value as a social tool, especially regarding status and power (Eatwell et al., 1992). According to Ingham and Zelizer (2004, 1994), money and its meanings are socially constructed. This means the value measure depends on human judgment resulting from social interaction and agreement. Three scholars, Weber, Parsons and Simmel dominated the initial sociological theories of money. Aside from sociological issues, Weber did not devote much attention to monetary theory and money, and he largely relied on Knapp's (1924) *State Theory of Money*. Weber integrated economics and social aspects of money in an integrated manner where supply and demand determine the price of a commodity, and money plays an important role in ensuring individuality, personal freedom and intellectualism in society. In his view, money is not just a medium of exchange but an instrument for assigning values to all products and services in society. Talcott Parson dominated sociological thought for many years with his view of money. Parson viewed money as a tool for controlling resource processes and emphasized its power relationship. The value of money can function as a measure of value and an exchange medium, and it can also serve as a reward and a facility. As a control mechanism, power is a step above money since it can control a monetary system. According to Ingham (2004), the Parsonian sociology of money failed to consider that dominance is not only the result of money's position but also of states' and banks' control over the process of money production.

According to Habermas (1979), Luhmann (1988) and Giddens (1990), money is a symbolic token of exchange (see Ingham, 2004). In Simmel's view, money represents abstract value that does not derive from the cost of its production, supply and demand, or labor time value—rather, it represents "the value of things without the things themselves" (Simmel, 2004/1900, p. 21). Turner (1999) points out that Simmel viewed money as a medium that promotes individuality, freedom and intellectualism within a society (Turner, 1999).

Other researchers also began to examine the concept of money from a cultural perspective. Mauss (1914/2015) observed that money is "essentially a social fact" and attaches to various social relations rather than individuals. Mauss (1914/2015) critiqued Mill's (1862) view of money from an individual perspective and insisted that the meaning of money was derived from social arrangements that were taken for granted by individuals. The idea that cultural values and social relationships shape money's meaning has accumulated consensus among sociologists (e.g., Baker & Jimmerson, 1992; Poggi, 1993; Zelizer, 1989, 1994; Dodd, 1994; Carruthers & Babb, 1996; Wuthnow, 1996; Singh, 1997). Zelizer (1994, p. 18) contended that money can be seen as socially constructed, shaped by social relations, and as something that also "exists outside of the market and is profoundly influenced by cultural and social structures. In addition, 'values and social relations reciprocally transmute money by investing it with meaning and social positions.'" The meaning of money changes depending on use: domestic (shopping/grocery), investment, inherited and gifted uses, for example. Money that enters the household can come from income from employment, welfare money and other sources. Each type of money is regarded as different, and use and status can differ (Bohannan, 1955; Douglas, 1967; Zelizer, 1994). Singh (1997) also suggests that money has a different meaning across different contexts. For instance, a joint account in marriage shows trust and togetherness. Cultural identity also shapes the meaning of money (Demosthenous et al., 2006). Fleming et al. (1997) suggest that the meaning of money changes based on the payment method. The study contrasted forms of payment using credit card payment and cash payment for the ritual of a Maori funeral in New Zealand. Pahl (1999) indicates that literacy and gender play a role in how the meaning of money is derived within social class.

History and Origin of Money

Early Period

The known history of money is traced to the Bronze Age in Mesopotamia through discoveries by archaeological studies. The Bronze Age saw irrigation and farming shaping the organization of community settlements in one place. Division of labor fueled the expansion and growth of Babylonian economies. The surplus of agricultural produce further exploited the expansion of trade with other communities. These increased interactions and exchanges contributed to the rise of social structures. As a result, keeping records of these exchange activities was necessary for the era. The necessity to organize compelled early civilizations to rely on recording activities and transactions on stones, tree barks and even tallying sticks to record debt and credits (Rosenswig, 2024). Over time, these recordings of debit and credit became the fundamental basis of trade and exchange (Van de Mieroop, 2005). Ancient Mesoamerica is one such example of organized communities. Others can be found in the Americas such as Olmec, Zapotec, Maya, Toltec and Aztec (Urban & Schortman, 2024). The ancient Egyptian, Mesopotamian, Greek, Indus and Chinese civilizations document and provide evidence of money and economic recording systems. In the same way, Mesoamerica flourished through farming and domestication of animals, resulting in various professións, mythologies, numeric record keeping, farming and ball playing (Carrasco & Sessions, 2000).

The archaeological evidence of such recordkeeping exists from the Mesopotamian and Egyptian societies (c. 3000 to 500 BC). "Primitive societies used clay tokens stored in sealed clay balls, called bullae, a kind of contract that specified the commitment of future payments (e.g., tribute to the temple, taxes, or loans)" (Goetzmann, 2017, p. 24). Abstract symbols on the surface of hollow and fist-sized clay envelopes depicted the number and types of tokens inside. These evolved into inscribing pictographs into clay tablets and accounting symbols into a cuneiform, the world's first writing (Van de Mieroop, 2005). The cuneiform, a clay certificate, was used to record agricultural surpluses and deficits in production. These clay tokens symbolize economic commodities and record transactions traded with other organized societies. Chinese clay money (*ní qián*), a special type of burial money, was unearthed recently. It dates to 1300 BCE and indicates recording and transactions within organized societies. The first known (gold) coins date from c. 640 BC in the Near Eastern Kingdom of Lydia, with gold and silver accorded the highest value (Davies & Davies, 1998).

Graeber (2011) investigated how clay tokens may have been symbolic of organizing exchange activities as debts within social relations, such as marriage, barter, friendship, slavery, war and statesmanship. The organization of the debt economy relied on a promise to pay it back. His idea of debt traces back to the Sumerian civilization around 3500 BCE, where priests and temples were the political and administrative center. The clay tablets recorded the contribution and distribution of commodities such as barley, cattle and individuals' obligation to pay the temples, marriage payments and the capital invested in trade with other communities. These temples may have been the predecessor of modern-day banks. The credit economy was typically organized through advances in agricultural goods and interest-bearing pay. Often, interest was paid in the form of labor or pledged by family members or servants who, at times, were added to the balance of payments. Similarly, the risk and transportability of these commodities for high-value transactions gave way to representative money, e.g., gold and silver. Representative money was socially regarded as valuable because of its intrinsic qualities and entered circulations as a means of payment. Advance payment was an innovation whereby private contractors, such as tax farmers (middlemen), would balance and convert payments in kind using gold and silver. This god and silver became the standard unit of currency in which governments and societies set the price of commodities and labor payments (Graeber, 2011).

The next major upheaval in the history of money is related to the axial period (Jaspers, 1953), in which religious and philosophical thought coincided in various locations from about the 8th to 3rd century BCE. Religions including Buddhism, Hinduism, Daoism, Judaism, Christianity, Islam and philosophers such as Socrates, Pythagoras, Buddha, Mahavira, Confucius and Lao Tse (Baumard et al., 2015, p. 2) enlightened societies during times and places where there was a heavy reliance on gold and silver coins. This period coincided with the growth of the military coinage slave complex (Graeber, 2011) based on war and violence, the use of mercenary armies, looting and prisoners cut off from their societies. They were sold as slaves in major empires (Chamberlin, 1983). The extreme violence of the period produced great empires in China, India and the Mediterranean. The war strategy in China, India and the Mediterranean was to amass a large number of slaves, use gold coins for soldiers' salaries and taxes, and trade with other nations using gold/silver currencies.

At the height of the axial period, Greek philosophers begin systematically thinking about money in general within the context of society and the state, focusing on the nature of monies and their functions within societies. Plato was credited with considering money in its symbolic form as a means of exchange, and Aristotle thought of coins (gold and silver) as a social innovation constituting superior quality and a commodity that has intrinsic exchange value and function as measure, medium and store of value (Fuller, 2020). Aristotle's coinage concept of representative money prevailed as it led to the practical concerns of the time—the debasement of coinage by authorities.

The Middle Age

The Middle Ages saw the developmental period of the banking system. This included promissory notes, paper money, letters of credit, bills of exchange and cheques. This also aligned with advancing legal systems, public institutions and technological inventions to enforce standard rules and contractual commitments. The concept of banking developed in the port of Piraeus in Greece, where 'trapezitai' (ancient bankers) took deposits and provided loans for maritime traders (Ferguson, 2008). This period oversaw the written contracts to document loans and commitments from debtors to repay. This was the basis for letters of credit and bills of exchange, which first appeared in India and Rome and later led to cheques by Arab merchants to settle accounts. Due to access to transactions throughout its vast empire, the Roman Empire is officially credited with banking services such as money transfers or lending services.

Paper money was a Chinese invention in the 9th century, initiated by private merchants issuing bills of exchange (Jiaozi) in paper circulation. The empire supported paper money by controlling its issuance and operation within a large, unified territory. However, this later became unpopular due to excessive use and associated inflation.

In the 16th century, colonial conquest and the slave trade from West Africa across the Atlantic to work in plantations and mines resulted in a massive amount of gold and silver extracted from the American continent. This stimulated the emergence of a bullion economy for international trade. From the mid-16th century, lawyers acted as loan brokers and started issuing nontransferable personal credit letters on deposits. Goldsmiths turned to the issue of endurable promissory notes for their trade-in bullion (Cassis & Cottrell, 2015). In Amsterdam, the "Wisselbank" was founded in 1609 and started denominating accounts in standardized currency (Fergusson, 2008, p. 48). In Stockholm, the Sveriges Riksbank issued banknotes, and London's private bank, the Bank of England, issued cash notes payable to bearers on demand in 1694; this period saw the true emergence of representative paper money backed by bullion.

Post-World War II

The collapse of the Bretton Woods system in the 1970s ended the bullion economy, and the US government abandoned the gold standard in 1971. Representative money led to fiat money—the type used today. Fiat money does not represent an asset; its value comes from being a legal tender backed by the issuing government. This includes money in circulation, such as paper money or coins. Fiat money is backed by countries or a union of states. Here, the government, rather than a physical commodity or financial instrument, guarantees the value of these tokens. This passage of money returns to credit money with derivatives, speculations and uncertainties. The US dollar dominates world currencies. As a result, the dollar has acquired this status because of its ability to increase its quantity through debts and deficits and, most significantly, because the Federal Reserve has unrestrained authority to create money, enabling the United States to accumulate 34 trillion dollars of debt by 2024. The prominence of the US dollar as the world reserve currency continues if the United States maintains its status as the world's preeminent military power and the client states trust the currency and are eager to pay seignories for US government bonds.

Next, we discuss the tribulations of commodity-backed representatives and the advancement of fiat money to digital currencies. This treatment will bring us nearly to the current day.

Tribulations of Commodity-Backed Representative Money

Graziani (2004) describes paper money as a unit of account and a means to store and transport abstract value (Keynes, 1930; Hicks, 1989). This abstract value is stored and transported by the monetary system, according to Weber (1920). The value of these notes and coins can only be embodied through social agreement, eliminating the need to anchor the token's value to the time and space of any particular transaction. The representative paper money was more accessible and safer than gold. Through the usage of cash and coins, people grew to trust paper certificates as much as gold.

When cash crops (commodities), such as tobacco or tea, serve as the medium of exchange, this poses a problem that farmers, in their self-interest, would grow the commodity in abundance and beget inflation within the society. Also, given the variability in the quality of cash crops, there was a tendency for lower quality commodities to replace the higher quality commodities. Gresham's law distills the notion: "the tendency for a lower quality commodity (bad money) to drive a higher quality commodity (good money) out of circulation." According to Gresham's law, "bad money drives out good money." It is possible, for instance, for the more valuable commodity to gradually disappear if two forms of commodity money have similar face values and are circulated and accepted by law.

The issues of the quality of commodities as money encourage the issuance of gold and silver money. One of the significant problems with gold and silver was that they were scarce metals and the scarcity or abundance of gold inflated or deflated the economy. For example, the city of Sardis of ancient Lydia, some 25,000 years ago, issued pure coins into circulation and was primarily immune to inflation. It did not take long for rulers to discover that adding small amounts of other base metals can significantly increase wealth. The Roman currency, the denarius, saw its value gradually decrease as Roman rulers altered the coin's size and silver content (Malanima, 2009). The original silver content was nearly pure, weighing about 4.5 grams, reduced to 4.0 grams during the Julio-Claudian dynasty, and almost lost 1.0 grams by the rule of Nero. The denarius continued to shrink in size and purity until it had only 2% silver content before being replaced by the Argenteus (Harl, 1996). Debasement lowers the intrinsic value of the coinage to allow more coins to be minted with the same quantity of precious metal (Redish, 2000). Gold and silver declined and became unpopular within societies because of debasement. Similarly, gold discoveries in certain countries aggravated the situation for others who did not have gold deposits (Goodman, 1981). Countries lacking gold experienced the inflation set off by the increase in the supply of gold in circulation in other countries. Until the mid-20th century, most coins used as currency were made of rugged, cheap metals such as steel, copper or a copper–nickel alloy, reducing wear and making it difficult and unprofitable to debase them (Desjardins, 2016).

Understandably, societies agreed on representative paper money (certificates), which have no intrinsic value but represent something of value, such as gold or silver, following the gold standard. The gold standard in modern times lasted from the 1870s to the early 1920s and from the late 1920s to 1932 (Eichengreen, 2019). Following the Second World War, the Bretton Woods system pegged all currencies to the US dollar and the dollar to a gold reserve, which led to the collapse of the gold standard. At the official price of $35 per ounce, the United States promised to provide gold on demand in exchange for dollars accruing from foreign central banks (Bernholz, 2006). Gold was the fixed value of all currencies pegged to the dollar. Although the system worked well initially, problems emerged when deficit countries with overvalued currencies refused to devalue their national currency. Similarly, surplus countries enjoyed trade competitiveness and had no incentive to revalue their national currencies (Bernstein, 1984). This situation led to the crash of the Bretton Woods system in 1971, when the world reserve currency, the US dollar, abandoned the gold standard, and all major currencies turned to fiat money. Fiat money is not backed by a precious metal, such as gold or silver, though the value is pegged to world reserve currency, such as the US dollar, and risk assurance by the issuing government. Fiat money has value through social agreement, which individuals use as a unit of account (Dror, 2001).

Electronic-Fiat Currencies

Bank-Issued Payment Card

Technological advancement in the financial sector produced magnetic cards, ATMs and, importantly, SWIFT after the Bretton Wood Agreement in the 1970s. SWIFT stands for Society for Worldwide Interbank Financial Telecommunications and is a member-owned cooperative of safe and secure financial transactions worldwide banking network. The first bank cards were issued by Barclays in London in 1967 (Wonglimpiyara, 2017) and Chemical Bank in Long Island, New York, in 1969 (Wonglimpiyara, 2017). Using a personal identification number for security, Lloyds Bank issued the first bank card with a magnetic strip that encoded information. In the mid-1980s, credit and debit cards became more widely used.

The electronic payment system brought an additional set of social agreements (Khan et al., 2015), one placed on the SWIFT network and banking system and the second issuing government role in creating and safeguarding monetary system within societies. This moves to an electronic form of money instituted trust in the banking institutions, which safeguards user data safety and security of the payment networks. The system assigns each member of the bank a unique code (e.g., BIC), which identifies the bank name and the country, city and branch. The SWIFT system accommodates all electronic banking, including credit and debit cards, mobile banking and online banking. While the United States championed the SWIFT system reliant on back-based magnetic stripped and chip-based card systems, China leapfrogged the card system with its own QR code (two-dimensional bar codes) and the software to allow the new payment system to operate via mobile devices.

Third-Party Mobile Payments

Mobile payment is a platform-based payment system used mainly with WeChat and Alipay. They dominate the Chinese market, and Jingdong Pay is prevalent in the e-commerce platform J.D.com, which competes with the dominant players (Auer et al., 2021). WeChat Pay and Jingdong Pay dominate the retail market, and Alipay controls the business-to-business market. Convenience, ease of use, trust and app design facilitate mobile payments. Mobile transactions reached ¥110.4 trillion in 2019 and ¥500 trillion in 2023. The COVID-19 pandemic in 2020 facilitated mobile payments in China.

The mobile payment system disintermediates banks from payment transactions and places users' trust in a third-party merchant, removing banks' role as transaction clearing agencies. The third-party payment service links buyers and sellers via the platform. Consumer trust is placed in the platform, which clears those transactions. Consumers can pay retailers indirectly via third-party payment, which charges commissions for payments and then transfers the rest to the retailers. Decoupling the bank from the consumer and seller adds data safety and security risks.

Past 2008 Financial Crisis and Emergence of Cryptocurrencies

Fast forward to 2008 and the emergence of cryptocurrencies; the financial crisis of 2008 caught the world by surprise and caused a significant loss of public confidence in the current monetary system and the institutions supporting it. It undermined the legitimacy of the global financial systems, and the mechanism utilized to deal with such a crisis led to a movement to find an alternative monetary system. Against this backdrop, the promotion of Bitcoin on the global stage established the first peer-to-peer electronic cash, which was introduced by someone using the name Satoshi Nakamoto to develop "a purely peer-to-peer digital cash which would allow online payments to be sent directly from one party to another without going through financial institutions" (Nakamoto & Bitcoin, 2008, p. 8). Nakamoto proposed a blockchain ledger system that does not rely on the trust of third-party agents, thus fundamentally questioning money as a social agreement. The system placed the 'trust' element on cryptographic proofs that verify the integrity of information about a transaction in a decentralized network of computers. Bitcoin provides automation of trust through blockchain and distributed ledger technology. Using cryptographic signatures, the algorithm records transactions in blocks and adds them to the chain of existing blocks. Distributed ledgers require that all or permission groups of participants validate new blocks and maintain the entire history of transactions. The system's security is strengthened by repeatedly replicating the same ledger (Berg et al., 2019). Satoshi Nakamoto disappeared and has never been identified (Humayun & Belk, 2018).

Digital Currencies

A rapid shift in technological innovation transmuted the global economy and initiated the digital age. The most recent transformation has been central bank digital currency, a shift in focus from cryptocurrency and fintech. The cryptocurrency boom 2017–2021 witnessed the incursion of private currencies, such as Bitcoins, Ethereum and Litecoin, as a media of exchange or investment. Limited supply to demand led to price hikes, making crypto-based assets volatile, vulnerable and incidental fluctuations, eroding their prospects as a media of exchange in day-to-day transactions (Katsiampa et al., 2019). Central banks and some governments worldwide placed immediate bans on crypto assets. China, Bolivia, Indonesia, Turkey and Egypt were the first to ban it. The United Kingdom, Singapore and Kenya warned citizens of the potential risk of using cryptocurrencies. The movement toward the central bank's authority over controlling money in society was brought back with digital currency. Cryptocurrencies crashed in 2022 but rose again in 2024, as we write this, partly because crypto funds were legalized in the United States.

China's digital RMB was the first digital currency issued by a major economy. Carapella and Flemming (2020) define CBDC digital currency as the digital equivalent of central bank-issued cash. One main difference with physical cash is that it remains digital, not pegged to any physical commodity (Ozili, 2021). Central banks issue these currencies to support financial services and commercial banking. The central government controls monetary policies, such as issuance and interest rates, and regulates digital currency issuance, operation and flow within the financial market (Kiff et al., 2020). Currently, China has launched its central bank digital currency. Fifteen are in the piloting path, another 26 countries are currently developing and 45 are in the development phase of the digital currency for their nation (Badaik et al., 2024). The People's Bank of China (PBOC) launched the first digital currency in the world. The PBOC began researching digital fiat currencies in 2014 and experimented in several cities only (Xu, 2022). Due to China's economic environment, people have gradually become accustomed to cashless payments (Xu, 2022), rapidly shifting to electronic payments.

References

Auer, R., Frost, J., Gambacorta, L., Monnet, C., Rice, T., & Shin, H. S. (2021). Central bank digital currencies: Motives, economic implications and the research frontier. *SSRN Electronic Journal*, *976*(976), 1–28. https://doi.org/10.2139/ssrn.3922836

Badaik, D., Chinnaraju, K. T., Kamath, S., Ramesh, V. L., Sathiyamoorthy, R., Namachivayam, L., & Kamath, R. (2024). Development of research on continuous usage intention of M-Wallets: A systematic review of literature from 2011 to 2021. *Journal of Advanced Research in Applied Sciences and Engineering Technology*, *35*(1), 156–172.

Baker, W. E. (1987). What is money? A social structural interpretation. In Mizruchi, M. S. & Schwartz, M. (Eds.), *Intercorporate relations* (pp. 109–144). Cambridge University Press.

Baker, W. E., & Jimerson, J. B. (1992). The sociology of money. *American Behavioral Scientist*, *35*(6), 678–693.

Baumard, N., Hyafil, A., Morris, I., & Boyer, P. (2015). Increased affluence explains the emergence of ascetic wisdoms and moralizing religions. *Current Biology*, *25*(1), 10–15. https://doi.org/10.1016/j.cub.2014.10.063

Berg, C., Davidson, S., & Potts, J. (2019). *Understanding the blockchain economy: An introduction to institutional cryptoeconomics*. Edward Elgar Publishing.

Bernholz, P. (2006). *Monetary regimes and inflation: History, economic and political relationships*. Edward Elgar.

Bohannan, P. (1955). Some principles of exchange and investment among the Tiv. *American Anthropologist*, *57*(1), 60–70. https://doi.org/10.1525/aa.1955.57.1.02a00080

Carapella, F., & Flemming, J. (2020, November 09). *Central bank digital currency: A literature review*. FEDS Notes. Board of Governors of the Federal Reserve System. https://doi.org/10.17016/2380-7172.2790

Carrasco, D., & Sessions, S. (2000). *Mesoamerica's classic heritage: From Teotihuacan to the Aztecs*. University Press of Colorado.

Carruthers, B. G., & Babb, S. (1996). The color of money and the nature of value: Greenbacks and gold in postbellum America. *American Journal of Sociology*, *101*(6), 1556–1591. https://doi.org/10.1086/230867

Cassis, Y., & Cottrell, P. L. (2015). *Private banking in Europe: Rise, retreat, and resurgence* (Vol. 1). Oxford University Press.

Chamberlin, R. (1983). *Loot! The heritage of plunder*. Thames and Hudson.

Davies, G., & Davies, R. (1998). A comparative chronology of money: Part 1: From the origins of agriculture to the industrial revolution. *Journal of Management History*, *4*(3), 160–185.

Demosthenous, C., Robertson, B., Cabraal, A., & Singh, S. (2006, October 25–26). *Cultural identity and financial literacy: Australian aboriginal experiences of money and money management*. In *Financial Literacy, Banking and Identity Conference*, Storey Hall, RMIT University, Melbourne, Australia. http://bit.ly/3Arzlr1

Desjardins, J. (2016). This infographic shows how currency debasement contributed to the fall of Rome. *Business Insider*. https://www.businessinsider.com/how-currency-debasement-contributed-to-fall-of-rome-2016-2

Dodd, N. (1994). *The sociology of money: Economics, reason and contemporary society*. Polity Press.

Douglas, M. (1967). Primitive rationing. In R. Firth (Ed.), Themes in economic anthropology (pp. 119–145). Tavistock.

Dror, D. M. (2001). Reinsurance of health insurance for the informal sector. *Bulletin of the World Health Organization*, *79*(7), 672–678.

Eatwell, J., Milgate, M., & Newman, P. (1992). *The new Palgrave dictionary of money and finance*. Springer.

Eichengreen, B. (2019). *Globalizing capital: A history of the international monetary system*. Princeton University Press.

Ferguson, N. (2008). *The ascent of money: A financial history of the world*. Penguin.

Fleming, R., Taiapa, J., Pasikale, A., & Easting, S. K. (1997). *The common purse*. Auckland University Press.

Friedman, M. (1953). *Essays in positive economics*. University of Chicago Press.

Fuller, E. W. (2020). Introduction: The Aristotelian monetary tradition. In Fuller, E. W. (Ed.), *A source book on early monetary thought* (pp. 1–7). Edward Elgar Publishing.

Furnham, A., & Lewis, A. (1986). *The economic mind: The social psychology of economic behaviour*. Wheatsheaf.

Giddens, A. (1990). *The consequences of modernity*. Polity Press.

Goetzmann, W. N. (2017). *Money changes everything: How finance made civilization possible*. Princeton University Press.

Goodman, G. J. W. (1981). Paper money. Summit Books.

Gough, I. (1936). *The social contract*. Oxford University Press.

Graeber, D. (2011). *Debt: The first 5,000 years*. Melville House.

Graziani, A. (2003). *The monetary theory of production*. Cambridge University Press.

Graziani, A. (2004). *Money, credit, and the role of the state: Essays in honour of Augusto Graziani*. Ashgate Publishing.

Grierson, P. (1977). *The origins of money*. Athlone Press.

Habermas, J. (1979). *Communication and the evolution of society*. Heinemann.

Harl, K. W. (1996). *Coinage in the roman economy, 300 B.C. to A.D. 700*. Johns Hopkins University Press.

Helfferich, K. (1927). *Money* (Vol. 1). Adelphi Company.

Hicks, J. (1989). *A market theory of money*. Clarendon Press.

Humayun, M., & Belk, R. W. (2018). "Satoshi is dead. Long live Satoshi": The curious case of bitcoin's creator. In Cross, S. N. N., Ruvalcaba, C., Venkatesh, A., & Belk, R. W. (Eds.), *Consumer culture theory* (Vol. 19, pp. 19–35). Emerald Publishing Limited.

Ingham, G. (1998). Money is a socialrelation. In Fleetwood, S. (Ed.), *Critical realism in economics* (pp. 117–138). Routledge.

Ingham, G. (2004). *The nature of money*. Polity.

Jaspers, K. (1953). *The origin and goal of history* (M. Bullock, Trans., 1st English ed.). Routledge.

Jevons, W. S. (1879). *The theory of political economy*. Macmillan.

Katsiampa, P., Corbet, S., & Lucey, B. (2019). High-frequency volatility co-movements in cryptocurrency markets. *Journal of International Financial Markets, Institutions and Money*, *62*, 35–52. https://doi.org/10.1016/j.intfin.2019.05.003

Keynes, J. M. (1930). *A treatise on money*. Macmillan & Co.

Khan, J., Belk, R. W., & Craig-Lees, M. (2015). Measuring consumer perceptions of payment mode. *Journal of Economic Psychology*, *47*, 34–49. https://doi.org/10.1016/j.joep.2015.01.006

Kiff, J., Alwazir, J., Davidovic, S., Farias, A., Khan, A., Khiaonarong, T., Malaika, M., Monroe, H., Sugimoto, N., Tourpe, H., & Zhou, P. (2020). A survey of research

on retail central bank digital currency. *IMF Working Papers*, *20*(104), 130. https://www.imf.org/en/Publications/WP/Issues/2020/06/26/A-Survey-of-Research-on-Retail-Central-Bank-Digital-Currency-49517
Knapp, G. F. (1924). The state theory of money. Macmillan.
Laughlin, J. L. (1924). The quantity-theory of money. *Journal of Political Economy*, *32*(3), 265–281.
Luhmann, N. (1988). *Die wirtschaft der gesellschaft* (Vol. 2). Suhrkamp.
Malanima, P. (2009). Premodern European economy: One thousand years (10th–19th centuries). *European Review of Economic History*, *13*(2), 189209.
Mauss, M. (1914/2015). *The gift: Forms and functions of exchange in Archaic societies*. Andesite Press.
Mill, J. S. (1862). *Principles of political economy: With some of their applications to social philosophy* (2 Vols.). Verlag Wirtschaft u. Finanzen.
Mill, J. S. (1871). *Principles of political economy*. Longmans, Green, Reader, and Dyer.
Moore, C. (2020). *It's money* (Vol. 3). Charles.
Nakamoto, S. (2008). *Bitcoin: A peer-to-peer electronic cash system*. https://bitcoin.org/bitcoin.pdf
Bernstein, E. M. (1984). Bretton woods at forty: Do we need a new Bretton woods? *IMF eLibrary*, *21*(3), 5–9. www.elibrary.imf.org/display/book/9781451973495/ch04.xml
Nowzad, B., Nawaz, S., Landell-Mills, J., Meehan, S., Stoddard, R., & Salzer, D. (2021). *Annual report on exchange arrangements and exchange restrictions*.
Ozili, P. K. (2021, October). Financial inclusion research around the world: A review. *Forum for Social Economics*, *50*(4), 457–479.
Pahl, J. (1999). *Invisible money: Family finances in the electronic economy*. Policy Press.
Parsons, T. (1937). *The structure of social action*. Free Press.
Petty, W. (1963). *The economic writings of Sir William Petty*. Routledge.
Poggi, G. (1993). Money and the modern mind: George Simmel's philosophy of money. *The British Journal of Sociology*, *44*(4), 716–718.
Redish, A. (2000). *Bimetallism: An economic and historical analysis*. Cambridge University Press.
Rosenswig, R. M. (2024). The first economic record keepers: The earliest evidence of accounting and writing in Mesoamerica. *Antiquity*, *98*(379), 1833.
Roy, D. (2012). *The power of money*. Vij Books India Pvt. Ltd.
Simmel, G. (2004/1900). *The philosophy of money* (3rd enlarged ed.; D. Frisby & T. Bottomore, Eds.). Routledge.
Singh, S. (1997). *Marriage money: The social shaping of money in marriage and banking*. Allen & Unwin.
Snelders, H. M. J. J., Hussein, G., Lea, S. E. G., & Webley, P. (1992). The polymorphous concept of money. *Journal of Economic Psychology*, *13*(1), 71–92. https://doi.org/10.1016/0167-4870(92)90053-a
Turner, B. S. (1999). *Classical sociology*. Sage.
Urban, P. A., & Schortman, E. M. (2024). The sociopolitical organization of Mesoamerican cities: A comparative perspective. *Journal of Urban History*, *50*(2), 198–217.
Van de Mieroop, M. (2005). *The invention of writing in Mesopotamia*. Cambridge University Press.

Weber, M. (1978 [1920]). *Economy and society* (Vol. 2), Roth, G. & Wittich, C. (Eds.). University of California Press.

Wonglimpiyarat, J. (2017). Fintech banking industry: A systemic approach. *Foresight, 19*(6), 590–603.

Wuthnow, R. (1996). Poor Richard's principle: Recovering the American dream through the moral dimension of work, business, and money. *American Journal of Sociology, 101*(6), 1641–1642.

Xu, J. (2022). Digital payments and e-CNY: The future of payments in China. *Journal of Payment Systems and Strategy, 16*(3), 187–202.Zelizer, V. A. (1989). The social meaning of money: "Special monies." *American Journal of Sociology, 95*(2), 342–377. https://doi.org/10.1086/229272

Zelizer, V. A. (1994). The creation of domestic currencies. *The American Economic Review, 84*(2), 138–142.

2 Money in Digital Assets

Jashim Khan and Russell Belk

Definitions of Digital Assets

> Van Niekerk (2006, p. 53) *defines a digital asset as "any text or media items that have been formatted into a binary source and include the right to use." The key characteristics of digital assets imply security, transparency, flexibility, and control, all of which define an asset.*
>
> Kaal (2020, p. 911) *refers to "digital currency as digital assets that cover all types of virtual and electronic assets, regardless of how they are otherwise named or categorized by regulatory agencies, including cryptocurrencies, security tokens, utility tokens, virtual assets, virtual collectibles, stablecoins, altcoins, among others." Digital assets can be distinguished from stocks because stocks are not inherently digital and have strong ties to the world of hard assets. "Bitcoin is a purely digital asset because it only exists in the virtual world."*
>
> In another definition, "*Digital financial assets can be represented by instruments such as cash, equity instruments, or contractual rights. The concept of "Digital assets" is identical to the concept of "electronic assets" or "virtual assets." It is substantiated that digital financial assets include such groups of digital assets represented by payment tokens and tokens in securities, and utilitarian tokens are not financial assets*".
>
> (Havva & Haponiuk, 2023, p. 246)

Digital assets initially referred to physical media, such as photos, videos and documents, which were later converted into digitized formats during the 1980s and 1990s (Newell, 2012). This transition from analog to digitization in various industries and government sectors led to the development of global databases and infrastructure supporting digital transformation, enabling data to be created, stored and shared in digital environments as an asset (Lafioune et al., 2024). At the start of the 21st century, the global financial crisis of 2008 and the emergence of distributed ledger technologies and decentralized cryptocurrencies hyped interest in 'digital assets' among financial market participants and stakeholders. Havva and Haponiuk (2023) focused on tokenized electronic or virtual assets representing financial assets.

DOI: 10.4324/9781003425021-2

These financial digital assets lack clarity on what constitutes the classification of non-financial assets. Van Niekerk (2006) broadly classified all digital content as digital assets, while Kaal (2021) differentiated financial digital assets from stocks. The present research demystifies digital assets by categorizing them into financial and non-financial logic.

Financial Digital Asset

Digital financial assets are assets that exist in digital form and are traded or held electronically (Girich et al., 2022). They are usually created using decentralized ledger technologies, which ensure security, transparency and immutability (Antal et al., 2021) (see the types of digital financial assets in the Addendum of Chapter 2, Appendix 1).

Kochergin (2022, p. 7) states that:

> crypto assets are.... private digital assets ... not issued and are not guaranteed by state authorities...., embody values or rights recorded electronically in a distributed ledger... protected cryptographically and are used as a means of payment and savings and/ or for investment....

These characteristics of crypto assets distinguish them from other financial assets, such as central bank digital currency (Bullmann et al., 2019). The term 'digital assets' is typically associated with financial assets and can be traced back to Nick Szabo, who first introduced the term 'bitgold' in 1998 (Lubogo, 2022). Bitgold was intended to be a decentralized digital currency that operates independently of central bank control and serves as a store of value (Raskin & Yermack, 2018). Its proof-of-work method allowed for the recording and verifying of time-stamped blocks, like the Bitcoin blockchain. Bitgold's cryptographic and mining properties contributed to its decentralization, but Szabo never implemented its scalability characteristic (De Filippi & Loveluck, 2016).

Ten years later, Satoshi Nakamoto introduced Bitcoin as a cryptocurrency in a white paper. Bitcoin is a peer-to-peer digital currency powered by blockchain technology and operates outside the central bank authority. Distributed ledger technology (DLT) provides both security and efficiency when transferring non-fungible tokens (NFT) (Singh, 2024). Following the rise in popularity of Bitcoin, numerous alternative virtual currencies, also known as 'altcoins,' were introduced, such as Litecoin in 2011—the first altcoin. Challenging Bitcoin's consensus process, Litecoin utilized a new proof-of-work algorithm called Scrypt, which consumed significantly less energy and enabled much faster transactions (Cagli, 2019).

In 2014, stablecoins were introduced to overcome issues with Bitcoin volatility. They aim to eliminate the risk of unpredictability while still retaining the advantages and innovations of cryptocurrencies (Ferreira, 2021). Stablecoins allow for smooth and secure peer-to-peer cross-border transaction capability and exhibit lower volatility because they are pegged to fiat currency (Li & Shen, 2021). With the introduction of stablecoins, central bank digital currencies (CBDCs) and tokenized securities, it is expected that the market capitalization of stablecoins will continue to grow. However, in the long term, CBDCs may surpass stablecoins. Ethereum was the first public blockchain to introduce smart contracts, which led to the rise of decentralized finance (DeFi) and NFTs. Like Litecoin, Ethereum switched to a faster, more energy-efficient proof-of-stake verification method in 2022.

The term 'digital assets' has been used to describe financial innovations and cryptocurrency since Bitcoin was introduced in 2008. However, the emergence of terms like 'cryptocurrency,' 'digital assets,' 'crypto assets' and 'virtual assets' has confused the general population. This creates a need to clarify how digital financial assets are characterized and categorized, especially with the rise of DLT and central bank digital currency.

Based on the literature in Table 2.1, we define digital financial assets as

> Digital financial assets, representing e-money in a digital format, are considered financial assets that can be converted to other financial assets when the owner wishes to do so (Zatti & Barresi, 2024). Other assets, such as gold or silver, are also realizable and convertible with tokenization applications and may represent fungible non-fungible and semi-fungible tokens.
>
> (Hofmann, 2020; Mowbray et al., 2023)

Digital financial assets include central bank digital currencies, cryptocurrencies and tokens, which convey financial value as universally accepted and supported by the market's supply-and-demand principles.

Types of Financial Digital Assets

Cryptocurrencies and NFTs are two different types of investable and financial digital assets. NFTs, asset-backed NFTs and tokenized real estate are transforming the digital asset market. The definition of financial digital assets has expanded to include assets backed by a distributed ledger. This means that physical assets like real estate and commodities can be tokenized for digital trading, creating new opportunities for financial digital asset marketplaces. The emergence of investable financial digital assets in the financial services industry presents a new opportunity for investment in a rapidly growing sector supported by scalable technology that can digitally transform into financial digital assets.

Cryptocurrencies

One of the most well-known forms of digital financial assets is cryptocurrency, such as Bitcoin and Ethereum. Blockchain technology secures these

Table 2.1 Characteristics of Financial Digital Assets

Characteristics	*Definition*	*Explanation and Examples*	*Key Reference*
Distributed ledger technology	Using distributed ledger technology (DLT), decentralized applications can be created without a central authority that registers, shares and synchronizes digital asset transactions. (Antal et al., 2021)	**Blockchain:** Records transactions in multiple networks to provide security and transparency (Wijesekara & Gunawardena, 2023) **Hashgraph:** Uses consensus called gossip about gossip and virtual voting to achieve consensus (Hoxha, 2019) **Tangle:** A directed acyclic graph (DAG) aims to solve scalability and transaction fee issues (Hellani et al., 2021) **Holochain:** Designed to be agent-centric rather than data-centric (Parmar & Vaghani, 2022) **Corda:** Designed for financial institutions and allows central authority to view transactions (Panda et al., 2022) **Hyperledger Fabric:** Permissioned blockchain allows the creation of private, permissioned blockchains (Rao et al., 2020) **Quorum:** Ethereum-based permissioned blockchain for financial institutions; allows for private transactions (Amiri et al., 2021)	Antal et al. (2021); Bokolo (2022); Huibers (2024); Bellaj et al. (2024); Cheng et al. (2024); Kizza (2024); Inshakova et al. (2024)
Interoperability	Interoperability refers to the ability of blockchain networks or distributed ledger technologies (DLTs) to communicate, interact and transact with each other seamlessly (Belchior et al., 2023). Also refers to the ability to use avatars and other digital assets across platforms.	**Cross-Chain Transactions:** Allows assets or tokens to move between different blockchains or DLT protocols, e.g. Ethereum to Binance (Belchior et al., 2023) **Standardization of Protocols:** Provide common standards to communicate using Interledger Protocol (ILP) for cross-border payments and Atomic Swaps for direct transfer (Ren et al., 2023) **Wrapped Tokens:** Wrapped tokens are digital financial assets pegged to the value of another digital financial asset (Gottschalk, 2023) **Smart Contract:** Smart contracts execute transactions and interact with assets across different blockchains (Khan et al., 2021) **Regulatory and Compliance Interoperability:** Ensure compliance with regulatory requirements across different jurisdictions (McIntosh et al., 2024) Platforms: Polkadot, Cosmos, Wanchain, Chainlink	Diallo et al. (2024); Barbu et al. (2024); Bokolo (2022); Pillai et al. (2019); Chiu and Wong (2022); Milkau and Bott (2015)

Tokenization	A token is a digital representation of an asset in physical or online form. Blockchain can represent cryptocurrencies like Bitcoin or Ether and can be fungible, non-fungible, or semi-fungible assets (Mazzei et al., 2020).	**Real Estate:** Tokenization enables investors to own fractions of properties, offering access to real estate markets with lower entry barriers (Gupta et al., 2020) **Stocks and Equities:** Companies tokenize shares, allowing for fractional ownership such as dividend payments and shareholder voting (Baum, 2021) **Commodities:** Tokenization of commodities, such as gold or oil, can simplify trading and settlement on blockchain platforms (Tian et al., 2022) *Art and Collectibles:* Investors can own and trade shares of valuable artworks or collectibles through tokenization (Barbereau et al., 2022)	Chaleenutthawut et al. (2021); Efimova et al. (2024); Stankevich and Vlasov (2024); Zhang et al. (2024)

digital currencies through cryptography. Cryptocurrencies can be used for various purposes, such as investing, speculation and payment (Lewis, 2018).

NFTs

NFTs mean that the asset's unique token can be authenticated to prove it belongs to its owner. NFTs allow users to own unique assets such as artworks and media recordings (Popescu, 2021).

Asset-Backed Tokens

Physical assets such as gold and oil can be tokenized and traded among users on the blockchain using asset-backed tokens. By doing this, liquidity problems can be solved, and a broader range of investors and users can access these assets (Benedetti & Rodríguez-Garnica, 2023).

Tokenized Commercial Real Estate

As with asset-backed tokens, commercial real estate can now be tokenized. This process may allow more investors to access ownership opportunities with improved liquidity, more transparency for proofs of ownership and simplified transaction procedures (Gupta et al., 2020).

DeFi

Decentralized digital ledgers record asset ownership and exchanges as a core component of digital assets. A central party maintains a private ledger of assets that contrasts with traditional assets recorded in a private ledger. This change describes a system allowing consumers to trade digital assets without needing a traditional financial institution like a bank.

Anything digitally stored and uniquely identifiable that organizations can use as a source of value is considered a digital asset. Examples of non-financial digital assets are documents, audio, video, logos, slide presentations, spreadsheets and websites (Kaal, 2020).

Non-Financial Digital Asset

A non-financial digital asset is any digital document, audio file, video, or other relevant digital data that resides on a computer, laptop, portable media player, tablet, or data storage device that is not linked to a financial transaction (Mauthe & Thomas, 2004; Seel, 2022). This encompasses any devices currently in existence or those that will be developed to support new forms of digital assets (Bekaert et al., 2006). This applies regardless of the ownership of the physical device where the digital asset is stored.

We define non-financial digital assets based on Belk's (2020) commodification and Bardhi and Eckhardt's (2017) liquid consumption. A non-financial digital asset is any digital asset that does not represent a traditional financial instrument, such as currency, stocks, bonds, or commodities. Instead, they are digital collectibles, intellectual property, domain names, identities and digital profiles, decentralized governance systems and NFTs containing ownership of proof. These assets are intangible and liquid, rendering value-added services and consumption in modern life involves resources, such as efforts, time and money, to establish digital possessions. This often includes transforming non-material goods into sellable content with market value. For instance, a host on Airbnb may compete with other hosts for super host status to attain the super host status and demand better service and guest ratings in the reputation rating system. The associated reputation rating influences the marketability of shared accommodation on the Airbnb platform, and the super host status is an asset manifesting in financial rewards. With market competition and the accessibility of digital tools, individuals seize the opportunity to overcome financial constraints by creating non-financial digital content, hoping to capitalize on its value in their personal and private businesses.

Yi et al. (2023) illustrate non-financial digital assets such as sales promotion in live-stream commerce: private sales of previously unmarketable agricultural products in e-commerce platforms. The growth of digital content is linked to evolving lifestyles in a technology-driven environment, increased digital content creation and engagement in private businesses. This process described by Belk (2020) as commodification involves rendering goods saleable or exchangeable, suggesting that they can be replaced by something of equal value, whether money or something else. This interchangeable nature means that time and effort spent on creating digital content could be capitalized in digital business. Commodification can transform personal digital content into assets that can be traded in the market (Belk, 2020). Digital content brings flexibility, adaptability, fluidity, lightness, detachment and speed to people's daily lives (Bradhi & Eckhardt, 2017).

From these two perspectives, digital content involves sharing intangible possessions without permanently transferring ownership, though shared documents over the platform must follow the terms of service of the platform owners. With the increasing recognition of digital ownership rights and the emergence of virtual goods, our concept of what can be owned expands to the digital context. Photos, videos and memes are emerging as parts of digital collections on digital platforms. The collection of digital gifts, mementos, souvenirs, heirlooms, monuments and pets is becoming part of everyday digital life (Belk, 2013). This form of digital ownership, such as sharing, leasing, communal ownership and collaborative consumption, expresses our identity and creates sociality, though it hinders the inheritance of digital content (Belk, 2014). This sharing occurs over the platform, and the terms of service of the service provider limit the rights of the content creator, as rightly explained by Beier and Porter (2013, p. 5):

> It is the worst nightmare for a parent. Seemingly out of nowhere, your 15-year-old son commits suicide. You search for answers, finding none. Like all teenagers his age, your son spent much time on his computer, particularly on the Facebook website. So, you hope to find some answers by accessing his account. The problem is that Facebook refuses your request, stating that you have no rights to access or obtain a copy of the content within your own son's account.

A digital non-financial asset involves digital content or files stored on a computer that can be accessed or shared with others. These files are typically stored on a storage drive, website, or in an online account. Digital assets can take various forms, including privately created or publicly curated music, videos, medical records, tax documents, financial records and photographs. Accessing most of this digital content requires a login ID and password. Other non-market assets include social media accounts used for social interaction, messaging and connecting with other individuals. These accounts are considered digital content. We often use secure access accounts in our daily lives, such as email accounts, private domain names, or blogs. However, these may become inactive once we are no longer present.

In summary, a non-financial digital asset is a digital representation of something that has value or utility but is not directly related to traditional financial instruments such as currencies or securities (Table 2.2).

The definition of non-financial digital assets includes:

- Non-financial digital assets that do not function as payment instruments may potentially act as stores of value; the value of these assets arises from their usefulness, uniqueness, or scarcity in digital business.
- Non-financial digital assets can be digital collectibles, website or domain names, digital content, online reputation and customer databases. With the ubiquitous nature of digital innovations, this list will grow.
- Non-financial digital assets gain value through collaborative efforts, and market forces determine the value. As a result, any digital content itself is not a financial asset.
- Non-financial digital assets are non-fungible, and their ownership is possessed by individuals and the platforms that store the digital content. If left unprotected, these assets eventually become public goods once made available to the world.

Ownership

Ownership in the market determines whether assets are traded, leading to financial transactions influenced by the interaction of supply and demand

Table 2.2 Characteristics of Digital Non-financial Assets

Characteristics	*Definition*	*Explanation and Examples*	*Key Reference*
Collectibles	Digital collectibles are unique digital items that can be collected, bought and sold. They often exist on blockchain platforms, including digital art, trading cards, or virtual pets (Fairfield, 2022).	**Blockchain:** Ownership or proof of authenticity of a particular item or piece of content is assigned by blockchain technology (Ali & Bagui, 2021) **Ownership and Authenticity:** NFTs enable creators and owners to verify ownership and authenticity of their digital assets transparently and securely (Popescu, 2021) **Value and Speculation:** The value of digital collectibles can vary widely based on factors such as scarcity, demand and the reputation of the creator (O'Dwyer, 2020) **Virtual Games:** Often integrated into online games, serve as status symbols, in-game assets and virtual commodities (Macák & Šašalová, 2022) **Types:** Digital art, virtual trading cards, virtual real estate, digital fashion items, virtual pets and more. Any digital file or representation tokenized and owned can be a digital collectible. **Platforms:** Some popular platforms include OpenSea, Rarible and NBA Top Shot	Varadarajan and Seeni (2024); Wong (2022); Nagpal (2021); Allen et al. (2022)
Website/ domain name	Website addresses that can be bought and sold, often for significant sums depending on their perceived value (Toygar et al., 2013; Soukupová, 2024)	**Ownership and Control:** A domain name or website address is registered to gain ownership and control over a website or platform address. It is considered a digital asset for its unique address (McConaghy & Holtzman, 2015). **Value:** Domain names with short, memorable, or popular keywords hold significant financial value (Kesmodel, 2008) **Intellectual Property:** Domain names are intellectual property and can be protected by trademark laws (Johnson, 2001) **Liquid Asset:** Domain names can be relatively liquid assets compared to physical properties, as they can be transferred or sold relatively quickly (Sun, 2022)	Cheng (2024); Hamroun et al. (2024); Vitalii (2024)

(*Continued*)

Table 2.2 (Continued)

Characteristics	*Definition*	*Explanation and Examples*	*Key Reference*
Digital content	Digital content is any information or material developed and distributed via the Internet or other digital networks.	**Textual Content:** Articles, blogs, eBooks, digital magazines and other written materials are distributed electronically. **Visual Content:** Images, photographs, infographics, illustrations and digital art. **Audio Content:** Music tracks, podcasts, audiobooks and sound recordings. **Video Content:** Short videos, films, documentaries, tutorials, vlogs and animations **Interactive Content:** Games, quizzes, interactive stories, simulations and virtual reality experiences. **Educational and Training Content:** Online courses, tutorials, webinars and educational resources. **Types:** Digital media such as eBooks, online courses, music, videos, podcasts and software programs sold, licensed, or distributed online.	Kaal (2020); Berlin (2024); Zalan and Toufaily (2024)
Online reputation	Search engine results, social media profiles, online reviews and the influence of digital communities are all parts of online reputation, which is considered a digital asset.	**Digital Identity:** The culmination of all online activities, such as blogs, webpages, social media profiles and other digital footprints (Mario Lavizzari et al., 2021; Church, 2015) **Online Testimonials:** A positive online reputation is bolstered by reviews and testimonials on sites like Youku, Facebook, Yelp, Google, Baidu and LinkedIn. (Sharad et al., 2024) **Digital Networking:** Connections and relationships formed online through professional networking platforms like LinkedIn **Search Engine Visibility:** Search engine results for relevant keywords related to profiles can enhance reputation online (Morrison, 2024) **Content Ownership and Creation:** Content such as articles, videos, podcasts, or digital artwork contribute to online presence (Gandini, 2016)	Lefebvre and Vershinina (2024); Arshad and Bukhari (2024)
Customer databases	Customer contacts, user databases and analytical data provide insights about customers.	**Customer Information:** Customer databases store valuable information such as contact details, purchase history, preferences, demographics and other relevant data (Park & Youm, 2021). **Blockchain-based Certificates:** Digital certificates stored on a blockchain provide proof of ownership, authenticity, or provenance for physical or digital assets.	Gu et al. (2017)

(Ho, 2023). Non-market ownership refers to assets that are not primarily traded in a marketplace or do not have a value determined by market forces (Watkins et al., 2016; Fia, 2021). These assets may be held for reasons other than financial gain and managed under different ownership models, such as access-based ownership, leasing, communal and collaborative ownership (Belk, 2014, 2018). The distinction between financial and non-financial digital assets is significant regarding ownership and possession (Kochergin, 2022). Ownership of financial assets is conducted through transfer or exchange due to established markets and legal frameworks (Athanassiou, 2016). Non-market ownership restricts non-financial digital assets' ability to transfer outside the digital community (Watkins et al., 2016), requiring value-adding additives to transform non-final digital assets into financial ones.

Market ownership of financial digital assets has a clear market value based on supply and demand, whereas non-financial digital assets lack a universally agreed exchange rate. NFTs may be relevant to gaming, art, cultural exploration and other areas where the sharing of emails and database information does not fit into traditional supply-and-demand algorithms. However, non-fungible assets may still enter competitive marketplaces, challenging dominant central bank digital currency. Profit motives often drive market ownership of non-financial digital assets.

In other large economies globally, governmental control and regulation over non-financial digital assets are limited due to a lack of legislation or legal precedent (Bull, 2020). Individuals and firms maintain most of the control issues related to access and transferability. In summary, non-financial digital assets encompass various digital representations of value and ownership, revolutionizing finance, commerce and digital interactions. They offer new opportunities for innovation and economic empowerment while presenting challenges that require careful consideration and management.

Meaning of Money with Digital Assets

The word cloud below (Figure 2.1) was designed using Python to visualize the dataset's most frequently occurring words related to digital assets. This visual representation highlights the collective focus on digital currency and the economy underlying the idea that people equate digital assets with money. The public discourse focuses on financial technology like Web3, blockchain, NFTs and cryptocurrencies. People equate non-financial digital assets as investments, digital collections, data and people. Similarly, trading platforms, metaverse and game tokens were viewed as assets.

The most frequent occurrences in the digital asset word cloud are those most often mentioned in discussions about digital currencies, such as 'bitcoin,' 'blockchain' or 'cryptocurrency.' In the face of this concept, words like 'secure,' 'unstable' or 'innovative' appear prominently, indicating the focus of public discussion around the security, stability and novelty of digital financial and non-financial digital assets. In addition, words like 'investment,'

Figure 2.1 Word Cloud: Digital Assets

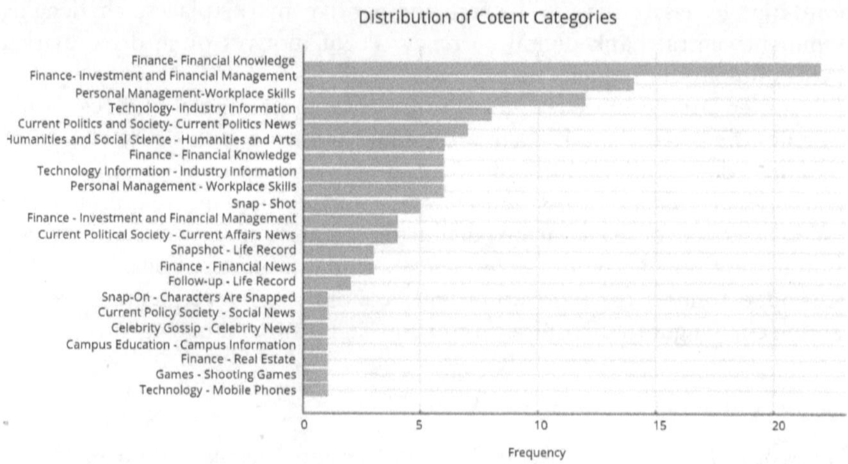

Figure 2.2 Average Likes within Themes

'technology' and 'future' are prominent, which may indicate optimism that financial digital and non-financial digital are our future.

Figure 2.2 represents the average number of likes and comments for each topic and it can be noticed that the number of likes and comments show a positive correlation. In terms of attitude, users were more likely to respond with statements about the uncertainty of non-financial digital assets.

In summary, a central theme is the intangibility of both financial and non-financial digital assets. Unlike traditional money, digital assets have no physical form and exist digitally. The innovation of financial technology supporting digital assets is a precursor to the shift to a more decentralized asset and tokenization. Digital assets are not only financial instruments, but also they have relevance to social and psychological significance, influencing people's identity, social status and personal sense of security and affluence.

References

Ali, M., & Bagui, S. (2021). Introduction to NFTs: The future of digital collectibles. *International Journal of Advanced Computer Science and Applications*, *12*(10), 50–56.

Allen, S., Juels, A., Khaire, M., Kell, T., & Shrivastava, S. (2022). *NFTs for art and collectables: Primer and outlook*. https://osf.io/preprints/socarxiv/gwzd7

Amiri, M. J., Agrawal, D., & El Abbadi, A. (2021, June). Permissioned blockchains: Properties, techniques and applications. In *SIGMOD/PODS '21: International Conference on Management of Data Virtual Event China* (pp. 2813–2820). https://dl.acm.org/doi/proceedings/10.1145/3448016

Antal, C., Cioara, T., Anghel, I., Antal, M., & Salomie, I. (2021). Distributed ledger technology review and decentralized applications development guidelines. *Future Internet*, *13*(3), 62.

Arshad, A., & Bukhari, H. (2024). Corporate branding and reputation management: Cultivating trust and competitive advantage in a digital age. *Review Journal for Management & Social Practices*, *1*(3), 20–27.

Athanassiou, P. L. (2016). *Digital innovation in financial services: Legal challenges and regulatory policy issues*. Kluwer Law International BV.

Barbereau, T., Sedlmeir, J., Smethurst, R., Fridgen, G., & Rieger, A. (2022). Tokenization and regulatory compliance for art and collectibles markets: From regulators' demands for transparency to investors' demands for privacy. In Lacity, M. C. & Treiblmaier, H. (Eds.), *Blockchains and the token economy: theory and practice* (pp. 213–236). Springer International Publishing.

Barbu, M., Vevera, A. V., & Barbu, D. C. (2024). Standardization and interoperability—Key elements of digital transformation. In Cioca, L. I., Ivascu, L., Filip, F. G., & Doina, B. (Eds.), *Digital transformation: Technology, tools, and studies* (pp. 87–94). Springer Nature Switzerland.

Bardhi, F., & Eckhardt, G. M. (2017). Liquid consumption. *Journal of Consumer Research*, *44*(3), 582–597.

Baum, A. (2021). Tokenization—The future of real estate investment. *The Journal of Portfolio Management*, *47*(10), 41–61.

Beier, J. C., & Porter, S. (2013). The digital asset dilemma. *NYSBA Trusts and Estates Law Section Newsletter* [Electronic resource], *46*(2), 34–42.

Bekaert, J., Kooning, E. D., & Sompel, H. V. D. (2006). Representing digital assets using MPEG-21 Digital Item Declaration. *International Journal on Digital Libraries*, *6*, 159–173.

Belchior, R., Riley, L., Hardjono, T., Vasconcelos, A., & Correia, M. (2023). Do you need a distributed ledger technology interoperability solution? *Distributed Ledger Technologies: Research and Practice*, *2*(1), 1–37.

Belk, R. (2014). You are what you can access: Sharing and collaborative consumption online. *Journal of Business Research*, *67*(8), 1595–1600.

Belk, R. (2018). Ownership: The extended self and the extended object. In Peck, J. & Shu, S. (Eds.), *Psychological ownership and consumer behavior* (pp. 53–67). Springer.

Belk, R. (2020). Commodification as a part of marketization. In Roy Chaudhuri, H. & Belk, R. (Eds.), *Marketization: Theory and evidence from emerging economies* (pp. 31–72). Springer.

Belk, R. W. (2013). Extended self in a digital world. *Journal of Consumer Research*, *40*(3), 477–500.

Bellaj, B., Ouaddah, A., Bertin, E., Crespi, N., & Mezrioui, A. (2024). Drawing the boundaries between blockchain and blockchain-like systems: A comprehensive survey on distributed ledger technologies. Proceedings of the IEEE, 112(3), 247–299. https://doi.org/10.1109/JPROC.2024.3386257

Benedetti, H., & Rodríguez-Garnica, G. (2023). Tokenized assets and securities. In Baker, H. K., Benedetti, H., Nikbakht, E., & Smith, S. S. (Eds.), *The Emerald handbook on cryptoassets: Investment opportunities and challenges* (pp. 107–121). Emerald Publishing Limited.

Berlin, J. (2024). Charting the course: Essential elements of a digital asset management governance framework. *Journal of Digital Media Management*, *12*(4), 308–314.

Bokolo, A. J. (2022). Exploring interoperability of distributed ledger and decentralized technology adoption in virtual enterprises. *Information Systems and e-Business Management*, *20*(4), 685–718.

Bull, A., & Harttraft, T. (2020). Cryptocurrency and blockchain law: SEC's heightened enforcement against digital assets. *Richmond Journal of Law & Technology*, *27*, 1.

Bullmann, D., Klemm, J., & Pinna, A. (2019). In search for stability in crypto-assets: Are stablecoins the solution? Available at SSRN 3444847.

Cagli, E. C. (2019). Explosive behavior in the prices of Bitcoin and altcoins. *Finance Research Letters*, *29*, 398–403.

Chaleenutthawut, Y., Davydov, V., Kuzmin, A., & Yanovich, Y. (2021, December). Practical blockchain-based financial assets tokenization. In ICBTA 2021: 2021 4th International Conference on Blockchain Technology and Applications (pp. 51–57). Xi'an China December 17–19, 2021.

Cheng, Q., Gong, Y., Qin, Y., Ao, X., & Li, Z. (2024). Secure digital asset transactions: Integrating distributed ledger technology with safe AI mechanisms. *Academic Journal of Science and Technology*, *9*(3), 156–161.

Chiu, J., & Wong, T. N. (2022). Payments on digital platforms: Resiliency, interoperability and welfare. *Journal of Economic Dynamics and Control*, *142*, 104173.

Church, C. (2015). Your digital identity and assets are important: So what can you do to protect them. *Waikato Law Review*, *23*, 151.

Coinbase. (n.d.a). *AvalancheAVAX*. Retrieved May 6, 2024, from https://www.coinbase.com/price/avalanche

Coinbase. (n.d.b). *BitcoinBTC*. Retrieved April 14, 2024, from https://www.coinbase.com/price/bitcoin

Coinbase. (n.d.c). *Cardano*. Retrieved May 6, 2024, from https://www.coinbase.com/price/cardano

Coinbase. (n.d.d). *DogecoinDOGE*. Retrieved April 27, 2024, from https://www.coinbase.com/price/dogecoin

Coinbase. (n.d.e). *EthereumETH*. Retrieved April 27, 2024, from https://www.coinbase.com/price/ethereum

Coinbase. (n.d.f). *SandboxSAND*. Retrieved June 11, 2024, from https://www.coinbase.com/price/the-sandbox

Coinbase. (n.d.g). *SHIBA INUSHIB*. Retrieved May 6, 2024, from https://www.coinbase.com/price/shiba-inu

Coinbase. (n.d.h). *SolanaSOL*. Retrieved April 27, 2024, from https://www.coinbase.com/price/solana

Coinbase. (n.d.i). *TetherUSDT*. Retrieved April 27, 2024, from https://www.coinbase.com/price/tether

Coinbase. (n.d.j). *USDCUSDC*. Retrieved April 27, 2024, from https://www.coinbase.com/price/usdc

Coinbase. (n.d.k). *XRPXRP*. Retrieved April 27, 2024, from https://www.coinbase.com/price/xrp

Coinbase. (n.d.l). *Decentraland. MANA*. Retrieved April 27, 2024, from https://www.coinbase.com/price/decentraland

De Filippi, P., & Loveluck, B. (2016). The invisible politics of bitcoin: Governance crisis of a decentralized infrastructure. *Internet Policy Review*, *5*(4). https://doi.org/10.14763/2016.3.427

Diallo, E. H., Dieye, M., Dib, O., & Valiorgue, P. (2024). An agnostic and secure interoperability protocol for seamless asset movement. *Journal of Network and Computer Applications*, *230*, 103930.

Efimova, L., Sizemova, O., & Chub, D. (2024). Digital financial assets: Concept and legal nature. *BRICS Law Journal*, *11*(1), 32–57.

Fairfield, J. A. (2022). Tokenized: The law of non-fungible tokens and unique digital property. *Indiana Law Journal*, *97*, 1261.

Ferreira, A. (2021). The curious case of stablecoins-balancing risks and rewards? *Journal of International Economic Law*, *24*(4), 755–778.

Fia, T. (2021). An alternative to data ownership: Managing access to non-personal data through the commons. *Global Jurist*, *21*(1), 181–210.

Gandini, A. (2016). *The reputation economy: Understanding knowledge work in digital society*. Palgrave Macmillan.

Girich, M. G., Ermokhin, I. S., & Levashenko, A. D. (2022). Comparative analysis of the legal regulation of digital financial assets in Russia and other countries. *Bulletin of International Organizations*, *17*(4), 176–192.

Gottschalk, S. (2023). International financial regulation of cryptoassets and asset-backed tokens. In Kim, S. J. (Ed.), *Fintech, pandemic, and the financial system: Challenges and opportunities* (pp. 145–181). Emerald Publishing Limited.

Gu, X., Yang, L., Liang, Y., & Cao, S. (2017, December). Design and implementation of digital assets management system based on WeChat. In *2017 IEEE 2nd Information Technology, Networking, Electronic and Automation Control Conference (ITNEC)* (pp. 394–398). IEEE.

Gupta, A., Rathod, J., Patel, D., Bothra, J., Shanbhag, S., & Bhalerao, T. (2020). Tokenization of real estate using blockchain technology. In *Applied Cryptography and Network Security Workshops: ACNS 2020 Satellite Workshops, AIBlock, AIHWS, AIoTS, Cloud S&P, SCI, SecMT, and SiMLA, Rome, Italy, October 19–22, Proceedings 18* (pp. 77–90). Springer International Publishing.

Hamroun, C., Amamou, A., Haddadou, K., Haroun, H., & Pujolle, G. (2024). A review on lexical based malicious domain name detection methods. *Annals of Telecommunications*, *79*, 457–473.

Havva, V., & Haponiuk, M. (2023). Digital financial assets: Definition and classification. *Ekonomichnyy Analiz*, *33*(3), 238–246.

Hellani, H., Sliman, L., Samhat, A. E., & Exposito, E. (2021, October). Tangle the blockchain: towards connecting blockchain and DAG. In *2021 IEEE 30th International Conference on Enabling Technologies: Infrastructure for Collaborative Enterprises (WETICE)* (pp. 63–68). IEEE.

Ho, K. J. M. (2023). Towards an idea of digital asset ownership. Cambridge Law Review, 8(1), 41–71.

Hofmann, C. (2020). The changing concept of money: A threat to the monetary system or an opportunity for the financial sector?. European Business Organization Law Review, 21, 37–68.

Hoxha, L. (2019). Hashgraph the future of decentralized technology and the end of blockchain. *European Journal of Formal Sciences and Engineering*, *2*(1), 39–45.

Huibers, F. (2024). Distributed ledger technology and the future of money and banking: Banking is necessary, banks are not. Bill Gates 1994. *Accounting, Economics, and Law: A Convivium*, *14*(2), 213–249.

Inshakova, E. I., Kalinina, A. E., & Zabezhailo, M. I. (2024). Standardization of Blockchain distributed ledger technology: Global trends, opportunities and challenges for remote investment transactions. In Inshakova, A., Matytsin, D., & Inshakova, E. (Eds.), *Remote investment transactions in the digital age: Perception, techniques, law regulation* (pp. 11–25). Springer.

Johnson, S. T. (2001). Internet domain name and trademark disputes: Shifting paradigms in intellectual property. *Arizona Law Review*, *43*, 465.

Kaal, W. A. (2020). Digital asset market evolution. *Journal of Corporation Law*, *46*, 909.

Kaal, W. A. (2021). Digital asset market evolution. *Journal of Corporation Law*, *46*(4), 909–964.

Kesmodel, D. (2008). *The domain game: How people get rich from Internet domain names*. Xlibris Corporation.

Khan, S., Amin, M. B., Azar, A. T., & Aslam, S. (2021). Towards interoperable blockchains: A survey on the role of smart contracts in blockchain interoperability. *IEEE Access*, *9*, 116672–116691.

Kizza, J. M. (2024). Blockchains, cryptocurrency, and smart contracts technologies: Security considerations. In Kizza, J. M. (Ed.), *Guide to computer network security* (pp. 575–600). Springer International Publishing. https://doi.org/10.1007/978-3-031-47549-8_26

Kochergin, D. A. (2022). Crypto-assets: Economic nature, classification and regulation of turnover. *International Organisations Research Journal*, *17*(3), 75–130.

Lafioune, N., Poirier, E. A., & St-Jacques, M. (2024). Managing urban infrastructure assets in the digital era: Challenges of municipal digital transformation. *Digital Transformation and Society*, *3*(1), 3–22.

Lefebvre, V., & Vershinina, N. (2024). 15 Growing up in the digital era: Creating digital assets by digital new ventures. In Lamine, W., Jack, S., Fayolle, A., & Audretsch, D. B. (Eds.), *De Gruyter handbook of digital entrepreneurship* (p. 327). De Gruyter.

Lewis, A. (2018). *The basics of bitcoins and blockchains: An introduction to cryptocurrencies and the technology that powers them*. Mango Media Inc.

Li, C., & Shen, Y. (2021). The potential impacts and risks of global stablecoins. *China Economic Journal*, *14*(1), 39–51.

Lubogo, I. C. (2022). *Digital money: The law of cryptocurrency and cryptography*. Jescho Publishing House.

Macák, M., & Šašalová, V. (2022). Digital games, collectors and (artificial) scarcity: The digital future might be a bit physical after all. *Communication Today*, *13*(2), 4–23.

Mario Lavizzari, M. G., Luzio, M. D., & Tommasino, C. (2021). The development of digital identity in the financial service industry: From an element that enables digital transactions to a new strategic asset for business. *Journal of Digital Banking*, *6*(1), 57–65.

Mauthe, A., & Thomas, P. (2004). *Professional content management systems: Handling digital media assets*. John Wiley & Sons.

Mazzei, D., Baldi, G., Fantoni, G., Montelisciani, G., Pitasi, A., Ricci, L., & Rizzello, L. (2020). A Blockchain Tokenizer for industrial IOT trustless applications. Future Generation Computer Systems, 105, 432–445.

McConaghy, T., & Holtzman, D. (2015). Towards an ownership layer for the internet. *Ascribe GmbH*.

McIntosh, T. R., Susnjak, T., Liu, T., Watters, P., Xu, D., Liu, D., Nowrozy, R., & Halgamuge, M. N. (2024). From COBIT to ISO 42001: Evaluating cybersecurity frameworks for opportunities, risks, and regulatory compliance in commercializing large language models. *Computers & Security*, *144*, 103964.

Milkau, U., & Bott, J. (2015). Digitalisation in payments: From interoperability to centralised models? *Journal of Payments Strategy & Systems*, *9*(3), 321–340.

Morrison, R. (2024). Making the invisible visible: Critical discourse analysis as a tool for search engine research. *Journal of the Association for Information Science and Technology*, *75*(5), 600–612.

Mowbray, N., & Kramer, S. (2023). Chapter 68. Bitcoin, virtual currencies, and digital assets (pp. 1–58). *Taxes The Tax Magazine*. https://bit.ly/4e0nk9P

Nagpal, Y. (2021). Non-fungible tokens (NFT's): The future of digital collectibles. *International Journal of Law Management & Humanities*, *4*(5), 758.

Newell, J. (2012). Old objects, new media: Historical collections, digitization and affect. *Journal of Material Culture*, *17*(3), 287–306.

O'Dwyer, R. (2020). Limited edition: Producing artificial scarcity for digital art on the blockchain and its implications for the cultural industries. *Convergence*, *26*(4), 874–894.

Panda, S. K., Daliyet, S. P., Lokre, S. S., & Naman, V. (2022). Distributed ledger technology in the construction industry using corda. In Panda, S. K., Mohapatra, R. K., Panda, S., & Balamurugan, S. (Eds.), *The new advanced society: Artificial intelligence and industrial internet of things paradigm* (pp. 15–41). Wiley Online Library.

Park, K., & Youm, H. Y. (2021). Proposal for customer identification service model based on distributed ledger technology to transfer virtual assets. *Big Data and Cognitive Computing*, *5*(3), 31.

Parmar, J. K., & Vaghani, K. G. (2022). A conceptual study on holochain and blockchain technology. In Hiranwal, S. & Mathur, S. (Eds.), *Artificial intelligence and communication technologies* (pp. 331–341). SCRS.

Pillai, B., Biswas, K., & Muthukkumarasamy, V. (2019). Blockchain interoperable digital objects. In *Blockchain – ICBC 2019: Second International Conference, Held as Part of the Services Conference Federation, SCF 2019, San Diego, CA, June 25–30, Proceedings 2* (pp. 80–94). Springer International Publishing.

Popescu, A. D. (2021). Non-fungible tokens (NFT) –innovation beyond the craze. In *5th International Conference on Innovation in Business, Economics and Marketing Research* (Vol. 32, pp. 26–30). Proceedings of Engineering & Technology – PET.

Rao, K. V., Teja, M. S., Reddy, P. P., & Saikrishna, S. (2020). Building permissioned blockchain networks using hyperledger fabric. In Panda, S. K., Elngar, A. A., Balas, V. E., & Kayed, M. (Eds.), *Bitcoin and blockchain* (pp. 193–235). CRC Press.

Raskin, M., & Yermack, D. (2018). Digital currencies, decentralized ledgers and the future of central banking. In Conti-Brown, P., & Lastra, R. M. (Eds.), *Research handbook on central banking* (pp. 474–486). Edward Elgar Publishing.

Ren, K., Ho, N. M., Loghin, D., Nguyen, T. T., Ooi, B. C., Ta, Q. T., & Zhu, F. (2023). Interoperability in blockchain: A survey. *IEEE Transactions on Knowledge and Data Engineering, 35*(12), 12750–12769.

Seel, P. B. (2022). *Digital universe: The global telecommunication revolution*. John Wiley & Sons.

Sharad Mangrulkar, R., & Vijay Chavan, P. (2024). Beyond Blockchain. In Blockchain *essentials: Core concepts and implementations* (pp. 229–248). Apress.

Singh, S. (2024). Bitcoin's genesis: A catalyst for digital currency. In Kaur, G., Lekhi, P., & Popli, S. (Eds.), *Exploring Central Bank digital currencies: Concepts, frameworks, models, and challenges* (pp. 21–32). IGI Global.

Soukupová, J. (2024). Virtual property, digital assets, data, digital content and others – An analysis of the fragmented terminology. *Charles University in Prague Faculty of Law Research Paper No.*

Stankevich, V. S., & Vlasov, A. V. (2024). Review of digital assets. Trends in the development of digital financial assets in the Russian Federation and forecast. *Russian Journal of Economics and Law, 2024*(2), 422–452.

Sun, K. (2022). Digital asset valuation: A study on domain names, email addresses, and NFTs. arXiv preprint arXiv:2210.10637.

Tian, Y., Wang, C., Asutosh, A., Woo, J., & Adriaens, P. (2022). Blockchain-enabled tokenization for sustainable and inclusive infrastructure investment. arXiv preprint arXiv:2208.04709.

Toygar, A., Rohm, Jr., C. E., & Zhu, J. (2013). A new asset type: Digital assets. *Journal of International Technology and Information Management*, 22(4), 7.

Van Niekerk, A. (2006). A methodological approach to modern digital asset management: An empirical study. In *Allied Academies International Conference. International Academy for Case Studies. Proceedings* (Vol. 13, No. 1, p. 53). Jordan Whitney Enterprises, Inc.

Varadarajan, M. N., & Seeni, S. K. (2024). Innovative digital ownership and collectibles via proof of stake (PoS) and non-fungible tokens (NFTs). *International Journal of Advances in Signal and Image Sciences, 10*(1), 22–34.

Vitalii, V. (2024). Legal aspects related to intellectual property protection in the field of digital E-Commerce technologies. *International Journal of Religion, 5*(3), 413–420.

Watkins, R. D., Denegri-Knott, J., & Molesworth, M. (2016). The relationship between ownership and possession: Observations from the context of digital virtual goods. *Journal of Marketing Management, 32*(1–2), 44–70.

Wijesekara, P. A. D. S. N., & Gunawardena, S. (2023). A review of blockchain technology in knowledge-defined networking, its application, benefits, and challenges. *Network, 3*(3), 343–421.

Wong, A. L. (2022). NFTs and digital collectibles: Creating systems of ownership for digital objects. In Edizioni, M. (Ed.), *Visual culture studies: Rivista Semestrale di Cultura Visuale: 3/4, special double issue, 2022* (pp. 225–251). http://digital.casalini.it/9788857595900

Yi, Q., Khan, J., Su, Y., Tong, J., & Zhao, S. (2023). Impulse buying tendency in live-stream commerce: The role of viewing frequency and anticipated emotions influencing scarcity-induced purchase decision. *Journal of Retailing and Consumer Services*, *75*, 103534.

Zalan, T., & Toufaily, E. (2024). A nascent market for digital assets: Exploration of consumer value of NFTs. *Digital Business*, *4*(1), 100084.

Zhang, Y., Gong, B., & Zhou, P. (2024). Centralized use of decentralized technology: Tokenization of currencies and assets. *Structural Change and Economic Dynamics*, *71*, 15–25.

Addendum to Chapter 2

Top 10 Cryptocurrencies in 2024

Cryptocurrencies have transformed the financial landscape by offering decentralized and secure digital assets, gaining immense popularity in recent times. Some of the most prominent cryptocurrencies include Bitcoin (BTC), Ethereum (ETH), Tether (USDT), Solana (SOL), USDC, XRP, Dogecoin (DOGE), Cardano (ADA), Shiba Inu (SHIB) and Avalanche (AVAX). These cryptocurrencies serve diverse purposes, such as stores of value, decentralized applications and stablecoins. With a combined market capitalization in the trillions, these digital assets have captured the attention of investors, traders and technologists worldwide. Each cryptocurrency possesses unique features and value propositions, contributing to the dynamic blockchain technology ecosystem. As we explore the history and mechanisms of each coin, we will uncover the innovations and developments that have shaped the cryptocurrency market and its impact on the global economy. In the following sections, each cryptocurrency mentioned above is introduced, starting with its basic information, followed by its history, how it functions and, finally, its current market status.

Bitcoin (BTC)

Bitcoin is the world's first cryptocurrency, stored and exchanged online via a digital ledger called blockchain. Recognized as one of the initial cryptocurrencies to appear on the market, Bitcoin was initially described by an individual or a group using the alias Satoshi Nakamoto in a 2008 whitepaper, and it encouraged the emergence of thousands of competing projects after that. Bitcoin was officially launched in January 2009 and is a peer-to-peer online currency that allows transactions to happen directly between independent and equal participants without any intermediary. It has created a worldwide community and brought about a brand-new industry of millions of enthusiasts who create and utilize Bitcoin and other cryptocurrencies daily. Bitcoin is also a decentralized medium of exchange, providing ownership rights as a physical asset or a unit of account. With an increasing value, 'high divisibility' has become a critical attribute of Bitcoin. There will only be 21 million Bitcoins worldwide, and 1 Bitcoin can be divided into 100,000,000 Satoshi (or 'sat').

Bitcoin's core innovation was the blockchain—a piece of software that works like a ledger, logging each transaction ever made using Bitcoin. Unlike a regular bank's ledger, the Bitcoin blockchain is distributed and verified across a network of computers, meaning that nobody can control it, and anyone can become part of the network. To enter new bitcoins into circulation, challenging puzzles must be solved computationally to discover a new block added to the blockchain. The first individuals to present a solution to the puzzle are compensated with a certain number of bitcoins. Finally, anyone can receive, send and hold Bitcoin using the public version of their key wherever they have Internet access.

According to the latest data provided by Coinbase (n.d.b) and other third-party market vendors (2024), Bitcoin is now the highest-market-cap asset, with a value of £1.0 trillion. It has a volume of approximately £47.6 billion and a circulating supply of 19.7 million. Its price has been rising overall over the past year, and the highest price since it was launched in the market is £59,248.47. The typical hold time for Bitcoin customers is 85 days.

Ethereum (ETH)

Up to 2023, Ethereum was the second-largest cryptocurrency (after Bitcoin) by market cap. It is also a decentralized computing platform that can function with applications, including a set of DeFi apps and services. In 2013, a highly flexible blockchain, which can support nearly all kinds of transactions, was proposed in a whitepaper by a 19-year-old computer programmer called Vitalik Buterin, who co-founded Bitcoin Magazine. In 2014, Buterin and other co-founders sold $18 million in pre-launch tokens to fund this project. The first public version of the Ethereum blockchain was launched in July 2015, and the smart contract functionality started working. Ethereum has been upgraded several times to improve the project's ongoing development and forward-thinking nature. In 2022, Ethereum experienced a significant upgrade: switching from proof-of-work to proof-of-stake to become a more energy-efficient blockchain. Ethereum can transfer value and enable the support of decentralized applications on the platform. Ethereum also allows the creation and exchange of NFTs, a unique digital asset that can represent the ownership of various items and content.

Ethereum is a decentralized computing platform that uses ETH (also known as Ether) to pay transactions (or 'gas'). It runs via a network of computers that works as a supercomputer. Miners in the network solve complicated problems to confirm transactions and add them to the blockchain. Developers can run decentralized applications and issue new crypto assets. According to the latest data provided by Coinbase (n.d.e) and other third-party market vendors (2024), Ethereum is currently the second most popular cryptocurrency. It has the second-highest market cap of £304.3 billion. It has a volume of £8.9 billion and a circulating supply of 122.1 million. Its highest price since it was launched in the market is £3,779.59. The typical hold time for Ethereum customers is 44 days. It is used heavily on metaverse platforms.

Tether (USDT)

Tether (USDT, also known as a stablecoin) is an Ethereum token pegged to the US dollar's value. It aims to provide an alternative to the conventional financial system with a digital approach to money by facilitating the usage of traditional fiat currencies digitally. Unlike other highly volatile cryptocurrencies, Tether is relatively historically stable, and beginners who want to enter the cryptocurrency community could be attracted by this trait. Tether is the first blockchain-enabled platform that facilitates the digitalization of traditional currencies. It was initially launched in 2014 by Brock Pierce, Reeve Collins and Craig Sellars and has allowed users to transact with conventional currencies across the blockchain over the past few years. Despite some controversies, Tether continues operating. Till November 2023, there have been more than 88.8 billion US dollar tokens in circulation. With the launch of MXNT (a new stablecoin supported by the Mexican peso), Tether entered the Latin American market in 2022. Tether USDT functions as a digital token built on multiple blockchains. Tether reserves back 100% of each Tether token and maintains transparency via publishing records of its current reserve assets. Tether sustains USDT's value by being pegged to the US dollar, as the company would allocate the same amount of US dollars to its reserve whenever new USDT tokens are issued. Tether offers a way to transact a US dollar equivalent across regions, countries and continents through blockchain without traditional intermediaries such as banks and financial service providers.

According to the latest data provided by Coinbase (n.d.i) and other third-party market vendors (2024), Tether has a market value of £88.5 billion and a volume of £36.5 billion. Its current circulating supply is 110.6 billion, and its historical highest price is £0.97. The typical hold time for Tether customers is one day.

Solana (SOL)

Like Ethereum, Solana is both a cryptocurrency and a flexible platform for operating decentralized apps or mining NFTs. It uses SOL to pay for transactions and intends to enhance blockchain scalability by combining proof-of-stake consensus and so-called evidence of history. As one of many new crypto solutions aiming to make crypto networks faster and more scalable, Solana utilizes clever technologies and claims to finish 50,000 transactions per second without sacrificing decentralization. The initial idea of Solana existed in 2017, and the official launch was in March 2020 by the Solana Foundation, headquartered in Geneva, Switzerland. Anatoly Yakovenko is the most significant person to Solana, who worked with his Qualcomm colleagues and founded the Solana Lab project. Solana's protocol targets serving both small-time users and enterprise customers alike. Solana combines proof-of-history (PoH) and proof-of-stake (PoS) consensus mechanisms. The PoH component is the central element of the Solana protocol and processes most transactions. It records successful operations and the time elapsed between them to maintain the trustless nature of blockchain. The PoS consensus works as a monitoring tool for the PoH process, which validates all sequences of blocks it produces. This combination distinguishes Solana from other approaches in the blockchain industry. According to the latest data provided by Coinbase (n.d.h) and other third-party market vendors (2024), Solana has a current market cap of £48.7 billion and a volume of £2.1 billion. Its circulating supply is 447.2 million, and its historical highest exchange price is £208.15. The typical hold time for Solana customers is 146 days.

USDC

USDC is a stablecoin redeemable on a one-to-one basis for US dollars. It is supported by dollar-denominated assets in segregated accounts with US-regulated financial institutions. USDC aims to reduce volatility while making transactions cheaper and faster. The launch of USDC was backed by a collaboration between Coinbase (n.d.j) and Circle via the co-funding of the CENTRE Consortium. USDC is a new type of cryptocurrency whose price is often fixed to a reserve asset such as the US dollar at a 1:1 ratio. These stablecoins are one of the most popular and versatile categories of cryptocurrency to emerge over the past few years, as their prices are usually powered by one or several reserve assets.

USDT operates on Ethereum. This decentralized and programmable blockchain allows users to establish various tokens and applications. USDC is designed to become a very useful form of digital currency that would not see value swing hugely during a transaction. USDC can be applied to facilitate blockchain payments and value transfer in Ethereum smart contracts, which enables customers to keep cryptocurrencies in their wallet before sending them to others or interacting with decentralized tools and services, as well as minimize the risk of their holding's dropping in price before they are spent. According to the latest data as of July 2024 provided by Coinbase (n.d.j) and other third-party market vendors (2024), USDC currently has a market cap of £26.8 billion and a market volume of £5.1 billion. Its circulating supply in the market is 33.5 billion, and its all-time high price is £0.8. The typical hold time for USDC customers is four days.

XRP (XRP)

XRP is the native token of the XRP ledger and is used by the Ripple payment network. It is created for worldwide enterprise use and supports cost-efficient cross-border payments. In 2012, David Schwartz, Jed McCaleb and Arthur Britto launched XRP and XRP Ledger (XRPL), which focus on speed and energy efficiency and can be an alternative to the Bitcoin blockchain.

In September of the same year, they established Ripple with Chris Larsen. The XRP Ledger architects give vast amounts of XRP to Ripple for its use cases around digital assets. Since 2020, Ripple Labs, the creators of XRP tokens, has been arguing with the US Security and Exchange Commission over the security trait of XRP. XRP runs on the XRP Ledger, using a unique Federated Consensus mechanism to validate transactions. These transactions are confirmed via a consensus protocol in which independent servers (known as validators) agree on the order and result of the transaction. Each server in this network processes the transactions following the same rule, and any transaction under the protocol can be confirmed immediately. The XRP Ledger is public and transparent, so everyone can run it as a validator. This mechanism is designed to process the verified transactions without failure, as all participants are dependent when deciding. The XRP Ledger is highly useful and flexible for enterprises and developers. It is currently applied in five main methods: payments, tokenization, DeFi, CBDCs and stablecoins. According to the latest data provided by Coinbase (n.d.k) and other third-party market vendors (2024), the current capital size of the XRP market is £22.9 billion, with a volume of £835.1 million. XRP's circulating supply is 55.2 billion, and its historical highest price is £3.08. The typical hold time for XRP customers is 70 days.

Dogecoin (DOGE)

Created in 2013, Dogecoin is a lighthearted alternative to traditional cryptocurrencies such as Bitcoin. Like the Shiba Lnu logo (see below), the name 'Dogecoin' is also based on a meme. In 2021, Dogecoin became one of the largest cryptocurrencies by market cap, although each individual coin is worth very little. Dogecoin is intentionally designed to be abundant, with 10,000 new coins mined every minute, and there is no maximum supply. Like most prominent cryptocurrencies, including Bitcoin and Ethereum, Dogecoin is also secured by mining. Every day there are thousands of computers around the globe competing to mine Dogecoin to add millions of new coins to the supply and validate and process network transactions simultaneously. Early in Dogecoin's history, any computer could be used to mine Dogecoin. As it became increasingly popular later, mining competition became intense, and small-scale miners with regular hardware found mining more difficult. A miner could earn Doge with powerful graphics processor units. However, he or she needs a more robust and specialized computer named ASIC to conduct more profitable mining. In 2021, Dogecoin's price was significantly increased as celebrities like Mark Cuban, Snoop Dogg and Elon Musk showed great interest in it. According to the latest data provided by Coinbase (n.d.d) and other third-party market vendors (2024), Dogecoin's market cap is currently £16.8 billion, with a volume of £739 million. Its circulating supply is 144.1 billion, and its all-time high price is £0.59. Dogecoin customers' typical hold time for it is 85 days.

Cardano (ADA)

Cardano is one of the largest cryptocurrencies by market cap. It is created to be the next-gen evolution of Ethereum's idea to be flexible, sustainable and scalable. Aiming to be the third-generation blockchain (Bitcoin is the first-generation and Ethereum is the second-gen), Cardano was launched in 2017 by Charles Hoskinson, the co-founder of Ethereum. On March 1, 2021, the Cardano blockchain introduced the function of creating native tokens, meaning the Cardano native assets can work like Ethereum tokens do, which can teach things like NFTs and stablecoins. They can be made and distributed on the blockchain and interact with smart contracts. To be the most environmentally sustainable blockchain platform, Cardano uses a unique proof-of-stake consensus mechanism named Ouroboros (after a mythical creature that eats its tail), which is opposed to the energy-intensive proof-of-work system used by Bitcoin. The Ouroboros consensus mechanism originates from the research by computer scientists and cryptographers from the University of Edinburgh, Tokyo University, and other institutions to build a decentralized network that can validate transactions stably and securely. As decentralized cryptocurrency networks must ensure all transactions are legitimate, a proof-of-stake system uses a network of invested participants named validators rather than 'miners.' According to the latest data provided by Coinbase (n.d.c) and other third-party market vendors (2024), ADA's current market cap is £13 billion, its volume is 180 million and its circulating supply is 36.7 billion. ADA's historical highest price is £2.47, and customers' typical hold time is 294 days.

Shiba Inu (SHIB)

Shiba Inu (SHIB) is a token that could be an alternative to Dogecoin (DOGE), a popular Ethereum-based memecoin. Unlike Bitcoin, which is designed to be scarce, SHIB is intentionally abundant, with a total supply of one quadrillion. SHIB was created by an individual or a group pseudonymized 'Ryoshi' in August 2020. It gained traction quickly, and its popularity surged even further, especially when a considerable portion of its supply was burned, which increased its rarity. SHIB's history is empowered by its community-led approach, and Ryoshi emphasized the significance of a decentralized community-driven project. SHIB runs on the Ethereum blockchain, using smart contracts to facilitate diverse operations, including transactions. The Shiba Inu ecosystem consists of Shiba-Swap, a decentralized exchange on which users can swap tokens, provide liquidity and stake the holdings to gain compensation. The ecosystem also introduced Shibarium, a Layer-2 solution that has processed millions of transactions. According to the latest data provided by Coinbase (n.d.g) and other third-party market vendors (2024), SHIB's current market cap is £11.6 billion, and the volume is 290.5 million. Its current circulating supply is 589.3 trillion, and the all-time-high value is £0.000072 per token. It has been the 11th most popular token so far, and the typical hold time for its holders is 212 days.

Avalanche (AVAX)

Avalanche is an open and programmed smart contact platform for decentralized applications. Its own token, AVAX, can be used to pay transactions and stakes in the network. There will only ever be 720 million AVAX coins in circulation. Avalanche was launched by Ava Labs and founded by Emin Gün Sirer, a Cornell University professor, Kevin Sekniqi and Maofan 'Ted' Yin, two computer science PhDs. The project closed a seed round in February 2019 with investors like Polychain, Andreessen Horowitz and Balaji. Avalanche completed its initial coin offering in 2020 within 24 hours. Avalanche runs via its unique mechanism, consisting of three blockchains—the X-chain, the C-chain and the P-chain. The X-chain can create and exchange assets, including native AVAX tokens. The C-chain can operate smart contracts and decentralized applications through its Avalanche Virtual Machine, enabling developers to fork EVM-compatible decentralized applications. The P-chain coordinates can coordinate network validators, track active subnets and support the creation of new subnets. Such task division allows Avalanche to complete higher workloads without affecting decentralization. Several projects have integrated with Avalanche as the unique modular structure enhances Avalanche's interoperability with other blockchains. According to the latest data provided by Coinbase (n.d.a) and other third-party market vendors (2024), AVAX is currently the 12th most popular cryptocurrency by market cap, which is £13 billion. Its current volume is £180 million, with a circulating supply of 35.7 billion. AVAX's historical highest price is £2.47, and the typical hold time for its customers is 294 days.

Decentraland (MANA)

Decentraland (MANA) is an Ethereum token that enables users to create, experience and generate value from content and applications within a virtual world. On Decentraland, users can acquire LAND which can be navigated, built upon and generate value. As the virtual world is totally owned by its users, the platform is a truly decentralized platform. MANA and LAND are two tokens used by Decentraland.

Decentraland was established in 2015 by Ariel Meilich and Esteban Ordano and officially launched in 2020. The platform was first designed to function as a proof of concept for dividing the ownership of a digital real estate to blockchain users. It has been evolving from a 2D experiment into a full-fledged 3D world. The virtual world launched its closed beta in 2019 and opened to the public in 2020. Since then, users continued to create diverse experiences on their LAND such as interactive games and sprawling

3D scenes. LAND can be acquired by using MANA, and MANA can be used to acquire avatars, wearables, names, etc.

Decentraland operates on the three-layer protocol on Ethereum smart contracts. The ownership of LAND is tracked and managed by the consensus. The content of virtual world is displayed on the land content layer and the real-time layer enables users to interact with each other. By allowing a range of activities of participants, Decentraland provides a powerful platform for content generators, businesses and people that look for new artistic medium, business opportunities and sources of entertainment.

According to the latest data provided by Coinbase (n.d.l) and other third-party market vendors (2024), Decentraland MANA is now the 100th popular cryptocurrency by market cap. Its market cap is £620.2 million with a volume of £115.7 million. The circulating supply of MANA is 1.9 billion. All-time high price of MANA is £4.65 and the customers' typical hold time is 81 days.

The Sandbox (SAND)

The Sandbox (SAND) is a blockchain-based virtual world which creates a multiplayer metaverse where players can create, monetize and participate in blockchain-based gaming experiences. In Sandbox, game designers can create custom 3D NFTs to use in the ecosystem. SAND can be used to purchase and sell NFTs or other items in the game and vote on the future of the platform.

The Sandbox was initially introduced by Pixowl which was co-founded by Arthur Madrid and Sebastien Borget in 2011. The Sandbox was first supported by numerous parties in the gaming industry, including brands such as Atari, Helix and CryptoKitties. Till March 2021, there have been approximately 680,266,194 active SAND tokens in circulation, which represent 23% of the total SAND supply.

The Sandbox operates through integrating blockchain technologies into the gaming world and offers a universe where participants can create and collect blockchain-based assets. The Sandbox works on user-created content and provides a metaverse to participants who can contribute to its future development. The SAND token allows decentralized governance and enables users to exchange their thoughts about the project's advancement. The SAND token uses the PoS consensus mechanism, meaning owners can stake it and gain benefits from its awards.

According to the latest data provided by Coinbase (n.d.f) and other third-party market vendors (2024), the Sandbox SAND has a market cap of £737.6 million and a volume of 143.4 million. Its circulating supply is 2.3 billion and its all-time high price is £5.28. SAND holders' typical hold time is 40 days.

3 Money in Digital Currencies

Jashim Khan and Russell Belk

Introduction

The rise of central bank digital currency is associated with the rise of stablecoins and cryptocurrencies, demonstrating the technological possibilities of creating an alternative payment system (Cunha et al., 2021). Cryptocurrencies have also caused policymakers and regulators to face pressure because they may negatively impact society and financial system stability (Liu & Serletis, 2019). Similarly, big tech firms, such as Facebook's Diem initiative and China's mobile payment platforms, such as WeChat and Alipay, are challenged in entering the payment market and incentivized initiatives in central bank digital currency development (Gronwald, 2019). Central bank digital currency takes the form of retail and wholesale currency. Consumers use retail central bank digital currencies, whereas banks and licensed financial institutions use wholesale digital currencies for interbank payments and securities transactions (Schumacher, 2024). According to Maryaningsih et al. (2022), countries with developed financial markets and greater cross-border/international transactions will adopt the wholesale central bank digital currency, while countries with less financial inclusion and large informal economies will adopt the retail central bank digital currency. Some observers (Zams et al., 2020; Shirai, 2019) view central bank digital currency as a tool for financial inclusion due to more accessible access to financial assets and digitally traced economic activities that minimize informal economy-boosting tax collection.

Central bank digital currency may use centralized ledger technology, though the chosen technology will likely be adapted to each nation's requirements. A distributed ledger technology (DLT) is stored on separate, connected devices to ensure data security and accuracy, bypassing third-party transactions like the SWIFT system (Scardovi, 2016). Distributed ledger technology is advantageous; for example, it enables the system to synchronize data automatically, provide data traceability and make transactions faster (Parlour et al., 2020). Peer-to-peer retail payment and third-party authentication are complex payment systems that are difficult for central banks to supervise. According to Qian (2019), adopting retail central bank digital currency

DOI: 10.4324/9781003425021-3

reduces complexities and makes it easier for the central bank to supervise the retail payment system. At the same time, digital money is quickly adopted in peer-to-peer payment systems following retail central bank digital currency, enabling exchange for goods and services. The availability of 24 hours a day, seven days a week, pegged to national currency, has the function of interest rates the same as cash (Barrdear & Kumhof, 2022). In a central bank digital currency, a trusted authority can only update transaction data (Davoodalhosseini, 2022). On the other hand, in a decentralized digital currency, all participants can update transaction data simultaneously (Kiff et al., 2020).

DLT in Central Bank Digital Currency

Distributed Ledger Technology (DLT)

Distributed ledger technology (DLT) builds on the invention of database technology developed by IBM in the 1970s. DLT used the IBM model of the database and extended it to peer-to-peer technology (Giblin, 2011). The DLT is a secure decentralized infrastructure that allows simultaneous access, validation and record updating across a networked database (Jagrič et al., 2022). One example of distributed ledger technology is Bitcoin, and another is Ethereum. Although they both rely on blockchain technology, they have several differences. The Ethereum platform supports smart contracts, which execute automatically when certain conditions are met. This capability is not available with Bitcoin. Unlike Bitcoin, Ethereum uses a less energy-intensive method of verifying transactions called proof of stake instead of the energy-intensive proof of work method (Buterin, 2014). DLT, a chronological transaction, is recorded on a network of computers permanently and immutably, allowing for a continual historical record. Technically, it is a back-end database that maintains a distributed ledger that anyone can inspect. Ethereum is a programmable platform on which other applications can run. Essential properties of distributed ledgers:

- The concept of decentralization implies moving control and decision-making from one centralized entity to another (Sunyaev & Sunyaev, 2020).
- Data immutability: Data is stored securely with cryptography, and encrypted signatures and keys ensure that only authorized users can access the data. In immutability, information is not deleted once it has been stored, and any updates are permanently recorded (Gray & Gray, 2021).
- The term distributed refers to a digital system for recording asset transactions in which details are simultaneously recorded in multiple locations (Farahani et al., 2021). A centralized entity does not guide the DLT either.

From a financial perspective, the network records financial transactions and assets between peers without needing third-party intermediaries to replace the validator role of trusted third parties (Mougayar & Buterin, 2016), like banks, governments and credit and lending institutions. DLT is associated with financial transactions and cryptocurrencies (McConaghy et al., 2017) and emerged as a bottom-up rather than top-down sequence of activities (O'Dair, 2018). The DLT system leapfrogs with no requirement for third-party entities. By using this approach, people who do not know or trust each other can reach a consensus on the occurrence of a particular transaction (Swan, 2015; Tresise et al., 2018). In the early days of DLT, cryptocurrencies dominated, followed by smart contracts introduced by Ethereum (self-executing and tamper-resistant code that turns distributed ledgers into financial operating systems (Bonnet & Teuteberg, 2023). Smart contracts serve as a prototype for defining service and usage. Participants can control interactions and transactions within the system (Tapscott & Tapscott, 2016). The latest development phase has expanded to decentralized applications (dApps) designed for flexibility, transparency and distribution of transactions. The dApps are flexible, potentially permissionless or public, and open to everyone without compromising decentralization. The dApps are programmed to be permissioned or private (also known as enterprise), with access control mechanisms that restrict access to specific users (Rupa et al., 2022). They focus on efficiencies, privacy, confidentiality and modularity to improve existing systems rather than replace them. According to Wang et al. (2018), distributed ledgers can even be clustered (also called federated), combining the best features of permissionless and permissioned systems. Central bank digital currencies are likely to adopt the permissioned or private DLT which requires the nodes in the system permitted to join, hence centralizing the control over distribution. For example, Corda is a permissioned, open source dApp that provides strict privacy for recording and managing smart contracts between participants. They have introduced 'Notary' stamps for every transaction to avoid double spending. Quorum is based on Ethereum is another such example. Bitt is another development that provides solutions for central banks to develop and implement central bank digital currency.

Central Bank Digital Currency

Central Bank Digital Currency (CBDC) is in its infancy and countries and regulators are learning about digital currency's potential advantages and risks. The experimentation with central bank digital currency explores whether to trial retail or wholesale digital currencies, and the decision question is whether to adopt one of them, both or neither. A retail digital currency for public use, the wholesale currency is used among banks and licensed financial institutions for interbank payments and securities transactions (Waliczek & Nili, 2024). Countries are careful not to disrupt their established and mature intermediary systems based on real-time gross settlement systems. The potential risk is crowding out bank deposits, increasing credit interest rates, losing fiscal control of the economy and contracting commercial banking credit to the fiat currency (Agur et al., 2022). The central bank's digital currency risks disrupting money creation by commercial banks, as the public could shift to digital currency from traditional loan deposits when acquiring mortgages for property. It can potentially lower loan disbursement by commercial banks (Agur et al., 2022).

The Bahamas, China, Ecuador, Cambodia, Ukraine and Uruguay have carried out retail central bank digital currency pilot projects. Canada, France, the United Kingdom, Hong Kong, Japan and Singapore have completed wholesale central bank digital currency pilot projects (Boar et al., 2020). A World Economic Forum's white paper suggests that retail central bank digital currency is most widely explored in 11 countries (Waliczek & Nili, 2024). *According to* Atlantic Council's CBDC Tracker (2024),

> six central banks have launched a CBDC: the Central Bank of The Bahamas (Sand Dollar), the Eastern Caribbean Central Bank (DCash), the Central Bank of Nigeria (e-Naira), the Bank of Jamaica (JamDex), the People's Bank of China (e-CNY), Reserve Bank of India (Digital Rupee), and Bank of Russia (Digital Ruble). Since March 2023, the Brazilian Central Bank has been testing a digital currency (Drex). As a result of a two-year study phase, the ECB and Eurozone decided to move forward with the preparation phase for introducing a digital euro in October 2023. Central banks in Latin America and the Caribbean prioritize CBDC research and development and have several critical reasons for releasing their central bank digital currency in the future, according to the World *Economic Forum's white paper* on Central Bank Digital Currency Global Interoperability *Principles.*
>
> (Waliczek & Nili, 2024)

In the Asia-Pacific, China, with its e-CNY, has piloted many retail payments. The Bank of Thailand is also testing a retail CBDC. The European Central Bank (ECB), Bank of England and Bank of Japan are working on prototypes and running consultations on potential privacy and financial stability issues, according to think tank the Atlantic Council's CBDC Tracker. The progress of developing a retail CBDC in the US is currently being researched.

Case Example e-CNY or Digital RMB

The need for digital currency aligns with Chinese developments in big data, cloud computing, artificial intelligence, blockchain and the Internet of Things, contributing to the digital economy. According to the People's Bank of China (PBOC) white paper (2022), the PBOC initiated a task force comprising researchers, experts, government representatives and entrepreneurs to study digital fiat currency in 2014. The PBOC established its Digital Currency Institute in 2016, and in 2017, pilot tests were launched.

A digital fiat currency, also known as e-CNY, is a value-based, quasi-account based on a hybrid payment instrument with legal tender status. A unit of account, a medium of exchange and a store of value are all functions performed by e-CNY. e-CNY is China's legal tender, just as RMB is in its physical form. China's fiat currency is available in digital form. While e-CNY has the same issuance and circulation as physical RMB, its value is transferred electronically. A central bank's e-CNY is its public liability. E-CNY is a legal tender backed by sovereign credit. e-CNY is a state-issued currency. In the operational system of e-CNY, the PBOC plays a central role. In addition to issuing e-CNY to commercial banks, it manages the whole life cycle of the currency. A central bank can revoke the expiration of issued digital e-CNY to align fiscal and monetary policies with market conditions (Arslanian, 2022). Meanwhile, authorized operators and other commercial institutions exchange and circulate e-CNY. Both e-CNY and physical RMB are liabilities of the PBOC to the public, regardless of their legal status or economic value. The PBOC will consider e-CNY and physical RMB when collecting, analyzing and managing daily data. The e-CNY is a CBDC issued to the public for retail use. By issuing e-CNY, China will meet its daily payment needs, improve the efficiency of its retail payment system and reduce its retail payment costs. With the development of digital technology and electronic payments, retail payments have become less cash based. As a result of the digitalization of cash, the central bank must ensure the public's direct access to cash and ensure the unit of account is consistent with the digital economy. In various scenarios, an e-CNY system will make financial services more accessible and provide fiat money for a large population. A list comparing e-CNY with other digital currencies is presented in Table 3.1.

A handful of studies have attempted to understand centralized digital currency consumption. Mainly, extant literature considers central bank digital currency adoption (Qian, 2019; Bindseil, 2020; Lee et al., 2021) payment choice (Shy, 2020), and the summary of factors considered are ease-of-use, security and transaction cost. Bijlsma et al. (2024) highlight trust, price, exchange, privacy and security. The present study considers a broader set of economic, technological, social and cultural factors compared to previous studies. For brevity and simplicity, in this chapter, we categorize digital currency as being defined by the property of centralization, such as central bank digital currencies. The chapter explores the meaning of money in digital currency within the social, economic and technological domains. It also discusses the role of social, technological and financial processes in attaining value and what money became—the discourse and examination aid in understanding the meaning of digital currencies.

Methodology

This research aims to uncover the meaning of money in central bank digital currency (CBDC). Gathering perceptions and probing discourse about what the public and communities perceive about central bank digital currency is essential. Discourse occurring in public space reveals the structure and expression of public conversation. Therefore, the investigation uses netnography and videography data gathered using AI-generated algorithms and extracted data from publicly available forums of videos and live broadcasts.

Table 3.1 Central Bank Digital Currency

Central Bank	*Year*	*CBDC*	*Type*	*Structure*	*Provider*	*Technology*	*DLT*
Launched							
Central Bank of Nigeria	2021	e-Naira	Retail	*USSD	Bitt Inc.	Hyperledger	DLT
Central Bank of Bahamas	2017	Sand Dollar	Retail	Token	Movmint	NZIA Cortex	DLT
Reserve Bank of Zimbabwe	2021	ZIG	Retail, Wholesale	**GBDT	—	—	Non-DLT
Bank of Jamaica	2023	Jam-Dex	Retail	Account	eCurrency Mint	DSC	Non-DLT
Pilot							
Bank of Russia	2019	D-Ruble	Retail	Account	—	—	Non-DLT
National Bank of Kazakhstan	2020	D-Tenge	Retail, Wholesale	Token	R3 Corda, Binance	—	DLT
Reserve Bank of India	2020	D-Rupee	Retail, Wholesale	Token	—	—	DLT
People's Bank of China	2014	e-CNY	Retail	Account	Feitian Technologies	—	Non-DLT
People's Bank of China, Bank of Thailand	2022	*m-Bridge	Wholesale	Token	—	Dashing Protocol	DLT
Saudi Arabian Monetary Authority	2019	Aber	Wholesale	Account	IBM	—	DLT
The Bank of Ghana	2018	E-Cedi	Retail	Token	Giesecke+Devrient	Filia	Non-DLT
Central Bank of Tunisia, Banque de France	2021	Properus	Wholesale	Token	Prosperus	—	DLT
Central Bank of the Republic of Turkey	2018	Digital Lira	Retail	Token	TÜBITAK	—	DLT
Central Bank of Hungary	2020	Hungary CBDC	Retail	Token	***MNB	***MNB	DLT
Banque de France	2021	French CBDC	Wholesale	Token	IBM	DL3S	DLT

(*Continued*)

Table 3.1 (Continued)

Central Bank	*Year*	*CBDC*	*Type*	*Structure*	*Provider*	*Technology*	*DLT*
Swiss National Bank	2020	Helvetia	Wholesale	Token	SIX Digital Exchange	—	DLT
Proof of Concept							
USA (Project Hamilton), Canada (Jasper, Jasper-Ubin), Brazil (Drex), Sweden (e-Krona), Norway (CBDC), Ukraine (e-hryvnia), Georgia (D-Lari), Iran (D-Rial), UAE, Israel (e-Shekel), Laos (CBDC), Malaysia (e-Ringgit), Philippines (Agila), Japan (D-Yen), South Korea, Australia (e-AUD), New Zealand, Palau, Hong Kong (e-HKD), Singapore (Jasper-Ubin, Inthanon-LionRock), Thailand (Inthanon, Inthanon-LionRock)							
Research Stage							
44 countries in the world in research phase							
Cancelled							
Six countries have been canceled: Finland (Avant), Denmark (e-Kroner), Kenya CBDC, Philippines CBDC, Ecuador and Curacao.							

Source: https://cbdctracker.org/

Note: * Unstructured Supplementary Service Data code on mobile phones, ** Gold-backed digital token, *** Central Bank of Hungary (MNB) own technology.

The digital disruptions in financial services have caused public discourse about the possibility of digital currency, and this chapter utilizes the public discourse to develop the meaning of money in digital currency. This discourse occurs in public, like a brainstorming effect where millions think and feel about a central topic. The network effect brings a uniqueness to making sense of the central phenomenon, the meaning of money in the form of digital currency. While money and technology make space for discussion, digitalization provokes security concerns and highlights risks associated with digital currency. The existing body of research on the meaning of money and its value (Belk & Wallendorf, 1990; Carruthers & Babb, 1996; Zelizer, 1994) highlights how individuals derive the meaning of money by embedding it within social, political and economic conditions. It requires investigation and interpretations of public opinion.

Research Context

Chinese e-CNY, or Digital RMB, launched in January 2019 is the context of this study (Popper & Li, 2021). It is the first central bank digital currency whose value is aligned to the fiat renminbi and is being tested as legal tender in a significant economy (Areddy, 2021). In April 2020, testing began in four Chinese cities (Shenzhen, Suzhou, Chengdu and Xiong'an) to improve the currency's functionality (Wu, 2020). It has been verified that e-CNY is reliable, stable, easy to use and prevents money laundering, tax evasion and terror financing in several pilot programs in various cities (Chen, 2021). Five additional regions have been added to the pilot program since 2022: Jinan, Fangchenggang, Nanning, Kunming and Xishuangbanna (Feng, 2023). Twenty-six Chinese cities serve as test beds, and 5.6 million merchants registered in 2023 (Nulimaimaiti, 2023). In 2023, Changshu, in the province of Jiangsu, conducted a rollout to government employees, state-owned companies and public institutions (L. He, 2023). During the same period, prime banks and telecommunication companies such as the Bank of China, China Telecom and China Unicom jointly launched SIM card-based e-CNY wallets to access offline payments by applying near-field communication (NFC) (Chhangani, 2023).

Data Collection

To explore public opinion about the "meaning of money as a central bank-issued digital currency," our research adopted videography (short videos on the TikTok platform) and netnography (focusing on understanding the concept, keywords, likes and comments) as research approaches. Netnography and videography enabled the researchers to explore and understand diverse communities and interest groups nationally and globally. This method allows for studying topics online in virtual communities that might not be easily accessible through other means (Belk & Kozinet, 2017). This investigation aims to analyze publicly available verbatims of what was said and how it is used to uplift or critique the central meaning of digital currency in social settings.

Xinbang (https://xd.newrank.cn) is a multifaceted digital platform aggregating creative content and real-time e-commerce data, including videos, background music, challenges and product rankings based on various metrics such as sales and public opinion. The category includes content marketing, live streaming e-commerce, training operations, copyright distribution and other services, focusing on digital marketing and helping Chinese enterprises acquire and manage digital content assets. It offers tools for precise targeting and analysis of all WeChat (Official Account message template, WeChat Channels), Douyin, Xiaohongshu, B station, Kuaishou, People, Toutiao, Douyin, Kuaishou, Xiaohongshu, B station, Tencent watch, Baijia, NetEase, Sohu, a little information, Qu Toutiao, Sina watch, Youhao Video, Xigua Video, Sohu Video, Ximalaya, Dragonfly FM, Litchi FM, Evernote, Understand Chedi, Mafengwo and other mainstream content platforms, videos with extensive data indicators, live broadcast tracking and account searching with multiple filters. Additionally, Xindou facilitates the discovery of famous locations and trends, provides insights into brand dynamics and hosts a range of resources like updates, reports and communities for user engagement and knowledge sharing. Membership in these communities is free and anonymous in data extraction, though participants can identify themselves within the platform.

Data Cleaning and Analysis Procedure

The data consisted of discussion threads between April 2023 and April 2024 on 'Digital Currency.' The dataset comprises publicly available posts in 110 categories comprising 500,000 posts. A second search term, 'perception,' was superimposed on digital currency, which required further narrowing down to 'finance,' 'technology,' 'economics' and 'humanities and social sciences.' 'Humanities and social sciences' and 22 subcategories were generated through manual filtering. Post messages, text, timestamps and topics or comments were analyzed. Within each category, we developed scripts using Python to scan the dataset and filter outposts by identifying those that contained specific keywords (e.g., 'assets,' 'currency,' 'finance' and 'social impact') related to the categories we refined. After keyword filtering, we performed text analysis to identify thematic trends across posts and assess how people's views on digital currencies differ across academic and practical contexts. Additionally, we applied sentiment analysis to assess the emotional tone of the discussions to gain insights into the wide range of public sentiment toward digital currencies in different domains. Through this approach, we distilled the dataset into 160 posts specifically related to digital currencies. The combined analysis of these posts produced a 10,000-word document.

Coding clip

```
def categorize_perception(text):
tangible = any(keyword in text for keyword in
tangible_keywords)
intangible = any(keyword in text for keyword in
intangible_keywords)
social = any(keyword in text for keyword in social_keywords)
economic = any(keyword in text for keyword in
ieconomic_keywords)
gold = any(keyword in text for keyword in gold_keywords)
stability = any(keyword in text for keyword in
istability_keywords)
security = any(keyword in text for keyword in
security_keywords)
privacy = any(keyword in text for keyword in
privacy_keywords)
asset = any(keyword in text for keyword in asset_keywords)
if tangible and intangible and social and economic and gold
and stability and security and privacy and asset:
return 'all'
else:
return 'None'
df['Perception'] = df['text'].apply(categorize_perception)
```

Results and Discussion

The idea of decentralized digital money distributed the task of maintaining a ledger of transactions to multiple miners to validate the transactions based on the proof of work or proof of stake and incentivized individual miners to participate in the mining activities mainly based on the processing power of the networks of computers. This process of digital money leapfrogs the role of government and banking institutions. The blockchain-based approach sidelined the role of banking institutions and placed importance on 'trustless' protocols that verified the creation of digital cash with the consensus of all the nodes in the network. In this sense, trustlessness refers to the quality of a decentralized blockchain, whereby there is no need to rely on trust from a third party. Unlike traditional networks operated by centralized financial institutions such as SWIFT, mobile payment via platforms such as WeChat and Alipay, Digital currency bypasses such institutions, media and platforms. Bitcoin was created as a system where anyone with a computer and an internet connection can participate in validating transactions. A public ledger keeps track of all transactions so anyone (designated) can view them. In place of trusting one central institution, code and economic incentives are carefully designed. This means that trust can be distributed and that its need is minimized.

Primitive society trusted gold and silver to have intrinsic value in use to serve as money. Modern societies perceive fiat currency as representing value and worth, and the exact nature of value is unknown since trust in the issuing authority encodes the value of money (Popper, 2015). Digital gold, such as

Bitgold, mimicked fiat currencies by hedging against them, creating unlimited money out of nothing (Sharma, 2021), the exception being cryptocurrencies, such as Bitcoin, which utilizes decentralized money creation. The commonality between fiat currencies and cryptocurrency performs the function of money but differs as the former is a legal tender, and the latter derives its value from the native blockchain (Abid et al., 2023). Commercial banks create credit under a regulatory framework, and the role of the central bank is to supervise commercial banks and manage monetary policies (Ioannidou, 2005). On the contrary, protocols, codes, blockchain and distributed users govern cryptocurrencies.

Using decentralized blockchain technology, the system uses decentralized networks to access 'trustless' transactions (Chohan, 2019). The trustless protocol of cryptocurrencies is distinct from trust-based fiat currencies (Harz & Boman, 2019). 'Trustless' is a quality of decentralized blockchain technology, meaning there is no need to place trust in third-party agencies (Truong et al., 2021, p. 68). What makes cryptocurrency unique is its ability to ensure anonymity in transactions and global reach, and it is often criticized as a tool for money laundering. Möser (2013) contends that digital currency based on blockchain design ensures all transactions are publicly stored and that encrypted transactions cannot be bundled and forwarded anonymously since the origin must always be specified to prevent double spending. Androulaki et al. (2013) similarly discredit cryptocurrency that privacy in multi-input transactions with system-generated shadow addresses can neither hide privacy nor be anonymous since user profile and online behavior occurs in the public domain (Reid & Harrigan, 2013). In 1985, Chaum designed an e-cash system embedding anonymity using a blind signature. Similarly, Levin et al. (2011) tried electronic currencies as a credit network, where users can create digital credit bonds that guarantee collateral for the transaction. The hindsight of blind signature and digital credit bonds rely on trust in a third party to prevent double spending, leaning toward fiat currency in circulation. The risk of hacking this system made it unpopular. The 2008 financial crisis spurred a drive to a decentralized alternative payment system on top of the existing banking system, resulting in the launch of Bitcoin in 2009. The origin of alternative payment systems, such as Bitcoin and, eventually, in recent times, central bank digital currency, share its roots in the 2008 financial crisis.

Cryptocurrencies, as a decentralized system, inherently encounter instability of price. One is viewed as an alternative currency and used as a speculative tool, and participation has not gained global acceptance (Phan et al., 2021). According to Zhang et al. (2024), the stability of cryptocurrency is correlated with economic policy uncertainty; that is, investors in the cryptocurrency market perceive liquidity volatility as risk or as a desired speculative gamble. Under economic policy uncertainty, cryptocurrencies will be prone to instability. For example, Bitcoin experienced a rise from $0 in 2009 to $68,000 in 2023. Cryptocurrencies crashed in 2022 but rose again in 2024, demonstrating the unstable nature of the liquidity dependent in the parallel speculative stock market.

Figure 3.1 Central Bank Digital Currency Stability

Stability

Figure 3.1 presents the keywords that were prominent to digital currency consumption stability of central bank digital currency branching antecedents to adoptions of digital currency relies on conversion economy, that in the ease people move between different payment method, and trust and reliability with stability of the payment method (see Figure 3.1). Central Bank digital currency centralizes and controls the governance of the digital money supply. Schilling and Seuring (2024, p. 3) argue that central bank digital currency would struggle to achieve 'price stability though it is possible to achieve a socially efficient allocation, financial stability.' The argument is based on speculation. According to Diamond and Dybvig (1983) (bank runs and related financial crises), socially efficient allocation leads to bank runs (i.e., when a bank or other financial institution customers withdraw their deposits over concerns about the bank's solvency at the same time). An example of this would be a central bank digital currency offering nominal savings accounts to households and acting as the intermediary in the financial market (Bagehot, 1873). Spending runs and their associated inflations pose a risk to a central bank concerned with price stability. This argument echoes Schilling and Seuring (2024, p. 3), who argue that a

> *"central bank's primary tasks are maintaining stable prices and ensuring financial stability through their role as lenders of last resort, raises*

> *concern as central bank digital currency may become an attractive alternative to traditional demand deposits in private banks for all households and firms."* As a result, the central bank may be transformed into a financial intermediary that must confront classic banking issues and the exposure to a demand for liquidity induced by "spending" shocks (runs) of its private customers.

Next, we focus on digital currency and discourse in the public domain, broadly covering economic, technological, social and cultural contexts.

Economics and Finance

In the digital economy, digital currency is central to connecting individuals, businesses, devices, data and operations through digital technology (Miao, 2022). There are multiple requirements of an economy to be a digital economy and sufficiently have e-business synergies based on established e-business infrastructure and sound e-commerce in the private sector; in these senses (Minich, 2023), China's e-business model is well grounded in the success of the 5G Internet network and e-commerce platforms (Jiang & Murmann, 2022). Keyword analysis reveals digital RMB, digital wallets, smartphones, digital currency and assets and the infrastructure-defining digital economy in China.

Third-party payment performs functions as store, exchange and unit of account of value functions (Khan, 2011). Perhaps digital currency pegged to a fiat currency ensures stability. This contrasts with decentralized cryptocurrencies, which fluctuate as a store of value, as evidenced by the Bitcoin crash in early 2022. The public conversation surrounds fluctuations in the exchange rates, akin to the stock market. The central bank's digital currencies remain trustworthy and stable with a guarantee from the government (Lotz, 2014). Cryptocurrencies would gain stability with increased adoption, and variability in the exchange rate should stabilize with Central Bank Digital Currencies (Phillips & Pohl, 2024).

The horizontal bar graph in Figure 3.2 shows the distribution of content categories related to digital currencies. This chart shows categories in which digital currencies are a topic of interest in multiple domains. However, digital currencies stand out by appearing more frequently in the economic and technology fields, suggesting that digital currencies have the potential to be discussed more broadly and have a more significant impact on the financial market.

The count data reveals that e-CNY or Digital RMB was the most discussed topic in the TikTok platform in 2024, following third-party payment apps. Data reveals that China's economy is ripe for the rollout of e-CNY or digital RMB with established digital economy infrastructure and smartphone penetration. Approximately 72% of Chinese people own smartphones as of 2022 (Statista, 2022). The most relevant theme to imposed keywords reveals people's interest and concerns about third-party apps or digital wallets. The public discourse analysis reveals interest in digital assets that people equated with digital gold and e-CNY (see Figure 3.3).

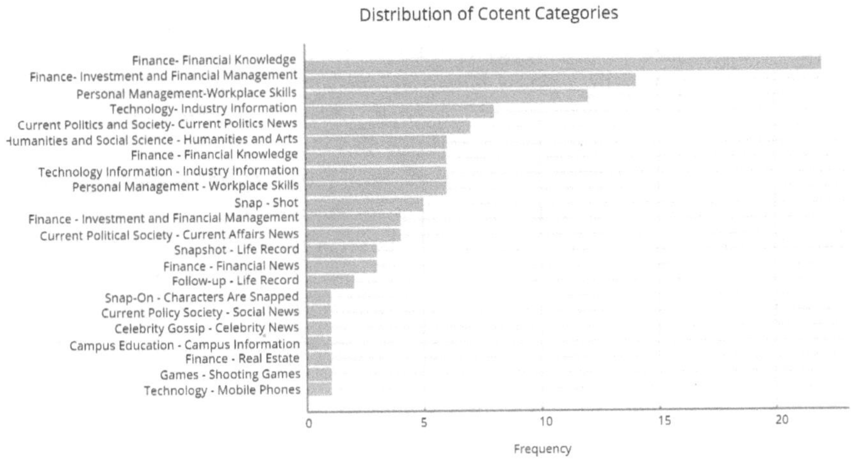

Figure 3.2 Central Bank Digital Currencies Content Categories

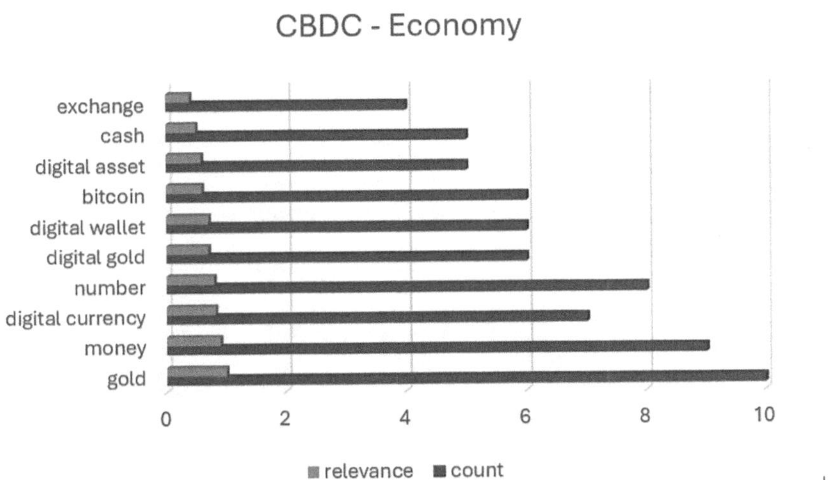

Figure 3.3 Central Bank Digital Currency Economy

Economy and Technology

Within this discourse (see Figure 3.3), central bank digital currency appears more frequently in the economy and technology, suggesting that digital currencies have the potential to impact the digital economy. The double national currency model (fiat and CBDC), to which the digital currency is pegged to the national currency, instills confidence in the public. The view is *that e-CNY is new, young, and promising [He] has a potential but careless, intangible digital gold* (see Appendix 3.1, comments appear in TikTok under the e-CNY category). The reference to gold in the data may have been related to its value as a reserve currency globally. The extant opinion of the public assures that the digital economy is here to stay, with digital currency playing a significant part in the future development of the economy. Gold is viewed as a barometer of value and asset and the measure of economic value. Commentary analysis in TikTok reveals that "compared to cash, digital RMB is an asset like gold ... have a higher level of liquidity and anonymity" (see Appendix 3.1). The digital economy is based on the digitalization of economic value. This justifies the shift in the digital economy in which economic activities are measured against computational power used to generate digital currencies rather than the simple economic theory of labor. The value chain would entail electricity and energy consumption to run and maintain blockchain and digital currency technologies (Abakah et al., 2024). As seen in the word frequency counts, digital gold appears to be associated with asset, safety and original investment. Similarly, Bitgold links with code, numbers, mining and worth. These words highlight the difference in the meaning of money when it is a legal tender issued by the government.

Digital Money

Figure 3.4 Digital Currency Consumption

Digital Money and Consumption

Figure 3.4 presents the community discourse on digital currency and expresses a solid connection to socio-economic concepts in which people tend to equate money with the intrinsic value of gold. Similarly, exchangeability for goods and services is associated with the source of value. The economics derives the meaning of money in digital currency situated on the source of intrinsic value, and the symbolic intrinsic value appears as digital gold. The earliest digital currency depicting gold was Nick Szabo's Bitgold. The attempt was to create a decentralized virtual currency based on blockchain in 1998 (Frisby, 2014). Szabo saw data as bits of gold encrypted to perform financial transactions representing value without relying on a trust-based third party. The idea was to develop a system that does not rely on third-party 'trust' to free money from manipulating central banks and governments. Thus, unlike Bitcoin, Bitgold was not seen as being related to money itself but rather an alternative to reserve currency to back other forms of electronic currency simulating the gold standard before the collapse of the Bretton Woods agreement. A decade later, Satoshi Nakamoto's Bitcoin, using proof of work and limits on minting Bitcoins, dealt with the most significant issue: fiat currency is accused of causing recessions. Szabo attempted to align Bitgold closely with the gold standard in cyberspace, which is that people place their trust in precious metals. Unlike gold and silver, both fiat currencies and Bitgold lacks the intrinsic value in use that gold stands for (Peck, 2012). A decade later, Nakamoto (2009), in a white paper, emphasized designing a system of value exchange that was decentralized and trustless, taking away the control of money from government and central banks. In doing so, Nakamoto's Bitcoin imitates the look of digital gold resembling gold color. Contrarily, the Chinese e-CNY logo features a Yen sign surrounded by a digital renminbi in a dark red color. Some observers (Zakir et al., 2023; Maouchi et al., 2024; Qin et al., 2024) claim digital currency is digital gold because it has the characteristics of a safe haven asset like gold. Others consider it a speculative bubble or fad (Bajra & Aliu, 2023; Meider, 2023; Qin et al., 2024). Bitcoin has shown remarkable resilience during periods of turmoil, highlighting its potential hedging and safe haven grounding in gold symbolism, which was not only critical to the design of Bitcoin but also played a significant role in its initial adoption. The word count and relevance of categories to digital currencies suggest a collective focus on digital currencies, such as 'digital money,' 'digital wallet,' 'digital gold,' 'bitcoin,' 'transactions' and 'cash.' In the face of this finding, words like 'secure,' 'unstable,' 'innovative,' 'intangible' and 'trust' appear prominently, indicating the focus of public discussion around digital currencies' security, stability and novelty. Words like 'investment,' 'technology' and 'future' are prominent, which may indicate optimism that digital currencies are future-proof and integral to technological advances and investment strategies. However, more discussion is gathered on sensible expectations of digital currencies, which suggests that digital currencies are more controversial but more appealing to TikTok users and deserve further discussion and studies of Generation Z's perceptions of digital currency.

Conclusion

A central theme of central bank digital currency is its stability, which is the assurance of pegging digital currency to national currency. Digital currencies may not reference intrinsic value in use reflected in public conversation regarding digital gold and assets. This highlights that people seek security and stability of their money stored in digital currency. The digital currency has no physical form and exists purely in the digital realm. Therefore, regulators must ensure that people feel that digital currency is stable and secure. Intangibility challenges the concept of trustworthiness and reliability since third-party payment experiences similar challenges of being nonphysical. Terms related to innovation, technology and the future are associated with digital currencies. The analysis also revealed that a dual system of traditional fiat currency running parallel to central bank digital currency is positive in instilling the value of stability and security, avoiding the risk associated with adoption. This reflects an understanding that digital currencies require new approaches to ensure trust, reliability and protection against fraud or loss. Digital currencies are often discussed in terms of their accessibility and global utility. This suggests that currencies have implications beyond national borders and traditional banking systems, providing a more inclusive financial system globally. It demonstrates the democratization of finance, where anyone with access to the internet can access money in the form of digital currency. Public discourse reveals that third-party payment systems are deeply embedded in people's lives; therefore, enacting interoperability between different payment methods is deemed necessary to adopt digital currency successfully in the coming days.

References

Abakah, E. J. A., Tiwari, A. K., Abdullah, M., Ji, Q., & Sulong, Z. (2024). Monetary policy uncertainty and ESG performance across energy firms. *Energy Economics*, *136*, 107699.

Abid, I., Bouri, E., Galariotis, E., Guesmi, K., & Mzoughi, H. (2023). Bitcoin vs. fiat currencies: Insights from extreme dependence and risk spillover analysis with financial markets. *International Review of Financial Analysis*, *90*, 102806. https://doi.org/10.1016/j.irfa.2023.102806

Agur, I., Ari, A., & Dell'Ariccia, G. (2022). Designing central bank digital currencies. *Journal of Monetary Economics*, *125*, 62–79.

Androulaki, E., Karame, G. O., Roeschlin, M., Scherer, T., & Capkun, S. (2013). Evaluating user privacy in bitcoin. In *Financial Cryptography and Data Security: 17th International Conference, FC 2013,* Okinawa, Japan, April 1–5, *Revised Selected Papers 17* (pp. 34–51). Springer Berlin Heidelberg.

Areddy, J. T. (2021, April 5). China creates its own digital currency, a first for major economy. *Wall Street Journal*. https://www.wsj.com/articles/china-creates-its-own-digital-currency-a-first-for-major-economy-11617634118

Arslanian, H. (2022). Central bank digital currencies. In Arslanian, H. (Ed.), *The book of crypto: The complete guide to understanding bitcoin, cryptocurrencies and digital assets* (pp. 171–184). Springer International Publishing.

Atlantic Council. (2024). CBDC tracker. *Atlantic Council*. https://www.atlanticcouncil.org/cbdctracker/

Bagehot, W. (1873). *Lombard street*. King.

Bajra, U. Q., & Aliu, F. (2023). Deciphering the cryptocurrency conundrum: Investigating speculative characteristics and volatility. *Finance Research Letters*, *58*, 104589.

Barrdear, J., & Kumhof, M. (2022). The macroeconomics of central bank digital currencies. *Journal of Economic Dynamics and Control*, *142*, 104148.

Belk, R., & Kozinetz, R. (2017). Videography and netnography. In Kubacki, K. & Rundle-Thiele, S. (Eds.), *Formative research in social marketing: Innovative methods to gain consumer insights* (pp. 265–279). Springer.

Belk, R., & Wallendorf, M. (1990). The sacred meanings of money. *Journal of Economic Psychology*, *11*, 35–67.

Bijlsma, M., van der Cruijsen, C., Jonker, N., & Reijerink, J. (2024). What triggers consumer adoption of central bank digital currency? *Journal of Financial Services Research*, *65*(1), 1–40.

Bindseil, U. (2020). Tiered CBDC and the financial system. *SSRN Electronic Journal*. https://doi.org/10.2139/ssrn.3513422

Boar, C., Holden, H., & Wadsworth, A. (2020). Impending arrival – A sequel to the survey on central bank digital currency. *BIS paper* (107).

Bonnet, S., & Teuteberg, F. (2023). Impact of blockchain and distributed ledger technology for the management of the intellectual property life cycle: A multiple case study analysis. *Computers in Industry*, *144*, 103789.

Buterin, V. (2014). A next-generation smart contract and decentralized application platform. *White Paper*, *3*(37), 2–1.

Carruthers, B. G., & Babb, S. (1996). The color of money and the nature of value: Greenbacks and gold in postbellum America. *American Journal of Sociology*, *101*(6), 1556–1591.

Chen, S. (2021). Progress of research and development of E-CNY in China. *Working Group on E-CNY Research and Development,* People's Bank of China, *16*.

Chhangani, A. (2023, November 6). Central bank digital currency evolution in 2023: From investigation to preparation. *Atlantic Council*. https://www.atlanticcouncil.org/blogs/econographics/central-bank-digital-currency-evolution-in-2023-from-investigation-to-preparation/

Chohan, U. W. (2019). Are cryptocurrencies truly trustless? In Goutte, S., Guesmi, K., & Saadi, S. (Eds.), *Cryptofinance and mechanisms of exchange: The making of virtual currency* (pp. 77–89). Springer.

Cunha, P. R., Melo, P., & Sebastião, H. (2021). From bitcoin to central bank digital currencies: Making sense of the digital money revolution. *Future Internet*, *13*(7), 165.

Davoodalhosseini, S. M. (2022). Central bank digital currency and monetary policy. *Journal of Economic Dynamics and Control*, *142*, 104150.

Diamond, D. W., & Dybvig, P. H. (1983). Bank runs, deposit insurance, and liquidity. *Journal of Political Economy, 91*(3), 401–419.

Farahani, B., Firouzi, F., & Luecking, M. (2021). The convergence of IoT and distributed ledger technologies (DLT): Opportunities, challenges, and solutions. *Journal of Network and Computer Applications*, *177*, 102936.

Feng, H. (2023, November). The application of blockchain technology in e-CNY in China. In 2023 International Conference on Finance, Trade and Business Management (FTBM 2023) (pp. 479–486). Atlantis Press.

Frisby, D. (2014). *Bitcoin: The future of money?* Unbound Publishing.

Giblin, R. (2011). Physical world assumptions and software world realities (and why there are more P2P software providers than ever before). *The Columbia Journal of Law & the Arts*, *35*, 57.

Gray, G. R., & Gray, G. R. (2021). DLT types and design trade-offs. In Gray, G. R. (Ed.), Blockchain technology for managers (pp. 165–172). Springer.

Gronwald, M. (2019). Is bitcoin a commodity? On price jumps, demand shocks, and certainty of supply. *Journal of International Money and Finance*, *97*, 86–92.

Harz, D., & Boman, M. (2019). The scalability of trustless trust. In *Financial Cryptography and Data Security: FC 2018 International Workshops, Bitcoin, voting, and WTSC*, Nieuwpoort, Curaçao, March 2, 2018, *Revised Selected Papers 22* (pp. 279–293). Springer Berlin Heidelberg.

He, A. J. (2023). Scaling-up through piloting: Dual-track provider payment reforms in China's health system. *Health Policy and Planning*, *38*(2), 218–227.

He, L. (2023, April 24). China makes major push in its ambitious digital yuan project | CNN Business. *CNN*. https://www.cnn.com/2023/04/24/economy/china-digital-yuan-government-salary-intl-hnk/index.html

Ioannidou, V. P. (2005). Does monetary policy affect the central bank's role in bank supervision? *Journal of Financial Intermediation*, *14*(1), 58–85.

Jagrič, T., Fister, D., Amon, A., Jagrič, V., & Beloglavec, S. T. (2022). The banking industry in the ecosystem of digital currencies and digital central bank currencies. In Grima, S., Özen, E., & Boz, H. (Eds.), *The new digital era: Digitalisation, emerging risks and opportunities* (pp. 89–115). Emerald Publishing Limited.

Jiang, H., & Murmann, J. P. (2022). The rise of China's digital economy: An overview. *Management and Organization Review*, *18*(4), 790–802.

Khan, J. (2011). *Cash or card: Consumer perceptions of payment modes* (Doctoral dissertation, Auckland University of Technology).

Kiff, J., Alwazir, J., Davidovic, S., Farias, A., Khan, A., Khiaonarong, T., Malaika, M., Monroe, H. K., Sugimoto, N., Tourpe, H., & Zhou, P. (2020). *A survey of research on retail central bank digital currency*. Repec.org. IMF Working Papers, no. 20/104. https://econpapers.repec.org/paper/imfimfwpa/2020_2f104.htm

Lee, D. K. C., Yan, L., & Wang, Y. (2021). A global perspective on central bank digital currency. *China Economic Journal*, *14*(1), 52–66.

Levin, D., Schulman, A., LaCurts, K., Spring, N., & Bhattacharjee, B. (2011, June). Making currency inexpensive with iOwe. In *Proceedings of the workshop on the economics of networks, systems, and computation (netecon)*. Workshop on the Economics of Networks, Systems, and Computation Vancouver British Columbia Canada 3 October 2010. https://www.cs.umd.edu/~dml/papers/iowe_netecon11.pdf

Liu, J., & Serletis, A. (2019). Volatility in the cryptocurrency market. *Open Economies Review*, *30*(4), 779–811.

Lotz, C. (2014). *The capitalist schema: Time, money, and the culture of abstraction*. Lexington Books.

Maouchi, Y., Fakhfekh, M., Charfeddine, L., & Jeribi, A. (2024). Is digital gold a hedge, safe haven, or diversifier? An analysis of cryptocurrencies, DeFi tokens, and NFTs. *Applied Economics*, Advance Publication Online, 1–16.

Maryaningsih, N., Nazara, S., Kacaribu, F. N., & Juhro, S. M. (2022). Central bank digital currency: What factors determine its adoption? *Bulletin of Monetary Economics and Banking*, *25*(1), 1–24.

Meider, E. (2023). Crypto currencies: Speculative bubble or disruptive technology? In Užík, M., Schmitz, C., & Block, S. (Eds.), *Financial innovation and value creation: The impact of disruptive technologies on the digital world* (pp. 21–41). Springer International Publishing.

McConaghy, M., McMullen, G., Parry, G., McConaghy, T., & Holtzman, D. (2017). Visibility and digital art: Blockchain as an ownership layer on the Internet. *Strategic Change*, *26*(5), 461–470.

Miao, Z. (2022). Industry 4.0: Technology spillover impact on digital manufacturing industry. *Journal of Enterprise Information Management*, *35*(4/5), 1251–1266.

Minich, S. A. (2023). Improving the system of mandatory requirements to business under the digital transformation of economy. *Journal of Digital Technologies and Law*, *1*(3), 775–802.

Möser, M. (2013, July). Anonymity of bitcoin transactions. In University of Münster *(Ed.), Münster bitcoin conference* (pp. 17–18). University of Münster.

Mougayar, M., & Buterin, V. (2016). Blockchain for business.

Nakamoto, S. (2009). *Bitcoin: A peer-to-peer electronic cash system Bitcoin: A peer-to-peer electronic cash system*. Bitcoin. org. https://bitcoin.org/en/bitcoin-paper

Nulimaimaiti, M. (2023, October 10). How is China's digital yuan roll-out progressing in 2023? *South China Morning Post*. https://www.scmp.com/economy/china-economy/article/3237317/whats-state-chinas-digital-yuan-2023

O'Dair, M. (2018). *Distributed creativity: How blockchain technology will transform the creative economy*.

Parlour, C. A., & Rajan, U. (2020). Contracting on credit ratings: Adding value to public information. *The Review of Financial Studies*, *33*(4), 1412–1444.

Peck, M. E. (2012). The cryptoanarchists' answer to cash. *IEEE Spectrum*, *49*(6), 50–56.

People's Bank of China (PBOC). (2022). *Payment system report (2021)*. http://www.pbc.gov.cn/en/3688110/3688172/4437084/4525787/2022040622295461615.pdf

Phan, M., & Nordal, T. L. (2021). *Bitcoin in a pandemic: Did COVID-19 cases or other factors affect Bitcoin's return during the pandemic and did Bitcoin provide diversification benefits during this period?* (Master's thesis).

Phillips, P. J., & Pohl, G. (2024, January 19). Bitcoin, 2022, crash. *Crash*.

Popper, N. (2015). *Digital gold: Bitcoin and the inside story of the misfits and millionaires trying to reinvent money* (Cane, J., Murphy, D., Titunik, V., Gillen, D., & Lattman, P., Eds.). http://bit.ly/3UqvpxF

Popper, N., & Li, C. (2021, March 1). China charges ahead with a national digital currency. *The New York Times*. https://www.nytimes.com/2021/03/01/technology/china-national-digital-currency.html

Qian, Y. (2019). Central bank digital currency: Optimization of the currency system and its issuance design. *China Economic Journal*, *12*(1), 1–15.

Qin, M., Su, C. W., Wang, Y., & Doran, N. M. (2024). Could "digital gold" resist global supply chain pressure? *Technological and Economic Development of Economy*, *30*(1), 1–21.

Reid, F., & Harrigan, M. (2013). *An analysis of anonymity in the bitcoin system* (pp. 197–223). Springer.

Rupa, C., MidhunChakkarvarthy, D., Patan, R., Prakash, A. B., & Pradeep, G. G. (2022). Knowledge engineering–based DApp using blockchain technology for protract medical certificates privacy. *IET Communications*, *16*(15), 1853–1864.

Scardovi, C. (2016). *Restructuring and innovation in banking* (p. 36). Springer International Publishing.

Schilling, L., & Seuring, S. (2024). Linking the digital and sustainable transformation with supply chain practices. *International Journal of Production Research*, *62*(3), 949–973.

Schumacher, L. V. (2024). Architecting a wholesale CBDC. In Schumacher, L. V. (Ed.), *Decoding digital assets: Distinguishing the dream from the dystopia in stablecoins, tokenized deposits, and central bank digital currencies* (pp. 313–334). Springer Nature Switzerland.

Sharma, R. (2021, October 24). *Bit gold.* Investopedia. https://www.investopedia.com/terms/b/bit-gold.asp

Shirai, S. (2019). *Money and central bank digital currency.* Asian Development Bank Institute, ADBI Working Paper 922. https://papers.ssrn.com/sol3/papers.cfm?abstract_id=3362952

Shy, O. (2020). Low-income consumers and payment choice. *Research in Economics*, *74*(4), 292–300.

Statista. (2022, June 15). Smartphone penetration rate in China from 2018 to 2022 with forecasts until 2027 [Graph]. *Statista.* Retrieved July 31, 2024, from https://www-statista-com.surrey.idm.oclc.org/statistics/321482/smartphone-user-penetration-in-china/

Sunyaev, A., & Sunyaev, A. (2020). Distributed ledger technology. In *Internet computing: Principles of distributed systems and emerging internet-based technologies* (pp. 265–299). Springer.

Swan, M. (2015). *Blockchain: Blueprint for a new economy.* O'Reilly Media, Inc.

Tapscott, D., & Tapscott, A. (2016). *Blockchain revolution: How the technology behind Bitcoin is changing money, business, and the world.* Penguin.

Tresise, A., Goldenfein, J., & Hunter, D. (2018). What blockchain can and can't do for copyright. *28 Australian Intellectual Property Journal 144.* https://ssrn.com/abstract=3227381

Truong, N., Lee, G. M., Sun, K., Guitton, F., & Guo, Y. (2021). A blockchain-based trust system for decentralised applications: When trustless needs trust. *Future Generation Computer Systems*, *124*, 68–79.

Waliczek, S., & Nili, C. (2024, February 6). *Wholesale and retail CBDCs – What exactly is the difference?* World Economic Forum. https://www.weforum.org/agenda/2024/02/wholesale retail cbdcs-difference/

Wang, Z., Liffman, D. Y., Karunamoorthy, D., & Abebe, E. (2018, October). Distributed ledger technology for document and workflow management in trade and logistics. In *Proceedings of the 27th ACM International Conference on Information and Knowledge Management* (pp. 1895–1898). Association for Computing Machinery.

Wu, Y. (2020, November). The impact of the issuance of central bank digital currency on the effectiveness of monetary policy. In *2020 2nd International Conference on Economic Management and Cultural Industry (ICEMCI 2020)* (pp. 35–39). Atlantis Press.

Zakir, M. A. B. M., Zakaria, M. Z. B., Salleh, A. Z., Ismail, A. M., Hasbullah, M., & Majid, M. N. A. (2023). Digital gold investment platform in shariah perspective: A case study of quantum metal. In Rafiki, A. (Ed.), *Digitalization in halal management* (pp. 47–64). Springer Nature Singapore.

Zams, B. M., Indrastuti, R., Pangersa, A. G., Hasniawati, N. A., Zahra, F. A., & Fauziah, I. A. (2020). Designing central bank digital currency for Indonesia: The Delphi–analytic network process. *Bulletin of Monetary Economics and Banking*, *23*(3), 413–440.

Zelizer, V. A. (1994). The creation of domestic currencies. *The American Economic Review*, *84*(2), 138–142.

Zhang, P., Kong, D., Xu, K., & Qi, J. (2024). Global economic policy uncertainty and the stability of cryptocurrency returns: The role of liquidity volatility. *Research in International Business and Finance*, *67*, 102165.

Appendix 3.1

Keywords, Category and Selected Comments

Keywords	*Category*	*Selected Comments*	*Likes*	*Comment*
Episode 8	Web3.0 helps you regain your digital assets #web3 #NFT #digital economy				
Episode 9	The next 25 years of explosive wealth growth will be the era of the digital economy. 5557 193				
['is,' 'gold,' 'economy,' 'universe,' 'virtual,' 'time,' 'comparison,' 'troubled times,' 'liquidity,' 'Numbers,' 'We,' 'Hundreds of thousands']	Financial knowledge	*e-CNY is new, young, and promising [He] has potential but careless, intangible but digital gold*	1307	183
Episode 41	China's digital asset trading platform will officially launch on January 1, 2023! This concept may usher in an explosion! What are digital collections?				
['number,' 'leader,' 'good,' 'self,' 'culture,' 'digital gold,' 'share,' 'economy,' 'people's daily life online']	Financial Management	*Compared to cash, digital RMB is also an asset like gold … have a higher level of liquidity and anonymity*	2739	348
Episode 261	An asset that everyone can create, the sixth largest asset in the world, was born out of nowhere and can be inherited from generation to generation				
['China,' 'pay,' 'fortune,' 'already,' 'awesome,' 'asset,' 'really,' 'gold,' 'always,' 'enjoy']	Finance-Investment	*No paper money, convenient feels like gold, and a beauty [she] is adorable*	2716	190
Episode 40	The Web 3.0 era is to use digital wallets				
['identity,' 'codes,' 'digital assets,' 'digital wallet,' 'NFTs,' 'intangible'	Technology	*A modern and efficient person, a young person who is very fashionable and up to date with technology*	50	19
Episode 31	Artificial Intelligence #Metaverse #Web3				

['Artificial intelligence,' 'Metaverse,' 'Web3']	Technology	*This wave of technological revolution must be the biggest variable of digital assets in 2023!*	48	9
Episode 26 | The first year of virtual assets and digital economy				
['is,' 'gold,' 'economy,' 'can,' 'universe,' 'virtual,' 'time,' 'teacher,' 'comparison,' 'troubled times,' 'no,' 'liquidity,' 'Drumming,' 'Still,' 'Don't play,' 'Numbers,' 'We,' 'Teahouse,' 'Playing mahjong,' 'Hundreds of thousands']	Economics	*Cash has a more physical feel Digital assets are just numbers You can't see or touch them*	1461	257
Episode 30 | How to convert your data into assets?				
['Digitalization,' 'digital economy,' 'digital currency']	Economic	*Digital collection, blockchain, encryption, and digital assets is our future*	2016	30
Episode 69 | Use digital technology to build a win-win ecology in rural areas				
['hehe,' 'participation,' 'how,' 'take off,' 'make money,' 'good people,' 'experience exchange,' 'warm heart,' 'ordinary people,' 'same,' 'content,' 'worthy'	Social	*Help the construction of rural data systems the new digital forces for people's livelihood stability and social prosperity.*	747	250

Appendix 3.2
Central Bank Digital Currency Tracker

Name	*CBDC Status*	*Use Case*	*Architecture*	*Crossborder Projects*	*Technology*	*Infrastructure*	*Access*	*Technology Partnerships*
The Bahamas	Launched	Retail	Intermediated		NZIA Limited	Both	Undecided	NZIA Limited
Jamaica	Launched	Retail	Intermediated			Conventional	Undecided	eCurrency Mint
Nigeria	Launched	Retail	Intermediated		Fabric	DLT	Undecided	Bitt Inc.
Anguilla	Pilot	Retail	Intermediated	DCash		DLT	Undecided	Bitt Inc.
Saint Kitts and Nevis	Pilot	Retail	Intermediated	DCash	Fabric	DLT	Undecided	Bitt Inc.
Antigua and Barbuda	Pilot	Retail	Intermediated	DCash	Fabric	DLT	Undecided	Bitt Inc.
Montserrat	Pilot	Retail	Intermediated	DCash		DLT	Undecided	Bitt Inc.
Dominica	Pilot	Retail	Intermediated	DCash		DLT	Undecided	Bitt Inc.
Saint Lucia	Pilot	Retail	Intermediated	DCash	Fabric	DLT	Undecided	Bitt Inc.
Saint Vincent and the Grenadines	Pilot	Retail	Intermediated	DCash	Fabric	DLT	Undecided	Bitt Inc.
Grenada	Pilot	Retail	Intermediated	DCash	Fabric	DLT	Undecided	Bitt Inc.
Brazil	Pilot	Retail, Wholesale	Intermediated			DLT	Undecided	
Euro Area	Pilot	Retail, Wholesale	Intermediated	Digital euro		Both	Undecided	Caixabank, Worldline, Amazon, EPI and Nexi

Spain	Pilot	Retail	Undecided	Digital euro		Undecided	Undecided	
Sweden	Pilot	Retail	Intermediated	Project Icebreaker		DLT	Undecided	Svenska Handelsbanken
Ghana	Pilot	Retail	Intermediated			Undecided	Undecided	Giesecke + Devrient
South Africa	Pilot	Wholesale	Undecided	Project Dunbar		Undecided	Undecided	
Tunisia	Pilot	Wholesale	Undecided			Undecided	Undecided	ProsperUs
Ukraine	Pilot	Retail	Undecided			Undecided	Undecided	Stellar Development Foundation
Turkey	Pilot	Retail	Undecided			Both	Undecided	Aselsan, Havelsan, Tubitak Bilgem
Israel	Pilot	Retail, Wholesale	Intermediated		Ethereum	Both	Undecided	Project Icebreaker
Saudi Arabia	Pilot	Wholesale	Undecided	Project Aber	Fabric	DLT	Undecided	
United Arab Emirates	Pilot	Retail, Wholesale	Undecided	mBridge	Fabric	DLT	Undecided	
Iran	Pilot	Retail	Undecided			Undecided	Undecided	
Mauritius	Pilot	Retail, Wholesale	Undecided			Undecided	Undecided	
Kazakhstan	Pilot	Retail	Intermediated		R3 Corda	Both	Undecided	Binance
Russia	Pilot	Retail, Wholesale	Intermediated			Both	Undecided	
China	Pilot	Retail, Wholesale	Intermediated	mBridge		Both	Undecided	
India	Pilot	Retail, Wholesale	Intermediated			Both	Undecided	
Hong Kong	Pilot	Retail, Wholesale	Intermediated	mBridge, Project Aurum		Undecided	Undecided	

(Continued)

Name	*CBDC Status*	*Use Case*	*Architecture*	*Crossborder Projects*	*Technology*	*Infrastructure*	*Access*	*Technology Partnerships*
Laos	Pilot	Retail, Wholesale	Undecided			Undecided	Undecided	Soramitsu
Thailand	Pilot	Retail, Wholesale	Intermediated	mBridge		Both	Undecided	Giesecke + Devrient
Singapore	Pilot	Both	Undecided	Project Cedar, Project Dunbar, Project Jasper, Onyx/ Multiple wCBDC, Project Mariana		Undecided	Undecided	
Malaysia	Pilot	Wholesale	Undecided	Project Dunbar		Undecided	Undecided	
South Korea	Pilot	Retail	Intermediated		Ethereum	DLT	Undecided	Samsung; Ground X
Japan	Pilot	Retail, Wholesale	Intermediated	Project Stella		Undecided	Undecided	
Palau	Pilot	Retail, Wholesale	Undecided		Ripple	DLT	Undecided	Ripple
Australia	Pilot	Retail, Wholesale	Undecided	Project Dunbar	Ethereum	Undecided	Undecided	
Solomon Islands	Pilot	Retail, Wholesale	Undecided			Undecided	Undecided	Soramitsu
Mexico	Development	Retail	Undecided			Undecided	Undecided	
United States	Development	Retail, Wholesale	Intermediated	Project Cedar		Undecided	Undecided	
Canada	Development	Retail, Wholesale	Intermediated	Project Jasper		Both	Undecided	

Colombia	Development	Undecided	Intermediated		Undecided	Undecided	Undecided	Ripple
Haiti	Development	Retail, Wholesale	Intermediated			Both	Undecided	EMTECH, HaitiPay
United Kingdom	Development	Retail, Wholesale	Intermediated			Undecided	Undecided	
Norway	Development	Retail, Wholesale	Undecided	Project Icebreaker	Ethereum	Undecided	Undecided	
Ireland	Development	Undecided	Undecided			Undecided	Undecided	
France	Development	Retail, Wholesale	Intermediated	Digital euro		Undecided	Undecided	
Netherlands	Development	Retail	Intermediated	Digital euro		Both	Undecided	
Luxembourg	Development	Wholesale, Retail	Undecided	Venus Initiative			Undecided	
Switzerland	Development	Wholesale	Undecided	Project Jura, Project Mariana		Undecided	Undecided	SIX
Italy	Development	Wholesale, Retail	Intermediated	Digital euro		Both	Undecided	
Austria	Development	Retail, Wholesale	Undecided			DLT	Undecided	
Germany	Development	Wholesale, Retail	Intermediated	Digital euro		Both	Undecided	
Montenegro	Development	Retail	Undecided			Undecided	Undecided	Ripple
Belarus	Development	Undecided	Undecided			Undecided	Undecided	
Georgia	Development	Retail	Undecided			Undecided	Undecided	Ripple
Rwanda	Development	Undecided	Undecided			Undecided	Undecided	
Bahrain	Development	Wholesale	Intermediated			Both	Undecided	JP Morgan Onyx
Sri Lanka	Development	Retail	Undecided			Undecided	Undecided	
Bhutan	Development	Retail, Wholesale	Undecided		Ripple	Undecided	Undecided	Ripple
Cambodia	Development	Undecided	Intermediated			DLT	Undecided	Soramitsu

(Continued)

Name	*CBDC Status*	*Use Case*	*Architecture*	*Crossborder Projects*	***Technology***	***Infrastructure***	***Access***	***Technology Partnerships***
Indonesia	Development	Retail, Wholesale	Undecided			Undecided	Undecided	
Macau	Development	Undecided	Undecided	e-CNY		Undecided	Undecided	
Taiwan	Development	Retail, Wholesale	Undecided			Undecided	Undecided	
Philippines	Development	Wholesale	Undecided			Undecided	Undecided	
Finland	Development	Retail, Wholesale	Intermediated	Digital euro		Both	Undecided	
Estonia	Development	Retail	Intermediated	Digital euro		DLT	Undecided	
Lithuania	Development	Retail	Undecided		Ethereum	Undecided	Undecided	
Honduras	Research	Retail	Undecided			Undecided	Undecided	
Trinidad and Tobago	Research	Undecided	Undecided			Undecided	Undecided	
Peru	Research	Retail, Wholesale	Undecided			Undecided	Undecided	
Paraguay	Research	Undecided	Undecided			Undecided	Undecided	
Argentina	Research	Undecided	Undecided			Undecided	Undecided	
Chile	Research	Retail	Undecided			Undecided	Undecided	
Morocco	Research	Undecided	Undecided			Undecided	Undecided	
Mauritania	Research	Undecided	Undecided				Undecided	
Algeria	Research	Undecided	Undecided			Undecided	Undecided	
Andorra	Research	Retail	Undecided			Undecided	Undecided	
Czech Republic	Research	Undecided	Undecided			Undecided	Undecided	
Hungary	Research	Retail	Undecided			Undecided	Undecided	
Chad	Research	Undecided	Undecided			Undecided	Undecided	
Cameroon	Research	Undecided	Undecided			Undecided	Undecided	
Central African Republic	Research	Undecided	Undecided			Undecided	Undecided	

Equatorial Guinea	Research	Undecided	Undecided	Undecided	Undecided	
Gabon	Research	Undecided	Undecided	Undecided	Undecided	
Egypt	Research	Undecided	Undecided	Undecided	Undecided	
Jordan	Research		Undecided	Undecided	Undecided	
Namibia	Research		Undecided	Undecided	Undecided	
Botswana	Research	Undecided	Undecided	Undecided	Undecided	
Zimbabwe	Research	Undecided	Undecided	Undecided	Undecided	
Eswatini	Research	Retail, Wholesale	Undecided	Undecided	Undecided	Giesecke + Devrient
Madagascar	Research	Retail	Undecided	Undecided	Undecided	
United Republic of Tanzania	Research		Undecided	Undecided	Undecided	
Kenya	Research	Retail	Undecided	Undecided	Undecided	
Uganda	Research		Undecided	Undecided	Undecided	Temtum group
Ethiopia	Research		Undecided		Undecided	
Armenia	Research	Undecided	Undecided	Undecided	Undecided	
Azerbaijan	Research		Undecided	Undecided	Undecided	Visa
Qatar	Research	Wholesale, Retail	Undecided	Undecided	Undecided	
Oman	Research	Retail, Wholesale	Undecided	Undecided	Undecided	
Uzbekistan	Research	Undecided	Undecided	Undecided	Undecided	
Pakistan	Research	Retail	Undecided	Undecided	Undecided	
Nepal	Research		Undecided	Undecided	Undecided	
Bangladesh	Research	Undecided	Undecided	Undecided	Undecided	
Myanmar	Research	Undecided		Undecided	Undecided	
Vietnam	Research		Undecided	Undecided	Undecided	Soramitsu
Vanuatu	Research		Undecided	Undecided	Undecided	Soramitsu
New Zealand	Research	Retail	Undecided	Undecided	Undecided	
Fiji	Research	Undecided	Undecided	Undecided	Undecided	Soramitsu

(Continued)

Name	*CBDC Status*	*Use Case*	*Architecture*	*Crossborder Projects*	***Technology***	***Infrastructure***	***Access***	***Technology Partnerships***
Tonga	Research		Undecided			Undecided	Undecided	Soramitsu
Guatemala	Inactive		Undecided			Undecided	Undecided	
Belize	Inactive	Undecided	Undecided			Undecided	Undecided	Bitt Inc.
Costa Rica	Inactive	Undecided	Undecided			Undecided	Undecided	
Sint Maarten	Inactive	Retail	Intermediated			Conventional	Undecided	Bitt Inc.
Bermuda	Inactive	Undecided	Undecided			Undecided	Undecided	
Curaçao	Inactive	Retail	Intermediated			Conventional	Undecided	Bitt Inc.
Venezuela	Inactive	Retail, Wholesale	Undecided			Undecided	Undecided	
Uruguay	Inactive	Retail	Intermediated			Conventional	Undecided	
Iceland	Inactive	Retail	Undecided			Undecided	Undecided	
Denmark	Inactive	Retail	Undecided			Undecided	Undecided	
Benin	Inactive	Undecided	Undecided			Undecided	Undecided	
Zambia	Inactive		Undecided			Undecided	Undecided	
Lebanon	Inactive	Retail	Undecided			Undecided	Undecided	
Palestine	Inactive	Retail	Undecided			Undecided	Undecided	
Kuwait	Inactive	Retail	Undecided			Undecided	Undecided	
North Korea	Inactive	Undecided	Undecided			Undecided	Undecided	
Ecuador	Cancelled	Retail	Undecided			Conventional	Undecided	CNT
Senegal	Cancelled	Retail	Direct			Undecided	Undecided	eCurrency Mint

Appendix 3.3

Central Bank Digital Currency Development

One hundred thirty-four countries and currency unions, representing 98% of global GDP, are exploring a CBDC. In May 2020, that number was only 35. Currently, 68 countries are in the advanced exploration phase—development, pilot or launch.

There is a new high of 36 ongoing CBDC pilots, including the digital euro. The European Central Bank (ECB) is now in the preparation phase, conducting practical tests with some transactions settled in a controlled environment. The digital euro is in a two-year preparation stage, ending in 2025.

Nineteen of the Group of 20 (G20) countries are now in the advanced stages of CBDC development. Of those, 11 countries are already in the pilot stage. This includes Brazil, Japan, India, Australia, South Korea, South Africa, Russia and Turkey.

Progress on retail CBDC has stalled in the US. There is a widening gap between the US and G7 banks, including the Bank of England and the Bank of Japan. CBDC has become an issue in the ongoing US presidential campaign, with several candidates speaking out against its development.

Three countries have fully launched a CBDC—the Bahamas, Jamaica and Nigeria. The Eastern Caribbean Currency Union—consisting of eight countries—halted the availability of DCash due to technical issues and is developing a new pilot.

In every country with an advanced retail CBDC project, CBDCs are intermediated, meaning they are distributed through banks, financial institutions and payment service providers. In China, there is also an option for a direct CBDC—which can be accessed through a central bank application.

Brazil, Russia, India, China and South Africa—the founding members of BRICS—are in the pilot phase of CBDC exploration. Several of the new members—Saudi Arabia, Iran and the UAE—are also exploring cross-border wholesale CBDCs. Since last year, BRICS has actively promoted developing an alternate payments system to the dollar.

Since Russia's invasion of Ukraine and the resulting G7 sanctions response, wholesale CBDC developments have doubled. There are currently 13 cross-border wholesale CBDC projects, including mBridge, which connects China, Thailand, the UAE and Hong Kong, and will enter a new phase, expanding to 11 more countries this year.

As the largest CBDC pilot in the world, China's digital yuan (e-CNY) reaches 260 million wallets across 25 cities. Since 2022, it has been used in a range of settings from transit and healthcare to buying crude oil. In 2024, the pilot is focused on optimizing overseas tourist use and expanding cross-border applications of e-CNY.

Appendix 3.4
Addendum to Chapter 3
Cross-Border CBDC Projects

Project Jura

Participating Countries

France and Switzerland.

Overview

The Bank for International Settlements (BIS) Innovation Hub, Banque de France and Swiss National Bank launched Project Jura that, together with a private sector consortium led by Accenture, will conduct an experiment using wholesale CBDC (wCBDC) for cross-border settlement on a distributed ledger technology (DLT) platform.

Use Case

Wholesale.

Source

https://www.bis.org/about/bisih/topics/cbdc/jura.htm

Project Icebreaker

Participating Countries

Israel, Norway, Sweden and Bank for International Settlements Innovation Hub.

Overview

In September 2022, the Bank of Israel, Central Bank of Norway, Sveriges Riksbank and BIS Innovation Hub Nordic Centre announced Project Icebreaker, which would test interlinking and interoperability between different retail CBDCs. The project explores a model for permitting retail CBDC payments across borders and is run through the end of 2022. A report is expected in 2023.

Use Case

Retail.

Source

https://www.bis.org/about/bisih/topics/cbdc/icebreaker.htm

Digital Euro

Participating Countries

Euro area countries.

Overview

The European Central Bank began its digital euro project in July 2021 with the aim to create a CBDC to be used throughout countries in the Eurozone. The project is currently in a two-year preparation phase, which includes finalizing legislation, selecting private-sector partners and some testing and experimentation.

Use Case

Retail, Wholesale.

Source

https://www.ecb.europa.eu/paym/digital_euro/html/index.en.html

DCash

Participating Countries

Eastern Caribbean Central Union: Anguilla, Antigua and Barbuda, Dominica, Grenada, Montserrat, Saint Kitts and Nevis, Saint Lucia and Saint Vincent and the Grenadines.

Overview

In March 2021, the Eastern Caribbean Central Bank launched DCash, a digital currency for the seven countries aimed at financial inclusion. As of January 2024, the ECCU has closed the DCash and initiated a request for vendor information to explore the development of a more advanced CBDC, referred to as DCash 2.0.

Use Case

Retail.

Source

https://www.eccb-centralbank.org/d-cash

Project Mariana

Participating Countries

France, Switzerland, Singapore and Bank for International Settlements Innovation Hub.

Overview

In November 2022, Banque de France, the Monetary Authority of Singapore and the Swiss National Bank, in partnership with the Eurosystem and BIS Innovation Hub, announced a project exploring the use of public and permissioned blockchains alongside DeFi AMMs for wholesale CBDC experiments. The final report concluded that while the project demonstrated how blockchain could address FX market settlement risks, it also highlighted challenges with liquidity requirements and implementing bridges for cross-chain transactions. Additionally, the report emphasized that Project Mariana was a proof of concept and not an endorsement of DeFi or any specific technology.

Use Case

Wholesale.

Source

https://www.bis.org/about/bisih/topics/cbdc/mariana.htm

Project Cedar x/Ubin+

Participating Countries

United States (NY Fed) and Singapore.

Overview

In November 2021, the Federal Reserve Bank of New York and the Monetary Authority of Singapore launched Project Cedar/Ubin+. This joint experiment explores cross-border multi-currency transactions with DLT. Their May 2023 report found that DLT can enhance interoperability and achieve 30-second atomic settlement in cross-border multi-currency payments—reducing settlement times and risk.

Use Case

Wholesale.

Source

https://www.newyorkfed.org/aboutthefed/nyic/project-cedar https://www.newyorkfed.org/medialibrary/media/nyic/project-cedar-phase-two-ubin-report.pdf

Venus Initiative

Participating Countries

France, Luxembourg and European Investment Bank.

Overview

In 2022, the Banque de France and the Central Bank of Luxembourg collaborated on the Venus initiative, supporting the European Investment Bank in issuing a €100 million digital native bond, using an experimental CBDC for secure settlement.

Use Case

Wholesale.

Source

https://www.banque-france.fr/en/press-release/banque-de-france-and-banque-centrale-du-luxembourg-jointly-conducted-successful-wholesale-central

Project Helvetia

Participating Countries

Switzerland and Bank for International Settlements Innovation Hub.

Overview

Project Helvetia was a collaboration between the Swiss National Bank, the BIS and a commercial infrastructure operator, SIX. In 2020, Project Helvetia explored the feasibility of issuing a wholesale CBDC onto SIX's distributed digital asset platform. In January 2022, it was announced that Project Helvetia was successful in integrating the wholesale CBDC to the core banking infrastructure of the country.

Use Case

Wholesale.

Source

https://www.bis.org/about/bisih/topics/cbdc/helvetia.htm

Project Polaris

Participating Countries

Bank for International Settlements Innovation Hub—Nordic Centre.

Overview

In February 2023, the Bank for International Settlements Nordic centre designed Project Polaris to explore security and resilience in CBDC systems. The project will begin with an analytical report on offline payment possibilities and functionalities for CBDC platforms. This will be followed by a 'deep-dive' event, late 2023, where invited vendors discuss their solutions to risks and scalability options for offline CBDCs.

Use Case

Retail.

Source

https://www.bis.org/about/bisih/topics/cbdc/polaris.htm

Project Rosalind

Participating Countries

United Kingdom and Bank for International Settlements Innovation Hub.

Overview

In June 2022, the Bank of England partnered with the BIS Innovation Hub in London to create prototypes for a CBDC application program for retail CBDC, which is based on two-tier, intermediated model. The project is aimed at understanding how central bank ledgers can effectively communicate with private sector vendors. The project released their final report in June 2023 detailing CBDC could make payments between individuals cheaper and more efficient while allowing businesses to create new financial products to reduce fraud.

Use Case

Retail.

Source

https://www.bis.org/about/bisih/topics/cbdc/rosalind.htm

Project Dunbar

Participating Countries

Australia, Singapore, Malaysia and South Africa.

Overview

In March 2022, BIS Innovation Hub announced Project Dunbar in collaboration Reserve Bank of Australia, Central Bank of Malaysia, Monetary Authority of Singapore and South African Reserve Bank to investigate a potential shared platform for multiple central bank digital currencies. They built two prototypes, Corda and Partior, and will continue testing in 2023.

Use Case

Wholesale.

Source

https://www.bis.org/about/bisih/topics/cbdc/dunbar.htm

Project Aurum

Participating Countries

Hong Kong, Bank for International Settlements Innovation Hub—Hong Kong Centre.

Overview

Following the completion of a wholesale interbank system, e-wallet and retail CBDC prototype for Project Aurum, the BIS Innovation Hub Hong Kong Centre and the HKMA are entering a new phase to research the privacy of retail payments using CBDC.

Use Case

Retail.

Source

https://www.bis.org/about/bisih/topics/cbdc/rcbdc.htm

Project mBridge

Participating Countries

Thailand, China, Hong Kong, United Arab Emirates and Bank for International Settlements Innovation Hub.

Overview

In September 2021, the Bank for International Settlements (BIS) released a report on phase two of the mBridge project, aiming to create a multiple CBDC arrangement for faster, cheaper and more efficient transfers and foreign exchange operations. In October 2022, the project successfully conducted 164 transactions in collaboration with 20 banks across 4 countries, settling a total of $22 million. Instead of relying on correspondent banking networks, banks were able to link with their foreign counterparts directly to conduct payments and settlements across e-HKD, e-AED, e-THB and e-CNY. In their recent 2023 report, Project mBridge announced its collaboration with and 25 observing members. The observing members have access to mBridge's testing sandbox, however no production data or real-value transactions are involved in testing. More observing members are expected to join the project soon. The report confirmed that 11 countries have already actively engaged in sandbox testing. Until recently, mBridge operated on a proprietary blockchain based on Ethereum's Solidity language. However, in late 2023, Chinese media reported that mBridge would transition to the Dashing protocol, developed by the PBoC's Digital Currency Research Institute and Tsinghua University.

Use Case

Wholesale.

Source

https://www.bis.org/about/bisih/topics/cbdc/mcbdc_bridge.htm

Project Mandala

Participating Countries

Bank for International Settlements Innovation Hub—Singapore Centre, Australia, South Korea, Malaysia and Singapore.

Overview

In November 2023, the BIS Innovation Hub began Project Mandala. The project aims to revolutionize cross-border payments by developing a common protocol that automates and simplifies compliance with jurisdiction-specific regulatory requirements, enhancing efficiency, transparency and the integrity of international transactions. This project also addresses challenges identified during Project Dunbar, which developed a multiple central bank digital currency (mCBDC) platform.

Use Case

Wholesale.

Source

https://www.bis.org/about/bisih/topics/cbdc/mandala.htm

Project Sela

Participating Countries

Israel, Hong Kong and Bank for International Settlements Innovation Hub.

Overview

In June 2022, the Bank for International Settlements' Innovation Hub in Hong Kong announced a partnership between the Bank of Israel and the Hong Kong Monetary Authority (HKMA). The project is meant to explore the cybersecurity implications of two-tier, retail CBDC. It is meant to be completed by the end of 2022. In 2023, the experiment concluded that retail CBDC can support access, cyber security and competition, while retaining cash features.

Use Case

Retail.

Source

https://www.bis.org/about/bisih/topics/cbdc/sela.htm

Project Tourbillon

Participating Countries

Bank for International Settlements Innovation Hub—Swiss Centre.

Overview

Launched in November 2022 by the Bank for International Settlements' Swiss Centre, Project Tourbillon is a prototype platform that explores how to improve cyber resiliency, scalability and privacy in prototype CBDCs. In their final report in November 2023, the team produced two prototypes named eCash 1.0 and eCash 2.0, emphasizing payer anonymity and enhanced security respectively. The report concluded that implementing a CBDC with payer anonymity to combat illicit transactions is feasible, achieved through complete consumer anonymity during transactions with merchants.

Use Case

Both.

Source

https://www.bis.org/about/bisih/topics/cbdc/tourbillon.htm

e-CNY

Participating Countries

China, Hong Kong and Macau.

Overview

In 2022, the People's Bank of China (PBoC) began collaborating with the Hong Kong Monetary Authority to test the e-CNY for cross-border transactions in Hong Kong. It is most likely that Macau will also become a testing site for e-CNY cross-border payments in 2024.

Use Case

Retail.

Source

https://www.bis.org/publ/bppdf/bispap123_e.pdf

4 Psychological Ownership of Digital Currencies

Jashim Khan and Russell Belk

Introduction

Conventionally, the ownership of money should be independent of how a transaction is completed. Nevertheless, this does not happen, for instance, when money is perceived as cash versus non-cash (Peck & Luangarth, 2023; Khan & Belk, 2024). This distinction produces different cognitions, emotions and behavioral responses, such as spending versus saving (Liu et al., 2021; Khan, 2011). There is considerable evidence that perceptions of cash and non-cash impact psychological ownership of digital cash (Zhou et al., 2023), spending and saving behavior (Khan et al., 2015). According to Zhou et al. (2023), cash results in a greater sense of purchasing power than digital cash, and psychological ownership is related to payment methods. "A payment app is chosen by people who spend considerable time engaging with the app, and their skills, knowledge, and personalization constitute psychological ownership of the app" (Khan & Belk, 2024, p. 8). "It may be virtual, ungraspable, elusive, and unreal, but I have learned to manage this beast; it's mine" (Khan & Belk, 2024, p. 10). Sharma et al. (2021) document systematic differences in psychological ownership between borrowed and owned money in different payment methods. According to Galoni and Noseworthy (2015), our sense of ownership is influenced by physicality and touchability. According to Khan and Belk (2024), psychological ownership is manifested more in the app than in the legal ownership of money, and the digital apps that store people's money make them feel happy, confident, safe and secure. Physical attributes of cash trigger consumer emotions in that payment methods produce varying emotions, impacting psychological ownership and feelings of purchasing power (Zhou et al., 2023). Cash's physical and visceral nature (unlike cards or apps) leads to feelings of psychological ownership, which increases spending awareness. Khan and Belk (2024) argue that the transient nature of third-party apps facilitates impulsive and unnecessary spending due to the disconnect between awareness of spending and actual spending. The differential awareness of spending in cash and non-cash payment mode ramifies spending behavior. Compared with cash, digital money produces a lesser sense of psychological ownership

DOI: 10.4324/9781003425021-4

(Zhou et al., 2023). Consumers feel that purchases are more valuable with their cash than others' or borrowed money (Polman et al., 2018). People generally spend dirty cash faster, but value products purchased with clean cash more (Galoni & Noseworthy, 2015). Such perceptions of psychological ownership of money may also have implications for the central bank digital currency (CBDC) studied in this research.

People's financial behavior and payment choices suggest a linkage in that consumers overspend if they pay by card, irrespective of cash limits, and do not choose to constrain spending (Hernandez et al., 2017). The explanation provided in literature attributed to the pain of paying (Prelec & Loewenstein, 1998; Bechler et al., 2023), tangibility and pleasure of savings (Khan et al., 2015), transparency (Raghubir & Srivastava, 2008) and psychological ownership (Khan & Belk, 2024). These studies have implicated emotions such as the pain of spending (Soman, 2003) and the pleasure of saving (Khan et al., 2015) to explain spending behavior using different payment methods. In their study, Zhou et al. (2023) argue that the pain of paying may vary depending on how people pay for transactions, although more pain might be experienced when cash is used compared to digital payments. The pleasure of saving and associated psychological ownership of money is an underdeveloped research area needing exploration. The emotional associations with cash create a visceral and positive relationship that influences perceptions of cash and non-cash payment modes, as documented in Khan (2011) and Khan and Craig-Lees (2009) study.

Cash is physical, and ownership is straightforward, with the money in possession and the knowledge of savings in the bank accounts usually readily converted to cash. CBDC, which remains digital once minted digitally (Wang & Lau, 2023). This specific attribute of CBDC distinguishes it from others, such as cash, debit, credit cards, third-party payment apps, Bitcoin and other fungible cryptocurrencies. The notion is that cash is physical, and possession of the asset is experienced and felt physically when accounting for a conscious or unconscious sense of possession of value. Cash typically involves seeing, touching and counting money during each transaction. Consciousness and positive feelings of cash result in the sense of possession that is felt viscerally, potentially transferring a sense of ownership of cash as well (Khan & Belk, 2024) and even psychological ownership of the product purchased (Kamleitner & Erki, 2012). Cash stored digitally, such as debit and credit cards, third-party payment apps and cryptocurrencies, may be fungible; their ownership could be realized when converted to cash. CBDC cannot be realized physically (Bijlsma et al., 2024). The fungibility of money is a characteristic that contributes to the quality of money in that a unit of currency is exchanged for the same unit (Berg, 2020). Money is a prime example of a fungible asset because a ¥100 bill is easily convertible into different denominations in circulation. The main idea of fungibility is central to substitutability, which involves cash being convertible into physical and non-physical forms. Digital currencies may also be substitutable for cash in digital form but cannot be freely converted into physical form wherever transactions occur.

The attributes of cash and CBDC motivate this research to explore consumer emotions toward CBDC and their influence on psychological ownership and consumer spending. Evidence indicates that payment methods influence spending because of touchability, and our sensory perception seems to shape judgment and behavior (e.g., Soman, 2003; Khan et al., 2015). Khan and Belk (2024) and Zhou et al. (2023) establish the payment mode and psychological ownership linkage, i.e., perceiving an object as 'mine' is higher for cash. Peck and Luangarth (2023) reignited scholarly interest in studying the psychological ownership of money in various payment methods, leading to studies exploring social gratification and consumer need for touch. For Peck and Luangarth (2023), psychological ownership explains what happens when cash is used compared to other non-cash payment options.

A vital attribute of cash is its physicality, a trait that satisfies people's need for touch and social gratification for objects of prestige and power. Nevertheless, CBDC exists only in digital form. Therefore, this study investigated the touchability and social gratification associated with CBDC. Gonzáles-Benito et al. (2015) suggested that the need for touch is an essential human sensory need and serves as an evaluation mechanism to make spending decisions. CBDC diminishes the connection to touch-accepting cash. There is a call for research to study the consequences of the need for touch in CBDC and their impact on consumer spending (Peck & Luangarth, 2023; Khan & Belk, 2024). This research explores the impact of consumer touchability of money while studying CBDC and controlling emotions toward cash. Social gratification is the focal object of money in the relationship between consumer emotions and CBDC, influencing feelings of psychological ownership and spending behavior (Morewedge, 2021; Morewedge et al., 2021; Shu & Peck, 2011). The same is expected for touchability, though attributes of touchability potentially interact with consumer emotions toward money and how they retain ownership of the money in digital mode.

The existing literature commonly suggests that using cash to pay for purchases decreases spending (Wong & Lynn, 2017). Cash use heightens psychological ownership and feelings of value compared to non-cash payment instruments (Zhou et al., 2023). The emergence of CBDC highlights the lack of physicality and convertibility to cash, which may influence user behavior (Dinh & Dinh, 2022). Unlike cash, people may not mentally be tuned to the money spent. To address this knowledge gap, the main research question in this chapter: *Is there a relationship between consumer emotions, psychological ownership, and spending with CBDC? what relevant factors may influence the psychological ownership of CBDC and spending?*

This research extends our knowledge of CBDC. Specifically, it examines the role of social gratification and touchability in the relationship between feelings toward CBDC, psychological ownership and spending.

Subsequent sections will discuss the main theoretical framework and describe the factors associated with CBDC and psychological ownership.

Psychological Ownership

Money is generally accepted as a medium of exchange, unit of account, store of value and standard of deferred payment (Mauss, 1922). The connotation of money is cash, an object and value that circulates within societies (Khan et al., 2015). CBDC is defined as digital fiat currency pegged to the national currency that performs the functions of money digitally. Extensive research suggests the perceptions and ownership of money differ across payment methods (Allen & Gervais, 2017; Khan & Belk, 2024); the literature discusses emotions associated with spending, psychological ownership, social gratifications, the need for touch and associated ramifications for consumer spending.

Typically, psychological ownership refers to the idea that an object is 'theirs' or 'mine' (Pierce et al., 2003; Morewedge et al., 2021). An individual's subjective feeling of mine is construed as an emotional attachment to an object (Shu & Peck, 2011). (Peck & Shu, 2018) consider it to have cognitive and affective components, with the cognitive state subordinate to the emotional one. There are generally four motivations for owning things: effectance, signaling self-identity, home and stimulation (Pierce & Peck, 2018). Effectance refers to the feeling of possessing and directly controlling an object (Dawkins et al., 2017). Individuals use possessions to identify themselves (Pierce et al., 2003). Conversely, self-identity and psychological ownership emphasize 'what is mine' and 'what is me' and reflect identity. "The home as an object of ownership provides the self with a sense of familiarity, comfort, and security" (Pierce & Peck, 2018). The need for stimulation requires effectance motive for individuals in which positive arousal is possible (Pierce & Jussila, 2011).

Researchers (e.g., Dirks et al., 1996; Wagner et al., 2003) report that psychological ownership predicts workers' attitudes and behavior patterns. According to research in geography, philosophy, gerontology and law, psychological ownership also impacts how people behave in the workplace. Etzioni (2011) examines ownership from a legal and psychological perspective, and Kasser and Ryan (1993) examine ownership's relationship with people's identity, adjustment and happiness. According to Rochberg-Halton (1980), owning tangible objects like toys and intangible objects like ideas triggers feelings of psychological ownership. Belk (1989) asserts that the extended aggregated self is a sense of self by relating interactions with people and objects. Whenever their work is criticized, employees feel their identity is also attacked. Using Rousseau and Shperling (2003) as examples, they demonstrated teamwork, employee and psychological ownership. In their study, Peck and Shu (2009) found that even simple interactions between objects and persons, such as touching them to gain information and temporary control, can increase the perception of ownership and motivate purchase motivation.

These psychological ownership conditions suggest how we pay for purchases influences our cognitions, emotions and behavior (Khan et al., 2015). Cash is perceived as more valuable than digital money (Zhou et al., 2023). Payment mode affects how customers feel about the products they purchase; paying via cash produces greater felt ownership of the product purchased than digital money (Kamleitner & Erki, 2012). People also feel psychological ownership of money, such as perceiving an object as 'mine' (Pierce et al., 2003). With digital payment methods, consumers cannot touch, feel or physically access money (Liu et al., 2017). Payments of this type are associated with reduced sensory perceptions of spending and diminished psychological ownership of money (Peck & Luangrath, 2023). Our sense of ownership is influenced by the physicality or touchability of money and objects, according to Galoni and Noseworthy (2015). Due to a lack of psychological ownership produced by digital money, consumer spending is stimulated by their absence (Zhou et al., 2023). There is also evidence that digital possessions are perceived as less valuable than material possessions (Atasoy & Morewedge, 2017; Petrelli & Whittaker, 2010; Siddiqui & Turley, 2006). However, there is also evidence that digital possessions can be deeply meaningful and can even be seen as irreplaceable (Khan & Belk, 2024; Denegri-Knott et al., 2013; Kirk & Sellen, 2010; Mardon et al., 2022; Watkins & Molesworth, 2012).

As Kamleitner and Erki (2012) report, payment mode can influence psychological ownership via personal investment, with higher levels of personal investment indicating greater psychological ownership. It is found in Kamleitner and Hölzl's (2009) study that the benefits and costs of transactions may interact to influence perceptions of a transaction. Despite extensive research on payment modes, none has examined central bank digital currencies (Petare et al., 2024). As digital money takes center stage (Khan & Belk, 2024), it has gained attention for psychological ownership of money. Soman (2003) demonstrates that digital payment has a lower salience than paying with cash. Thus, digital money likely asserts lesser psychological ownership of money. Hence, we hypothesize that:

H1: *Feelings toward CBDC directly influence the psychological ownership of the digital currency.*

Emotions toward CBDC

The interest in emotions to explain financial behavior is credited to Jon Elster (1998), who pronounced the role of emotions in decision-making (Yi et al., 2023). Positive emotions facilitate approach behavior (Cacioppo et al., 1999), whereas negative emotions stimulate avoidance (or withdrawal) (Frijda et al., 1989). Emotions after decision-making could be classified as rejoicing or regret (Yi et al., 2023). When they are referred to during decision-making, emotions such as pleasure and pain are likely to influence consumer ownership of money and spending. Following Seligman and Csikszentmihalyi (2000), possessing money triggers positive emotions such as security, assurance, relaxation and confidence that are negatively related to spending (Khan et al., 2015). In contrast, spending causes negative emotions such as fear, anger, sadness and disgust (Oatley & Johnson-Laird, 1987). The immediate depletion of wealth caused by using cash results in a negative feeling—psychological pain affects money ownership psychologically. In addition to positive emotions like security, confidence, assurance and a relaxed state of mind, possessors are prone to saving behavior since they try to prolong possession of the objects that generate those feelings and emotions (Khan et al., 2015). Happiness, entertainment, enjoyment, ecstasy and euphoria are positive emotions, according to Berridge and Kringelbach (2008). In Cabanac et al. (2009), they distinguish between fundamental sensory pleasures (e.g., food intake and sex) and higher-order pleasures (e.g., money, friendship and altruism). Early childhood socialization lays the foundation for higher-order pleasures. According to this theory, we also strive to minimize the pain of regretting unnecessary spending, maximize the pleasure of saving money and feel confident, secure and relaxed (Khan et al., 2015). Cash arouses positive emotions inherent to its physical qualities, and likely possession is reinforced as psychological ownership of cash.

The emotional association with digital money also influences psychological ownership of the asset and spending behavior; presumably, consumers are influenced by the interplay of positive emotions and lack of transparency, as manifested in a psychological ownership of digital assets. The relationship between emotions, such as rejoicing and guilt, influencing purchases during livestream commerce has surfaced recently (Yi et al., 2023). Khan and Belk (2024) suggest that people form psychological ownership but with the app or the platform appropriating that technology as their own while personalizing it. Therefore, we hypothesize that:

H2: *There is a direct relationship between psychological ownership of CBDC and spending.*

Social Gratification

The perception of payment modes is influenced by social gratification (Khan, 2011). It is now widely recognized that social relationships are essential in understanding money (Rosenswig, 2024). Desmond (1962) argues that money is a miraculous talisman in everyday life, satisfying almost every desire we can imagine. Besides, as a social instrument, money is shaped by social relations, which define the meaning of money (Zelizer, 1994). With CBDC, people can still use their mobiles, platform-based payments and central bank digital currencies for convenience and to heighten their social status as belonging to tech-savvy people. Nevertheless, some people still hoard cash and, like Disney's Uncle Scrooge comic character (Khan & Belk, 2024), see their tangible wealth as a symbol of social status and achievement. Money and social status operate in the same brain region, and people position themselves in society according to their spending and wealth (Zink et al., 2008). CBDC, a new trend adopted among Generation Z and professionals, emphasizes more vital social gratification among peers than earlier generations. Over time, fewer people are likely to choose cash because it generates less gratification and more pain in paying. Traditionally, people show off their cash in social circles. However, the future is in the form of CBDC, which indicates that this behavior could give them gratification at the cost of incurring more debt. With this understanding, we propose that:

P3a: There is a direct relationship between emotions to CBDC and social gratification.
P3b: There is a direct relationship between social gratification and *psychological ownership of CBDC.*
P3c: There is a direct relationship between emotions to CBDC and *psychological ownership.*

Touchability

Touching products is crucial for consumers. Consumers often touch products even when the tactile interaction is unnecessary. For instance, many people caress, and fondle book covers even though there is no pertinent information on the covers (Underhill, 1999). Touching can create a sense of intimacy (McCabe & Nowlis, 2003) and closeness with the product. It has been suggested that people have varying needs for touch. Krishna et al. (2024) indicate that sensory information needs differ for each individual. Comparing in-store purchases to online shopping, Burke (1997) notes that online shoppers receive less information about the products they buy. Different motivations drive the urge to touch products (Peck & Childers, 2003a, 2003b). Peck and Childers (2006) discovered that individuals with a stronger motivation to touch fruits made more impulsive purchases than those with less motivation.

In digital money, individual differences in touching behavior are often overlooked (Khan & Belk, 2024). However, there has been an increasing interest in studying the impact of individual differences and the touchability of money in recent years (Zhou et al., 2023). Peck and Luangarth (2023) found that individuals with a high need for touch are more confident and less frustrated when they can touch products. On the other hand, those with a lower need to touch products are not expected to experience any impact on their confidence or frustration levels (Krishna et al., 2024). Our judgment and decision-making are also spontaneously influenced by haptic information, such as touch. According to Hulten (2012), visual and olfactory perception can positively influence consumers' touching behavior, purchase intentions and spending. Di Muro and Noseworthy (2013) demonstrate that money is more than just a collection of papers; it carries the meaning of ownership, and their findings suggest that customers' spending behavior can be significantly affected by the physical appearance of cash. Crisp currency symbolizes pride and is preferred, while the worn currency is disliked because it has been used and owned by others (Zenkić et al., 2024). Therefore, the need for touch will affect individuals who are accustomed to touching while switching to CBDC. The influence of touch on people's perceptions is widely acknowledged (Khan & Belk, 2024). According to Aristotle, touch mediates many types of sensory perception (Siegel, 1970), and Gibson (1966) defines touch as the sensation of one's body receiving information about the outside world. Burke (1997) notes that shopping from home cannot provide the same amount of product information as physical stores. Krishna et al. (2024) suggested that touchability differs from person to person; some need more touch sensation, and others need less. Similarly, Hulten (2012) concluded that visual and olfactory sensory cues positively affect shoppers' purchasing decisions.

According to Di Muro and Noseworthy (2013), money is more than just a valuable object; it also triggers emotional associations, and its physical appearance affects spending habits. People actively seek out new bills and take pride in having them, while discarding old, worn bills that are seen as dirty due to being handled by many people. This shows that the physical appearance of money matters more than conventionally thought, especially during COVID-19. Our perceptions of objects are closely tied to our sense of touch, which can influence our feelings toward those objects, such as money. Taking all these understandings together, we propose that:

P4a: There is a direct relationship between emotions to digital currency and touch.

P4b: There is a direct relationship between touch and psychological ownership of the owned money.

P4c: There is a direct relationship between emotions to digital currency and psychological ownership of the owned money.

Payment Method and Spending

Evidence shows that the perception of payment mode influences spending behavior (Hirschman, 1979). The converging evidence is that digital money lacks the quality of sensory input and increases spending behavior (e.g., Wong & Lynn, 2017). The payment method can significantly impact spending behavior (Khan et al., 2015). Research suggests that paying with cash feels more painful than using other less transparent payment methods (Raghubir & Srivastava, 2008). Soman (2001) argues that when consumers pay with cash, they instantly feel the depletion of their wealth, while digital payments can obscure the awareness of how much is being spent. This difference in payment methods lies in their transparency, with cash payments being the most transparent as customers can physically see and feel the amount spent, as pointed out by Soman (2003) and Raghubir and Srivastava (2008). This makes cash payments more salient and increases perceived costs. Conversely, digital payment may not feel as naturally salient as cash, reducing its impact on spending behavior. Overall, the transparency of payment methods is linked to the perceived pain of paying, influencing consumer spending habits.

Credit card research suggests its use induces spending (Wong & Lynn, 2017). When buying durable goods, Liébana-Cabanillas et al. (2014) identify that gender influences payment behavior and that more cash and checks are used in female-headed households than in male-headed households. Feinberg (1986) showed that credit card users pay larger restaurant tips. However, there is a lack of evidence on whether digital currency incurs higher spending since they are increasingly popular. A link has been found between the immediacy of payments and spending behavior. According to Soman (2001, 2003), paying in cash rapidly depletes a consumer's wealth. On the contrary, digital mobile payments decouples purchase experience and consumption at purchase. Usually, credit cards and checks cause a considerable temporal delay because of third-party processing of transactions. Thus, there is some 'float' before the bill comes due. However, it is also easier to pile up credit card debt. The cash purchase experience is direct, and one can see the depletion of money (Soman, 2001). CBDC users may view the purchase as a commitment rather than an actual spending (Runnemark et al., 2015). Soman (2003) also suggests that payment methods differ in transparency (in terms of physical form and amount), which impacts the pain of paying. Customers can see The payment amount immediately when they pay with cash. As a result, different payment methods greatly influence customers' spending behavior (Broekhoff et al., 2024). According to Raghubir and Srivastava (2008), the pain of paying is also related to payment transparency. Cash users are more likely to perceive their costs as real, and the pain of paying is significantly more than with other less transparent payment methods.

Method

A questionnaire was submitted to a panel of Chinese respondents who use cash and digital currency to pay restaurant bills in October 2023 as part of this cross-sectional study. Respondents were identified based on the method of payment in the screening question. Hair et al.'s (2009) suggestion of non-probability criterion-based judgment sampling was followed in this study since it allowed the researchers to select participants who had experience with the focal phenomenon. McGorry's (2000) double translation procedure was adapted for Chinese participants. Using a pilot sample of 27 respondents, it was edited in English and then translated into Chinese using a back translation process. The data were collected between October 2023 and May 2024. Ten student research assistants assisted in data collection. First, recruited participants via invitation to a social media network, completed a questionnaire online and then shared a photo of their weekly bill for eating out in a restaurant. The questionnaire was uploaded from https://www.credamo.world/#/ an international market research company that provides survey construction, distribution, management and analysis services. All participants gave informed consent, and the research obtained ethical approval from the author's institute. In return, the confidentiality of the identity of the participants was guaranteed. After discarding 54 incomplete questionnaires and receipts, 603 questionnaires were analyzed.

Sampling

The judgment sampling technique was deemed suitable as participants were chosen based on experience with the phenomenon under study. Seventy percent were between 18 and 25 years old, 12% were between the age of 26 and 30 years, 10% were between the age of 31 and 40 years and 7% were between the age of 41 and 50 years. Gender was distributed among 65% females and 35% males. Most responders (64%) used third-party payment apps, 20% reported using cash and 16% used CBDC. The pre-selection criteria to recruit participants determined whether participants used digital currency in the past week to pay for food and drinks.

To validate the research sample size, we conducted power analysis using the G-power tool. As the required sample size with effect size (f^2) of 0.9 (Faul et al., 2007) is 99, the sample size in this study is adequate. A sample size of 603 is sufficient for the analysis (Hoelter, 1983).

Construct Measurement

The constructs examined in this study were measured using a five-point Likert scale, ranging from strongly disagree (scored as one) to strongly agree (scored as five). The items were drawn from previous studies, namely emotions to payment mode (Khan et al., 2015), touch (Peck & Childers, 2003a, 2003b) and psychological ownership (Van Dyne & Pierce, 2004). Average weekly spending was measured in CNY (¥). The items were modified to fit the study's context.

Analyses

In order to ensure the accuracy of data entry and assess the normality of continuous variables, we performed basic data screening activities prior to conducting any analysis. A mean of the items from the subscale was used to replace missing data. For each variable, outliers were defined as values exceeding 3.5 standard deviations from the sample mean (Hair et al., 2013). A two-step CB-SEM approach using the SmartPLS4 package test the research hypothesis. The technique adopted is a bootstrapping procedure with replacement using 5,000 subsamples to calculate the statistical significance. Importance-performance analysis conducted to identify the factors influencing CBDC usage intention. In this research, the effect of feelings to cash, age, gender and income were controlled because they could influence the study result.

Results

Multicollinearity and Common Method Bias

To detect common method bias, Harman's single-factor, exploratory factor analysis is used (Fuller et al., 2016; Podsakoff et al., 2003). In this case, CMB was not an issue. Furthermore, Kock (2015) suggested checking variance inflation factor (VIF) values less than 3.3 to indicate that common method bias was not an issue—the VIF values in Table 4.1.

Table 4.1 Reliabilities and VIF Values

Construct with Items	*FL*	α	*rho_A*	*CR*	*AVE*	*VIF*
Emotions to (Khan et al., 2015) If I had (¥) 1,000 CBDC:		**.95**	**.96**	**.97**	**.88**	**3.0**
I would feel relaxed	.95					3.0
I would feel assured	.93					3.1
I would feel confident	.92					2.8
I would feel secure	.94					2.5
Emotions to cash (Khan et al., 2015) If I had (¥) 1,000 cash:		.93	.94	.95	.83	2.7
I would feel relaxed	.91					3.3
I would feel assured	.93					2.9
I would feel confident	.91					2.8
I would feel secure	.90					3.1
Psychological ownership (Van Dyne & Pierce, 2004) When I use CBDC:		**.92**	**.92**	**.95**	**.83**	**3.3**
I feel that this is my product	.86					2.4
I sense that this is my product.	.93					3.3
I feel a very high degree of ownership	.92					3.7
I feel I own the product	.92					3.5
Touch (Peck & Childers, 2003a,b)		**.89**	**.90**	**.91**	**.60**	**1.0**
When walking through stores, I can't help touching products	.79					2.0
The only way to ensure a product is worth it is to touch it	.81					2.0
I would only buy if I could touch them before purchase	.79					1.3
I find myself touching all kinds of products in stores	.77					2.5
Social gratification (Khan et al., 2015)		**.82**	**.82**	**.89**	**.74**	**1.6**
CBDC gives higher social status	.78					1.4
CBDC is pleasurable to use	.87					2.4
I Like the sensation of CBDC	.91					2.7

Note: FL = factor loading; α = Cronbach alpha; CR = composite reliability; AVE = average variance extracted; VIF = variance inflation factor.

Bold represents value for the composite factor.

Table 4.2 Discriminant Validity

	FC	*FD*	*PO*	*SG*	*SP*	*TO*
Heterotrait-Monotrait (HTMT)						
Feelings digital currency	0.84					
Psychological ownership	0.44	0.43				
Social gratification	0.47	0.60	0.75			
Spending	0.64	0.66	0.24	0.33		
Touch	0.07	0.13	0.37	0.32	0.03	
Touch × Feelings digital currency	0.12	0.05	0.42	0.34	0.02	0.17
Fornell-Larcker Criterion						
Feelings digital currency	-0.79	0.93				
Psychological ownership	0.41	-0.41	0.90			
Social gratification	0.41	-0.53	0.65	0.85		
Spending	0.61	-0.64	0.23	0.29	1.00	
Touch	0.07	-0.12	0.33	0.26	-0.02	0.78

Note: FD = feelings to CBDC; PO = psychological ownership; SG= social gratification; TO = touch; SP = spending.

Reliability: The questionnaire items with loadings greater than 0.70 are considered suitable for further study (Hair et al., 2011). Generally, internal consistency reliability is greater than 70. In this study, factor loadings (FL), Cronbach's alpha, Rho A and composite reliability (CR) all exceeded 0.70 (see Table 4.1), indicating acceptable reliability.

Validity: Henseler et al. (2015) recommend using the average variance extracted (AVE) to assess convergent validity (Campbell & Fiske, 1959). According to Sarstedt et al., 2020, the AVE threshold should be 0.50 or higher. Discriminant validity measures the degree of discrimination between two constructs within a model (Campbell & Fiske, 1959). The Fornell and Larcker (1981) criteria were met: the construct's AVE was greater than its correlation with any other construct and the item correlated with the related construct the most. The HTMT ratio of less than one recommended by Henseler et al. (2015) also met the discriminant validity threshold (See Table 4.2).

Structural Model

The structural model was tested using the coefficient of effect size (f^2) and determination (R^2) (Sarstedt et al., 2020). R^2 examines the endogenous variable, and a score of 0.2 is deemed acceptable. In this study, the R^2 values for psychological ownership, social gratification, spending and touch are .53, .29, .42 and .14, respectively. The threshold for f^2 is 0.02, deemed as a small effect, 0.15 as a medium effect and 0.35 as a large effect (Cohen, 1988). Results indicate that feelings to cash (f^2 = .04), feelings to CBDC (f^2 = .02), social gratification (f^2 = .40), psychological ownership (f^2 = .29), touch (f^2 = .07) and spending (f^2 = .63).

In SmartPLS3, key values for model fit include SRMR, d_ULS, d_G and NFI, which are .07, 1.2, .40 and .87, respectively (Hair et al., 2019). A satisfactory result was obtained for all values, confirming the suitability of the current model for this study. In order to assess the overall quality of the research model, we calculated the goodness of fit (GOF), as recommended by Tenenhaus et al. (2005). GOF is 0.44, which exceeds the threshold value of 0.36 (Wetzels et al., 2009), indicating high quality in the research model. Several control variables were considered in the analysis. The first control variable was feelings toward cash since people attribute cash to the concept of money. The second control variable was gender, as several studies suggest payment mode perceptions differ by age, gender and income (see Khan, 2011).

Path Coefficients

As shown in Table 4.3, Feelings toward CBDC do not result in psychological ownership directly, and H1 is rejected. Results show a direct relationship between psychological ownership and spending. The relationship between feelings of CBDC and psychological ownership is indirectly influenced by social gratification (H3) and the need for touch (H4). In other words, a full mediation. Therefore, after testing, H2, H3, H4 and H5 are all supported

Table 4.3 Path Coefficients Results

# Hypothesis	*Paths Coefficients*	*Standard Deviation*	*T Statistics*	*P Value*
Direct Relationship				
CBDC → PO	.05	.06	0.90	.340
PO → SP	.24	.04	6.22	.000
CBDC → SP	-.66	.03	22.9	.000
CBDC → SG	-.54	.03	16.4	.000
CBDC → TO	-.15	.04	3.60	.000
SG → PO	.47	.04	11.2	.000
TO → PO	.18	.03	5.90	.000
Indirect Relationship				
CBDC × TO → PO	-.22	.03	6.53	.000
CBDC → TO → PO	-03	.09	2.98	.000
CBDC → SG → PO	-.25	.03	8.63	.000
Control Factor				
FC → PO	.22	.05	4.50	.000
Age → PO	-.04	.03	1.80	.069
Gender → PO	-.01	.07	.010	.994
Income → PO	-.03	.03	1.07	.284

Note: CBDC = feelings to CBDC; PO = psychological ownership; SG = social gratification; TO = touch; SP = grocery spending/week.

Table 4.4 Important-Performance Analysis

Constructs	*Importance*	*Performance*
Psychological Ownership		
Feelings digital currency	–.40	34
Social gratification	.48	58
Touch	.17	64
Spending		
Feelings digital currency	–.09	34
Social gratification	.11	58
	.04	64
Touch		
Psychological ownership	.24	56

and accepted; feelings toward digital currency and psychological ownership are mediated via social gratification and touchability. We assessed the moderating role of touchability in the relationship between feelings toward CBDC and psychological ownership. We found that support touchability also moderates the relationship between feeling toward digital currency and psychological ownership.

Aside from testing the research hypotheses, it's important to identify the most influential factors driving consumer spending performance. According to Ringle and Sarstedt (2016), an increase in the predecessor variable's performance leads to an increase in the target variable's performance by the size of its importance. In the current research, psychological ownership and consumer spending are the target variables predicted by social gratification, feelings of digital currency and touchability.

The results indicate that touch significantly drives psychological ownership of digital currency. Social gratification has the highest importance score (.48), suggesting that consumers' psychological ownership of digital currency improves if they focus on social gratification. Moreover, the data shows that touch drives consumer spending and that psychological ownership of digital currency remains the priority (Table 4.4).

Discussions and Contributions

This research was designed to examine the relationship between feelings about digital currency and the effect of these feelings on psychological ownership and spending. It contributes to unpacking the mediating role of social gratification and the touchability of digital currency. This extends our understanding of how social gratification and touch indirectly influence the relationship between feelings toward digital currency and psychological ownership. A positive feeling about digital currency alone is insufficient to enact psychological money ownership. Previous studies have emphasized the role of psychological ownership of money and how consumers value digital currency less than its counterpart in cash (Zhou et al., 2023). The physical and visceral nature of cash (but not cards or apps) has been expanded (Khan & Belk, 2024, p. 18), and they state that "the transient nature of cards and apps leads to impulsive spending and a lack of awareness of spending." CBDC is an app-based customization experience that heightens psychological ownership of the app more than an appreciation of the value of money. It is evident that feelings toward CBDC are not directly associated with psychological ownership in this research. However, a direct relationship exists between psychological ownership of the mobile app that facilitates digital transactions and that this may influence consumer spending. We tested feelings about CBDC and psychological ownership while statistically controlling the perceptions of cash. The psychological ownership factor is the physicality and social gratification that affect our emotions, cognitions and behavior.

This research tackles a crucial area when the landscape of what money is becoming is unstable. Governments are experimenting with digital currencies, and private companies are entering digital money creation. Therefore, testing the assumption that touchability influences psychological ownership is needed information and worth knowing. This is a unique contribution to the existing body of knowledge, as it enhances our understanding of CBDC. The importance of touchability is demonstrated in this study as it moderates the mediated relationship between feeling to CBDC and psychological ownership, which has implications for consumer spending.

This study also provides several practical implications. Firstly, the government should actively regulate CBDC, especially when money creation is decentralized. Instead of displaying numbers alone, digital transactions might display a graphical representation of how much has been spent and how much remains. Using this method should make calculating the bill more intuitive for users. Future research must replicate the study, expand the sample group and test the theory in other cultural contexts. Data and sampling techniques remain the primary limitation of the study. As a non-probability sampling method, judgment sampling cannot generalize findings beyond the participants. Probability-based sampling techniques are suggested for further research. Future research should consider adopting experimentation. It is also suggested that future studies explore the psychological ownership of private currencies.

Appendix: Conceptual Model

See Figure 4.1.

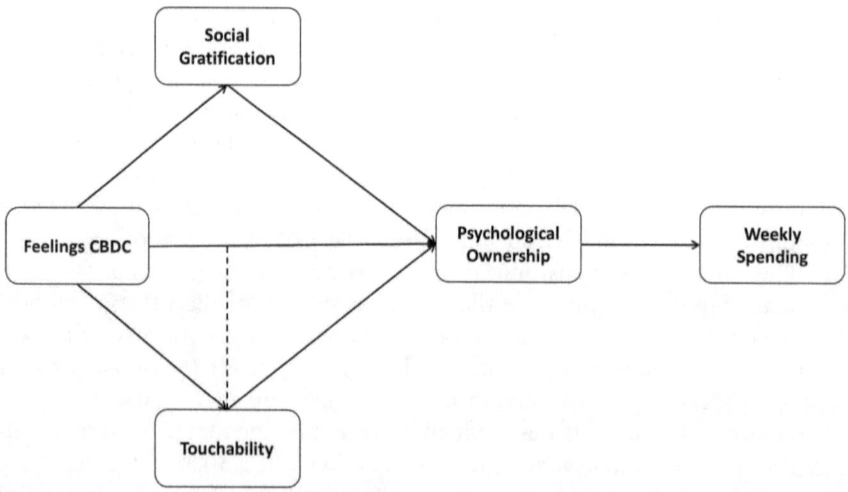

Figure 4.1 Conceptual Model

References

Allen, J., & Gervais, S. J. (2017). The femininity–money incongruity hypothesis: Money and femininity reminders undermine women's cognitive performance. *Psychology of Women Quarterly*, 41(4), 407–419.

Atasoy, O., & Morewedge, C. K. (2017). Digital goods are valued less than physical goods. *Journal of Consumer Research*, *44*(6), 1343–1357. https://doi.org/10.1093/jcr/ucx102

Bechler, C. J., Huang, S. C., & Morris, J. I. (2023). Purchase justifiability drives payment choice: consumers pay with card to remember and cash to forget. *Journal of the Association for Consumer Research*, 8(4), 452–464.

Belk, R. W. (1989). Extended self and extending paradigmatic perspective. *Journal of Consumer Research*, 16(1), 129–132.

Berg, A. (2020). The identity, fungibility and anonymity of money. *Economic Papers: A Journal of Applied Economics and Policy*, 39(2), 104–117.

Berridge, K. C., & Kringelbach, M. L. (2008). Affective neuroscience of pleasure: Reward in humans and animals. *Psychopharmacology*, *199*, 457–480.

Bijlsma, M., van der Cruijsen, C., Jonker, N., & Reijerink, J. (2024). What triggers consumer adoption of central bank digital currency? *Journal of Financial Services Research*, *65*(1), 1–40.

Broekhoff, M. C., & van der Cruijsen, C. (2024). Paying in a blink of an eye: It hurts less, but you spend more. *Journal of Economic Behavior & Organization*, *221*, 110–133.

Burke, R. R. (1997). Do you see what I see? The future of virtual shopping. *Journal of the Academy of Marketing Science*, *25*(4), 352–360.

Cabanac, M., Cabanac, A. J., & Parent, A. (2009). The emergence of consciousness in phylogeny. *Behavioural Brain Research*, *198*(2), 267–272.

Cacioppo, J. T., Gardner, W. L., & Berntson, G. G. (1999). The affect system has parallel and integrative processing components: Form follows function. *Journal of Personality and Social Psychology*, *76*(5), 839.

Campbell, D. T., & Fiske, D. W. (1959). Convergent and discriminant validation by the multitrait-multimethod matrix. *Psychological Bulletin*, *56*(2), 81.

Cohen, J. (1988). *Statistical power analysis for the behavioral sciences* (2nd ed.). Lawrence Erlbaum Associates.

Dawkins, S., Tian, A. W., Newman, A., & Martin, A. (2017). Psychological ownership: A review and research agenda. *Journal of Organizational Behavior*, 38(2), 163–183.

Denegri-Knott, J., Watkins, R., & Wood, J. (2013). Transforming digital virtual goods into meaningful possessions. In *Digital virtual consumption* (pp. 83–98). Routledge.

Desmonde, W. H. (1962). *Magic, myth, and money*. New York: Free Press of Glencoe.

Di Muro, F., & Noseworthy, T. J. (2013). Money isn't everything, but it helps if it doesn't look used: How the physical appearance of money influences spending. *Journal of Consumer Research*, *39*(6), 1330–1342.

Dinh, H. T. L., & Dinh, T. C. (2022). Verification of the impact of Central Bank Digital currency (CBDC) issuance on net interest income of vietnamese commercial banks. In *2022 IEEE/ACIS 7th international conference on big data, cloud computing, and data science (BCD)* (pp. 301–305). IEEE.

Dirks, K. T., Cummings, L. L., & Pierce, J. L. (1996). Psychological ownership in organizations: Conditions under which individuals promote and resist change. In Woodman, R. W. & Pasmore, W. A. (Eds.), *Research in organizational change and development* (pp. 1–23). JAI Press.

Elster, J. (1998). Emotions and economic theory. *Journal of Economic Literature*, *36*(1), 47–74.

Etzioni, A. (2011). Privacy merchants: What is to be done? *Journal of Constitutional Law*, *14*, 929–951. http://bit.ly/4e3cpfq

Faul, F., Erdfelder, E., Lang, A. G., & Buchner, A. (2007). G* Power 3: A flexible statistical power analysis program for the social, behavioral, and biomedical sciences. *Behavior Research Methods*, *39*(2), 175–191.

Feinberg, R. A. (1986). Credit cards as spending facilitating stimuli: A conditioning interpretation. *Journal of Consumer Research*, *13*(3), 348–356.

Fornell, C., & Larcker, D. F. (1981). Evaluating structural equation models with unobservable variables and measurement error. *Journal of Marketing Research*, *18*(1), 39–50.

Frijda, N. H., Kuipers, P., & Ter Schure, E. (1989). Relations among emotion, appraisal, and emotional action readiness. *Journal of Personality and Social Psychology*, *57*(2), 212.

Fuller, C. M., Simmering, M. J., Atinc, G., Atinc, Y., & Babin, B. J. (2016). Common methods variance detection in business research. *Journal of Business Research*, *69*(8), 3192–3198.

Galoni, C., & Noseworthy, T. J. (2015). Does dirty money influence product valuations? *Journal of Consumer Psychology*, *25*(2), 304–310.

Gibson, J. J. (1966). *The senses considered as perceptual systems*. Houghton Mifflin.

González-Benito, Ó., Martos-Partal, M., & San Martín, S. (2015). Brands as substitutes for the need for touch in online shopping. *Journal of Retailing and Consumer Services*, *27*, 121–125. https://doi.org/10.1016/j.jretconser.2015.07.015

Hair, J. F. (2009). *Multivariate data analysis* (7th ed.). Prentice-Hall.

Hair, J. F., Ringle, C. M., & Sarstedt, M. (2011). PLS-SEM: Indeed a silver bullet. *Journal of Marketing Theory and Practice*, *19*(2), 139–152.

Hair, J. F., Sarstedt, M., & Ringle, C. M. (2019). Rethinking some of the rethinking of partial least squares. *European Journal of Marketing*, *53*(4), 566–584.

Henseler, J., Ringle, C. M., & Sarstedt, M. (2015). A new criterion for assessing discriminant validity in variance-based structural equation modeling. *Journal of the Academy of Marketing Science*, *43*, 115–135.

Hernandez, L., Jonker, N., & Kosse, A. (2017). Cash versus debit card: The role of budget control. *Journal of Consumer Affairs*, *51*(1), 91–112.

Hirschman, E. C. (1979). Differences in consumer purchase behavior by credit card payment system. *Journal of Consumer Research*, *6*(1), 58. https://doi.org/10.1086/208748

Hoelter, J. W. (1983). The analysis of covariance structures: Goodness-of-fit indices. *Sociological Methods & Research*, *11*(3), 325–344.

Hultén, B. (2012). Sensory cues and shoppers' touching behaviour: The case of IKEA. *International Journal of Retail & Distribution Management*, *40*(4), 273–289.

José Liébana-Cabanillas, F., Sánchez-Fernández, J., & Muñoz-Leiva, F. (2014). Role of gender on acceptance of mobile payment. *Industrial Management & Data Systems*, *114*(2), 220–240.

Kamleitner, B., & Erki, B. (2012). Payment method and perceptions of ownership. *Marketing Letters*, *24*(1), 57–69. https://doi.org/10.1007/s11002-012-9203-4

Kamleitner, B., & Hölzl, E. (2009). Cost–benefit associations and financial behavior. *Applied Psychology*, *58*(3), 435–452.

Kasser, T., & Ryan, R. M. (1993). A dark side of the American dream: Correlates of financial success as a central life interest. *Journal of Personality and Social Psychology*, *65*(2), 410–422. https://doi.org/10.1037/0022-3514.65.2.410

Khan, J. (2011). *Cash or card: Consumer perceptions of payment modes* (Doctoral dissertation, Auckland University of Technology).

Khan, J., & Belk, R. (2024). Money you could touch: Cash and psychological ownership. *Qualitative Market Research: An International Journal*. 27(5), 820–840.

Khan, J., Belk, R. W., & Craig-Lees, M. (2015). Measuring consumer perceptions of payment mode. *Journal of Economic Psychology*, *47*, 34–49. https://doi.org/10.1016/j.joep.2015.01.006

Khan, J., & Craig-Lees, M. (2009). 'Cashless' transactions: Perceptions of money in mobile payments. *International Business and Economics Review*, *1*(1), 23–32.

Kirk, D. S., & Sellen, A. (2010). On human remains: Values and practice in the home archiving of cherished objects. *ACM Transactions on Computer-Human Interaction (TOCHI)*, *17*(3), 1–43.

Kock, N. (2015). Common method bias in PLS-SEM: A full collinearity assessment approach. *International Journal of e-Collaboration (ijec)*, *11*(4), 1–10.

Krishna, A., Luangrath, A. W., & Peck, J. (2024). A review of touch research in consumer psychology. *Journal of Consumer Psychology*, *34*(2), 359–381.

Liu, W., Batra, R. & Wang, H. (2017). Product touch and consumers' online and offline buying: The role of mental representation. *Journal of Retailing*, *93*(3), 369–381.

Liu, Y., Luo, J., & Zhang, L. (2021). The effects of mobile payment on consumer behavior. *Journal of Consumer Behaviour*, *20*(3), 512–520.

Mardon, R., Denegri-Knott, J., & Molesworth, M. (2022). Kind of mine, kind of not: Digital possessions and affordance misalignment. *Journal of Consumer Research*. https://doi.org/10.1093/jcr/ucac057

Mauss, M. (1922). *The gift: Forms and functions of exchange in archaic societies*. Routledge.

McCabe, D. B., & Nowlis, S. M. (2003). The effect of examining actual products or product descriptions on consumer preference. *Journal of Consumer Psychology, 13*(4), 431–439.

McGorry, S. Y. (2000). Measurement in a cross-cultural environment: Survey translation issues. *Qualitative Market Research: An International Journal, 3*(2), 74–81. https://doi.org/10.1108/13522750010322070

Morewedge, C. K. (2021). Psychological ownership: Implicit and explicit. *Current Opinion in Psychology, 39*. https://doi.org/10.1016/j.copsyc.2020.10.003

Morewedge, C. K., Monga, A., Palmatier, R. W., Shu, S. B., & Small, D. A. (2020). Evolution of consumption: A psychological ownership framework. *Journal of Marketing, 85*(1), 196–218. https://doi.org/10.1177/0022242920957007

Oatley, K., & Johnson-Laird, P. N. (1987). Towards a cognitive theory of emotions. *Cognition and emotion, 1*(1), 29–50.

Peck, J., & Childers, T. L. (2003a). Individual differences in haptic information processing: The "need for touch" scale. *Journal of Consumer Research, 30*(3), 430–442.

Peck, J., & Childers, T. L. (2003b). To have and to hold: The influence of haptic information on product judgments. *Journal of Marketing, 67*(2), 35–48.

Peck, J., & Childers, T. L. (2006). If I touch it I have to have it: Individual and environmental influences on impulse purchasing. *Journal of Business Research, 59*(6), 765–769.

Peck, J., & Luangrath, A. W. (2023). A review and future avenues for psychological ownership in consumer research. *Consumer Psychology Review*, 6(1), 52–74.

Peck, J., & Shu, S. B. (2009). The effect of mere touch on perceived ownership. *Journal of Consumer Research*, 36(3), 434–447.

Peck, J. & Shu, S. B. (2018). Psychological *ownership and consumer behavior*. Springer Publishing.

Petare, P. A., Josyula, H. P., Landge, S. R., Gatala, S. K. K., & Gunturu, S. R. (2024). Central bank digital currencies: Exploring the future of money and banking. *Migration Letters, 21*(S7), 640–51.

Petrelli, D., & Whittaker, S. (2010). Family memories in the home: Contrasting physical and digital mementos. *Personal and Ubiquitous Computing, 14*(2), 153–169. https://doi.org/10.1007/s00779-009-0279-7

Pierce, J. L., & Jussila, I. (2011). *Psychological ownership and the organizational context: Theory, research evidence, and application*. Edward Elgar Publishing.

Pierce, J. L., Kostova, T., & Dirks, K. T. (2003). The state of psychological ownership: Integrating and extending a century of research. *Review of General Psychology*, 7(1), 84–107. https://doi.org/10.1037/1089-2680.7.1.84

Pierce, J. L., & Peck, J. (2018). The history of psychological ownership and its emergence in consumer psychology. In Peck, J. & Shu, S. (Eds.), *Psychological ownership and consumer behaviour* (pp. 1–18). Springer. https://doi.org/10.1007/978-3-319-77158-8_1

Podsakoff, P. M., MacKenzie, S. B., Lee, J. Y., & Podsakoff, N. P. (2003). Common method biases in behavioral research: A critical review of the literature and recommended remedies. *Journal of Applied Psychology, 88*(5), 879.

Polman, E., Effron, D. A., & Thomas, M. R. (2018). Other people's money: Money's perceived purchasing power is smaller for others than for the self. *Journal of Consumer Research*, 45(1), 109–125.

Prelec, D., & Loewenstein, G. (1998). The red and the black: Mental accounting of savings and debt. *Marketing Science*, *17*(1), 4–28.

Raghubir, P., & Srivastava, J. (2008). Monopoly money: The effect of payment coupling and form on spending behavior. *Journal of Experimental Psychology: Applied*, *14*(3), 213–225. https://doi.org/10.1037/1076-898x.14.3.213

Ringle, C. M., & Sarstedt, M. (2016). Gain more insight from your PLS-SEM results: The importance-performance map analysis. *Industrial Management & Data Systems*, *116*(9), 1865–1886.

Rochberg-Halton, E. W. (1980). *Cultural signs and urban adaptation: The meaning of cherished possessions* (Doctoral dissertation, University of Chicago, Dissertation Abstracts International), *40*(8A), 4754–4755.

Rosenswig, R. M. (2024). Money, currency, and heterodox macroeconomics for archaeology. *Current Anthropology*, *65*(2), 235–266.

Rousseau, D. M., & Shperling, Z. (2003). Pieces of the action: Ownership and the changing employment relationship. *Academy of Management Review*, 28(4), 553–570.

Runnemark, E., Hedman, J., & Xiao, X. (2015). Do consumers pay more using debit cards than cash?. *Electronic Commerce Research and Applications*, *14*(5), 285–291.

Sarstedt, M., Ringle, C. M., Cheah, J. H., Ting, H., Moisescu, O. I., & Radomir, L. (2020). Structural model robustness checks in PLS-SEM. *Tourism Economics*, *26*(4), 531–554.

Seligman, M. E., & Csikszentmihalyi, M. (2000). *Positive psychology: An introduction* (Vol. 55, No. 1, p. 5). American Psychological Association.

Sharma, E., Tully, S., & Cryder, C. (2021). Psychological ownership of (borrowed) money. *Journal of Marketing Research*, *58*(3), 497–514.

Shu, S. B., & Peck, J. (2011). Psychological ownership and affective reaction: Emotional attachment process variables and the endowment effect. *Journal of Consumer Psychology*, *21*(4), 439–452. https://doi.org/10.1016/j.jcps.2011.01.002

Siddiqui, S., & Turley, D. (2006). Extending the self in a virtual world. *Advances in Consumer Research*, *33*, 647.

Siegel, R. E. (1970). IV. Organ and perception of taste. In Siegel, R. E. (Ed.), *Galen on sense perception* (pp. 158–173). Karger Publishers.

Soman, D. (2001). Effects of payment mechanism on spending behavior: The role of rehearsal and immediacy of payments. *Journal of Consumer Research*, *27*(4), 460–474. https://doi.org/10.1086/319621

Soman, D. (2003). The effect of payment transparency on consumption: Quasi-experiments from the field. *Marketing Letters*, *14*(3), 173–183 https://doi.org/10.1023/a:1027444717586

Tenenhaus, M., Vinzi, V. E., Chatelin, Y. M., & Lauro, C. (2005). PLS path modeling. *Computational Statistics & Data Analysis*, *48*(1), 159–205.

Underhill, P. (1999). *Why we buy: The science of shopping*. Simon and Schuster.

Van Dyne, L., & Pierce, J. L. (2004). Psychological ownership and feelings of possession: Three field studies predicting employee attitudes and organizational citizenship behavior. *Journal of Organizational Behavior: The International Journal of Industrial, Occupational and Organizational Psychology and Behavior*, *25*(4), 439–459.

Wagner, S. H., Parker, C. P., & Christiansen, N. D. (2003). Employees that think and act like owners: Effects of ownership beliefs and behaviors on organizational effectiveness. *Personnel Psychology*, *56*(4), 847–871.

Wang, M., & Lau, N. (2023). NFT digital twins: A digitalization strategy to preserve and sustain Miao silver craftsmanship in the metaverse era. *Heritage*, 6(2), 1921–1941.

Watkins, R., & Molesworth, M. (2012). Attachment to digital virtual possessions in videogames. In Belk, R. W., Askegaard, S., & Scott, L. (Eds.), *Research in consumer behavior* (Vol. 14, pp. 153–170). Emerald Group Publishing Limited.

Wetzels, M., Odekerken-Schröder, G., & Van Oppen, C. (2009). Using PLS path modeling for assessing hierarchical construct models: Guidelines and empirical illustration. *MIS Quarterly*, 33(1), 177–195.

Wong, K.-Y., & Lynn, M. (2017). The easy-money effect: Credit card spending and hard-work reminders. *Journal of Consumer Marketing*, *34*(7), 541–551. https://doi.org/10.1108/jcm-07-2016-1868

Yi, Q., Khan, J., Su, Y., Tong, J., & Zhao, S. (2023). Impulse buying tendency in live-stream commerce: The role of viewing frequency and anticipated emotions influencing scarcity-induced purchase decision. *Journal of Retailing and Consumer Services*, *75*, 103534.

Zelizer, V. (1994). *The social meaning of money*. Basic Books.

Zenkić, J., Lei, J., Millet, K., & Rotman, J. D. (2024). Reversing the denomination effect in tipping contexts. *Journal of Consumer Psychology*, *34*(2), 351–358.

Zhou, K., Ye, J., Liu, X. (2023). Is cash perceived as more valuable than digital money? The mediating effect of psychological ownership and psychological distance. *Marketing Letters*, *34*(1), 55–68.

Zink, C. F., Tong, Y., Chen, Q., Bassett, D. S., Stein, J. L., & Meyer-Lindenberg, A. (2008). Know your place: Neural processing of social hierarchy in humans. *Neuron*, *58*, 273–283.

Appendix 4.1

Post-hoc Sample and Effect Size Determination

See Figure 4.2.

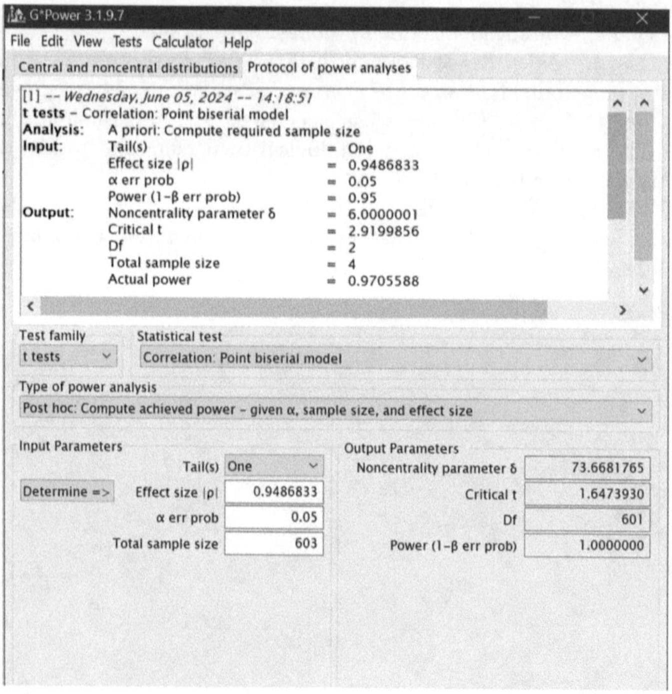

5 Pushes and Pulls in Switching to Digital Currencies

Jashim Khan and Russell Belk

Introduction

Bitcoin challenged the dominant fiat currency; since 2009, many central banks have researched and piloted the concept of digital currency. Cryptocurrencies, stablecoins and central bank digital currencies (CBDCs) are the three main categories of digital currency (Geva & Muraj, 2024). One hundred thirteen countries were exploring digital currencies in 2024, of which three launched, 30 were in development, 44 were researching, 17 were inactive and two countries canceled (Atlantic Council, 2024), representing 58% of the total countries and accounting for 98% of the global economy (Bank for International Settlements, 2024). China has been leading the way in developing a central bank digital currency, with the People's Bank of China initiating research in 2014. In 2021, the People's Bank of China extended the trial program. It is officially named China's digital currency, e-CNY or digital Renminbi, and the People's Bank of China issues it and holds legal tender status. The digital Renminbi can be used for everyday transactions, including payments, remittances and transfers. The year 2024 has accounted for over 9.5 million transactions, totaling approximately ¥87 billion ($13.7 billion at the time) in transaction value (Huang, 2024).

Extant research indicates that people consider attributes such as perceived convenience and ease of use (Fepetu & Adewumi, 2024; Kasowaki & William, 2024), security (Xia et al., 2023; Tan, 2023) and risk (Abu Elbeh, 2024; Wan, 2024; Tian et al., 2023) to determine the perceived value of the digital currency (Bijlsma et al., 2024; Liébana-Cabanillas et al., 2018). Liébana-Cabanillas et al. (2018) suggest that perceived risk and security remain the significant impacts of adopting digital payment. The convenience of digital currency accelerates its widespread use. The convenience of using digital currency is based on transaction costs via mobile phones, eliminating the need to carry cash or bank cards (Sleiman et al., 2021). Current research examines consumers' perceptions and emotions toward digital currency, influencing their willingness to switch it. Khan and Belk (2024) propose that positive emotions toward digital currency are critical to widespread adoption. Factors such as perceived trust and social influence evoke

DOI: 10.4324/9781003425021-5

positive emotions toward digital currency (Rabaai, 2021). Therefore, this study examines the impact of perceived convenience and positive emotions as pull factors. Perceived security and risk are critical push factors; determining the perceived value of a digital currency is a mooring effect evaluating consumer willingness to switch digital currency over third-party payment apps. This study uses the push–pull–mooring (PPM) framework to elucidate the importance of perceived security, convenience, risk and positive emotions in assessing the perceived value of digital currency.

While Western countries led the global adoption of magnetic striped credit and debit cards using SWIFT payment networks of central banks, China led the mobile payment, hereafter third-party payment apps, leapfrogged magnetic cards and disintermediated the banking system with the QR codes on smartphones. The adoption of QR codes allows merchants to connect over a platform via a mobile network, and as long as one party accesses the platform, the transaction can be completed. Third-party mobile payment accounted for approximately ¥ 350 trillion in 2019 via 100 billion mobile payment transactions in the country. A third-party payment refers to paying for goods, services and bills using a wireless or QR code (quick-response code), a two-dimensional matrix barcode scanned using mobile devices to complete transactions (Moon et al., 2022). Against the backdrop of the mature mobile payment ecosystem in China, this research aims to study consumer willingness to switch to central bank digital currency over third-party payment apps. Central digital currency will inevitably prevail and become a dominant payment method integrated into consumers' daily lives (Holden, 2024). Boar and Wehrli (2021) surveyed central bank digital currency adoption, revealing that in many countries, 113 out of 195 in the world (58% involved), 3 launched 36 in the pilot stage, 30 in development and 44 in the research stage (Atlantic Council, 2024).

Central bank digital currency adoption has been investigated in a study by the International Monetary Fund (IMF), which reports that when more households adopt central bank digital currency, it is likely that more firms will accept central bank digital currency, incentivizing both households and firms will result in greater adoption (Tan, 2023). The incentives prioritize the adoption cost per transaction and the efficiency of the payment system; other factors incentivizing adoptions are tax exemption, subsidies and results in financial inclusion at the cost of a third-party payment system. Our study contributes to understanding consumer willingness to switch to digital currency over third-party payment apps by examining the push–pull factors determining the perceived value of digital currency in China.

Existing literature uses the PPM framework to investigate switching behavior, which serves as a theoretical lens unveiling the influential antecedents of user willingness to switch digital currency over third-party payment apps. In this framework, push factors drive users away from the incumbent payment methods, pull factors attract users to new (alternative) payment methods and mooring factors hinder or facilitate switching behavior (Bansal et al., 2005). The PPM framework has been adapted to investigate switching behavior in many contexts instant messaging services (Sun et al., 2017); and mobile payment (Wang et al., 2019). Wang et al. (2019) suggest that QR code-based mobile payment is disintermediated, accessed by a third-party platform and entails private entity handling transactions. In contrast, central bank digital currency may bypass private bank intermediation, money creation is centrally managed, and all transactions remain digital where digital currency is a legal tender. These contextual differences may influence switching behavior, which remains to be studied. Governments and organizations formulating digital currency strategies are encouraged to integrate perceived security, risk, convenience and positive emotions as influential factors in digital currency usage and adoption.

Digital Currency

Digital currency, or e-CNY, is a form of digital legal tender encompassing all essential features of traditional money. The People's Bank of China (PBOC) has defined e-CNY as an alternative to physical cash and ensures its security, creation and management. Unlike third-party digital payments such as WeChat and Alipay, e-CNY is unique (Shin, 2018). While payment methods like WeChat Pay and Alipay mobilize smartphones, commercial banks function as intermediaries and are not involved in money creation (Know et al., 2017). People can choose to use WeChat Pay and Alipay, but e-CNY provides a better alternative with its support for offline transactions (Niu, 2021). Central bank digital currency offers improved payment security compared to third-party platform-based payments, lower transaction costs and enhanced payment efficiency. It also possesses unique monetary characteristics such as ensuring anonymity, preventing counterfeiting, enabling traceability and allowing for programmability. These attributes make it more effective in monetary policy and maintaining financial stability. However, digital currency cannot fully replace current payment methods despite its competing applications. Adopting legal digital currency faces habitual and technical resistance (Xia et al., 2023).

Network effects are a phenomenon that occurs in the market when third-party payments are intensely competitive (Wang et al., 2019). Depending on the number of buyers, sellers or users, the network effect produces value for a product, service or platform. A platform creates more value for its users when there are more buyers, sellers or users (Balachandran et al., 2024). Third-party platforms, such as Alipay and WeChat, pay rides on the network effect to create value for their users and potentially have such leverage that they potentially direct competitors of digital currency. Additionally, third-party payment systems add switching costs when consumers personalize mobile payment apps and feel psychological ownership of them rather than the money in them. According to Khan and Belk (2024), psychological ownership manifests more in the app than in the ownership of money itself.

Apps that stored money made people feel happy, confident, safe and secure. Central bank digital currency has the hurdle of circumventing people's affinity for these apps. Users may continue using third-party apps, even if it is not the best (Wang et al., 2019). Digital currency likely has the advantage of a lower cost-per-transaction than third-party apps, and the central bank issues greater confidence in the currency's stability. Digital currency represents critical factors such as convenience, perceived ease of use and usefulness (Ooi & Tan, 2016), as well as positive emotions that enhance user experience; therefore, willingness to switch will be dynamic because the push factors such as security and risk hinder realizing the perceived value of digital currency.

The PPM Framework

According to Bansal et al. (2005), the PPM framework is a dominant theory in studies exploring switching behavior. It implies that push, pull and mooring factors influence users' decisions to migrate from one service application to another. Pull factors, also known as attractor factors, represent the advantages of the alternatives, whereas push factors, also known as stressors, make consumers away from the items or services. Since switching involves mooring, it represents the supplementary constraints that facilitate or hamper behavior (Fan et al., 2021). People may switch between third-party mobile payment and digital currency usage and push–pull–mooring helps understand the underlying mechanism (Wang et al., 2019). This framework has been used to analyze various aspects of user behavior, such as mobile services (Calvo-Porral & Lévy-Mangin, 2015), travelers' switching intentions (Lehto et al., 2015), social network sites (SNS) switching intentions (Chiang & Chen, 2014), web browser switching behavior (Ye & Potter, 2011) and users' switching behavior of mobile instant messaging (Sun et al., 2017) and third-party payment (Xia et al., 2023). However, the application of this framework in digital currency switching behavior is limited. Considering digital currency's uniqueness, we propose several critical variables that can either facilitate or impede user switching behavior.

Push Factor: Perceived Risk

Perceived risk is often defined as the uncertainty surrounding the potential negative consequences of using a specific program or service. Inadequate or unreliable security measures can heighten the level of risk for users, leading to reduced satisfaction within the context of digital currency. Bauer (1960) introduced the concept of perceived risk within psychological research, arguing that perceived risk influences consumer decision-making. When purchasing or using newly acquired products or services, consumers expect uncertainties and may experience doubts about whether the outcomes will be satisfactory. According to Amarullah et al. (2022), perceived risk is usually generated when there is uncertainty about the decision-related purchase behavior or when unpleasant outcomes are possible. The study identifies two types of perceived risk: inherent and operational. Currim and Sarin (1983) further categorized perceived risk as physical, financial, social, time, functional and psychological. Research has shown that increased privacy concerns lead to lower trust levels and higher perceived risk, preventing mobile payment system adoption (Chin et al., 2020).

Perceived risk about digital currency is attributed to potential losses or uncertain adverse outcomes that may occur during the transactions. These risks include network failures, missing keywords, operating system incompatibility and poor user experience (Chen et al., 2020). Furthermore, perceived risk also encompasses concerns about privacy, platform flaws and the loss of essential data (Chao, 2019). In the context of digital currency, the risk pertains to one that is inherent in the digital nature of the currency, such as once invested, the money remains in digital form and operational aspects, such as the possibility that the central bank may enforce the expiration of digital currency during periods of inflation, forcing people to spend their digital currency within a specified timeframe. Considerably fewer studies have investigated perceptions of digital payment (Laukkanen, 2016) and the risk as barrier embraces topics such as security (Dimitrova et al., 2022).

Push Factor: Perceived Security

According to Linck et al. (2006), perceived security is the perception and subjective evaluation of a system's security and protection against potential risks. Electronic payments involving financial assets raise concerns about consumer security. The concerns stem from data and privacy issues associated with self-conducted transactions over a network. According to De Luna et al. (2019), individuals effectively use mobile payment systems when they believe they can manage the security of these technologies. The customer authentication system for electronic payments is based on knowledge of the system and management of passwords, personalization of the payment app, how a user receives a double authentication code on their mobile phone and user biometric data such as fingerprints in the app. These measures were adopted for a successful model of their third-party payment system. One of the main reasons in digital currency adoption is concerns about security (Presthus & O'Malley, 2017; Roussou et al., 2019). People are most concerned about protecting their financial assets and privacy (Bucko et al., 2022). Individuals may view digital currency as risky, influencing their inclination to accept and place trust in these currencies (Mendoza-Tello et al., 2018). To protect themselves, prospective users may mitigate security risks by refraining from adoption (Schuh & Shy, 2016). Digital currency is not an outside security risk. For example, cross-border cyber threats should not be ignored. Further transparency and data privacy are issues. For example, Yao and Li (2022) suggested that central banks control and administer the following transactional data and those data falling into the wrong hands pose security challenges.

Additionally, potential danger comes from legal issues such as breaches of rules and regulations, cyberattacks and network flaws. The main security concerns regarding digital currencies include cyberattacks carried out by hackers or criminals (Saif Almuraqab, 2020), e-thefts (Mendoza-Tello et al., 2018) that happen without identification, transparency or traceability (Roussou et al., 2019) and problems related to the identification, privacy and anonymity of users (Abraham et al., 2019). Dimitrova and Öhman (2024) confirm that increasing convenience and usefulness influences privacy, security and access.

Pull Factor: Perceived Convenience

Convenience is "anything that enhances comfort or reduces effort; a useful, convenient or helpful tool, item, service" (Webster Dictionary, 2024). It can be described as how consumers perceive the time and effort they need to spend while buying or utilizing a service (Berry et al., 2002). Jiang et al. (2013) conceptualized five dimensions of convenience: access, search, evaluation, transaction and possession/post-purchase convenience. The concept of the convenience of digital currency is appreciated as follows: third-party payment apps and digital currency afford convenience by minimizing time and effort costs while accessing, searching, evaluating and transaction through ownership and gratification.

The desire for convenience drives consumer willingness to switch to mobile payment (Boden et al., 2020). In this study, convenience is defined as faster payments, low cost per transaction, remittance benefits, new investment avenues and decentralization than the current means accessible 24/7. The convenience of digital currency accommodates all the benefits of mobile payment, plus additional stability backed by central banks. It enhances user comfort while minimizing the time and effort required to utilize this advanced technology.

According to Boden et al. (2020), digital payment provides direct utility from the incentivized lower transaction cost, may entail tax benefits due to reduced fees and can derive utility from faster payments. Digital currency affords convenience in paying without carrying cash or using traditional wallets with credit and debit cards. Convenience has been studied as the driver of willingness to use payment methods (Ting & Ahn, 2023). Digital currency builds on the infrastructure of their third-party mobile payment utilizing the QR code to access payment, which does not require a memorizing pin but rather facial recognition or figure prints, and biometrics act as PIN codes (Boden et al., 2020). Perceived convenience of payment method is associated with the choice of payment mode in that convenience and speed of transaction influence willingness to use digital currency (Xia et al., 2023). This research asserts that the perceived convenience of digital currency acts as a pull factor in determining the perceived value of digital currency as a chosen payment mode over third-party mobile payment.

Pull Factor: Positive Emotions

The concept of positive emotions, as defined by Seligman and Csikszentmihalyi (2000), is based on a scientific study of positive human functioning and flourishing on various levels, including biological, personal, relational, institutional, cultural and global dimensions. Zaleskiewicz and Traczyk (2020) suggest that emotions and perception influence financial decision-making. Based on their study, Dew et al. (2015) tracked positive emotions after consumers made decisions.

As people's incomes increase and their purchasing power grows, they value money, convenience, security and safety in their lifestyle. According to a study by Simon et al. (2000), when consumers' perceptions and experiences of consumption exceed their expectations, they are more likely to develop an emotional attachment to the payment method, resulting in positive emotions. Khan and Belk (2024) agree that the customization experience of third-party payment apps increases psychological ownership of the app more than an appreciation of the value of money. People feel happy, confident, safe and secure while using apps that store their money, leading to positive associations with payment methods since they represent digital assets. Xu and Tang (2021) argue that the use of e-CNY in people's day-to-day transactions may lead to positive emotions (Xu & Tang, 2021).

Mooring Factor: Inertia

Inertia is an unconscious process that leads a person to repeat the same behavior due to habits and attachments. It can also be defined as resistance or a tendency to stick to norms and habits (Xiao & Yue, 2018; Gao et al., 2020). The PPM theory considers inertia to have a moderating effect on the push–pull factors (Wang et al., 2020; Zeng et al., 2021). Therefore, inertia enables consumers to execute and complete repeat tasks with minimal effort, which is closely related to the willingness to switch to new technology, processes or products (Chang et al., 2017).

Due to the early stage of digital currency development, only a small number of people use digital currency at this stage. People have likely not yet formed a habit of using digital currency. To ensure that people's perception of digital currency's value and willingness to switch are accurately understood, this study statistically controls the influence of inertia.

Mooring Factor: Consumer Perceived Value

Mooring factors are intervening or facilitating factors that comprise personal, social or cultural forces that either facilitate the movement of potential migrants to a new origin or hinder migration to a new location (Bansal et al., 2005). Mooring factors influence users to forgo switching, even if there are significant push and pull factors (Wang et al., 2019). Factors such as habit and monetary incentives can influence users to stick with their current choices instead of switching, even when compelling reasons exist (Bansal et al., 2005). This behavior, termed 'behavioral inertia,' is influenced by internal and external factors (Limayem et al., 2007). Instead of choosing better alternatives, consumers consciously decide to continue with their current choice (Wang et al., 2019). Despite the benefits of alternatives outweighing those of the incumbent service, people tend to rely on experience to guide their current and future choices (Fan et al., 2021). The decentralized mobile payment platform has already built-up significant network effects. People may find the switching cost from a third-party platform to digital currency incredibly high when their peers and networks are already psychologically embedded in that platform. On the other hand, digital currency incentivizes finance, payment and convenience, security, utility and the close relationship between digital currency and consumer perceived value (Sharma & Sharma, 2015) may impact willingness to switch to third-party payment apps. Therefore, we consider the inertia (tussle between the push–pull factor) and consumer perceived value of the digital currency as a mooring factor to understand the underlying mooring effect.

Existing research defines perceived value from various perspectives. Zeithaml et al.'s (2013) work focuses on the subjective aspects of perceived value, which involve trade-offs between the benefits and costs of products and services. The notion of perceived value is based on equity theory (Carrell & Dittrich, 1978). It refers to how customers assess the benefits they expect to receive in relation to the costs incurred (Bolton & Lemon, 1999). Perceived value represents a balance between the perceived advantages and disadvantages or potential risks associated with a product or service (Barbu et al., 2021).

Sweeney and Soutar (2001) identify four key components contributing to perceived value, which combines both intrinsic and extrinsic attributes: quality value, the value for money, emotional value and social value. Quality value denotes the extrinsic benefits derived from the product based on its quality and performance (Dangelico et al., 2024). The value for money corresponds to the benefits received from using the product relative to the cost (Haverila et al., 2024). Emotional value arises from the product's capacity to evoke positive emotions in consumers (Albornoz et al., 2024). Social value represents the benefits of the product's ability to enhance social gratification (Khan et al., 2015). The perceived value is a precursor to satisfaction (Katt & Meixner, 2020) and repurchase intention (Satriandhini et al., 2020).

Research on perceived value has been conducted in various sectors, such as the hospitality and tourism industry (Kim et al., 2023), the service industry (Hariguna et al., 2020; Saif Almuraqab, 2020) and the digital payment industry (Wu et al., 2022; Xie et al., 2021; Ronaghi, 2023). Coutelle-Brillet et al. (2014) found a positive relationship between perceived value and the intention to use a product or service. Xie et al. (2021) found that perceived value and risk were determinants of individuals' intention to adopt FinTech services. According to Hasan et al. (2022), perceived benefits, perceived risks, perceived value and structural provisions affect behavioral intention to adopt cryptocurrency, similar to findings from Pakrou and Amir (2016), Karjaluoto et al. (2019) and Lin et al. (2020) regarding mobile payment adoption. Perceived value was found to be an important factor in the intention to use mobile payment services in these studies.

With this understanding, we define digital currency is associated with perceived value; this judgment entails quality, deriving positive emotions and harnessing social gratification with a minimum cost of digital currency over third-party apps to users. When evaluating the perceived value of digital currency, the extrinsic and intrinsic attribute values will affect the perception of consumer values to third-party payment apps (Yu & Lee, 2019). Therefore, Perceived value is the difference between the total value of benefits obtained by consumers from using and the total costs incurred for the payment method (Zeithaml et al., 2013; Yu & Lee, 2019).

Current research investigates the perceived value of digital currency as a mooring factor influencing willingness to switch over to third-party payment apps (Figure 5.1).

Research Framework

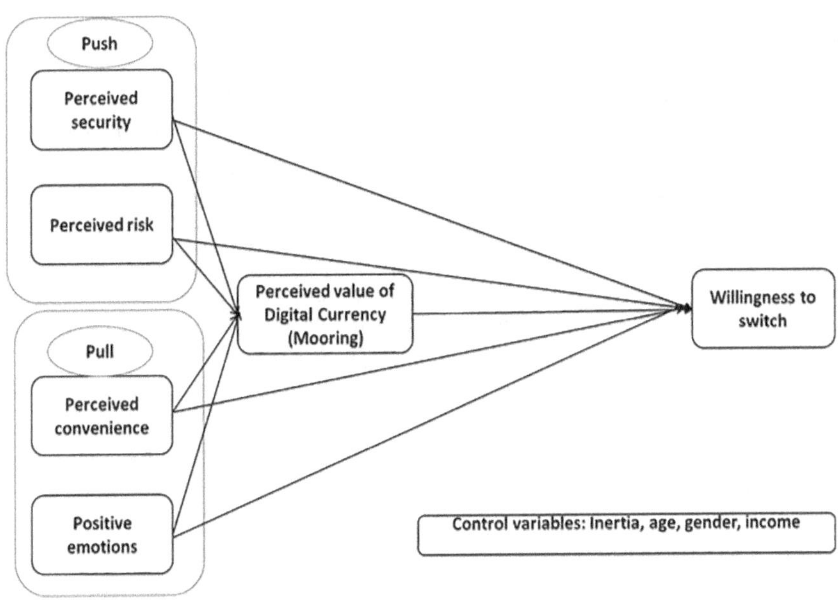

Figure 5.1 Proposed Conceptual Model

Conceptual Development

Push Factor: Perceived Security

Perceived security refers to consumers' subjective belief in protecting their personal information during its transmission and storage, with the expectation that unauthorized parties will not access or manipulate it (Flavián et al., 2006). Consumers' perception of security holds more weight than the actual security measures in place, as it is primarily influenced by the perceived value of the payment choice used to make the transaction in the context of mobile payment (Gao & Waechter, 2017). Though the link exists in third-party and private mobile payment, In the context of this article, perceived security pertains to consumers' placed value on payment technology; it is most likely the relationship between perceived security and digital currency may be stronger as it is backed by the central bank, thus enhancing the perceived value of digital currency. Privacy and perceived value are interconnected during the transaction process, as compromising value also compromises security. Researchers have found a strong positive link between perceived security and the perceived value of the payment method (Singh & Sinha, 2020). Therefore, we propose the following hypothesis:

H1a: There is a relationship between perceived security and perceived value of digital currency.
H1b: There is a relationship between perceived security and willingness to switch to digital currency over third-party payment apps.

Push Factor: Perceived Risk

Perceived risk refers to consumers' uncertainty about new technology and their willingness to accept it to ensure the safety of their transactions in digital currency or other payment modes. Consumers find it difficult to assess the quality of new technology, which causes uncertainty (Derbaix, 1983). Perceived risk is a vital component in assessing the value of new technology (Liébana-Cabanillas et al., 2019). It represents consumers' perception of uncertainty and potential consequences of digital currency (Ma et al., 2022), which may impact their decision to use digital currency over third-party payment apps. Therefore, we propose the following hypothesis:

H2a: There is a relationship between perceived risk and perceived value of digital currency.
H2b: There is a relationship between perceived risk and willingness to switch to digital currency over third-party payment apps.

Pull Factor: Convenience

Perceived value is the consumer's overall assessment of the utility of a product or service based on perceptions of benefit–cost evaluation (Zeithaml, 1988).

The cost entails non-monetary, such as time and effort to use services. A third-party payment app, as does digital currency, brings convenience when carrying out transactions. The perceived value of a digital currency is associated with convenience, which reflects that the time and effort required to use digital currency is less than cash and is the same as third-party payment apps (Xie et al., 2021; Ronaghi, 2023). However, the transaction cost is relatively lower than the third-party payment due to the disintermediation of commercial banks and third-party agents; the perceived value of a digital currency is superior to third-party payment apps. Since the convenience of conducting transactions is an essential consideration for customers, people will likely pay attention to convenience when evaluating the perceived value of digital currency. WE hypothesize that:

H3a: There is a relationship between convenience and the perceived value of the digital currency.
H3b: There is a relationship between convenience and willingness to switch to digital currency over third-party payment apps.

Pull Factor: Positive Emotions

Positive emotions are the enjoyable experiences that occur when an individual's needs are fulfilled. Research has shown that regardless of its form, money triggers positive emotions (Khan et al., 2015) while parting with money incurs discomfort (Zellermayer, 1996). Studies have demonstrated that ownership of money typically brings about positive feelings (Khan & Belk, 2024), and digital payment serves to access money and a store of value (Oatley & Johnson-Laird, 1987).

In a state of positive emotion, it has been found that consumers are more likely to actively engage with their environment, explore novelty and influence consumption patterns (Menon & Kahn, 2002). Moreover, payment apps not only produce psychological ownership of the app itself but also evoke positive emotions such as happiness, confidence, safety and security, thus influencing the perceived value of the digital currency (Zhou & Huang, 2021; Khan & Belk, 2024). However, third-party payment apps may have less security compared to bank-issued digital currency, as anonymous transactions may fall into third-party hands. With centralized digital currency, data security remains in the hands of the issuing central bank. Therefore, the hypothesis is that:

H4a: There is a relationship between positive emotions and the perceived value of the digital currency.
H4b: There is a relationship between positive emotions and willingness to switch to digital currency over third-party payment apps.

Willingness to Switch

Intentions represent likely behavior (Ajzen, 1991); in marketing literature, intention represents consumers' positive attitudes influencing future purchases. Willingness to buy represents a consumer's probability and likelihood of purchasing (Schiffman & Wisenblit, 2019). Possibly, intention describes how much effort is put into planning a behavior. Pomery et al. (2009) argue that willingness explains customers' openness to opportunities and their willingness to perform certain behavior. Intention and willingness predict behavior, but willingness involves less planning or pre-planning than intention (Jun & Arendt, 2016). The influence of willingness on behavior has been studied in different fields (Hukkelberg & Dykstra, 2009). Therefore, the willingness to switch from their-party payment to digital currency is driven by the perceived value of digital currency. This study investigates the PPM effects on consumers' willingness to switch to digital currency behavior. The hypothesis is:

H5: There is a relationship between the perceived value of and willingness to switch to digital currency over third-party payment apps.

Consumers undergo perceived cost–benefit analysis, and their willingness to use a digital currency is associated with security, risk, convenience and a positive attitude toward the payment mode. The risk may entail transactions or information leakage, while the benefits are reduced transaction costs.

Research Method

The purpose of this study is to investigate the impact of PPM factors on willingness to switch to digital currency over third-party payment apps. To address its aim and objective, this study utilized a cross-sectional survey approach. Any person who is familiar with e-CNY and has used third-party payment apps, such as WeChat or Alipay, was targeted. Research participants were recruited by an international market research company based in Beijing, China: https://www.credamo.world/#/. Survey questionnaires were provided to an agency that specializes in data collection, construction, distribution and analysis. In addition to an incentive of USD 1 per participant, the research agency billed USD 500 for hosting the survey on their platform. McGorry's (2000) double translation procedure was adapted to suit Chinese participants and translation. The questionnaire was validated through a six-member expert panel (two marketing professors and four doctoral students) that assessed clarity, understandability and readability. A robust Kappa coefficient was executed between bilingual translator groups (0.89, $p < .0001$). The research sample size was validated using the G-power tool. The results demonstrated that the sample size in this study was sufficient to achieve the effect size (f^2) 0.15 at .05 significance level (Faul et al., 2007) (see Appendix I). A mask was imposed on research objectives during questionnaire preparation to reduce the demand artifacts bias (Khan, 2011). Moreover, social desirability bias was minimized by acknowledging the confidentiality of the responses (Podsakoff et al., 2003). Since e-CNY is not widely used, a short video of a digital currency link was included in the online survey. Further earmark digital currency images of third-party payment apps and e-CNY were used to ensure participants do not confuse these two payment methods. Data was gathered between December 2023 and April 2024. Participant Profile in Table 5.1.

Participants Profile

Table 5.1 Respondent Profile

Characteristics	*Categories*	*Percentage*
Gender	Male	41
	Female	59
Age	18–24	18
	25–34	45
	35–44	29
	45 and over	8
Education level	Undergraduate	32
	Postgraduate	60
	Doctoral	8

Measurements

The constructs were measured using a five-point Likert scale, ranging from strongly disagree (scored 1) to strongly agree (scored 5). All of the items were drawn from previous studies, namely, perceived security (Kim et al., 2010), convenience (Xu & Gutiérrez, 2006), positive emotions (Khan et al., 2015), perceived risk and perceived value (Unni & Harmon, 2007) and willingness to switch (Xu et al., 2011). All items were modified to suit the context of this study. The control variables were inertia (Polites & Karahanna, 2012), age, gender, education and monthly disposable income.

Analysis

The data was validated through a two-step PLS-SEM in the SmartPLS4 package. PLS-SEM method is suitable for exploratory studies having multiple latent independent and dependent variables. Anderson and Gerbing (1988) commend the measurement of the reflective model confirmed reliability and validity of scale before testing the hypothesis with a two-stage analytical process adopted in this study. Hypotheses testing followed the procedure suggested by Zhao et al. (2010).

Measurements Model Assessment

Reliability: All the construct items on the scale had a loading greater than the required threshold of 0.60 (Hair et al., 2011). Internal consistency crossing Cronbach's alpha (α) and composite reliability met the threshold. Thus, internal consistency and reliability are not an issue in this study internal consistency and reliability (Hair et al., 2011, 2010). The results are in Table 5.2.

Table 5.2 Reliability and Validity

Measurement Items	*λ*	*VIF*	*α*	*CR*	*AVE*
Perceived Security (Kim et al., 2010)			.802	.803	.835
e-CNY shows accurate payment amounts and transactions compared to third-party payment	0.91	1.8			
e-CNY's security is superior to third-party payment	0.91	1.8			
Surprises and errors occur when paying with e-CNY (r)	0.89	1.0			
Perceived Risk (Unni & Harmon, 2007)			0.819	0.833	.733
I do not think there is a significant risk with e-CNY	0.86	1.7			
I do not think there is a significant loss with e-CNY	0.84	1.9			
I do not think there is uncertainty with e-CNY	0.87	1.8			
Convenience (Xu & Gutiérrez, 2006)			0.785	0.791	.700
I believe e-CNY is easy to use	0.83	1.6			
The steps to pay in e-CNY are simple	0.87	1.8			
I can cancel my payment anytime	0.81	1.5			
Positive Emotions (Khan et al., 2015)			0.850	.853	.770
e-CNY makes me feel relaxed	0.87	2.0			
e-CNY makes me feel confident	0.88	2.1			
e-CNY makes me feel assured	0.87	2.1			
Perceived Value (Unni & Harmon, 2007)			.710	.706	.634
e-CNY payment is faster than a third-party payment system	0.74	1.2			
e-CNY purchasing and paying is easier than third-party payment	0.82	1.6			
I think e-CNY's cost is lower than third-party payment	0.81	1.6			
Willingness to Switch (Xu et al., 2011)			.844	.844	.762
I would love to use e-CNY payments in the near future	0.81	1.9			
I would switch to e-CNY payments if I had the opportunity	0.87	2.0			
I will use more e-CNY than third-party payments	0.87	2.0			
I will spend time to learn and understand e-CNY payments	0.87	2.0			
Inertia (Polites & Karahanna, 2012)			.820	.830	.763
It will be stressful to change to e-CNY	.71	1.3			
Third-party payment is part of my life	.75	1.2			
I will continue to my current app payment even I know is not best	.78	1.1			

Abbreviations: λ: factor loading; VIF: variance inflation factor; α: Cronbach's alpha; CR: composite reliability; AVE: average variance extracted.

Table 5.3 Discriminant Validity

Fornell-Larcker Criterion						
	1	*2*	*3*	*4*	*5*	*6*
1. Perceived Convenience	**0.84**					
2. Positive Emotions	0.36	**0.88**				
3. Perceived Risk	-0.34	-0.36	**0.86**			
4. Perceived Security	0.36	0.37	-0.39	**0.91**		
5. Perceived Value	0.34	0.37	-0.32	0.36	**0.79**	
6. Willingness to Switch	0.27	0.25	-0.24	0.26	0.45	**.873**

Note: The square root of each construct's average variance extracted (AVE) is higher than the correlation among the constructs.

Bold font denotes that correlations are larger in the column hence discriminant validity is achieved according to Fornell and Larcker.

Convergent Validity: The extent to which a construct demonstrates its item's variance (Campbell & Fiske, 1959) was assessed employing average variance extracted (AVE) and all AVEs met threshold criteria (Hair et al., 2009). The results are in Table 5.2.

Discriminant Validity was examined employing Fornell and Larcker's (1981) criterion (the square root of each construct's AVE higher than the correlation among the constructs) also met (see Table 5.3).

Structural Model Assessment

We evaluated determination (R^2), effect size of coefficient (f^2) and predictive relevance (Q^2) (Sarstedt et al., 2022). The perceived value of digital currency and willingness to switch produced a moderate effect size. Similarly, the effect size of coefficient (f^2) values ranged within acceptable values. Consistent PLS-SEM provides the critical predictors for model fit, such as SRMR, d_ULS, d_G and NFI, which test model fits, and all were within the range. (Hair et al., 2019), and goodness of fit of the research model (Tenenhaus et al., 2005) suggest the model was acceptable to test for further assessments (Wetzels et al., 2009). The result values denoted the suitability of the research model for further assessment.

Structural Model Results

The results of this study reveal that push factors (e.g., perceived security and perceived risk) and pull factors (convenience and positive emotions) directly influence the perceived value of the digital currency but not the willingness to switch to digital currency. Push and pull factors are indirectly influenced by the perceived value of the digital currency, which determines the switching behavior to digital currency over third-party payment apps. Therefore, we did not find a direct relationship between H1b,

Table 5.4 Structural Model Results

Direct Effects	*Coefficient*	*t-statistics*	*p-values*	*Hypothesis*
Push Factors				
Perceived Security → Perceived Value	0.187	4.86	0.000	H1a: Accepted
Perceived Security → Willingness to Switch	-0.006	0.10	0.917	H1b: Rejected
Perceived Risk → Perceived Value	-0.113	2.81	0.005	H2a: Accepted
Perceived Risk → Willingness to Switch	-0.104	2.61	0.009	H2b: Accepted
Pull Factors				
Convenience → Perceived Value	0.167	4.04	0.000	H3a: Accepted
Convenience → Willingness to Switch	0.073	1.79	0.072	H3b: Rejected
Positive Emotions → Perceived Value	0.198	4.95	0.000	H4a:Accepted
Positive Emotions → Willingness to Switch	0.064	1.53	0.124	H4b: Rejected
Mooring Factor				
Perceived Value → Willingness to Switch	0.343	5.73	0.000	H5: Accepted
Indirect-Only Mediation				
Convenience → Value → Willingness to Switch	0.058	3.16	0.000	
Emotions → Value → Willingness to Switch	0.069	3.68	0.000	
Security → Value → Willingness to Switch	0.065	3.74	0.000	
Competitive Mediation				
Risk → Value → Willingness to Switch	-0.039	2.38	0.010	
Control Factors				
Inertia → Willingness to Switch	0.066	0.37	0.171	
Age → Willingness to Switch	0.001	0.02	0.988	
Qualification → Willingness to Switch	0.017	0.02	0.725	
Gender → Willingness to Switch	0.073	0.08	0.307	
Disposable Income → Willingness to Switch	0.048	1.20	0.195	

H3b and H4b. In other words, the perceived value of a digital currency is a critical factor that influences and connects the relationship between perceived security, convenience, positive emotions and willingness to switch to digital currency over third-party payment apps. In our result, the perceived risk seems to directly and negatively influence both the perceived value of the digital currency and the willingness to switch to digital currency, Zhao et al. (2010), classified as this situation as competitive mediation (Table 5.4).

Discussion and Conclusion

With time, the importance of digital currency is becoming more apparent around the globe. Our result shows that perceived security favors digital currency since the decentralized ledger technology (DLT) system ensures the security of payment and transactions. Perceived security could pose a concern for third-party payment networks. However, the central bank will most likely customize the DLT technology to maintain authority over their national currency. Convenience and positive emotions significantly impact consumers' perceived value of the digital currency. Central banks remain the priority in ensuring value is enhanced by reducing the cost of transactions and adding benefits, ensuring people have favorable emotions about digital currency. This may be tied to emotions about existing fiat currency, nationalism and patriotic feelings.

Consumers' perceived risk is negatively associated with the perceived value of digital currency and willingness to switch to digital currency over third-party payments. The competitive mediation in our result suggests that the risk we measured essentially is associated with trust in the national fiat currency. The risk in this research is that Chinese participants believe their money and assets are safe with the central bank authority. There is no risk associated with loss and uncertainty when adopting digital currency.

We used the PPM theory to explain why customers are moving from third-party payment apps to digital currency. By conducting a thorough review of existing literature, we focused on identifying the factors that influence people's willingness to switch to digital currency. We found that a crucial factor is the perceived risk of digital currency and the trust in the central bank, which can impact people's willingness to switch. To encourage widespread adoption of digital currency, it is important to enhance its security, convenience and overall positive user experience. People's perception of the risks associated with using e-CNY is based on their subjective assessment of potential insecurity or negative outcomes during payment transactions. The attributes of e-CNY can impact hidden expenses and negative consequences such as security risks, system performance, network connectivity and speed.

Digital currencies that offer enhanced security, convenience and positive user experience will be more highly valued, leading to increased adoption and switching from other digital payment methods. The e-CNY's security, convenience and attractive features will continue to influence consumer perception and drive willingness to switch from third-party payment apps.

This study aims to examine the factors influencing consumers' willingness to switch to digital currency. Data analysis and findings provide a detailed understanding of the relationship between consumers and e-CNY, and three practical recommendations are presented. It's important to note that many factors influence consumer behavior in digital currency, and we must consider external factors such as institutions, culture and social influence in future research. Additionally, the survey method and convenience sampling limit the generalizability of our results, making them applicable only to those who participated.

References

Abraham, R., Schneider, J., & Vom Brocke, J. (2019). Data governance: A conceptual framework, structured review, and research agenda. *International Journal of Information Management*, *49*, 424–438.

Abu Elbeh, I. M. (2024). E-Commerce and digital currencies risk management challenges. In R. E. Khoury & N. Nasrallah (Eds.), *Intelligent systems, business, and innovation research* (pp. 343–354). Springer. https://doi.org/10.1007/978-3-031-36895-0_28

Ajzen, I. (1991). The theory of planned behavior. *Organizational Behavior and Human Decision Processes*, *50*(2), 179–211. https://doi.org/10.1016/0749-5978(91)90020-T

Albornoz, R., García-Salirrosas, E. E., Millones-Liza, D. Y., Villar-Guevara, M., & Toyohama-Pocco, G. (2024). Using the theory of perceived value to determine the willingness to consume foods from a healthy brand: The role of health consciousness. *Nutrients*, *16*(13), 1995.

Amarullah, D., Handriana, T., & Maharudin, A. (2022). Ewom credibility, trust, perceived risk, and purchase intention in the context of e-commerce: Moderating role of online shopping experience. *Jurnal Ekonomi Bisnis Dan Kewirausahaan*, *11*(1), 61–83.

Anderson, J. C., & Gerbing, D. W. (1988). Structural equation modeling in p ractice: A review and recommended two-step approach. *Psychological Bulletin*, *103*(3), 411.

Atlantic Council. (2024). CBDC tracker. *Atlantic Council*. https://www.atlanticcouncil.org/cbdctracker/

Balachandran, D., Tan, G. W. H., Ooi, K. B., & Wei, J. (2024). What's stopping you from migrating to mobile payment? *International Journal of Human–Computer Interaction*, *40*(2), 295–314.

Bansal, H. S., Taylor, S. F., & St. James, Y. (2005). "Migrating" to new service providers: Toward a unifying framework of consumers' switching behaviors. *Journal of the Academy of Marketing Science*, *33*(1), 96–115.

Barbu, C. M., Florea, D. L., Dabija, D. C., & Barbu, M. C. R. (2021). Customer experience in fintech. *Journal of Theoretical and Applied Electronic Commerce Research*, *16*(5), 1415–1433.

Bauer, R. A. (1960). Consumer behavior as risk taking. *Dynamic Marketing for a Changing World*, *4*(1), 389.

Berry, L. L., Seiders, K., & Grewal, D. (2002). Understanding service convenience. *Journal of Marketing*, *66*(3), 1–17.

Bijlsma, M., van der Cruijsen, C., Jonker, N., & Reijerink, J. (2024). What triggers consumer adoption of central bank digital currency? *Journal of Financial Services Research*, *65*(1), 1–40.

Boar, C. (2021). Ready, steady, go? – Results of the third BIS survey on central bank digital currency. *BIS Papers*.

Boar, C., & Wehrli, A. (2021). Ready, steady, go?-Results of the third BIS survey on central bank digital currency. *BIS Papers*.

Boden, J., Maier, E., & Wilken, R. (2020). The effect of credit card versus mobile payment on convenience and consumers' willingness to pay. *Journal of Retailing and Consumer Services, 52*, 101910.

Bolton, R. N., & Lemon, K. N. (1999). A dynamic model of customers' usage of services: Usage as an antecedent and consequence of satisfaction. *Journal of Marketing Research, 36*(2), 171–186.

Bucko, J., Exenberger, E., & Héjjová, J. (2022). Balancing the segmentation and behavioral principles towards acquiring customer insight: Case of household management services and products. *Transnational Marketing Journal, 19*(2), 235–250.

Calvo-Porral, C., & Lévy-Mangin, J. P. (2015). Switching behavior and customer satisfaction in mobile services: Analyzing virtual and traditional operators. *Computers in Human Behavior, 49*, 532–540.

Campbell, D. T., & Fiske, D. W. (1959). Convergent and discriminant validation by the multitrait-multimethod matrix. *Psychological Bulletin, 56*(2), 81.

Carrell, M. R., & Dittrich, J. E. (1978). Equity theory: The recent literature, methodological considerations, and new directions. *Academy of Management Review, 3*(2), 202–210.

Chang, H. H., Wong, K. H., & Li, S. Y. (2017). Applying push-pull-mooring to investigate channel switching behaviors: M-shopping self-efficacy and switching costs as moderators. *Electronic Commerce Research and Applications, 24*, 50–67.

Chao, C. M. (2019). Factors determining the behavioral intention to use mobile learning: An application and extension of the UTAUT model. *Frontiers in Psychology, 10*, 1652.

Chen, S., Fan, L., Meng, G., Su, T., Xue, M., Xue, Y., ... & Xu, L. (2020, June). An empirical assessment of security risks of global android banking apps. In G. Rothermel & D.-H. Bae (Eds.), *Proceedings of the ACM/IEEE 42nd International Conference on Software Engineering* (pp. 1310–1322). Association for Computing Machinery, NY, United States. https://doi.org/10.1145/3377811.3380417

Chiang, H. S., & Chen, C. C. (2014). Exploring switch intention of users' reading behaviour: An e-book reader case study. *The Electronic Library, 32*(4), 434–457.

Chin, A. G., Onwujekwe, G., & Harris, M. A. (2020, March). Consumer trust in mobile payments: An initial review and synthesis. In *Proceedings of the Information Institute Conferences*. Las Vegas, NV, March 30-April 1.

Coutelle-Brillet, P., Riviere, A., & Des Garets, V. (2014). Perceived value of service innovation: A conceptual framework. *Journal of Business & Industrial Marketing, 29*(2), 164–172.

Cropanzano, R., & Mitchell, M. S. (2005). Social exchange theory: An interdisciplinary review. *Journal of Management, 31*(6), 874–900. https://doi.org/10.1177/0149206305279602

Dangelico, R. M., Fraccascia, L., & Strazzullo, S. (2024). Determinants of the intention to purchase sustainable beer: Do gender and type of sustainable solution matter? *Business Strategy and the Environment*, Advance online publication, 1–25. https://doi.org/10.1002/bse.3841

De Luna, I. R., Liébana-Cabanillas, F., Sánchez-Fernández, J., & Muñoz-Leiva, F. (2019). Mobile payment is not all the same: The adoption of mobile payment systems depending on the technology applied. *Technological Forecasting and Social Change*, *146*, 931–944.

Derbaix, C. (1983). Perceived risk and risk relievers: An empirical investigation. *Journal of Economic Psychology*, *3*(1), 19–38.

Dew, N., Grichnik, D., Mayer-Haug, K., Read, S., & Brinckmann, J. (2015). Situated entrepreneurial cognition. *International Journal of Management Reviews*, *17*(2), 143–164. https://doi.org/10.1111/ijmr.12051

Dimitrova, I., & Öhman, P. (2024). Flip that coin: Barriers, barrier-breakers, and full-adoption of digital payment methods. *Journal of Consumer Behaviour*, *23*(5), 2367–2378. https://doi.org/10.1002/cb.2343

Dimitrova, I., Öhman, P., & Yazdanfar, D. (2022). Barriers to bank customers' intention to fully adopt digital payment methods. *International Journal of Quality and Service Sciences*, *14*(5), 16–36.

Fan, A., & Mattila, A. S. (2021). Touch versus tech in service encounters. *Cornell Hospitality Quarterly*, *62*(4), 468–481.

Fan, L., Zhang, X., Rai, L., & Du, Y. (2021). Mobile payment: the next frontier of payment systems? – An empirical study based on push-pull-mooring framework. *Journal of Theoretical and Applied Electronic Commerce Research*, *16*(2), 155–169.

Faul, F., Erdfelder, E., Lang, A. G., & Buchner, A. (2007). G* Power 3: A flexible statistical power analysis program for the social, behavioral, and biomedical sciences. *Behavior Research Methods*, *39*(2), 175–191.

Fepetu, O., & Adewumi, P. A. (2024). Determinants of digital currency usage in Nigeria. In A. A. Balogun & Y. O. Oyedeko (Eds.), *Digital currency assets and challenges to financial system stability* (pp. 78–98). IGI Global.

Fornell, C., & Larcker, D. F. (1981). Evaluating structural equation models with unobservable variables and measurement error. *Journal of Marketing Research*, *18*(1), 39–50.

Gao, K., Yang, Y., Sun, L., & Qu, X. (2020). Revealing psychological inertia in mode shift behavior and its quantitative influences on commuting trips. *Transportation Research Part F: Traffic Psychology and Behaviour*, *71*, 272–287.

Gao, L., & Waechter, K. A. (2017). Examining the role of initial trust in user adoption of mobile payment services: An empirical investigation. *Information Systems Frontiers*, *19*, 525–548.

Geva, B., & Muraj, M. (2024). The digitization of money: Stablecoins and CBDC. *Banking & Finance Law Review*, *40*(1), 115–141.

Hair, J. F., Black, W. C., Babin, B. J., & Anderson, R. E. (2009). *Multivariate data analysis* (7th ed.). Prentice-Hall.

Hair, J. F., Ringle, C. M., & Sarstedt, M. (2011). PLS-SEM: Indeed a silver bullet. *Journal of Marketing Theory and Practice*, *19*(2), 139–152.

Hair, J. F., Sarstedt, M., & Ringle, C. M. (2019). Rethinking some of the rethinking of partial least squares. *European Journal of Marketing*, *53*(4), 566–584.

Hariguna, T., Adiandari, A. M., & Ruangkanjanases, A. (2020). Assessing customer intention use of mobile money application and the antecedent of perceived value, economic trust and service trust. *International Journal of Web Information Systems*, *16*(3), 331–345.

Hasan, S. Z., Ayub, H., Ellahi, A., & Saleem, M. (2022). A moderated mediation model of factors influencing intention to adopt cryptocurrency among university students. *Human Behavior and Emerging Technologies*, *2022*(1), 9718920.

Haverila, K., Haverila, M., & Rangarajan, A. (2024). The impact of the decision-making role on perceived satisfaction, value for money, and reinvest intentions at varying levels of perceived financial performance in the context of Big Data Marketing Analytics. *Journal of Marketing Theory and Practice*, Advance online publication, 1–21. https://doi.org/10.1080/10696679.2024.2305445

Holden, R. (2024). *Money in the twenty-first century: Cheap, mobile, and digital.* University of California Press.

Huang, R. (2024). A 2024 overview of the e-CNY, China's digital yuan. *Forbes.* https://www.forbes.com/sites/digital-assets/2024/07/15/a-2024-overview-of-the-e-cny-chinas-digital-yuan/

Hukkelberg, S. S., & Dykstra, J. L. (2009). Using the prototype/willingness model to predict smoking behaviour among Norwegian adolescents. *Addictive Behaviors*, *34*(3), 270–276.

Jiang, L. A., Yang, Z., & Jun, M. (2013). Measuring consumer perceptions of online shopping convenience. *Journal of Service Management*, *24*(2), 191–214.

Jun, J., & Arendt, S. W. (2016). Understanding healthy eating behaviors at casual dining restaurants using the extended theory of planned behavior. *International Journal of Hospitality Management*, *53*, 106–115.

Karjaluoto, H., Shaikh, A. A., Saarijärvi, H., & Saraniemi, S. (2019). How perceived value drives the use of mobile financial services apps. *International Journal of Information Management*, *47*, 252–261.

Kasowaki, L., & William, J. (2024). *Digital dollars: Maximizing the power of internet banking for seamless e-commerce transactions* (No. 11807). EasyChair.

Katt, F., & Meixner, O. (2020). A systematic review of drivers influencing consumer willingness to pay for organic food. *Trends in Food Science & Technology*, *100*, 374–388.

Khan, J. (2011). *Cash or card: Consumer perceptions of payment modes* (Doctoral dissertation, Auckland University of Technology).

Khan, J., & Belk, R. (2024). Money you could touch: Cash and psychological ownership. *Qualitative Market Research: An International Journal*, *27*(5), 820–840. https://doi.org/10.1108/QMR-04-2023-0049

Khan, J., Belk, R. W., & Craig-Lees, M. (2015). Measuring consumer perceptions of payment mode. *Journal of Economic Psychology*, *47*, 34–49. https://doi.org/10.1016/j.joep.2015.01.006

Kim, B., Chen, Y., & Kim, D. (2023). Key factors influencing customer loyalty in live commerce: The role of perceived value and perceived risk. *Social Behavior and Personality: An International Journal*, *51*(9), 1–10.

Kim, C., Tao, W., Shin, N., & Kim, K.-S. (2010). An empirical study of customers' perceptions of security and trust in e-payment systems. *Electronic Commerce Research and Applications*, *9*(1), 84–95. https://doi.org/10.1016/j.elerap.2009.04.014

Know, Y. M., Gui, X., & Cheng, W. (2017). Special digital monies: The design of Alipay and WeChat wallet for mobile payment practices in China. In *Human-Computer Interaction – INTERACT 2017*, [online] (pp. 136–155). https://doi.org/10.1007/978-3-319-68059-0_9

Lehto, X. Y., Park, O. J., & Gordon, S. E. (2015). Migrating to new hotels: A comparison of antecedents of business and leisure travellers' hotel switching intentions. *Journal of Quality Assurance in Hospitality & Tourism*, *16*(3), 235–258.

Liébana-Cabanillas, F., Higueras-Castillo, E., Molinillo, S., & Montañez, M. R. (2019). Assesing the role of risk and trust in consumers' adoption of online payment systems. *International Journal of Information Systems and Software Engineering for Big Companies*, *5*(2), 99–113.

Liébana-Cabanillas, F., Marinkovic, V., Ramos de Luna, I., & Kalinic, Z. (2018). Predicting the determinants of mobile payment acceptance: A hybrid sem-neural network approach. *Technological Forecasting and Social Change*, *129*, 117–130. https://doi.org/10.1016/j.techfore.2017.12.015

Limayem, M., Hirt, S. G., & Cheung, C. M. (2007). How habit limits the predictive power of intention: The case of information systems continuance. *MIS Quarterly*, *31*(4), 705–737.

Lin, W. R., Lin, C. Y., & Ding, Y. H. (2020). Factors affecting the behavioral intention to adopt mobile payment: An empirical study in Taiwan. *Mathematics*, *8*(10), 1851.

Linck, K., Pousttchi, K., & Wiedemann, D. G. (2006). Security issues in mobile payment from the customer viewpoint. In *14th European Conference on Information Systems (ECIS)* (Vol. 6, pp. 1–11). Göteborg/Schweden. https://mpra.ub.uni-muenchen.de/2923/1/MPRA_paper_2923.pdf

Ma, C., Jin, Z., Mei, Z., Zhou, F., She, X., Huang, J., & Liu, D. (2022). Internet of things background: An empirical study on the payment intention of central bank digital currency design. *Mobile Information Systems*, *2022*(1), 4846372.

Marangunić, N., & Granić, A. (2014). Technology acceptance model: A literature review from 1986 to 2013. *Universal Access in the Information Society*, [online] *14*(1), 81–95. https://doi.org/10.1007/s10209-014-0348-1

Mendoza-Tello, J. C., Mora, H., Pujol-López, F. A., & Lytras, M. D. (2018). Social commerce as a driver to enhance trust and intention to use cryptocurrencies for electronic payments. *IEEE Access*, *6*, 50737–50751.

Menon, S., & Kahn, B. (2002). Cross-category effects of induced arousal and pleasure on the Internet shopping experience. *Journal of Retailing*, *78*(1), 31–40.

Moon, I. T., Shamsuzzaman, M., Mridha, M. M. R., & Rahaman, A. S. M. M. (2022). Towards the advancement of cashless transaction: A security analysis of electronic payment systems. *Journal of Computer and Communications*, *10*(7), 103–129.

Niu, M. (2021). The influence of the development of digital currency on the central bank and the corresponding countermeasures. *Fortune Today*, *11*, 22–24.

Oatley, K., & Johnson-laird, P. N. (1987). Towards a cognitive theory of emotions. *Cognition & Emotion*, *1*(1), 29–50. https://doi.org/10.1080/02699938708408362

Ooi, K.-B., & Tan, G. W.-H. (2016). Mobile technology acceptance model: An investigation using mobile users to explore smartphone credit card. *Expert Systems with Applications*, *59*, 33–46. https://doi.org/10.1016/j.eswa.2016.04.015

Pakrou, M., & Amir, K. (2016). The relationship between perceived value and the intention of using Bitcoin. *Journal of Internet Banking and Commerce*, *21*(2), 1.

Podsakoff, P. M., MacKenzie, S. B., Lee, J. Y., & Podsakoff, N. P. (2003). Common method biases in behavioral research: A critical review of the literature and recommended remedies. *Journal of Applied Psychology*, *88*(5), 879.

Polites, G. L., & Karahanna, E. (2012). Shackled to the status quo: The inhibiting effects of incumbent system habit, switching costs, and inertia on new system acceptance. *MIS Quarterly*, 21–42.

Pomery, E. A., Gibbons, F. X., Reis-Bergan, M., & Gerrard, M. (2009). From willingness to intention: Experience moderates the shift from reactive to reasoned behavior. *Personality and Social Psychology Bulletin*, *35*(7), 894–908.

Presthus, W., & O'Malley, N. O. (2017). Motivations and barriers for end-user adoption of Bitcoin as digital currency. *Procedia Computer Science*, *121*, 89–97.

Rabaai, A. (2021). An Investigation into the acceptance of mobile wallets in the Fintech era: An empirical study from Kuwait. *International Journal of Business Information Systems*, *1*(1), 1. https://doi.org/10.1504/ijbis.2021.10038422

Radic, A., Quan, W., Ariza-Montes, A., Lee, J. S., & Han, H. (2022). You can't hold the tide with a broom: Cryptocurrency payments and tourism in South Korea and China. *Tourism Management Perspectives*, *43*, 101000.

Ronaghi, M. H. (2023). A contextualized study of blockchain technology adoption as a digital currency platform under sanctions. *Management Decision*, *61*(5), 1352–1373.

Roussou, I., Stiakakis, E., & Sifaleras, A. (2019). An empirical study on the commercial adoption of digital currencies. *Information Systems and e-Business Management*, *17*, 223–259.

Saif Almuraqab, N. A. (2020). Predicting determinants of the intention to use digital currency in the UAE: An empirical study. *The Electronic Journal of Information Systems in Developing Countries*, *86*(3), e12125.

Sarstedt, M., Radomir, L., Moisescu, O. I., & Ringle, C. M. (2022). Latent class analysis in PLS-SEM: A review and recommendations for future applications. *Journal of Business Research*, *138*, 398–407.

Satriandhini, M., Wulandari, S. Z., & Suwandari, L. (2020). *The effect of perceived value and service quality on repurchase intention through go-food consumer satisfaction: A study on the millenial generation*. Retrieved from http://bit.ly/40fAlt1

Schiffman, L. G., & Wisenblit, J. (2019). *Consumer behavior* (12th ed.). Pearson Education.

Schuh, S., & Shy, O. (2016, April). US consumers' adoption and use of Bitcoin and other virtual currencies. In *DeNederlandsche Bank, Conference Entitled "Retail Payments: Mapping Out the Road Ahead."* 2015/12/03, Frankfurt am Main, Germany.

Seligman, M. E., & Csikszentmihalyi, M. (2000). *Positive psychology: An introduction* (Vol. 55, No. 1, p. 5). American Psychological Association.

Sharma, A., & Sharma, B. R. (2015). The influence of education, occupation and income on perceived customer value. *International Journal on Customer Relations*, *3*(1), 36–44. https://doi.org/10.21863/ijcr/2015.3.1.006

Shin, H. S. (2018). Cryptocurrencies and the Economics of Money. In *Bank for International Settlements Lecture on the Occasion of the Bank's Annual General Meeting in Basel* (Vol. 24). Bank for International Settlements.

Simon, M., Houghton, S. M., & Aquino, K. (2000). Cognitive biases, risk perception, and venture formation. *Journal of Business Venturing*, *15*(2), 113–134. https://doi.org/10.1016/s0883-9026(98)00003-2

Singh, N., & Sinha, N. (2020). How perceived trust mediates merchant's intention to use a mobile wallet technology. *Journal of Retailing and Consumer Services*, *52*, 101894.

Sleiman, K. A. A., Juanli, L., Lei, H., Liu, R., Ouyang, Y., & Rong, W. (2021). User trust levels and adoption of mobile payment systems in China: An empirical analysis. *SAGE Open*, *11*(4), 215824402110565. https://doi.org/10.1177/21582440211056599

Sun, Y., Liu, D., Chen, S., Wu, X., Shen, X. L., & Zhang, X. (2017). Understanding users' switching behavior of mobile instant messaging applications: An empirical study from the perspective of push-pull-mooring framework. *Computers in Human Behavior*, *75*, 727–738.

Sweeney, J. C., & Soutar, G. N. (2001). Consumer perceived value: The development of a multiple item scale. *Journal of Retailing*, *77*(2), 203–220.

Tan, X. (2023, November). Security risk propagation and control strategies for complex tasks based on improved multi-signal flow graph. In *Proceedings of the 2023 3rd International Conference on Big Data, Artificial Intelligence and Risk Management* (pp. 171–175). Association for Computing Machinery.

Tenenhaus, M., Vinzi, V. E., Chatelin, Y. M., & Lauro, C. (2005). PLS path modeling. *Computational Statistics & Data Analysis*, *48*(1), 159–205.

Tian, S., Zhao, B., & Olivares, R. O. (2023). Cybersecurity risks and central banks' sentiment on central bank digital currency: Evidence from global cyberattacks. *Finance Research Letters*, *53*, 103609.

Unni, R., & Harmon, R. (2007). Perceived effectiveness of push vs. pull mobile location based advertising. *Journal of Interactive Advertising*, *7*(2), 28–40. https://doi.org/10.1080/15252019.2007.10722129

Wan, R. (2024, May). Analysis of the risks brought by the issuance of fiat digital currency in China and correlated strategy. In *9th International Conference on Financial Innovation and Economic Development (ICFIED 2024)* (pp. 612–617). Atlantis Press.

Wang, L., Luo, X. R., Yang, X., & Qiao, Z. (2019). Easy come or easy go? Empirical evidence on switching behaviors in mobile payment applications. *Information & Management*, *56*(7), 103150.

Wang, S., Wang, J., & Yang, F. (2020). From willingness to action: Do push-pull-mooring factors matter for shifting to green transportation? *Transportation Research Part D: Transport and Environment*, *79*, 102242.

Webster Dictionary. (2024). Definition of convenience. In *Webster Dictionary*. https://www.merriam-Webster.com. https://www.merriam-webster.com/dictionary/convenience

Wetzels, M., Odekerken-Schröder, G., & Van Oppen, C. (2009). Using PLS path modeling for assessing hierarchical construct models: Guidelines and empirical illustration. *MIS Quarterly*, *33*(1), 177–195. https://doi.org/10.2307/20650284

Wu, H., Zheng, H., & Zhang, M. (2022). Credit payment services and pricing strategy in the digital economy era. *Annals of Operations Research*, 1–18. https://doi.org/10.1007/s10479-022-04920-z

Xia, H., Gao, Y., & Zhang, J. Z. (2023). Understanding the adoption context of China's digital currency electronic payment. *Financial Innovation*, *9*(1), 63.

Xiao, S., & Yue, Q. (2018). Investors' inertia behavior and their repeated decision-making in online reward-based crowdfunding market. *Decision Support Systems*, *111*, 101–112.

Xie, J., Ye, L., Huang, W., & Ye, M. (2021). Understanding FinTech platform adoption: Impacts of perceived value and perceived risk. *Journal of Theoretical and Applied Electronic Commerce Research*, *16*(5), 1893–1911.

Xu, G., & Gutierrez, J. A. (2006). An exploratory study of killer applications and critical success factors in M-Commerce. *Journal of Electronic Commerce in Organizations*, *4*(3), 63–79. https://doi.org/10.4018/jeco.2006070104.

Xu, H., Luo, X. (Robert), Carroll, J. M., & Rosson, M. B. (2011). The personalization privacy paradox: An exploratory study of decision making process for location-aware marketing. *Decision Support Systems*, *51*(1), 42–52. https://doi.org/10.1016/j.dss.2010.11.017

Xu, Z., & Tang, C. (2021). Challenges and opportunities in the application of China's central bank digital currency to the payment and settle account system. *Financial Forum*, *9*(4), 233. https://doi.org/10.18282/ff.v9i4.1553

Yao, Y., & Li, J. (2022). Operational risk assessment of third-party payment platforms: A case study of China. *Financial Innovation*, *8*(1), 19.

Ye, C., & Potter, R. (2011). The role of habit in post-adoption switching of personal information technologies: An empirical investigation. *Communications of the Association for Information Systems*, *28*(1), 35.

Yu, S., & Lee, J. (2019). The effects of consumers' perceived values on intention to purchase upcycled products. *Sustainability*, *11*(4), 1034.

Zaleskiewicz, T., & Traczyk, J. (2020). Emotions and financial decision making. In T. Zaleskiewicz & J. Traczyk (Eds.), *Psychological perspectives on financial decision making* (pp. 107–133). Springer. https://doi.org/10.1007/978-3-030-45500-2_6

Zeithaml, V. A. (1988). Consumer perceptions of price, quality, and value: A means-end model and synthesis of evidence. *Journal of Marketing*, *52*(3), 2–22.

Zeithaml, V. A., Mary Jo Bitner, Gremler, D. D., & Pandit, A. (2013). *Services marketing: Integrating customer focus across the firm*. Mcgraw-Hill Education.

Zellermayer, O. (1996). *The pain of paying*. Carnegie Mellon University.

Zeng, Z., Li, S., Lian, J. W., Li, J., Chen, T., & Li, Y. (2021). Switching behavior in the adoption of a land information system in China: A perspective of the push–pull–mooring framework. *Land Use Policy*, *109*, 105629.

Zhao, X., Lynch Jr, J. G., & Chen, Q. (2010). Reconsidering Baron and Kenny: Myths and truths about mediation analysis. *Journal of Consumer Research*, *37*(2), 197–206.

Zhou, Y., & Huang, W. (2021). The analysis of Chinese people's recognition of digital currency electronic payment policy. In *2021 5th Annual International Conference on Data Science and Business Analytics (ICDSBA)* (pp. 433–438). Changsha, China. https://doi.org/10.1109/icdsba53075.2021.00090

6 The Meaning of Money in Cryptocurrency

Jashim Khan, Russell Belk and Ansar Abbass

Introduction to Cryptocurrencies

Cryptocurrency's primary function is to transfer value, ensuring safety and privacy. This aim is carried out by authorizing users to avoid the transaction fees imposed by financial institutions and regulatory authorities and perform the transaction with minimum service charges (Chaim & Laurini, 2018). The national and international financial institutions were discussing the emergence of digital instruments, which may replace the current financial reality with a decrease in the usage of central bank currency (Bibi & Canelli, 2023). From a technological view, technology development is the lurking potential of digital markets, the ways digital instruments are swapped and stored, as well as user applications. From the capital view, investment in the digital market continued to increase and fueled numerous novel advances. One of the latest digital instruments is cryptocurrency, which has gained much popularity in the current digital market (Levulytė & Šapkauskienė, 2021). Merriam-Webster defines it as:

> A form of digital currency which has no central authority but used decentralized mechanism to manage data and the issuance of new digital units that depends upon cryptography to forefend fake and bogus business dealings

As it stems from the definition 'a form of digital currency,' which is true, cryptocurrency is a big kind of digital instrument with huge capital in the current digital market. We will discuss the meaning of money in cryptocurrency and these payment instruments in this chapter but document that we cannot physically hold or touch cryptocurrency. On the other hand, non-digital assists are paper money or physical coins.

The Concept of Tokenization

Tokenization outlines how we exchange value things. Tokens are legal papers or certificates used to exchange value in our routine life, such as national

DOI: 10.4324/9781003425021-6

identity cards, driving licenses and airplane tickets. All these are token forms and used to exchange value; some are permanent, and some are temporary. Each token has distinct features, and these features are fixed on the universal blockchain-based system; for example, an airplane ticket has a certain value within a specific time frame. To seek this, a digital token is issued in the digital market with blockchain technology's help and showcases the value of digital assets, such as non-fungible tokens (NFTs). NFTs provide entrance rights to just a visual digital artwork proving validity to allowing participants to access a specific dealing case, like an airplane ticket contemplating diverse kinds of tokens such as access tokens, safety tokens, crypto collectibles, identity tokens and others (Voshmgir, 2020). An airplane token allows us to consume the services of an airplane; once the job is done, the token is not used again. In the case of NFTs, a similar philosophy is applied but in a digital nature. On the blockchain, once an NFT is minted, a certificate of validity is formed, which conveys to the digital world that no similar token exists. Such NFTs are unique and limited (Chohan, 2021). Brouard (2024) details how BYAC tokens are used to attend owner parties, mint other NFTs (Mutant Apes Yacht Club), and access BYAC merchandise. Owners can also use the Ape they own to start a business, and many have done so, selling such things as BAYC vodka, hot sauce and bags.

Cryptocurrency Properties

Leveraging our discussion of the historical view of money and the concept of tokenization, we are addressing the characteristics/properties of cryptocurrencies. Cryptocurrencies like Bitcoin are based on blockchain technology, having mathematical properties digitally instead of focusing on physical instruments. Moreover, cryptocurrencies have many qualities of money, including transportability, divisibility, durability, fungibility, scarcity, recognizability and utility. All these qualities are available in the fiat currency under certain legal authorities, but cryptocurrency works under a decentralized mechanism and transforms value from one person to another. Consequently, with the advent of cryptocurrencies, the idea of money is further fueled. Nevertheless, scholars disagree on whether they possess the characteristics inherent in what money will become in the coming days. Some scholars do not consider the currency viable to withstand pressure from government regulations and argue that it will become an abundance of fiduciary currency. In contrast, other scholars illustrate the features of commodities to cryptocurrency (Paule Vianez et al., 2020), and some others believe that cryptocurrency has no future in financial markets. A few studies recommend a neutral view of whether a cryptocurrency can be considered a currency and offer no evaluation of the details of currency attributes (e.g., Bouri et al., 2018; Ciaian et al., 2016). Most scholars believe that cryptocurrency is a new kind of digital currency, elucidating one or two functions of the currency. Similarly, numerous studies acknowledge that cryptocurrency covers the functions of currency (e.g., Hazlett & Luther, 2019). Notably, insights gleaned from the earlier literature of cryptocurrency is a digital currency with huge capital in the current digital markets, with money functions such as a unit of account, a source of payment and a store value (Bibi & Canelli, 2023). To seek this novel plethora, NFTs and Bitcoin are significant kinds of cryptocurrency in the current digital market with market capitalization.

This research is poised to document that cryptocurrencies would prevail in one way or another since government institutions refuse to accept cryptocurrencies as tax payment instruments. In addition, in countries such as China, crypto owners do not have Bitcoin or other crypto assets to measure the cost of products and services (unit of account), reimburse sellers for products and services (means of payment) or store value. Bitcoin is used only in these nation-states for rising investment collections (Bibi, 2023). It will create a series of challenges when a broad range of goods and services influence the digital paradigm with a massive interaction of blockchain-based payment systems (Roth et al., 2023). The global detonation of cryptocurrencies with the question about the appropriateness of crypto as a bill of exchange implies regulators and citizens discern certain features attributed to money proper. Cryptocurrencies such as 'crypto assets' have the essential nature of sovereignty to qualify as money or currency (Bibi & Canelli, 2023). Cryptocurrencies have been accepted by a few governments, such as Marshall Island and some industries worldwide (Fang et al., 2022). Crypto coins (i.e., Bitcoin and Ethereum) are helping to increase digital assets like NFTs. NFTs confirm the legality and properties of a specific digital object. NFTs represent an innovative course of thought about virtual assets and a circle of people by giving a podium to scholars to show their interest and opinion to the public. Some NFTs like Bored Apes Yacht Club (BAYC) and Nike tokens are used as admission to real-world events or as tokens for merchandise like Nike shoes (Brouard, 2024). It also authorizes people to join and show a common interest, and this community guides the global adoption of cryptocurrencies. The acceptance illustrates cryptocurrency as a socio-technical innovation that may challenge the financial and fiscal policy structure (Caliskan, 2020). Cryptocurrency makes use of a decentralized network of technologies to facilitate payments. Within the cryptocurrency payment method (decentralized financial network), no certain body or government authority oversees the transactions and monitors their growth (Lee et al., 2021).

NFTs trading increased rapidly during 2021, only to fall just as quickly in 2022 and again rise to new heights in 2024. Some unscrupulous individuals took advantage of the latest technology in the crypto market. However, the governing bodies and anti-money laundering (AML) communities must tackle the issues with new digital assets and decentralized financial networks. Bitcoin trading is illegal in some parts of the world, and regulations lag behind innovation. Trading NFTs and Bitcoin has been an emerging concern for governments and legal authorities partly due to the rise in digital cheating known as wash trading (An inside trade to raise value). NFTs have distinct features and are a new type of saleable crypto asset. They live virtually within the Ethereum blockchain system, protected by the computer protocol with cryptography techniques, and consist of a decentralized network (Rahman & Jin, 2023). Ethereum blockchain is very important for how NFTs work. The Ethereum network has smart contract functionality (contracts attached to the token so that corporations like Yuga (BAYC) get a percentage of the resale of the token) and can operate various decentralized applications; it offers a newly developed adoption of the early blockchain that powers Bitcoin and other digital currencies (Cho et al., 2023). NFTs are taken down within a tidy contract computer-coded agreement planned to perform instinctively when prearranged criteria have been fulfilled (Rahman & Jin, 2023).

Chinese blockchain technology is becoming more and more dominant as the country continues to develop its central bank digital currency (CBDC). However, dealing with cryptocurrencies is prohibited in China due to fear of various issues, including misuse of resources, financial misdeeds and market interference. The lack of use and regulations imposed by the Chinese NFT market is outside the NFT ecology. Recently, several laws and policies have been made by the Chinese government to protect the transactions of NFTs.

NFTs

Technological advancement curated the consumer lifestyle, adding new features to the needs and wants. With this alteration, the financial landscape is tough to compete within the current digital era. Financial institutions reduce the cost of their products and services following digital technologies to compete with their competitors. With the rapid growth of blockchain technology, traders and developers have imagined a new decentralized and democratized web for delegating digital property and reforming Web 3 (Murray-Rust et al., 2023). Web 3 is an up-to-date 3D AR/VR invention of web technologies that authority blockchain technology to attain decentralized property and management. As Nakamoto (2008) mentioned, a public blockchain technology is a distributed record used for a peer-to-peer system to process and verify the transaction, which empowers dealing without any intermediaries (Chen et al., 2021). The Web3 network, consisting of blockchains, attains public verifiability of crucial computing and decentralized property through shared ledgers of technology, peer-to-peer networks and digital tokens (Liu et al., 2021). Attaining Web3 technology, participants can make their own digital identity and ownership on a public blockchain using the same virtue as all the platforms and participate in dispersed governance to retrieve ownership and have power over it (Chen et al., 2021). NFTs are vital to Web3 (Li & Chen, 2023). NFTs are a rapidly growing technology available at the intersection of cryptocurrency and digital property. They lost this attention just as quickly when the market for NFTs and the value of cryptocurrencies crashed in early 2022. NFTs are pieces of digital data or tokens stored on the blockchain and cannot be exchanged into another digital asset (Chohan, 2021). On the other hand, is fungible, i.e., one coin of crypto like Bitcoin or ether has the same worth as the other crypto coin, but the NFTs do not have the same value as other NFTs (Chohan, 2021).

The notion of blockchain technology and the decentralized token have attained much popularity with the advent of NFTs as a digital asset in the cryptocurrency realm (Wang et al., 2021; Ante, 2022). This narrative builds on the technical background of NFTs, which have capital potential in the current digital market. NFTs authorize marketers to talk and join with customers/consumers through a digital dominion, and marketers have begun to explore the potential of NFTs for metaverse business. The early success of NFTs came with a sales value of more than 2.5 billion US dollars in 2021 (Howcroft, 2021). To seek this, retail brands such as i.e., Nike, Louis Vuitton, Burberry, are exploring opportunities in the NFT market (Belk, 2024). Nike's shoe 'Cryptokick' and Dolce & Gabbana's 'metajacket' are prominent examples of new market success. The worth of the NFTs market reached $41 billion capital in 2021, equal to the global fine art market. This was before the NFT and crypto market crashed in early 2022, leading to a situation in which 95% of NFTs were worth zero, and 79% of NFTs remained unsold. NFTs are developed by the same blockchain technology used for cryptocurrencies, but they differ from cryptocurrencies because they have a unique identity (Wilson et al., 2022). NFTs differ from other digital financial assets and have potential hedge and haven properties, as they are independent of the shock of standard asset classes (Karim et al., 2022). This hedge capability and safe haven property are in limited asset classes. NFTs give exchangeable rights to digital assets with distinctive features based on blockchain networks. It does not serve as money or currency, a commodity or even a technology but belongs to a digital asset and has a unique identity in the digital realm. NFTs are the unique agreement of digital assets based on blockchain technology or Web 3 and offer a unique identity code that discriminates them from other tokens used in virtual reality (Peres et al., 2023).

With the development of digital technologies, NFTs get more attention in the current digital market, where individuals become eligible to trade unique items like virtual real estate, collectibles and artwork on the blockchain, usually on exchange platforms like OpenSea and get the rights of ownership of digital property tackling the major challenge in the digital world. Despite the promise, it is improbable that you will be capable of receiving your avatar, plot, house and other digital properties (garments, vehicles and furniture) between platforms in the digital universe. NFTs give proof of ownership and realism to resolve the issue of origin and trust in digital properties (Belk et al., 2022). They can be transferred and traced safely, and their current and past ownership is recorded securely with the NTF. Blockchain technology is a distributed ledger technology (DLT) that provides a safe system for recording communication in a virtual realm (Mudgal, 2021). It first evolved into an enabling transportation that motorized Bitcoin, but now it is used in many industries, especially financial services. Moreover, with its unique properties, blockchain technology is gaining recognition through its applications in different lines of business, including health, finance, academia and others (Jain et al., 2021). On the other hand, blockchain technology is not compatible with Bitcoin or cryptocurrency. It is a life-changing technology that can be used in our daily routine life. Similarly, the internet allows for the sharing of knowledge and opinions, and blockchain allows us to share value from one place to another (Ragnedda & Destefanis, 2019).

NFT as a Financial Asset

The preceding literature review studies NFTs as a financial asset and investigates the potential relation among NFTs, cryptocurrencies and other digital assets. This study was the first to probe the cost of NFTs. The author demonstrates how price inefficiency and a gradual increase in value define the price series for the LAND token. Dowling (2022) investigated whether NFT pricing is linked to cryptocurrency price, given that the financial services sector was born out of cryptocurrencies. According to the wavelet coherence analysis, there was some movement between the two sets of markets (Grinsted et al., 2004). This suggests that knowing about the NFT pricing patterns may be an advantage to understanding bitcoin price habits. Moreover, the minor instability in communication also suggests that NFTs are different from cryptocurrencies as asset classes. The study finds that there was a minimal spillover impact amongst NFT submarkets, which is another significant insight. Vidal-Tomás (2022) observed an average long-term positive performance of non-fungible game tokens and an absence of notable co-movement with cryptocurrencies, as shown by the CCi30 index. This has been described as the takeback of the metaverse, and movement in the value of play to earn tokens does not generally exceed movement in cryptocurrency prices; nevertheless, a bubble burst in the NFT market in early 2022 as Bitcoin crashed. A subsequent rapid rise in Bitcoin value may signal the start of a new crypto bubble. Above all, the literature provides an idea about the relationship between market returns and NFT properties (sales, search and number of transactions), highlighting the divergence between the financial and real markets. This suggests that the positive rise of game tokens is not defensible by the real collapse of NFT sales and trader intentions. Also, some more mysterious elements may play a major role in boosting NFT prices. We can see that the Philippine Axie Infinity workers ('scholars') who could no longer afford to work when Bitcoin collapsed in early 2022 have returned with Bitcoin's resurgence in early 2024.

NFTs in Marketing

Using NFTs in marketing is an emerging topic and has generated significant interest in metaverse research. How NFTs work in marketing is a crucial question for the academic community. In a recent study, Colicev (2023) suggests that NFTs can translate the brand image into maverick brand elements and create value for the brand. The author gives two possibilities for NFTs and how they can work and create value in marketing; first, NFTs may give value by operating as an autonomous brand component, such as new supplies, which can be vital throughout the marketing channel and create brand equity. The companies may target new client demographics, such as Generation Z, by creating branded NFTs to enhance brand identification. Gen Z consumers (born between 1995 and 2010) are a key target for branded NFTs because they are very familiar with technological advancement. The first generation of people to be born in an environment where the internet is always available, this generation is also known as the 'digital natives.' Second, they now use NFT brand communities, especially in the metaverse. According to Colicev (2023), NFTs facilitate communication with consumers and increase awareness of brands. Businesses are using various means to provide engaging content and give incentives for applying NFTs. Furthermore, the author links these two strategies to the marketing funnel, demonstrating how customers are affected at each pre-purchase, purchase and post-purchase stage. A connection between customers and brands is created via the marketing channel. Traditional marketing is put to the test by NFTs. Hofstetter et al. define an NFT as a distinctive unit of data that is saleable through a decentralized, public blockchain. They identify three potential contexts for NFT-related queries. The first involves digital ownership, value and originality. Sharing, authenticity and status comprise the second sector, while branding and decentralized distribution comprise the third. According to Hofstetter et al. (2022), novel conclusions about crypto marketing may be reached by studying these domains. Additionally, they provide additional research issues in these fields (Hofstetter et al., 2022). NFTs have special qualities, including evidence of properties, scarcity, non-fungibility, direct distribution infrastructure, proven authenticity and royalties (Chohan & Paschen, 2023). They discuss NFT marketing and how NFTs might be used in marketing campaigns.

Marketing managers must be aware of NFT's implications for marketing. A personalized AIDA hierarchy is used to appraise these implications. AIDA stands for the four stages of consumer decision-making (Awareness, Interest, Desire and Action). Marketing managers utilize the improved AIDA hierarchy to enhance their understanding of NFTs and how to use them in marketing. This hierarchy provides a road map for how consumers can purchase the NFTs. Chohan and Paschen (2023) revive these hierarchy stages, attaining NFTs in consumer purchase decisions. The first stage is the cognitive stage, where the consumer collects information about the NFTs. Marketers emphasize the NFTs' scarcity and link them with the brand's goals using the cognitive stage of the AIDA hierarchy. For example, offering authenticity of the goods and services is a significant opportunity in the second stage, the affective stage, which is about the wish to acquire an NFT. Companies use multisensory NFTs to communicate with customers and share memories of the transaction. The cognitive stage concerns the pay for an NFT and includes the opportunity to sponsor and share NFTs. The authors have added the stage of post-purchase: recurring action. This stage outlines marketing spaces to sell NFTs that will, on the one hand, increase in value and get consumers to display them.

NFTs in the Fashion Industry

Metaverse advent revives the fashion industry, and NFTs gain much concern in the metaverse. Metaverse is a new digital bailiwick where consumers can spend a digital life and participate in activities similar to physical life. With this, consumer spending time increased on-screen, and the average daily spending time on screen recorded 6 hours and 38 minutes in 2023. To seek this, retail brands invest their resources to build a virtual world with the metaverse, such as Gucci, Burberry and Louis Vuitton, which rapidly use NFTs to engage consumer involvement with their brands. The consumer can use NFTs to purchase digital products for their counterpart in the metaverse and show the digital assets' legality. Moreover, innovative companies are expanding their digital products for the Metaverse (as opposed to several lowercase metaverses), some of which have existed since the early 2000s, such as Second Life and the game platform Roblox. However, the government banned NFTs dealings; China is not far behind; sellers acquire a set of laws by calling them digital figurines. Due to the high demand for these items, Singles Day, the biggest shopping event in the world, is developing into a huge platform for luxury businesses to reach Chinese customers. An example of this trend is a display of artwork on the Tmall/Taobao mobile app that incorporated eight NFTs, including Burberry and Kiehl's. Art entrepreneurs and artists who have achieved financial success using blockchain and NFT technologies have predicted the following paradigm change: the metaverse. The metaverse was derailed by generative AI in 2023, but many think it is merely dormant rather than dead.

NFT Customer Journey

NFTs are offered to customers and traded in a marketplace, typically arranged in collections (Clay Nation on Cardano, Bored Ape Yacht Club on Ethereum). An NFTs collection is a set of NFTs revealed by the creator (artists or founder) that includes only a few designs with varying attributes and shared characteristics. For instance, BAYC has 170 features, such as hats, skin colors and glasses (Brouard, 2024). The collections come in various forms, including virtual worlds, sports, games, artwork and collectibles. Currently, a few studies discuss the customer journey with NFTs. The description of the customer journey has evolved because of how important and easy it is to affect the customer experience at every stage with blockchain technology. We have studied the previous literature about the customer journey with NFTs (e.g., Schweidel et al., 2022) and our unreliable experiences to contemplate the critical steps connected with consumer interaction journeys with NFTs. Addressing the prior literature, we break the customer experience into three stages. These stages resemble the customer journey. The setup of preferences or likings is the first step in the pre-purchase process. Here, a collection frequently explains its artwork, a project plan, and other ways it provides value for a particular NFT user (such as particular functions, advantages, technology and utility). Many NFT projects publish their collections in a calendar specifically for NFTs (www.nextcnft.com, www.nftcalendar.io) and sometimes participate with other ventures to construct whitelists for early followers and create online movements (social media) and use marketing channels to draw the attention of people by illustrating the unique characters and advantages of a given collection. The 'purchasing' step occurs after the pre-purchase stage when preferences are developed. NFTs are 'minted' (printing a digital illustration of the given token as a distinctive identifier) during a collection's launch in secondary NFT marketplaces (JPG store on Cardano or OpenSea on Ethereum). This market is the same as Amazon's but built by digital assets. NFTs prove the owner can transfer or sell property in the secondary market. The post-purchase stage involves decisions about the 'holding' or 'selling.' NFTs have had a flourishing secondary market superior to the leading marketplace in size and purchasers. Traditionally, the consumer consumes the product or service, not necessarily to create value. However, NFTs show that consumers generally grasp and hold with the goal of profit. Selling NFTs is always a tricky part of the consumer journey with digital assets. Compared to purchasers of more traditional goods and services, who are least receptive to marketing messages, holders may thus be more receptive to creators' and the network of holders' attempts at influence in the post-purchase step of the process.

NFT and Fungible Digital Asset

The cryptocurrency market is related to speculation and bubble economy behavior dealing with digital assets (Belk, 2024). Decentralized finance and NFTs have become the center of attention in the digital market considering cryptocurrency; assembling them as autonomously as possible is necessary. Cryptocurrency is a digital asset formed with a decentralized system of several shared computer networks. Cryptocurrencies are used only in digital form, and blockchain technology has been adopted to build a decentralized webwork (Bouri et al., 2019). Due to their decentralized life, they will likely work autonomously from legislative and central authoritarian agencies. Some cryptocurrencies can be used to buy objects just as currency can. Some even believe governments use Bitcoin on a huge range to prevent sanctions (Tara, 2022). Other cryptocurrencies are used more like investment assets, meaning a price-explosive nature may exist. In recent years, governments, lawmakers, entrepreneurs and researchers have all noticed the cryptocurrency marketplace as a new digital asset class. As of March 2023, the number of digital assets transitioned has been over 9,100, as acknowledged by coinmarketcap.com. Despite the diversity of digital currencies, Bitcoin is considered the most extensive cryptocurrency worldwide. Over the decades, Bitcoin has gotten the leading position as a cryptocurrency, accounting for 46.23% of the whole market value of all digital assets. Furthermore, the Bitcoin market has endured extensive growth and fast development over the previous decade. Bitcoin and other cryptocurrencies have attracted the interest of practitioners and academics. Surveys and reports published by market practitioners have acknowledged an important rise in crypto investments by individual entrepreneurs and institutions over the years.

Bitcoin

Bitcoin is a famous and broad category of cryptocurrency around the globe, and its position and value volatility have been notorious (Koutmos., 2020). It was introduced by Nakamoto (2008) as a stare-to-start digital payment mechanism to create an innovative type of trust on blockchain technologies supporting decentralized operation with immediate payment to any party in the globe (Uddin. et al., 2020). Bitcoin holds the highest capitalization position in the cryptocurrency market, and blockchain technology makes it easier to create, distribute, transfer and retain a decentralized currency than traditional currency. Bitcoin's intrinsic value is created by its user.

Bitcoin's value crossed the $1.1 trillion figure in June 2022. With a growth rate of 40%, it has a finite supply and a decentralized system. In contrast, fiat currency supplies more than 170 fiat currencies under the regulatory authorities, just narrowly inching out of the Japanese yen and sitting at just above half of the volume of the US dollar. However, cryptocurrency is not monitored by any central authority. With the development of Bitcoin in the digital market, global financial communities and regulatory authorities are continuously exploring this controversial digital asset. Meanwhile, Bitcoin can be used for payment and as a store of value, like fiat currencies. Prior literature acknowledged that Bitcoin is a digital asset used for investment due to high price fluctuation in the cryptocurrency market (Charfeddine et al., 2020). Some researchers dispute that Bitcoin is a digital gold because it has the distinctive features of a haven asset, i.e., like gold (e.g., Selmi et al., 2018).

Nevertheless, Bitcoin is a pure digital currency, and its value unexpectedly increased from 2015 to 2017 due to global crises and uncertainty, such as the Greek and European sovereign debt crisis, the Cyprus banking crisis, China's currency depression and the Brexit referendum. Another rise in Bitcoin prices during 2020 happened with the COVID-19 eruption, which has destructively troubled the global economy. During the current war between Russia and Ukraine, cryptocurrency has benefited from different factors, compared to fiat currencies, regarding the worth shift. As such, they have been favored in specific national plans. In early 2024, the US SEC allowing crypto funds gave

Bitcoin another huge value boost, carrying it to its highest level. Thus, Bitcoin significantly impacts the financial market worldwide (Härdle et al., 2020). The cryptocurrency market introduces features of Bitcoin, such as futures options and backed bonds, which makes it closer to the world of high finance. However, it is potentially unprepared for the financial market due to its fast development and price instability. Now, it is compulsory to investigate how Bitcoin and other cryptocurrencies work in the digital market and develop a judgment for asset allocation, risk management and financial stability worldwide.

Conclusion

In this chapter, we have discussed the meaning of money in cryptocurrency, NFTs, Bitcoin and the concept of tokenization that ascertains consumer behavior in the current digital market. Money is an agreement between the people to use something as a source of trade. Cryptocurrency is a pure digital asset and is used as a source of trade. It has currency characteristics such as medium of exchange, unit of account and store value, which is known as the function of money. That is why it is considered money without physical instruments. Thus, cryptocurrency is a form of digital currency that is decentralized and depends on cryptography. NFTs and Bitcoin are the type of cryptocurrency that have achieved much transition in the current digital market.

References

Ante, L. (2022). The non-fungible token (NFT) market and its relationship with Bitcoin and Ethereum. *FinTech*, *1*(3), 216–224.

Belk, R. (2024). The digital frontier as a liminal space. *Journal of Consumer Psychology*, *34*(1), 167–173.

Belk, R., Humayun, M., & Brouard, M. (2022). Money, possessions, and ownership in the Metaverse: NFTs, cryptocurrencies, Web3 and Wild Markets. *Journal of Business Research*, *153*, 198–205. https://doi.org/10.1016/j.jbusres.2022.08.031

Bibi, S. (2023). Money in the time of crypto. *Research in International Business and Finance*, *65*, 101964.

Bibi, S., & Canelli, R. (2023). The interpretation of CBDC within an endogenous money framework. *Research in International Business and Finance*, *65*, 101970.

Bouri, E., Gupta, R., Lau, C. K. M., Roubaud, D., & Wang, S. (2018). Bitcoin and global financial stress: A copula-based approach to dependence and causality in the quantiles. *The Quarterly Review of Economics and Finance*, *69*, 297–307. https://doi.org/10.1016/j.qref.2018.04.003

Bouri, E., Shahzad, S. J. H., & Roubaud, D. (2019). Co-explosivity in the cryptocurrency market. *Finance Research Letters*, *29*, 178–183.

Brouard, M. (2024). Setting sail in a tokenized world: An exploration of the Bored Ape Yacht Club and the co-created consumer experience. *International Journal of Research in Marketing*. Advance online publication. https://doi.org/10.1016/j.ijresmar.2024.03.002

Caliskan, K. (2020). Data money: The socio-technical infrastructure of Cryptocurrency Blockchains. *Economy and Society*, *49*(4), 540–561.

Chaim, P., & Laurini, M. P. (2018). Volatility and return jumps in bitcoin. *Economics Letters*, *173*, 158–163. https://doi.org/10.1016/j.econlet.2018.10.011

Charfeddine, L., Benlagha, N., & Maouchi, Y. (2020). Investigating the dynamic relationship between cryptocurrencies and conventional assets: Implications for financial investors. *Economic Modelling*, *85*, 198–217.

Chen, Y., Richter, J. I., & Patel, P. C. (2021). Decentralized governance of digital platforms. *Journal of Management*, *47*(5), 1305–1337.

Cho, J. B., Serneels, S., & Matteson, D. S. (2023). Non-fungible token transactions: Data and challenges. *Data Science in Science*, *2*(1), 2151950.

Chohan, R., & Paschen, J. (2023). NFT marketing: How marketers can use nonfungible tokens in their campaigns. *Business Horizons*, *66*(1), 43–50.

Chohan, U. W. (2021). Non-fungible tokens: Blockchains, scarcity, and value. In U. W. Chohan (Eds.), *Non-fungible tokens* (pp. 1–11). Routledge.

Ciaian, P., Rajcaniova, M., & Kancs, D. A. (2016). The economics of BitCoin price formation. *Applied Economics*, *48*(19), 1799–1815.

Colicev, A. (2023). How can non-fungible tokens bring value to brands. *International Journal of Research in Marketing*, *40*(1), 30–37.

Dowling, M. (2022). Is non-fungible token pricing driven by Cryptocurrencies? *Finance Research Letters*, *44*, 102097.

Fang, F., Ventre, C., Basios, M., Kanthan, L., Martinez-Rego, D., Wu, F., & Li, L. (2022). Cryptocurrency trading: A comprehensive survey. *Financial Innovation*, *8*(1), 1–59. https://doi.org/10.1186/s40854-021-00321-6

Grinsted, A., Moore, J. C., & Jevrejeva, S. (2004). Application of the cross wavelet transform and wavelet coherence to geophysical time series. *Nonlinear Processes in Geophysics*, *11*(5/6), 561–566. https://doi.org/10.5194/npg-11-561-2004

Härdle, W. K., Harvey, C. R., & Reule, R. C. (2020). Understanding cryptocurrencies. *Journal of Financial Econometrics*, *18*(2), 181–208.

Hazlett, P. K., & Luther, W. J. (2019). Is Bitcoin money? (And what that means). *The Quarterly Review of Economics and Finance*, *77*, 144–149. https://doi.org/10.2139/ssrn.3387886

Hofstetter, R., De Bellis, E., Brandes, L., Clegg, M., Lamberton, C., Reibstein, D., ... & Zhang, J. Z. (2022). Crypto-marketing: How non-fungible tokens (NFTs) challenge traditional marketing. *Marketing Letters*, *33*(4), 705–711.

Howcroft, E. (2021, November 24). Virtual real estate plot sells for record $2.4 million. *Reuters*.

Jain, D., Dash, M. K., Kumar, A., & Luthra, S. (2021). How is Blockchain used in marketing: A review and research agenda. *International Journal of Information Management Data Insights*, *1*(2), 100044.

Karim, S., Lucey, B. M., Naeem, M. A., & Uddin, G. S. (2022). Examining the interrelatedness of NFTs, DeFi tokens and cryptocurrencies. *Finance Research Letters*, *47*, 102696.

Koutmos, D. (2020). Market risk and Bitcoin returns. *Annals of Operations Research*, *294*(1), 453–477.

Lee, M., Frank, L., & IJsselsteijn, W. (2021). Brokerbot: A cryptocurrency chatbot in the social-technical gap of trust. *Computer Supported Cooperative Work (CSCW)*, *30*(1), 79–117.

Levulytė, L., & Šapkauskienė, A. (2021). Cryptocurrency in context of fiat money functions. *The Quarterly Review of Economics and Finance*, *82*, 44–54.

Liu, Z., Xiang, Y., Shi, J., Gao, P., Wang, H., Xiao, X., ... & Hu, Y. C. (2021). Make web3. 0 connected. *IEEE Transactions on Dependable and Secure Computing, 19*(5), 2965–2981.

Mudgal, A. (2021). Introduction to blockchain. In S. S. Tyagi & S. Bhatia (Eds.), *Blockchain for business: How it works and creates value* (pp. 1–28). Scrivener Publishing LLC. https://doi.org/10.1002/9781119711063.ch1

Murray-Rust, D., Elsden, C., Nissen, B., Tallyn, E., Pschetz, L., & Speed, C. (2023). Blockchain and beyond: Understanding blockchains through prototypes and public engagement. *ACM Transactions on Computer-Human Interaction, 29*(5), 1–73.

Nakamoto, S. (2008). *Bitcoin: A peer-to-peer electronic cash system*. In S. Nakamoto (Ed.), bitcoin.org. https://bitcoin.org/bitcoin.pdf

Paule-Vianez, J., Prado-Román, C., & Gómez-Martínez, R. (2020). Economic policy uncertainty and Bitcoin. Is Bitcoin a safe-haven asset? *European Journal of Management and Business Economics, 29*(3), 347–363.

Peres, R., Schreier, M., Schweidel, D., & Sorescu, A. (2023). On ChatGPT and beyond: How generative artificial intelligence may affect research, teaching, and practice. *International Journal of Research in Marketing, 40*(2), 269–275.

Ragnedda, M., & Destefanis, G. (2019). Blockchain and Web 3.0. In M. Ragnedda & G. Destefanis (Eds.), Social, economic, and technological changes. Routledge.

Rahman, J., & Jin, Y. (2023). The control of tax corruption: Evidence from nonfungible token market in China. *Journal of Money Laundering Control* (ahead-of-print).

Roth, T., Stohr, A., Amend, J., Fridgen, G., & Rieger, A. (2023). Blockchain as a driving force for federalism: A theory of cross-organizational task-technology fit. *International Journal of Information Management, 68*, 102476.

Schweidel, D. A., Bart, Y., Inman, J. J., Stephen, A. T., Libai, B., Andrews, M., Rosario, A. B., Chae, I., Chen, Z., Kupor, D., Longoni, C., & Thomaz, F. (2022). How consumer digital signals are reshaping the customer journey. *Journal of the Academy of Marketing Science, 50*(50), 1257–1276. https://doi.org/10.1007/s11747-022-00839-w

Selmi, R., Mensi, W., Hammoudeh, S., & Bouoiyour, J. (2018). Is Bitcoin a hedge, a safe haven or a diversifier for oil price movements? A comparison with gold. *Energy Economics, 74*, 787–801.

Tara, O. (2022). *How North Korea launders money using cryptocurrency to evade sanctions, East Asia research center*. Retrieved July 28, 2024, from https://eastasiaresearch.org/2022/10/08/how-north-korea-launders-money-using-cryptocurrency-to-evade-sanctions/

Uddin, M. A., Ali, M. H., & Masih, M. (2020). Bitcoin—a hype or digital gold? Global evidence. *Australian Economic Papers, 59*(3), 215–231.

Vidal-Tomás, D. (2022). The new crypto niche: NFTs, play-to-earn, and metaverse tokens. *Finance Research Letters, 47*, 102742.

Voshmgir, S. (2020). *Token economy: How the Web3 reinvents the Internet* (Vol. 2). Token Kitchen.

Wang, Q., Li, R., Wang, Q., & Chen, S. (2021). Non-fungible token (NFT): Overview, evaluation, opportunities and challenges. *arXiv preprint arXiv:2105.07447*.

Wilson, K. B., Karg, A., & Ghaderi, H. (2022). Prospecting non-fungible tokens in the digital economy: Stakeholders and ecosystem, risk and opportunity. *Business Horizons, 65*(5), 657–670.

7 The Meaning of Money in Digital Game Currencies

Jashim Khan, Russell Belk, Na Zuo and Annie Banikema

> They could put as many microtransactions as they want; I have never bought any downloadable content in my life. Progression in a game must work on merit and not with a credit card.
>
> On the contrary, for me, microtransactions can improve my gaming experience and customize it to my taste. Microtransactions are the freedom to modulate a game at leisure.[1]

Introduction

These two verbatim extracts from an online forum of gamers highlight antagonistic positions about microtransactions in free-to-play mobile games. These *verbatims* illustrate the controversy related to microtransactions among gamers, which results in passionate debates about microtransactions. However, marketers have not shown much interest in this important phenomenon, which fundamentally explains how gamers consume free-to-play mobile games. This research aims to unpack microtransactions in free-to-play games by scrutinizing flow state, impulsive buying tendency and behavioral loyalty theories of consumer behavior.

Three broad streams of research in gaming behavior were identified by Seo et al. (2015): the first related to player–game interactions and experiences; the second related to purchasing decisions of games and the third deals with the impact of gaming within the context of addiction, gambling and impact to broader society. This research falls into the second stream of research on consumers' microtransactions on virtual tools in free-to-play mobile games. Microtransactions are a payment system in free-to-play games that allows gamers to purchase virtual tools that enable skipping stages and provide an advantage over other players (Ivanov et al., 2019). The underlying mechanism is that if gamers lack skills or time through regular gameplay, they can attain virtual tools through microtransaction and be on par with other players in the game (Civelek et al., 2018). Similarly, players can earn in-game virtual tools by playing for longer hours and exposure to in-game advertising. This research aims to provide an answer to the question of why some gamers choose to purchase virtual tools in free-to-play games while others do not.

DOI: 10.4324/9781003425021-7

This research explains the role of flow state, impulsive buying tendency and behavioral loyalty influencing gamers' microtransactions of in-game virtual tools.

Several studies suggest flow theory related to online purchase and continuance usage intention (Lee & Kim, 2017), online impulse buying (Wu et al., 2020), and flow is the underlying mechanism of pleasurable online consumer experience (Ding, 2011). Ming et al. (2021) found that the flow state triggers impulse buying in social commerce, and live streamers' power moderates the relationship between the flow state and impulse buying behavior. In the free-to-play gaming context, gamers experience a flow state. They also experience positive feelings and a sense of satisfaction, triggering impulse buying tendencies (Ming et al., 2021; Rook, 1987), which are influenced by personal situations (such as a lack of skills or time). Gamers deprived of these resources are tempted to attain hedonic satisfaction, viewed as the short-term goal (Widagdo & Roz, 2021), to act impulsively and engage in microtransactions of virtual tools. Those players, who are not hindered by time and skills, enjoy the positive feelings of playing games and may embark impulsively to make microtransactions of virtual tools (King et al., 2020). This research examines the relationship between flow state and microtransactions triggered by impulse buying tendencies.

Hamari and Lehdonvirta (2010) and Ryan and Rigby (2020) suggest that a well-designed game is a prime motivator for continuing to play. King and Delfabbro (2019) insisted that the gaming environment, usability, design and features enhance the microtransaction of virtual tools. The continuance to play the game repeatedly indicates behavioral loyalty (repeated purchase behavior for a specific choice of brand) (Back & Parks, 2003) that the gamers try to recreate the enjoyable moment by revisiting the game and probably recommend that pleasurable experience to their peers. While taking this view of the influence of the flow state, gamer loyalty may influence individual players' eagerness to purchase virtual tools while playing games that heightened enjoyment and experience in the past. In this research, we unpack the relationship between flow state and microtransactions triggered by gamer loyalty related to the enjoyment and pleasure players repeatedly draw from playing the game. This enjoyment and pleasure are reached through the experience of playing the game. Players in the flow state will likely be engulfed in games because they have enjoyable playing experiences (Chang et al., 2014). This positive state is rewarding, and players seek to experience this state again in the future.

Drawing on Hoffman and Novak's (1996) assertion that flow theory explains human–computer interaction, this study assumes that flow state may play a role in players' engagement and intention to make microtransactions in free-to-play mobile games. Nah et al. (2014) suggest that concentration in mobile games is associated with a flow state and that flow state evokes positive emotions during the playing (Quinn, 2005). However, Khan et al. (2015) claim that spending generally induces negative emotions, such as the pain of paying (Khan et al., 2015). This research proposes the flow state as a central concept explaining gamers' interest in purchasing virtual tools in free-to-play mobile games. The current study aims to investigate the relationship between flow state and microtransaction, examining the mediating role of impulse buying tendency and behavioral loyalty to influence the above relationship. This research extends our knowledge of flow state as the central concept demonstrating a gamer's willingness to purchase virtual tools in free-to-play mobile games. We address the main research question in our investigation: What is the relationship between flow state and microtransaction?

Why this Study?

We are particularly interested in free-to-play mobile games because their revenues are mainly based, and paradoxically, on the principle of punctual sales of virtual tools. Through this research, we combine two questions often addressed disjointedly: the influence of flow state on microtransactions and the role of impulse buying tendency and behavioral loyalty influencing microtransactions in free-to-play mobile games.

Research has shown the importance of flow theory in explaining gamers' behavior. Flow state predicts gamers' intention to play desktop games (Hsu & Lu, 2004); similarly, Huang and Hsieh (2011) suggest that flow state positively relates to gamers' loyalty toward online gaming. Shelstad's (2022) study highlights gamers' intention to purchase in-game virtual items in free-to-play games; Jiao et al. (2022) demonstrated the relationship between play duration and in-app purchase behavior in mobile games. These studies suggest that the purchase of a virtual item is related to the number of hours a gamer plays a game. For example, Hamari (2015) and Wang et al. (2022) suggest that attitude toward virtual tools in free-to-play mobile games depends on peers' attitudes and influence intention to purchase. Lehdonvirta (2009) suggests motivations for purchasing virtual tools dependent on gamer status, competitive advantage, being on par with other players, new content, customization and self-expression. This motivation explains why some players engage in the flow state and others are reluctant to engage in microtransactions (Garrett et al., 2023).

Raneri et al. (2022) report that a link exists between microtransactions, internet gaming disorder and gambling disorder. King et al. (2020) study contradicted gambling and addiction as the driver of microtransactions, claiming spending on virtual tools is associated with peers' purchasing behavior but not gaming disorder symptoms. They explained that the social influence of gamers predicts spending behavior, and gamers try to spend on virtual tools on par with their closest friends. This study also reports that gamers who engage in microtransactions are older and spend less time playing mobile games. However, the same study acknowledged that problematic gaming was associated with an impulse buying tendency (King et al., 2020). van Evers and Weeda (2015) liken microtransactions to gamers' status. Gamers who use microtransactions are perceived negatively by other gamers when their peers purchase an in-game advantage. However, we found no research on the influence of flow states on microtransactions in free-to-play games. This research seeks to fill this lacuna in the literature. It explains that gamers are triggered to make microtransactions when they draw on impulse buying tendencies and experience behavioral loyalty to free-to-play mobile games under the flow state. Klézl and Kelly (2023) studied gamer types based on gaming length and immersion in the game and their effect on purchase behavior. However, the study did not examine or control for impulse buying tendencies.

To understand why people do microtransactions in online games, Hamari (2015) argues that positive feelings of the flow state reduce the urge to make microtransactions while the flow state increases the desire to play mobile games for long hours. Continuation of playing the game, or behavioral loyalty, positively influences the making of microtransactions of virtual tools if gamers experience a lack of skills and/or time to play the game longer and earn those tools. Palmeira (2021) argues that microtransactions influence an individual's choice to play mobile games free-to-play, though money spent on games does not impact the number of hours spent playing games. Therefore, expressing a paradoxical consumer behavior concerning flow state, impulsive buying tendency and behavioral loyalty are worth researching.

Driven by a desire to understand the role of flow state and behavioral loyalty on microtransaction, we hypothesize that the impulsive buying tendency and behavioral loyalty mediate the relationship between flow state and microtransaction.

Literature Review

Mobile gaming content was worth approximately US dollars 140.5 billion in 2022, and it is projected to reach 173.4 billion by 2026 as smartphone adoption and usage continue to increase, comprising almost 30% of the world population. Mobile games (worldwide) are expected by revenue to be US dollars 315.90 billion in 2030, and almost half of this revenue originated in Asia Pacific, while the segment is reported to increase by 2,323.9 million mobile gamers globally in 2027. Microtransactions rapidly grew between 2012 and 2014 and matured in 2019, with 85.89% engaged with microtransactions during the survey period (Zendle et al., 2020).

The subsequent sections will discuss the theoretical framework of this study—the influence of impulsive buying tendency and behavioral loyalty in the relationship between flow state and microtransaction.

Microtransaction

Microtransaction is a business model bestowing gamers a choice of microtransactions to acquire in-game virtual tools. Microtransaction is a business model that allows gamers to acquire in-game virtual tools at a negligible cost.

Gamers who need more time or gaming skills purchase in-game virtual tools (Freeman et al., 2022). These virtual tools enhance gamers' ability, cosmetic appearance and status without influencing gamers' performance (Elmezeny, 2020). Zendle et al. (2020) reported a significant decline in one-time payment games during the survey between 2012 and 2019.

The microtransaction of virtual tools is studied from two different perspectives. First, studies examined the characteristics of virtual game items through a critical approach (Lehdonvirta, 2009). For example, Tan (2019) discussed the historical development of microtransactions and their impact on the industry and players. McCaffrey (2019) points out the controversy surrounding in-game microtransactions on the grounds that they are unfair and predatory. These studies converge that microtransaction gamers are helpless victims of microtransactions (Garrett et al., 2023), and they were judged negatively and disliked by other gamers and perceived as having inferior skills and status (van Evers & Weeda, 2015). Second, research was conducted from a player perspective, mainly to understand the motivation to engage in microtransactions (Wohn & Lee, 2013). Hamari and Keronen's (2017) meta-analysis reveals motives to purchase virtual tools, identifying attitude, social norms, network size and flow state as the factors that influence purchase intention. No previous study examined the direct and indirect relationship between flow state and microtransactions in free-to-play mobile games.

Flow State

Flow theory has been applied to impulse buying behavior (Jin et al., 2022; Zhang et al., 2018), website atmospherics (Lee et al., 2019; Ettis, 2017), mobile game adoption (Rauschnabel et al., 2017), free-to-play mobile games (Thomsen et al., 2016) gambling and addiction (Chang et al., 2014; Kim et al., 2017). The wide application of flow theory in the computer-mediated platform makes it imperative to study the flow state and gamers' microtransactions in free-to-play mobile games. Online games are likely to offer a flow experience, indicating a positive player experience, positive interaction and immersion. A higher immersion in the game increases the likelihood of creating a flow experience (Kaur et al., 2016).

Csikszentmihalyi (1975, p. 36) defined flow as "the holistic experience that people feel when they act with total involvement," and flow state refers to cognitive and affective, a conative component of mind activated for a highly focused activity and requires complete immersion in that activity (Biasutti, 2017). Trevino and Webster (1992) operationalized a flow state containing four characteristics: control, attention, curiosity and intrinsic interest, which involve enjoyment of the interaction (Webster et al., 1993). Gamers have a sense of loss of control, curiosity about the next level of the game, enjoyment and at the same time, devoting intrinsic interest to the game (Csikszentmihalyi, 1975).

This study of the flow state comprises intrinsic enjoyment and concentration (Ghani & Deshpande, 1994). Gamers primarily focus on the current task (playing games). This intrinsic concentration stimulated by the flow state triggers the impulsive buying tendency of microtransactions for gamers who lack time and skills (Guo & Poole, 2009). In other words, gamers who enjoy the flow state and lack resources (e.g., time or gaming skills) to maintain the flow may impulsively engage in microtransactions of virtual tools. Intrinsic enjoyment can increase gamers' immersion in playing, and these gamers tend to repeat that enjoyment by playing the game repeatedly. Hence, behavioral loyalty seems to trigger the relationship between the flow of joy and microtransactions. Serravalle et al. (2023) suggest that flow experience positively correlates with behavioral loyalty, meaning gamers who experience flow while playing a game are intrinsically interested in experiencing flow feelings again in the future (Hsiao & Chen, 2016). However, the direct effect of flow state in free-to-play games and engagement in microtransactions remain ignored in marketing literature.

Impulse Buying

Impulse buying tendency is a personality trait enthused by an abrupt, instinctive, unplanned, persistent urge to buy something immediately (Rook & Fisher, 1995; Rook & Gardner, 1993). An individual's emotional state is related to impulsive buying (Donovan & Rossiter, 1994). Positive emotions such as flow state and impulse buying are demonstrated in social commerce (Ming et al., 2021). Flow is recognized for enjoyment and concentration in gamer's mindset (Cheah et al., 2022), triggering a relationship between impulse buying tendency and purchase intention that reinforces the positive emotion of flow (Wu et al., 2020). The reinforcement of the flow state entices players to play the game repeatedly, drawing behavioral loyalty. The interplay of flow state, impulsive buying and gamer loyalty explains microtransactions of virtual tools in free-to-play games. Therefore, a priori logic suggests that a gamer's loyalty and impulse buying tendencies are essential factors that trigger spending behavior under the positive emotional state, e.g., the flow state.

Gamer Loyalty

Jacoby (1971) construed loyalty as embracing attitudinal and behavioral components. Kahn et al. (1986) and Ehrenberg et al. (1990) defined brand loyalty strictly from a behavioral perspective, supposing a surrogate measure such as repeat purchases or spending on a particular brand. Gamer loyalty extends brand loyalty to free-to-play mobile gaming context influenced by the gamer flow state and restricted by the availability of time and skills required to immerse in the game of choice. Generalized gamer loyalty metrics are when a gamer repeatedly returns to play a particular game without switching to other games (Kahn et al., 1986). The surrogate measure of gamer loyalty for a specific game is a first-choice trophy, recommending the game to other gamers, giving expert advice, spreading positive word of mouth and, importantly, spending time and money on the game—this type of loyalty surface from flow state triggering impulse tendency to engage in microtransaction.

Conceptual Development

This research examines the relationship between flow state and gamer's in-game virtual tools purchase behavior. The assumption is that flow experience does not necessarily influence gamers' microtransaction behavior. Gamer's impulse buying tendency and experience of playing the game connect the flow state and microtransaction in a free-to-play mobile game. Flow in mobile games is characterized by positive feelings, such as enjoyment and concentration (Kaur et al., 2016). It seemingly makes individuals forget or lose control and indulge impulsively (Supangan et al., 2019). Free-to-play mobile games elicit a flow state and evoke impulsiveness and repeat playing, drawing on loyalty to the game (see Figure 7.1).

Flow State and Microtransaction

The direct relationship between the flow state and spending 'money' in-game free-to-play mobile games needs investigation. To our knowledge, no study examined the above relationship. However, few studies suggest that spending 'time' playing mobile games highlights the importance of this relationship. For example, Cheung et al. (2015) indicated that players' engagement and time spent playing are determined by the money customers spend acquiring the gaming console. In the gambling context, Lavoie and Main (2019) demonstrate a direct relationship between the flow state and the amount

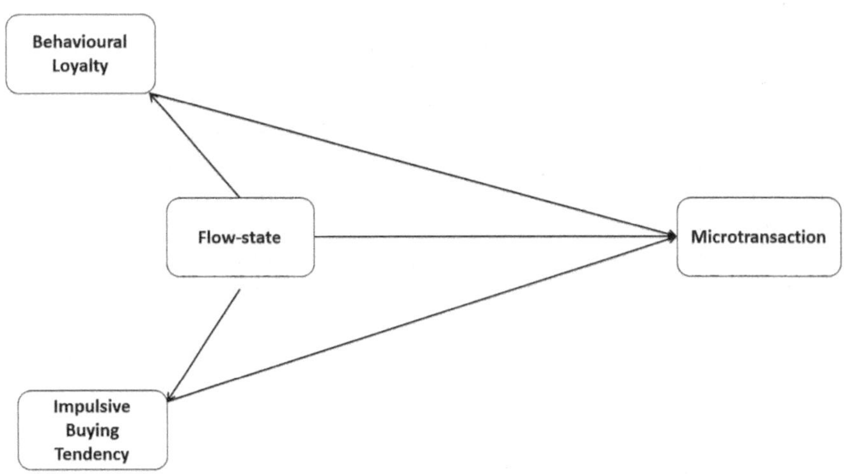

Figure 7.1 Microtransaction, Flow State, Impulse Buying Tendency

of time spent gambling. Liu and Shiue (2014) confirmed that the flow state significantly enhances game players' purchase intention of advertised products on social media such as Facebook. Spending time and money is a limited resource (Khan & Rivers, 2019), though research evidence that the flow state increases gaming time (Cheung et al., 2015).

Paradoxically, the flow influence on spending money in the free-to-play mobile game is sufficiently antagonistic: that flow state calls for concentration—enjoyment and, on the other hand, spending money on virtual tools is described as the pain of paying (Khan et al., 2015). However, Costes and Bonnaire (2022), within the context of Internet Gaming Disorder (IGD), reported flow being positively associated with spending and IGD, though the study sample underrepresented free-to-play gamers (17.9%). Lin and Sun (2007) found that gamers' concentration and enjoyment decrease with buying in-game virtual tools. Hamari (2015) confirms that positive feelings about the flow state reduce the urge to make microtransactions. With this understanding, we hypothesize that:

H1: There is a negative and no relationship between flow state and microtransaction in free-to-play games.

The Role of Impulse Buying Tendency

The enjoyment that gamers experience under the flow state increases the desire to play mobile games for long hours (Hamari, 2015). The flow state experience induces a sense of satisfaction triggering impulse buying tendencies (Ming et al., 2021). Gamers with time and skills are likely to extend the flow state by playing longer hours, but those who lack these resources are tempted to indulge in impulse buying of in-game microtransactions to maintain the flow state. Costes and Bonnaire (2022) demonstrate a positive relationship between impulse buying and spending on free-to-play games.

Given that free-to-play games request users to play for a more prolonged experience of enjoyment and immersion in the game, they may encounter a flow state likely to spend more time playing online games (King et al., 2020). On the contrary, a typical gamer deprived of time may engage in microtransactions to the continuance of the flow state, upgrading to a new level of challenge associated with maintaining the enjoyment related to the flow state. Thus, the concentration and enjoyment flow condition may lead to affective impulsive buying. In line with this reasoning, our research proposes that:

H2: Impulsive buying tendency mediates the relationship between flow state and microtransaction in free-to-play games.

The Role of Gamer Loyalty

The flow state is also likely to relate to behavioral loyalty since human nature revisits or recreates enjoyable experiences repeatedly (Whittaker et al., 2021).

Huang and Hsieh (2011) used flow theory to predict consumers' loyalty toward online gaming and found that flow positively influences loyalty toward a mobile game. However, in examining the role of flow experience in users' intention to continue using social network sites, Chang and Zhu (2012) found an influence of flow on consumer satisfaction but none in continuance intention. Yoo's (2015) study highlights that gamers are likelier to purchase in-game items and display loyalty to chosen games. Also, Individuals who experience flow states demonstrate a higher likelihood of satisfaction and loyalty (Ghazali et al., 2018).

Similarly, Chou and Ting (2003) suspected that people who enjoy the flow experience during an activity might tend to repeat the action. Flow increases playing time because its inherently enjoyable nature makes stopping difficult (Lavoie & Main, 2019). Similarly, Hsiao and Chen's (2016) study of mobile games found that gamer loyalty mediates the relationship between enjoyment and purchase of premium content. Therefore, we hypothesize:

H3: Gamer loyalty mediates the relationship between flow state and microtransaction in free-to-play games.

Methodology

Based on published literature, a cross-sectional survey adapts constructs to suit the study's context. Respondents who play League of Legends, a free-to-play game, were identified through the screening question. Respondents were recruited based on their participation in free-to-play games in the last month and their purchase of virtual tools in-game. Participants were selected based on a non-probability criterion-based purposive sampling technique (Hair et al., 2009). The data collection took place between February and August 2019. Qualtrix is an online survey platform used for survey construction, distribution and data management. Informed consent was obtained from all participants, and ethical approval was obtained. As a result, the participants' identities are kept confidential. There were 207 usable responses after discarding incomplete questionnaires.

Sample Profile

Ninety-three percent of the participants were aged between 18 and 25 years old; 4% were between the ages of 26 and 35; 3% were between 36 and 45, representing online in-game player characteristics. The majority were male (69%) and (31%) female, which coincides with free-to-play mobile gamer characteristics (Hainey et al., 2011). Of the 207 respondents surveyed, 41% played free games between 5 and 10 hours, 36% between 15 and 20 hours and the rest, 23%, played more than 20 hours per week. On average, participants spent US dollars 10 (£7) per week.

Construct Measurement

Participants viewed a 30-second video clip, League of Legends, and identified playing this game in the last 3 days. Questionnaire items were adapted to suit the context of this study, and perceptions were measured for the free-to-play mobile game League of Legends. Chang et al. (2014) study was the source of the flow state construct, measured using three items. The impulsive buying tendency was measured using three items and was adapted from (Wakefield & Inman, 2003); Gamer loyalty was adapted from Zeithaml et al. (1996) (see Table 7.1). Gamers' self-reported spending on in-game virtual items or tools in the last three months was the indicator of microtransactions.

Table 7.1 Convergent Validity Indexes

	Loading	α	*CR*	*AVE*
Flow State (Chang et al., 2014)		.94	.95	.85
I think I have experienced flow state while playing League of Legends	.97			
Every time I paly league of legends I experience the flow state	.85			
Most of the time I play League of Legends, I do not feel that I am in flow state	.95			
Impulsive Buying Tendency (Wakefield & Inman, 2003)		.93	.96	.88
While playing League of Legends, I often buy in-game items or gaming tools spontaneously	.95			
"I see it, I buy it" describes the way I buy in-game items or gaming tools of League of Legends	.91			
I buy in-game items of League of Legends because I like buying	.94			
Behavioral Loyalty (Zeithaml et al., 1996)		.75	.83	.51
I recommend League of Legends' in-game items or gaming tools to someone who seeks my advice in gaming websites	.91			
I will encourage friends and relatives to purchase in-game items or gaming tools of League of Legends	.59			
I consider League of Legends' in-game items or gaming tools as my first choice	.69			
I will purchase more in-game items or gaming tools of League of Legends in the next few years.	.68			
I make an effort to purchase League of Legends' in-game items or gaming tools for improving my gaming experiences	.67			

Note: α: Cronbach's alpha; AVE: average variance extracted; CR: composite reliability.

Analyses

Data screening ensured data quality and parametric test assumptions were met. Subscale means were used to replace missing data. In accordance with Hair et al. (2017), we examined outliers (values greater than 3.5 standard deviations from the sample mean were considered outliers). SmartPLS software (v.3.2.7) was used to test the statistical significance of path coefficient (Sarstedt et al., 2011). The statistical significance of the path coefficient was tested using a bootstrapping procedure with the replacement of 5,000 subsamples (Sarstedt et al., 2011).

Results

Factor Structure

To assess the reliability of each construct, we used Cronbach's alpha. A convergent validity assessment used factor loading, average variance extracted (AVE) and composite reliability (CR). Table 7.1 shows that all factors in this study met the convergent validity criteria AVE > 0.5 and CR > 0.7. To test discriminant validity, Fornell and Larcker (1981) compared the square root of each construct's AVE to the correlation between the constructs. Table 7.2 confirms discriminant validity. Hartman's single-factor technique revealed that the single factor explained less than .5 of the total variances, indicating a lesser likelihood of common method bias.

Structural Model Fit Index

The R^2 was 78.9% for impulsive buying tendencies, 68.5% for behavioral loyalty and 13.2% for microtransactions. Stone-Geisser's cross-validated redundancy $Q^2 > .0$ was observed in analysis, specifically .71 for impulsive buying tendency, .49 for behavioral loyalty and .09 for microtransactions. Wetzels et al. (2009) recommended a global goodness of fit threshold of 0.36 for microtransactions. According to these results, the structural model is predictive.

The significance, magnitude and direct and indirect effects are shown in Table 7.3. All three hypotheses (H2 and H3) were fully supported. We found a negative, albeit insignificant, direct relationship between flow state

Table 7.2 Discriminant Validity Indexes

	Behavioral Loyalty	*Flow State*	*Impulsive Buying*
Behavioral loyalty	.87		
Flow state	.82**	.93	
Impulsive buying	.85**	.92**	.94

Note: ** Correlation is significant at the 0.01 level (2-tailed). √ AVE in bold on the diagonal; AVE = average variance extracted; CR = composite reliability; α = Cronbach's alpha.

Table 7.3 Direct and Indirect Effects

	Coefficients	*T-value*	*P-value*	*Hypothesis*
Flow state → Behavioral loyalty	.83	35.3	.000	
Flow state → Microtransaction	-.31	1.6	.089	**H1** not supported
Flow state → Impulse buying tendency	.89	45	.000	
Impulse buying tendency → Microtransaction	-.39	3.6	.000	
Behavioral loyalty → Microtransaction	.50	2.7	.010	
Mediation Effect of Impulsiveness and Behavioral Loyalty (Full Mediation)				
H2: Flow state → Impulse buying tendency → Microtransaction	-.35	3.6	.010	H2 supported
H3: Flow state → Behavioral loyalty → Microtransaction	.41	2.7	.000	H3 supported

and microtransaction, indicating full mediation of impulse buying tendency and gamer loyalty. The negative relationship between flow state and microtransaction explains that the flow state enthuses positive emotions such as enjoyment and concentration in free-to-play mobile games, while microtransactions trigger the pain of payment (see Khan et al., 2015); it is possible that for enthusiast players, the pain of paying is more prevalent while riding on the flow state. The result is consistent with Lin and Sun (2007) and Hamari (2015) that gamers' concentration and enjoyment decrease with buying in-game virtual tools. It is understandable in this research that participants sought pride in being skillful gamers. Gamers purchased the virtual tool due to their impulse buying tendencies and loyalty to the game. Impulse buying tendencies and gamer loyalty fully mediated the flow state and microtransaction relationship. Our original result highlights that flow state and impulse buying tendency are not enough to incite microtransactions in free-to-play mobile games; gamer loyalty is necessary to initiate microtransactions. Results suggest that the interplay between flow state and spending depends on situational context, whether the individual goal is to seek a flow state by playing longer hours and seeking recognition within the gamer community or the goal is to experience a flow state for self-satisfaction. Our results suggest that individuals have plans to play free-to-play games to satisfy themselves or others. When a gamer is starved of time and skills and is loyal to the game will engage in microtransactions. When state flow persists, positive recommendations about the game are influencers within the gamers' community (close-knit circle) likely to encourage microtransactions.

Discussion and Conclusion

Results show no direct relationship between flow state and microtransactions. This result is consistent with Hoffman and Novak's negative consequences of flow (1996). Further attested in the study of microtransactions, the preference for free-to-play mobile games is related to time spent playing the game, which does not necessarily mean money is spent on games (Palmeira, 2021). The underlying explanation for the flow state is a positive emotion, and spending 'money' connotates negative emotions, such as the pain of paying (Zellermayer, 1996). However, when the flow state meshes with impulse buying tendency and gamers' loyalty, money spent on gaming tools is effortless in purchase-related activities. The flow state itself is a rewarding state that the player wishes to maintain that state's continuation. Our result indicates that preserving a flow state is more important (i.e., spending time playing a game), and when this state is combined with impulsiveness and behavioral loyalty, it manifests in microtransactions. Spending time in free-to-play games clearly indicates spending resources, preference and commitment over spending money buying virtual tools (Shaddy & Shah, 2018) for some gamers, thus supporting our finding that a flow state will not necessarily lead to microtransactions. Other factors, such as personality traits, impulse buying tendencies and gamer loyalty, are requirements for microtransactions.

In our study, players who experience a high level of flow while playing are 'enthusiasts and killers,' according to Klézl and Kelly's (2023, p. 7953) topology of free-to-play gamers. Our study identifies another segment searching to enhance their abilities in the game, e.g. identification seeker (Nacke et al., 2014). The gamer segment typifies the antagonistic relation between flow state and microtransactions. For identification seekers (Lopez & Tucker, 2019), buying in-game virtual tools may be perceived as an external reward because they may enhance players' abilities and identification. As such, this segment appears to be contradictory for players experiencing flow. Flow is a robust autotelic experience that might reduce external rewards' roles until they are perceived redundant (Csikszentmihalyi, 1996; Chang et al., 2014). Hamari (2015) stated that if players enjoy the game enough, there might not be a sufficient additional reason to buy virtual goods. Our study, on the contrary, finds that for identification seekers, external reward and gamer status are essential, and they engage in microtransactions to experience the gamer flow state.

Klézl and Kelly's (2023) 'economic enthusiasts' are gamers who do not enjoy the game but seek flow state, and this group incentivizes their gaming skills by purchasing virtual tools. This result supports the idea that flow requires higher skills (Liu & Chang, 2012). Therefore, gamer loyalty and impulse buying tendency is triggered to engage in microtransactions. Similarly, enthusiast gamers' experience flows state and are skills players who need less to buy virtual goods to enhance their game level and gratify their gaming experience.

Gamers engage in microtransactions when they are time-starved, especially if they experience a flow state, thus enjoying the game experience and being willing to prolong it. Our results show that economic aesthetes (Klézl & Kelly, 2023), coupled with impulse buying urges, are likely to engage in microtransactions when in the flow state. The results could explain the ego-depletion effect. Ego-depletion theory suggests humans have limited mental energy to make decisions; thus, the behavior should become more impulsive when prior exertions deplete the self (Baumeister, 2002). Vohs and Faber (2007) found that participants with depleted self-regulatory resources felt stronger urges to buy, were willing to spend more and spent more in unanticipated situations. In the context of our study, the flow state may act as the opposite of ego depletion. Flow state is attributed to a sense of concentration and enjoyment over the activity; individuals in this state have a thorough understanding of their activities and, as such, are more likely to resist the temptation of microtransactions and instead focus more on playing the game for a longer time. This group is atypical of game enthusiasts (Klézl & Kelly, 2023). Altogether, the enjoyment they feel when experiencing a flow state will instead act as a booster of energy that will prevent them from acting on impulse, contrary to the depletion that might lead to impulsive buying of virtual items in the game. In the latter group, deprived of time or gaming skills, the flow state triggers an impulse buying tendency to engage in microtransactions. Gamer loyalty mediates the relationship between the flow state and microtransactions within this microtransaction process. Gamers who experience a flow state are resistant to microtransactions. However, consistent with Hoffman and Novak (1996), a flow state influences the likelihood of loyalty to the game.

In conclusion, this study provides novel findings and weaves impulse buying tendencies and gamer loyalty as essential triggers to enact the relationship between flow state and microtransactions of the virtual in-gaming tool. Our research suggests that the flow state does not necessarily lead to in-game tool transactions. Still, it increases the likelihood of behavioral loyalty, and players who lack time and skills engage in microtransactions to attain enjoyment and experience the flow state.

Theoretical Implications

This research examined the direct relationship between flow state and microtransactions in free-to-play mobile games. The study reveals a negative and no direct relationship between flow state and microtransaction. The result is consistent with the extant literature, which shows that the flow state decreases when microtransaction engagement increases (Hamari, 2015; Lin & Sun, 2007).

This study theoretically and empirically focuses on the role of impulse buying tendency in the relationship between flow state and microtransaction, supporting the notion that when gamers lack time and gaming skills, the impulse buying tendency is activated to maintain the flow state by engaging in microtransactions. Gamers with impulse buying tendencies are searching for ways to enhance their gaming abilities (Nacke et al., 2014), though at the expense of reducing a flow state while engaging in microtransactions.

Our study reveals that impulse buying tendencies negatively mediate the relationship between flow state and microtransactions. The result highlights that identity seekers may sacrifice some aspect of the flow state when impulsively engaging in microtransactions.

Importantly, this study shows the paradoxical role of the flow state in the microtransaction process. On the one hand, impulse buying tendencies act as a trigger to enact a relationship between the flow state and gamers' resistance to microtransactions. On the other hand, gamer loyalty triggers the positive relationship between the flow state and microtransactions. For loyal gamers, purchasing virtual tools does not undermine the flow state; instead, the concentration and enjoyment of free-to-play mobile games increase the likelihood of loyalty to the game (Hoffman & Novak, 1996).

Our findings are consistent with research that shows that the flow state may be responsible for encouraging gamers to play games more and unlock virtual tools (Lavoie & Main, 2019). The result demonstrates that young gamers with high consciousness are more motivated to play to win virtual tools than engage in microtransactions, consistent with Klézl and Kelly's (2023) categorization of identification seekers. McCaffrey (2019) states that microtransaction users are judged negatively and disliked by other gamers and are perceived as having lower skills and status.

Managerial Implications

The managerial implication of this study is for game developers and mobile and telecommunications companies. Gaming companies package their game design to incorporate a flow state within existing features and add new features that maximize flow within the game. The result highlights a negative relationship between flow and microtransactions. The game designer must incorporate features that allure gamers' impulse tendencies to tap into those who lack time and gaming resources. The gaming mode allows recommendations from other gamers and rewards to maintain the loyalty of existing gamers. The micro price should be optimal and match the segment's purchasing power. Lastly, according to the mediating effect of impulsiveness, it can be concluded that some promotion activities designed to strengthen impulsiveness (such as time-limited discounts for in-game items) will have a limited impact on consumer experience flow.

Game designers will face a great dilemma with this blurred role of flow in microtransactions. On the one hand, how to facilitate gamers' flow experience (through game design) to generate gamer loyalty and impulse tendency to enhance greater probabilities of engaging in microtransactions. Nevertheless, at the same time, it does not allow them (also through game design) to feel higher levels of flow, giving them more self-control and the ability to resist the temptations of impulsively purchasing virtual goods.

Limitations and Future Research

The study's limitations are the cross-sectional survey, sampling technique, sample size and respondent recruitment. The survey focused on one game, League of Legends, and the findings from this study are generalizable to the participants and the game. Participants were recruited via posting questionnaires on social media; therefore, the sample frame was unknown. The self-report of daily and weekly microtransactions on free-to-play mobile games was gathered. Future studies should collect panel data of actual microtransactions as dependent measures. Further qualitative research methods could develop underlying reasons for the negative trigger of impulse buying tendency in the relationship between flow state and microtransaction.

The conceptual framework presented in this study may open up the opportunity for future research incorporating environmental factors as moderators and examining their effects on the relationships between antecedents and microtransactions. Furthermore, comparative studies involving several countries and regions would also contribute to generalizing the current research findings.

Note

1 https://www.jeuxvideo.com/news/1116275/gears-5-the-coalition-evoque-les-microtransactions.htm.

References

Back, K.-J., & Parks, S. C. (2003). A brand loyalty model involving cognitive, affective, and conative brand loyalty and customer satisfaction. *Journal of Hospitality & Tourism Research*, *27*(4), 419–435. https://doi.org/10.1177/10963480030274003

Baumeister, R. F. (2002). Yielding to temptation: Self-control failure, impulsive purchasing, and consumer behavior. *Journal of Consumer Research*, *28*(4), 670–676. https://doi.org/10.1086/338209

Biasutti, M. (2017). Flow and optimal experience. In M. A. Runco & S. R. Pritzker (Eds.), *Reference module in neuroscience and biobehavioral psychology*, San Diego: Academic Press, (pp. 522–528). https://doi.org/10.1016/B978-0-12-809324-5.06191-5

Chang, I.-C., Liu, C.-C., & Chen, K. (2014). The effects of hedonic/utilitarian expectations and social influence on continuance intention to play online games. *Internet Research*, *24*(1), 21–45. https://doi.org/10.1108/intr-02-2012-0025

Chang, Y. P., & Zhu, D. H. (2012). The role of perceived social capital and flow experience in building users' continuance intention to social networking sites in China. *Computers in Human Behavior*, *28*(3), 995–1001. https://doi.org/10.1016/j.chb.2012.01.001

Cheah, I., Shimul, A. S., & Phau, I. (2022). Motivations of playing digital games: A review and research agenda. *Psychology & Marketing*, *39*(5), 937–950. https://doi.org/10.1002/mar.21631

Cheung, C. M. K., Shen, X.-L., Lee, Z. W. Y., & Chan, T. K. H. (2015). Promoting sales of online games through customer engagement. *Electronic Commerce Research and Applications*, *14*(4), 241–250. https://doi.org/10.1016/j.elerap.2015.03.001

Chou, T.-J., & Ting, C.-C. (2003). The role of flow experience in cyber-game addiction. *CyberPsychology & Behavior*, *6*(6), 663–675. https://doi.org/10.1089/109493103322725469

Civelek, I., Liu, Y., & Marston, S. R. (2018). Design of free-to-play mobile games for the competitive marketplace. *International Journal of Electronic Commerce*, *22*(2), 258–288. https://doi.org/10.1080/10864415.2018.1441755

Costes, J. M., & Bonnaire, C. (2022). Spending money in free-to-play games: Sociodemographic characteristics, motives, impulsivity and internet gaming disorder specificities. *International Journal of Environmental Research and Public Health*, *19*(23), 15709. https://doi.org/10.3390/ijerph192315709

Csikszentmihalyi, M. (1975). *Beyond boredom and anxiety*. Jossey-Bass Publishers.

Csikszentmihalyi, M. (1996). *Creativity: Flow and the psychology of discovery and invention*. Harper Perennial.

Ding, D. X. (2011). Clues, flow channels, and cognitive states: An exploratory study of customer experiences with e-brokerage services. *Service Science*, *3*(2), 182–193. https://doi.org/10.1287/serv.3.2.182

Donovan, R., & Rossiter, J. (1994). Store atmosphere and purchasing behavior. *Journal of Retailing*, *70*(3), 283–294. https://doi.org/10.1016/0022-4359(94)90037-X

Ehrenberg, A. S. C., Goodhardt, G. J., & Barwise, T. P. (1990). Double jeopardy revisited. *Journal of Marketing*, *54*(3), 82. https://doi.org/10.2307/1251818

Elmezeny, A. (2020). Just 1€ to unlock this guide! How and why to study free-to-play game cultures. In Groen, M., Kiel, N., Tillmann, A., Weßel, A. (Eds.), *Games and ethics. Digitale Kultur und Kommunikation* (pp. 113–128). Springer V. https://doi.org/10.1007/978-3-658-28175-5_8

Ettis, A. S. (2017). Examining the relationships between online store atmospheric color, flow experience and consumer behavior. *Journal of Retailing and Consumer Services*, *37*, 43–55. https://doi.org/10.1016/j.jretconser.2017.03.007

Fornell, C., & Larcker, D. F. (1981). Structural equation models with unobservable variables and measurement error: Algebra and statistics. *Journal of Marketing Research*, *18*(3), 382–388. https://doi.org/10.1177/002224378101800313

Freeman, G., Wu, K., Nower, N., & Wohn, D. Y. (2022). Pay to win or pay to cheat: How players of competitive online games perceive fairness of in-game purchases. *Proceedings of the ACM on Human-Computer Interaction*, *6*(CHI PLAY), 1–24.

Garrett, E. P., Drummond, A., Lowe-Calverley, E., & Sauer, J. D. (2023). Current loot box warnings are ineffective for informing consumers. *Computers in Human Behavior*, *139*, 107534. https://doi.org/10.1016/j.chb.2022.107534

Ghani, J. A., & Deshpande, S. P. (1994). Task characteristics and the experience of optimal flow in human—computer interaction. *The Journal of Psychology*, *128*(4), 381–391. https://doi.org/10.1080/00223980.1994.9712742

Ghazali, E., Mutum, D. S., & Woon, M.-Y. (2018). Exploring player behavior and motivations to continue playing Pokémon GO. *Information Technology & People*, *32*(3), 646–667. https://doi.org/10.1108/itp-07-2017-0216

Guo, Y. M., & Poole, M. S. (2009). Antecedents of flow in online shopping: A test of alternative models. *Information Systems Journal*, *19*(4), 369–390. https://doi.org/10.1111/j.1365-2575.2007.00292.x

Hainey, T., Connolly, T., Stansfield, M., & Boyle, E. (2011). The differences in motivations of online game players and offline game players: A combined analysis of three studies at higher education level. *Computers & Education*, *57*(4), 2197–2211. https://doi.org/10.1016/j.compedu.2011.06.001

Hair, J. F., Black, W. C., Babin, B. J., & Anderson, R. E. (2009). *Multivariate data analysis*. Prentice Hall.

Hair, Jr., J. F., Matthews, L. M., Matthews, R. L., & Sarstedt, M. (2017). PLS-SEM or CB-SEM: Updated guidelines on which method to use. *International Journal of Multivariate Data Analysis*, *1*(2), 107. https://doi.org/10.1504/ijmda.2017.10008574

Hamari, J. (2015). Why do people buy virtual goods? Attitude toward virtual good purchases versus game enjoyment. *International Journal of Information Management*, *35*(3), 299–308. https://doi.org/10.1016/j.ijinfomgt.2015.01.007

Hamari, J., & Keronen, L. (2017). Why do people buy virtual goods: A meta-analysis. *Computers in Human Behavior*, *71*, 59–69. https://doi.org/10.1016/j.chb.2017.01.042

Hamari, J., & Lehdonvirta, V. (2010). Game design as marketing: How game mechanics create demand for virtual goods. *International Journal of Business Science and Applied Management*, *5*(1), 14–29. https://papers.ssrn.com/sol3/papers.cfm?abstract_id=1443907

Hoffman, D. L., & Novak, T. P. (1996). Marketing in hypermedia computer-mediated environments: Conceptual foundations. *Journal of Marketing*, *60*(3), 50–68. https://doi.org/10.2307/1251841

Hsiao, K.-L., & Chen, C.-C. (2016). What drives in-app purchase intention for mobile games? An examination of perceived values and loyalty. *Electronic Commerce Research and Applications*, *16*, 18–29. https://doi.org/10.1016/j.elerap.2016.01.001

Hsu, C.-L., & Lu, H.-P. (2004). Why do people play on-line games? An extended TAM with social influences and flow experience. *Information & Management*, *41*(7), 853–868. https://doi.org/10.1016/j.im.2003.08.014

Huang, L., & Hsieh, Y. (2011). Predicting online game loyalty based on need gratification and experiential motives. *Internet Research*, *21*(5), 581–598. https://doi.org/10.1108/10662241111176380

Ivanova, E., Magnusson, K., & Carlbring, P. (2019). Deposit limit prompt in online gambling for reducing gambling intensity: A randomized controlled trial. *Frontiers in Psychology*, *10*, 639.

Jacoby, J. (1971). A model of multi-brand loyalty. *Journal of Advertising Research*, *11*(3), 25–31.

Jiao, Y., Tang, C. S., & Wang, J. (2022). An empirical study of play duration and in-app purchase behavior in mobile games. *Production and Operations Management*, *31*(9), 3435–3456. https://doi.org/10.1111/poms.13772

Jin, Z., Sa, Y., Ke, S., Xin, Y., Hu, X., Kim, J., Lim, C-K., & Ju, S-W. (2022). The effect of emotional responses on reuse intention by impulse buying types: Focused on live shopping in China. *Journal of System and Management Sciences*, *12*(5), 487–504. https://www.aasmr.org/jsms/Vol12/JSMS%20OCT%202022/Vol.12.No.05.28.pdf

Kahn, B. E., Kalwani, M. U., & Morrison, D. G. (1986). Measuring variety-seeking and reinforcement behaviors using panel data. *Journal of Marketing Research*, *23*(2), 89–100. https://doi.org/10.2307/3151656

Kaur, P., Dhir, A., Chen, S., & Rajala, R. (2016). Understanding online regret experience using the theoretical lens of flow experience. *Computer and Human Behaviour*, *57*, 230–239. https://doi.org/10.1016/j.chb.2015.12.041

Khan, J., Belk, R. W., & Craig-Lees, M. (2015). Measuring consumer perceptions of payment mode. *Journal of Economic Psychology*, *47*, 34–49. https://doi.org/10.1016/j.joep.2015.01.006

Khan, J., & Rivers, G. (2019). Role of 'Owned' money and rational spending. In Gangl, K., & Kirchler, E. (Eds.), *A research agenda for economic psychology* (pp. 44–57). Edward Elgar Publishing. https://doi.org/10.4337/9781788116060.00009

Kim, H. S., Hollingshead, S., & Wohl, M. J. (2017). Who spends money to play for free? Identifying who makes microtransactions on social casino games (and why). *Journal of Gambling Studies*, *33*, 525–538. https://doi.org/10.1007/s10899-016-9626-6

King, D. L., & Delfabbro, P. H. (2019). Video game monetisation (e.g., 'loot boxes;): A blueprint for practical social responsibility measure. *International Journal of Mental Health and Addiction*, *17*, 166–179. https://doi.org/10.1007/s11469-018-0009-3

King, D. L., Russell, A. M. T., Delfabbro, P. H., & Polisena, D. (2020). Fortnite microtransaction spending was associated with peers' purchasing behaviors but not gaming disorder symptoms. *Addictive Behaviors*, *104*, 106311–106311. https://doi.org/10.1016/j.addbeh.2020.106311

Klézl, V., & Kelly, S. (2023). Negativists, enthusiasts and others: A typology of players in free-to-play games. *Multimedia Tools and Applications*, *82*(5), 7939–7960. https://doi.org/10.1007/s11042-022-13647-9

Lavoie, R. V., & Main, K. J. (2019, April). When losing money and time feels good: The paradoxical role of flow in gambling. *Journal of Gambling Issues*, *41*, 53–72. https://doi.org/10.4309/jgi.2019.41.4

Lee, S., & Kim, B. G. (2017). The impact of qualities of social network service on the continuance usage intention. *Management Decision*, *55*(4), 701–729. https://doi.org/10.1108/MD-10-2016-0731

Lee, Y. J., Ha, S., & Johnson, Z. (2019). Antecedents and consequences of flow state in e-commerce. *Journal of Consumer Marketing*, *36*(2), 264–275. https://doi.org/10.1108/JCM-10-2015-1579

Lehdonvirta, V. (2009). Virtual item sales as a revenue model: Identifying attributes that drive purchase decisions. *Electronic Commerce Research*, *9*, 97–113. https://doi.org/10.1007/s10660-009-9028-2

Lin, H., & Sun, C. T. (2007, January). Cash trade within the magic circle: Free-to-play game challenges and massively multiplayer online game player responses. In *Proceedings of DiGRA 2007 Conference: Situated Play*. Digital Games Research Association (DiGRA), National Taiwan University, Taipei, Taiwan.

Liu, C., & Chang, I. (2012). Measuring the flow experience of players playing online games. In *PACIS 2012 Proceedings*. Taiwan. https://aisel.aisnet.org/pacis2012/104

Liu, H. J., & Shiue, Y. C. (2014). Influence of Facebook game players' behavior on flow and purchase intention. *Social Behavior and Personality*, *42*(1), 125–134. https://doi.org/10.2224/sbp.2014.42.1.125

Lopez, C. E., & Tucker, C. S. (2019). The effects of player type on performance: A gamification case study. *Computers in Human Behavior*, *91*, 333–345. https://doi.org/10.1016/j.chb.2018.10.005

McCaffrey, M. (2019). The macro problem of microtransactions: The self-regulatory challenges of video game loot boxes. *Business Horizons*, *62*(4), 483–495. https://doi.org/10.1016/j.bushor.2019.03.001

Ming, J., Jianqiu, Z., Bilal, M., Akram, U., & Fan, M. (2021). How social presence influences impulse buying behavior in live streaming commerce? The role of S-O-R theory. *International Journal of Web Information Systems*, *17*(4), 300–320. https://doi.org/10.1108/IJWIS-02-2021-0012

Nacke, L. E., Bateman, C., & Mandryk, R. L. (2014). BrainHex: A neurobiological gamer typology survey. *Entertainment Computer*, *5*(1), 55–62. https://doi.org/10.1016/j.entcom.2013.06.002

Nah, F. F.-H., Eschenbrenner, B., Zeng, Q., Telaprolu, V. R., & Sepehr, S. (2014). Flow in gaming: Literature synthesis and framework development. *International. Journal of Information System Management*, *1*(1/2), 83–124. https://doi.org/10.1504/IJISAM.2014.062288

Palmeira, M. (2021). The interplay of micro-transaction type and amount of playing in video game evaluations. *Computers in Human Behavior*, *115*, 106609. https://doi.org/10.1016/j.chb.2020.106609

Quinn, R. W. (2005). Flow in knowledge work: High performance experience in the design of national security technology. *Administrative. Science Quarterly*, *50*(4), 610–641. https://doi.org/10.2189/asqu.50.4.610

Raneri, P. C., Montag, C., Rozgonjuk, D., Satel, J., & Pontes, H. M. (2022). The role of microtransactions in internet gaming disorder and gambling disorder: A pre-registered systematic review. *Addictive Behaviors Reports*, *15*, 100415–100415. https://doi.org/10.1016/j.abrep.2022.100415

Rauschnabel, P. A., Rossmann, A., & tom Dieck, M. C. (2017). An adoption framework for mobile augmented reality games: The case of Pokémon Go. *Computers in Human Behavior*, *76*, 276–286. https://doi.org/10.1016/j.chb.2017.07.030

Rook, D. W. (1987). The buying impulse. *Journal of Consumer Research*, *14*(2), 189–199. https://doi.org/10.1086/209105

Rook, D. W., & Fisher, R. J. (1995). Normative influences on impulsive buying behavior. *Journal of Consumer Research*, *22*(3), 305–313. https://doi.org/10.1086/209452

Rook, D. W., & Gardner, M. P. (1993). In the mood: Impulse buying's affective antecedents. *Research in Consumer Behavior*, *6*(7), 1–28.

Ryan, R. M., & Rigby, C. S. (2020). Motivational foundations of game-based learning. In Plass, J. L., Mayer, R. E., & Homer, B. S. (Eds.), *Handbook of game-based learning* (pp. 153–176). MIT Press.

Sarstedt, M., Henseler, J., & Ringle, C. (2011). Multi-group analysis in partial least squares (PLS) path modeling: Alternative methods and empirical results. *Advances in International Marketing*, *22*(1), 195–218. https://doi.org/10.1108/S1474-7979(2011)0000022012

Seo, Y., Buchanan-Oliver, M., & Fam, K. (2015). Advancing research on computer game consumption: A future research agenda. *Journal of Consumer Behaviour*, *14*(6), 353–356. https://doi.org/10.1002/cb.1557

Serravalle, F., Vanheems, R., & Viassone, M. (2023). Does product involvement drive consumer flow state in the AR environment? A study on behavioural responses. *Journal of Retailing and Consumer Services*, *72*, 103279.

Shaddy, F., & Shah, A. K. (2018). Deciding who gets what, fairly. *Journal of Consumer Research*, *45*(4), 833–848. https://doi.org/10.1093/jcr/ucy029

Shelstad, W. J. (2022). *The cost of playing the game: Modelling in-game purchase intention and investigating purchase behavior of mobile gamers* (Doctoral thesis, Embry-Riddle Aeronautical University). https://commons.erau.edu/edt/647

Supangan, R. A., Acosta, L. A. S., Amarado, J. L. S., Blancaflor, E. B., & Samonte, M. J. C. (2019). A gamified learning app for children with ADHD. In *ICIGP 2019: 2019 2nd International Conference on Image and Graphics Processing Singapore*. Singapore. https://doi.org/10.1145/3313950.3313966

Tan, E. L. P. (2019). Microtransactions in AAA video games–Are they really necessary? *Galactica Media: Journal of Media Studies*, *1*(1), 127–147. https://doi.org/10.24411/2658-7734-2019-00007

Thomsen, L. E., Petersen, F. W., Drachen, A., & Mirza-Babaei, P. (2016). Identifying onboarding heuristics for free-to-play mobile games: A mixed methods approach. In *Entertainment Computing-ICEC 2016: 15th IFIP TC 14 International Conference, Vienna, Austria, September 28–30, Proceedings 15* (pp. 241–246). Springer International Publishing.

Trevino, L. K., & Webster, J. (1992). Flow in computer-mediated communication. *Communication Research*, *19*(5), 539–573. https://doi.org/10.1177/009365092019005001

van Evers, E., & Weeda, D. (2015). The hidden cost of microtransactions: Buying in-game advantages in online games decreases a player's status. *International Journal of Internet Science*, *10*(1), 20–36.

Vohs, K. D., & Faber, R. J. (2007). Spent resources: Self-regulatory resource availability affects impulse buying. *Journal of Consumer Research*, *33*(4), 537–547. https://doi.org/10.1086/510228

Wakefield, K. L., & Inman, J. J. (2003). Situational price sensitivity: The role of consumption occasion, social context and income. *Journal of Retailing*, *79*(4), 199–212. https://doi.org/10.1016/j.jretai.2003.09.004

Wang, L., Luo, X. R., & Li, H. (2022). Envy or conformity? An empirical investigation of peer influence on the purchase of non-functional items in mobile free-to-play games. *Journal of Business Research*, *147*, 308–324. https://doi.org/10.1016/j.jbusres.2022.04.011

Webster, J., Trevino, K. L., & Ryan, L. (1993). The dimensionality and correlates of flow in human– computer interactions. *Computers in Human Behavior*, *9*(4), 411–426. https://doi.org/10.1016/0747-5632(93)90032-N

Wetzels, M., Odekerken-Schröder, G., & Van Oppen, C. (2009). Using PLS path modeling for assessing hierarchical construct models: Guidelines and empirical illustration. *MIS Quarterly*, *33*(1), 177–195. https://doi.org/10.2307/20650284

Whittaker, L., Mulcahy, R., & Russell-Bennett, R. (2021). Go with the flow for gamification and sustainability marketing. *International Journal of Information Management*, *61*, 102305. https://doi.org/10.1016/j.ijinfomgt.2020.102305

Widagdo, B., & Roz, K. (2021). Hedonic shopping motivation and impulse buying: The effect of website quality on customer satisfaction. *The Journal of Asian Finance, Economics, and Business*, *8*(1), 395–405. https://doi.org/10.13106/jafeb.2021.vol8.no1.395

Wohn, D. Y., & Lee, Y. H. (2013). Players of Facebook games and how they play. *Entertainment Computing*, *4*(3), 171–178. https://doi.org/10.1016/j.entcom.2013.05.002

Wu, L., Chiu, M., & Chen, K. (2020). Defining the determinants of online impulse buying through a shopping process of integrating perceived risk, expectation-confirmation model, and flow theory issues. *International Journal of Information Management*, *52*, 102099. https://doi.org/10.1016/j.ijinfomgt.2020.102099

Yoo, J. M. (2015). Perceived value of game items and purchase intention. *Indian Journal of Science and Technology*, *8*(7), 1–7. https://doi.org/10.17485/ijst/2015/v8i19/77148

Zeithaml, V. A., Berry, L., & Parasuraman, A. (1996). The behavioral consequences of service quality. *Journal of Marketing*, *60*(2), 31–46. https://doi.org/10.1177/002224299606000203

Zellermayer, O. (1996). *The pain of paying*. Carnegie Mellon University.
Zendle, D., Meyer, R., & Ballou, N. (2020). The changing face of desktop video game monetisation: An exploration of exposure to loot boxes, pay to win, and cosmetic microtransactions in the most-played steam games of 2010–2019. *PLoS One*, *15*(5), e0232780. https://doi.org/10.1371/journal.pone.0232780
Zhang, K. Z. K., Xu, H., Zhao, S., & Yu, Y. (2018). Online reviews and impulse buying behavior: The role of browsing and impulsiveness. *Internet Research*, *28*(3), 522–543. https://doi.org/10.1108/IntR-12-2016-0377

8 The Meaning of Money in Tipping Currencies

Jashim Khan and Russell Belk

Introduction

Live streaming involves streamers using smart devices to deliver real-time digital content to their followers and supporters on a platform (Zhou et al., 2019). It is popular due to its high interactivity, immersive experience, entertainment value and ability to retain user interest. Live-stream immersion involves feelings of physical and social presence while communicating with live streamers. Significantly, other viewers sometimes watch product use in real time (Yin et al., 2023); the level of absorption and engaged concentration produces positive emotions such as enjoyment, happiness and excitement likened to a flow state (the holistic sensation that people feel when they act with total involvement) (Koufaris, 2002). This induces impulse buying tendencies (Yi et al., 2023), suggesting that viewing frequency and past experiences with live streamers are related to impulse buying. That is, the flow state influences the

> impulse buying tendency and positive emotions in live-stream commerce, resulting in purchase decisions. For example, selling a perfume may arouse a certain atmosphere by showing a visual of a flower – from which the scent presumably originates. The idea of evoking positive emotions works in tandem to spark positive decision-making, carefully crafted by the live streamers during their show.
>
> (Yi et al., 2023)

While existing studies have generated important insights about live-stream shopping, an emergent stream of research investigates how the flow experience of positive emotions may influence impulsive buying tendencies while purchasing virtual gifts for favorite live streamers (Lin et al., 2021). Live-stream commerce represents a dynamic environment where viewers feel socially together with their favorite anchor and compete to gain the anchor's attention by purchasing virtual gifts. Several studies have examined virtual gifts or tipping in live-stream commerce, such as themes of poverty alleviation and building community trust (Zhao et al., 2023), leading to happiness and

DOI: 10.4324/9781003425021-8

smiles that beget virtual tips (Lin et al., 2021). Perceived pleasure, interaction with streamers, group interactions and support for streamers all predict virtual gifts (Xu et al., 2022), types of gifts (Jia et al., 2021), flow state and virtual gift-giving behavior (Li et al., 2021) in the context of impulsive buying in live-stream commerce (Yi et al., 2023). There is a lack of research exploring the meaning of money in tipping currency influencing virtual gift purchases in live-stream commerce. We find that it is driven by factors such as flow experience, emotions, impulsivity and the excitement of feeling prominent within the viewer community.

Tipping currencies are commonly used as a payment method in live-streaming platforms. These tipping currencies act as a medium of exchange and a store of value independent of real money. Fungible tokens, such as digital money stored in a digital wallet, are the most used tipping currency in live-stream platforms in China. Viewers typically exchange digital cash for platform-created tipping tokens and use them to make purchases within the platform. Live-stream commerce platforms like Douyin, Kuaishou and YY offer marketing services and live-streaming rewards and enhance e-commerce integration with platforms such as Taobao, JD and Tmall. This chapter focuses on live-streaming rewards, including virtual gifts that can be donated through tipping currency in live-stream commerce.

The audience purchases virtual gifts with the tipping currency and sends virtual gifts to streamers in live-streaming channels (Xu et al., 2022). Most virtual gifts have a value of US dollars 0.1–2000 (about US dollars 0.0014 to US dollars 285), and an animation and/or notification appears in the streamer's live-stream channel once the gift has been given (Zhou et al., 2019). As users give expensive virtual gifts, the streamer will recognize them, and the intimacy they may achieve with the streamer will increase (Zhou et al., 2019). Viewers are enticed to purchase these gifts to show their appreciation to live streamers (Li et al., 2024). Each type of gift has a different value, providing choices based on their budget and the level of support which the follower wishes to bestow. The gifts and tips received by the live streamer improve their popularity and enhance their ranking in a particular community. The revenue generated from these gifts is generally split between the live-streaming platform and the content creators (Chaudhry et al., 2024). While the percentage may differ by platform, live streamers typically receive a significant portion of the earnings, encouraging them to create compelling content. This model ensures that both the platform and the live streamers benefit financially from the interaction (Jhang-Li & Liou, 2024).

Live-streaming commerce allows users to record and broadcast in real time, sharing their video feed with others (Jhang-Li & Liou, 2024). A free-to-use model in live-stream commerce attracts more users by lowering the barrier to joining the live-stream platform (Tyrväinen & Karjaluoto, 2024). This approach encourages users to explore and engage with the platform without any initial investment. Additionally, offering free access can generate word-of-mouth promotion, as satisfied users recommend the service to others. Platforms like Douyin or Kuaishou have successfully implemented a free-to-use model, allowing users to join and participate in live-stream commerce without any upfront costs. This strategy has significantly contributed to the rapid growth and popularity of these platforms. The live-stream platform monetizes a free-to-use model by incorporating and generating revenue from advertising, subscriptions, donations and virtual gifts.

- Advertising—includes pre-roll clips on stream, and revenue accrues directly to the platform (Jhang-Li & Liou, 2024).
- Subscriptions—allow for improved viewing (i.e., ad-free) or increased interactivity (chat with streamers, emojis) (Wu et al., 2024).
- Donations and virtual gifts—viewers donate virtual gifts to their favorite streamers to have their name called out in the show. Platforms charge commissions on donations and virtual gifting revenues, although this varies significantly across platforms (Lin & Lee, 2024)

The global live-streaming market was valued at US dollars 37.48 billion in 2023 and is projected to increase to US dollars 139.41 billion by 2030 (Research Report World, 2024). Originating in China, Chinese live-stream commerce plays a crucial role in the growth of live-stream commerce, with the highest number of users and a market size projected to reach ¥5.86 trillion in 2024. The top companies in 2024 are Douyin (known as TikTok globally), Kuaishou and YY, with revenue ratios of 17.13%, 14.48% and 12.28%, respectively. These companies' success relies on their innovative algorithm that customizes content to individual preferences, ensuring high user engagement. The successful expansion into international markets significantly boosted monetization through ads, and in-app purchases played a crucial role. Live-stream tipping (donations and virtual gifts) will outpace advertising revenue by 2030 (Lu et al., 2022). Notably, the number of expensive virtual gifts purchased is much lower than that of micro-virtual gifts (Zhu et al., 2017). The number of expensive virtual gifts purchased in live streams is much lower than that of micro-virtual gifts. This trend suggests that viewers prefer to spread their contributions across multiple small tokens of appreciation rather than investing heavily in a single live streamer. This behavior could be due to a desire for recognition without a significant financial commitment. However, despite this, even small-value virtual gifts significantly impact the profit generation of live streamers. In 2023 alone, China's live-stream commerce was 5 trillion RMB, and 6 in 10 online shoppers engaged in live-stream commerce are expected to reach 430 million users by 2026 (Chevalier, 2024). Between 2021 and 2025, subscription revenues of media and digital content are expected to grow by 13.5% (Ceci, 2024), while advertising money may shift to subscriptions and virtual gifts (Xu et al., 2022). This stark contrast highlights virtual gifts' unique appeal and rapid adoption in live-stream commerce.

Virtual Gifts and Donations in Live-stream Commerce

Virtual gifts are available in various forms, such as animated stickers, digital flowers and virtual coins purchased using a digital wallet. The unique direct-to-creator model provides viewers with a more intimate and interactive experience. The gift is a way to show appreciation, leading to higher engagement and potential for higher earnings for content creators. For example, content creators like Nickmercs on Twitch and Pokimane on YouTube have built substantial followings and generate significant income through donations and virtual gifts. Nickmercs, known for his engaging gaming streams, regularly receives large donations from his dedicated fanbase. Similarly, Pokimane's interactive and personable streams encourage viewers to support her through various virtual gifts and donations. Jackie Li is the lipstick king and icon in Chinese live-stream commerce. Jackie Li became a sensation in Chinese live-stream commerce due to his impressive sales techniques and charismatic personality. His success is a testament to the power of social media and live-stream commerce. He has built a loyal following and driven substantial sales through engaging content and expert product knowledge.

There are two categories of virtual gifts in live-stream commerce, though variation exists in platforms: one has symbolic value and the other presents monetary worth; some platforms combine both. Symbolic virtual Fans give gifts to content creators to show appreciation, recognition and support. By sending gifts, loyal fans can express their admiration and engage with their favorites on a deeper level. Usually, these virtual gifts are animated icons, emojis or virtual currencies shaped like roses, diamonds, coins or gems. Live streamers' popularity and success increase with each gift they receive, and the more gifts they receive, the more successful. The second type of virtual gift has financial value for influencers and the live-stream platform. When a user buys a gift, the streamer receives a share of the value of the gift as money (Wang et al., 2019). There are significant differences between Chinese and Western live-streaming platforms, especially in terms of virtual gifting. According to Long and Tefertiller (2020), American streamers mainly rely on advertising, endorsements and subscription fees to generate revenue. The live-stream commerce platform has a unique set of virtual gifts, and the list generally includes coins, roses, unique effects (intimacy), beauty props and stickers. *Coins* are the most common virtual gifts that followers can buy in packs and trade for other virtual gifts. Streamers receive a share of the price of these coins.

- *Roses* are another virtual gift intended to express love, respect, affection, support or appreciation for the content.
- *Unique effects (intimacy)*—a special gift with animations or effects. Unique effect gifts include rainbows, sparkles, fireworks or an intimate hug or kiss on the cheek.

- *Beauty props and stickers* are entertaining and interactive features in the live streams, such as virtual hats, instruments and even virtual pets. The cost of these gifts varies from platform to platform.

Next, we discuss the influence of tipping currency and virtual gifts in live-stream commerce. This chapter explores the perceptions of tipping currency in donations and virtual gifts in live-stream commerce. Here, the focus is platform-issued tipping tokens rather than Bitcoins. Digital money is exchanged through the platform's in-app store using various payment methods, such as credit cards, WeChat, Alipay or PayPal. Once bought, the tipping currency is added to the user's account, ready to be spent on virtual gifts or donations during live streams or purchase discounted products from affiliated e-commerce platforms.

Tipping Currency in Live-stream Commerce

A live-streaming platform's tipping currency is a subset of virtual currency, which is a representation of value in digital form that can be exchanged, accounted for and stored. It could include cryptocurrencies like Bitcoin and Ethereum and stablecoins, utility tokens and security tokens (Moro-Visconti & Cesaretti, 2023). According to Claeys and Demertzis (2021), tipping currency enables fast and seamless transactions, eliminating the need for currency conversion and reducing costs. This feature of tipping currency enabled in live-stream commerce makes it popular among other payment methods. Tipping currency provides greater security and privacy, as transactions can be conducted anonymously using platform-issued tokens in live-stream commerce. It is created and held electronically within the platform ecosystem that offers an option to purchase the tipping tokens using their digital cash from a third-party wallet or Bitcoins, depending on the legality of those tokens in the geographic location. Despite government responses varying from bans to restrictions on Bitcoins, tipping currencies are expected to grow due to the popularity of live-stream commerce, regardless of how those coins are purchased. Canada, Australia, France, Denmark, Germany, Japan, Switzerland, Spain, the Bahamas and Austria legally use virtual currencies, e.g., Bitcoin. In contrast, it is illegal to mine and transact in virtual currency in China, Pakistan, Saudi Arabia, Tunisia, and Bolivia (Bajpal, 2021). The countries where it is legal are subject to taxation on purchases of virtual goods or services and investments (Bajpal, 2021).

Tipping currency in live-stream platforms varies significantly. Platforms like Kuaishou acquired Payeco in 2020 to integrate a payment system within the platform (Jingli, 2020). For example, YY uses its platform-issued coin, the intermediary currency that can be converted into tokens to use for virtual gifts or in interconnected e-commerce link and affiliates; these coins cannot be exchanged for fiat currency. Live-stream commerce platforms heavily rely on external payment methods such as WeChat and Alipay for tipping. Integrated tipping systems offer convenience for viewers as they can easily purchase the tipping currency and directly tip their favorite streamers within the platform (Jingli, 2020). This streamlines the tipping process and encourages more tipping activity. However, relying on external payment methods such as WeChat and Alipay allows for greater flexibility and accessibility for viewers with accounts on these platforms. Some viewers may prefer the convenience of integrated tipping systems, while others may feel more comfortable using external payment methods with which they are already familiar. By providing both options, the platforms can maximize their potential for tipping activity and ensure that viewers have the flexibility to support their favorite streamers in a way that suits them best. Some viewers may be more inclined to tip when presented with the convenience of an integrated tipping system. In contrast, others may be more motivated to tip when given the flexibility of using their preferred external payment method. Therefore, the tipping currency system adds another layer of engagement and convenience for viewers, who can easily acquire and use these tipping coins within the platform to show their appreciation and support.

Psychology of Tipping in Live-stream Commerce

Tipping and Payment Method

In the past, tipping was commonly done using cash or credit card receipts. Tipping jars and credit card processing machines have been the customary methods in full-service restaurants. Studies have shown that credit card users are likelier to leave more tips than those who pay with cash, possibly because credit cards have less emotional impact (Lynn & Latane, 1984). Feinberg (1986) compared the amount of tips left by patrons paying with cash versus credit cards at a restaurant and found that patrons using credit cards typically left more extensive tips. In replicating Feinberg's study, Shimp and Moody (2000) discovered that a credit card logo did not affect consumer spending on restaurant tips. Regardless of the level of materialism, the credit card did not influence tips payment in the Hunt et al. (1990) study. However, McCall and Belmont (1996) found that patrons who used cash left smaller tips than those with credit cards. According to Yi et al. (2023), impulsive buying tendencies are sparked using digital wallets. These studies suggest that how we pay impacts spending. A recent study of digital payment suggests that higher default tip suggestions lead to more significant tip amounts (Alexander et al., 2021). With this understanding, it is likely that in the context of live-stream commerce, it induces feelings of physical and social presence, and the live streamer's sales promotion technique likely influences followers to buy higher-value virtual gifts when using platform-issued tipping tokens compared to their regular habitual payment options. Khan and Belk (2024) suggest that psychological ownership does manifest in the app more than in the ownership of money itself. Hence, platform tokens may decouple the followers psychologically attuned to their money as a token compared to their owned money in payment apps.

Flow Experience in Live-Stream Commerce

Flow theory helps understand the mental state of individuals who engage in activities solely for pleasure (Csikszentmihalyi & LeFevre, 1989). It refers to the deep and complete immersion that people experience when fully engaged in an activity. This mental state is so enjoyable that individuals are willing to continue the activity even at significant personal cost (Csikszentmihalyi & LeFevre, 1989). Studies have shown that live-stream shopping involves interactivity and immediacy and is often associated with a sense of presence. This feeling encompasses both the feeling of being physically present on a live-stream platform and being personally (parasocially) connected to favorite streamers and socially connected to other viewers (Yin et al., 2023). Therefore, the flow theory helps to explain why audiences become more deeply immersed in live-stream commerce, particularly when they purchase virtual gifts for their favorite streamers (Ming et al., 2021).

Emotions

Live streamers' positive emotions induce positive viewer emotions, and similarly, positive viewer emotion enhances broadcaster emotions, suggesting that the dyads influence each other (Lin et al., 2021); this dyad of emotional exchange is commonplace in live-stream commerce. Lin et al. (2021) found that viewers are excited when a live streamer is in a happy mood, and more tips, chats and likes take place in the live-stream show. In general, viewers send more tips, buy virtual gifts and participate in comments and 'likes' when experiencing a flow state together (Hilvert-Bruce et al., 2018). Popular live streamers tend to smile more, create a joyful atmosphere and increase viewer tips (Lin et al., 2021). Khan and Belk (2024), in the context of third-party app payment, noted that the experience is a luxury or an indulgence; a pleasurable purchase is enjoyable and, indeed, as some of their participants point out, 'exciting' which echoes that purchasing virtual gifts in live-stream setting is a rewarding experience when viewers and streamer are together riding the flow state.

Impulsive Experience in Live-Stream Commerce

Impulse spending is making unplanned, instant, spontaneous purchases rather than deliberate, planned purchase decisions (Ahn & Kwon, 2022). This behavior becomes more spontaneous when individuals engage positively with the activity they enjoy and continue participating deliberately. Live-stream commerce is a fruitful ground for achieving a flow state. A positive live streamer and follower engagement entails real-time activities under a flow experience and is likely to trigger impulsivity. Viewers please the anchor by sending virtual gifts to show appreciation and emancipate social presence in the live-stream room. These virtual gifts often come as platform-issued tokens or items that can be purchased with real money. This not only boosts the anchor's morale but also creates a more engaging and interactive environment for all participants. According to Ahn et al. (2019), both external stimuli and psychological states influence impulse buying. It has been shown that live-stream commerce promotes impulse purchases of virtual gifts through its instant transactions and painless payment modes (Khan et al., 2015). Lee and Wan (2023) found that a viewer's intimate live experience, albeit digitally influenced by influencers' attractiveness and expertise, influences viewers to gratify their favorite anchor. Nevertheless, there is a gap exists in the literature regarding whether platform-issued tipping currency versus owned money in payment apps may influence virtual gift-buying behavior differently.

Personal and Social Gratification

The motivation to participate in live-stream commerce that is highlighted in the literature is that people tend to participate for live entertainment, enjoyment and for seeking personal gratification within a social setting (Hou et al., 2020; Kaur et al., 2020; Li & Guo, 2021). Ma (2021) explored the effects of viewer-streamer interaction strategies on product sales. In previous studies (Chiu & Huang, 2015) and Yin et al. (2023), streamer-follower interactions have been shown to satisfy individuals' needs for personal and social gratification. Xu et al. (2020) suggest that entertainment, responsiveness and personalization are the key factors motivating live-stream commerce's viewership. Entertainment is a joyous activity that entails positive emotions and may result in a positive flow state to maintain concentration and interest (Chen & Lin, 2018). Viewers have a feeling of immersion and get a sense of relaxation in live-streaming rooms. Responsiveness is the outcome of streamer–follower interaction, and the outcome is recognition and appreciation from the anchor (Wongkitrungrueng & Assarut, 2020). The viewers, when engaged, feel personal gratification with the live-stream room; they also seek social gratification by responding to anchors' calls frequently and purchasing high-value virtual gifts that set them apart from the rest of the viewers. In response to virtual gifts, anchors call out the donors' names and appreciate their gifts in public. The followers are gratified by the virtual special effects and intimate animation, and their social standing within the room is more prominent than that of others.

Method and Data Collection

This study employed a qualitative mixed-method approach using public discourse in a live-stream platform, participation, observation and semi-structured interviews (Migiro & Magangi, 2011). Data collection was conducted in two steps: first, participation and observation in live-stream from May 2023 to April 2024 in channels focusing on fast fashions, the digital economy and gift-giving. This participation enriched understanding of live-stream platforms, their anchors, viewer characteristics and their virtual gift-giving. It was deemed important to understand how viewers partake in appreciation, recognition and special effects animation. Participation ranged from 15 to 60 minutes weekly on the Douyin and Kuaishou platforms. The first author participated regularly and gathered insights into the live-stream platforms in this way, and by keeping an immersion journal. A semi-structured, in-depth interview protocol was developed with the key themes identified from participation in live-stream channels.

Seventeen face-to-face, in-depth interviews were conducted from April 2024 to May 2024, 6 of which were conducted by the first author and the remaining 11 by 5 trained research assistants. Each interview lasted for an hour, and three went over. We used a judgment sampling technique to recruit participants and sought participation via advertising on social networking sites such as the WeChat group. All participants had experience with Douyin or Kuaishou and subscription-based accounts with both live-stream platforms. The semi-structured interview protocol included general questions related to what people think and feel about virtual gifts in live-stream commerce, their emotions and their excitement during the live-stream session.

Participant Profiles—Semi-structured Interview

Seventy percent of the participants were between 18 and 25 years old, belonging to Generation Z. Twenty-one percent of respondents were between the ages of 26 and 38 (Millennials), and 9% were between the ages of 39 and 50 (Generation X). Sixty-seven percent of the respondents were women, and 33% were males. Each participant had a Douyin or Kuaishou subscription account. Only 30% of participants had postgraduate degrees, whereas all had undergraduate degrees.

Next, we purchased publicly available viewer and streamer comments and dialogues in March 2024 from Xinbang (https://xd.newrank.cn); it offers tools for precise targeting and analysis of all WeChat (Official Account message template), Douyin, Xiaohongshu, B station, Kuaishou, People, Toutiao, Tencent watch, Baijia, NetEase, Sohu, a little information, Qu Toutiao, Sina watch, Youhao Video, Xigua Video, Sohu Video, Ximalaya, Dragonfly FM, Litchi FM, Evernote, Understand Chedi, Mafengwo and other mainstream content platforms, videos with extensive data indicators, live broadcast tracking and account searching with multiple filters. The complete information was publicly posted in 80 categories comprising 400,000 posts, and after applying 'virtual gift,' 'donations' and tipping currency/'tipping,' the list was filtered down to 16,000 posts. The second round of filtering was applied with keyword searches such as impulse spending, emotions, flow experience and social gratification, which resulted in 300 posts.

Data Analysis

The transcripts of the in-depth interviews accounted for 61 pages and 13,000 words. To extract key themes from the verbatim transcriptions of all data, the Word document was formatted according to Nvivo 12 requirements. Themes were coded, classified, assessed and recorded using an exploratory thematic approach (Boyatzis, 1988). A comparison was made between in-depth interview data and online public discourse (Patton, 1999).

Public discourse data was analyzed using Python to scan the dataset and filter out posts by identifying those that contained specific keywords (e.g., impulse spending, emotions, flow experience and social gratification) produced word clouds and charts and figures.

Results

Using Python, the word cloud below highlights the most frequently used words when describing pieces related to the digital tipping currency on the live-streaming platforms, with larger fonts indicating more frequent use in public discourse.

Engagement with virtual gifts in humanities, social sciences and arts received significantly more likes and comments, indicating a higher audience appreciation of the topics concerning 'virtual gifts,' 'donations,' and tipping currency/'tipping.' The discourse within this category was stories about virtual gifts and tipping. One category that dominated was why people tip using virtual gifts in live-stream commerce. One of the most liked and commented expressions was that the sight of live streamers interactivity, their efforts and time spent or performance engaging followers were rewarded as virtual gifts. These performances were a choice of music, dance, visual arts, theater and literature. Creative appreciation ranked highest as followers felt tipping virtual gifts was a way to compensate for their time and show appreciation for their efforts during the live-stream show. The interactive experience is rated highest as the reason that followers send virtual gifts to influence the direction of the live-stream shows and performances. Another category that emerged as significant is support for the community since those anchors create community development goals and a portion of the proceeds is donated to societal cause-related campaigns (see Figure 8.1).

The difference between likes and comments suggests that users are more likely to express passive support or interest through likes than to participate in discussions actively. This was particularly visible when live streamers created content aligned with pro-social cause-related marketing rather than personal gain. Followers would refrain from commenting when they felt the topic in the live-stream room benefits only the anchor who is participating in achieving their personal goals (see Figure 8.2). The impact of content such as 'Helping a Streamer Save Her Ill Mother' generated more impact than beauty or fast-fashion topics. Sustainability-related topics were more popular and commented on more often.

Figure 8.1 Word-cloud Representation of Tipping Currency

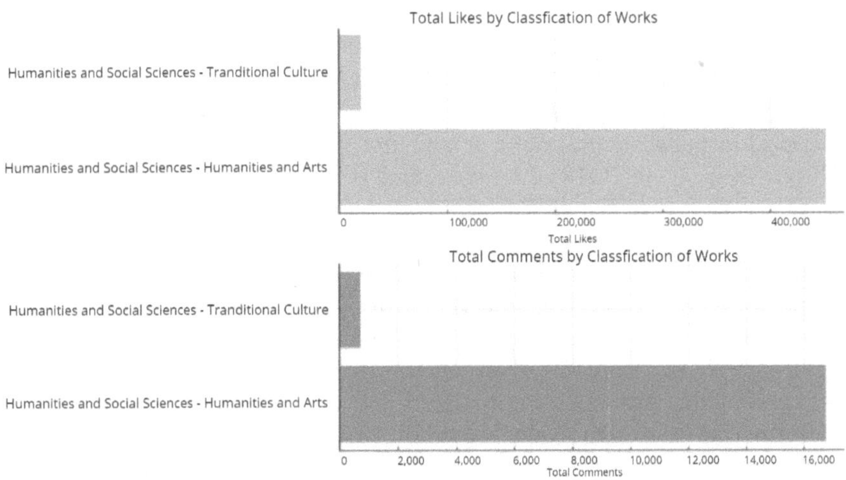

Figure 8.2 Likes by Classification of Category

Digital tipping empowers audiences by giving them agency in the creator–audience relationship. It allows viewers to actively participate in the success and continuation of the content they value, moving from passive consumption to active engagement and support. Secondly, financial contributions through tipping give creators the resources they need to maintain their creative freedom, thus increasing their autonomy. This independence is critical to the innovation and diversity of digital content, as it allows creators to pursue projects that resonate with their vision and values rather than being constrained by external funding sources or advertising revenue (see Figure 8.3).

In summary, tipping is an emotional exchange between anchor and follower, symbolizing gratitude, admiration and connection. It reflects the emotional value of entertainment, education, companionship, inspiration, community

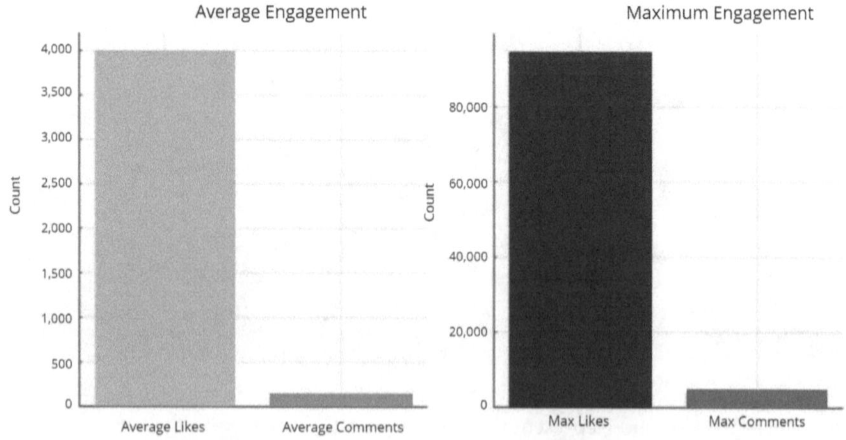

Figure 8.3 Public Engagement

building and sustainability. This highlights the importance of emotional relationships and monetary transactions imbued with emotion. The emotional relationship between the follower and the streamer influences virtual gifts (Hilvert-Bruce et al., 2018). Live streaming embeds social relationships where conversations occur in public places to monetize users' emotions and social gratification, which some may see as compensatory power achieved in the digital domain (Wohn et al., 2018). For example, a news article shows graphics of a food delivery person eating noodles costing ¥6 and purchasing ¥600 virtual gifts for their favorite live streamer on their mobile during lunchtime. It is important to note that users' emotions toward streamers play a significant role in promoting the purchase of virtual gifts (Lee et al., 2019). The live-streaming platform emphasizes the significance of virtual emotional relationships by using various virtual gifts to raise users' emotional awareness and encourage them to purchase virtual gifts (Wang, 2022). Additionally, streamers enhance users' attractiveness, improve entertainment feelings and trigger an emotional connection and flow experience, and the stronger the stimulation, the higher the impulse buying tendency with virtual gifts (Li & Peng, 2021).

In-depth Interview

The findings reveal that tipping and virtual gift-giving in live-stream commerce are self-image-enhancing activities. The transient nature of tipping currency decouples ownership of money, heightening one's gratifications through appreciation and support to alleviate the financial stress of the live streamers. *I use tipping currency to enhance my power in the broadcast room; I feel great when I get the most attention from the streamer, making me feel invincible* (Male, 24 years). *I felt tipping currency distant from me, like how I spend money in Alipay; it is easier to blow without realizing it at that moment, as you can't feel the loss of your money, only to wake up with regret the next morning. Am I rational or emotional?* (Female 29 years). The disconnection arises as followers convert their money to a token, alleviating the notion of ownership but heightening personal and social gratification, happiness, joy and companionship. Evidence of appropriation to emotions and engagement emerged in the data.

> *All platforms give special attention to those who have contributed the most, so there is competition among viewers in terms of ranking and face value. We feel honored and have a sense of existence. My favorite live streamer constantly receives gifts, and I compete with others in the room for her attention. I feel her in my heart and soul; I am emotional anyway. What I like about her ... she never asks me to tip; I feel like giving her gifts.*
>
> (*Male,* 42 years)

When viewers tip generously during a live-stream, anchors often feel more appreciated and motivated to deliver their best. This tipping boosts the performers' morale and creates connection and emotional engagement (See Table 8.1). It makes viewers feel like active participants in the performance, enhancing their overall experience. Anchors acknowledge their followers by giving them shout-outs during the live stream, making them feel recognized and valued. They can also offer special perks or exclusive content to those who contribute, further incentivizing audience engagement. Personalized thank-you messages or even small facial gestures and tones in voice touch the viewers emotionally. Recognition has a profound psychological effect on tippers, making them feel valued and esteemed. When live streamers acknowledge contributions publicly, tippers experience a boost in self-esteem and a sense of belonging and emotional connection with the anchor.

The appeal of virtual gifts to viewers lies in the instant gratification and recognition they receive from their favorite streamers. The excitement and feeling are prominent in the viewer community and empower people; though illusive, they feel overjoyed. The virtual gifts to the live streamer feeds maintain that prominent place within the live-stream room. For example, "to climb up to the 'number 1' ranking, gifting and tipping are a way to go. That feeling of number 1 makes me feel I have power" (Male 20) and another "It was exciting to see my name is number 1. I felt the sense of belongingness and existence which I don't get in real life" (Male 25). The empowerment in giving driven by the atmospherics of live streaming enchants a positive flow which, once ridden and experienced, calls for the continuation of meeting the favorite streamer. This virtual, though intimate partner can alleviate the hopelessness and frustrations people may experience daily.

> *I accidentally found this broadcasting room featuring beauty, which is my interest. We got along very well, so I spent a couple thousand*

Table 8.1 Codes, Category and Themes

Symbolic Worth

Final Codes	*Category*	*Main Theme*	*Selected Quotes*
Emotion		Symbolic worth	Quality content created by live streamer is liked and appreciated, I think tipping empowers you in the broadcast room (Male 22 years). It appears lack of thinking, and rationality in live-stream rooms … people are driven by emotion (Female 23 years) Driven by feelings of loneliness and bored in my life, I have found the room makes me feel connected, recognized and satisfied (Male 31 years). Tipping is a symbol of emotional connection to someone in your community, it good to help people and community, I do not agree to tip for those who think I am a fool (Male 32 years). Viewers should be more sensible instead of emotional, this would help stop unlawful and unethical behavior, there are lot of emotional blackmailing in livestream show (Female 27)
Excitement of feeling prominent within the viewer community		Symbolic worth	The news of students spending 3000 RMB rent on the female live streamer, says something about excitement of feeling prominent among others in that room (Male 36) It was exciting to see my name is number 1. I felt the sense of belongingness and existence which I don't get in real life (Male 25) To climb up to the 'number 1' ranking, gifting and tipping are a way to go. That feeling of number 1 make me feel I have power (Male 20)
Flow experience		Symbolic worth	I immerse myself, seeking fun, excitement, joy anytime and anywhere (Male 28) I was an entrepreneur. Things were not going well. I accidentally downloaded the Kuaishou, I was immersed in day 1, felt great and kept spending my time with her. I have wasted a lot of money by gifting and tipping. I have now come out of it (Male 40) I was encouraged to be the number one in the room. At the end, I lost control, initially it was before bed, and then, I stated spending the night with it (Male 26)

				I'm a software developer, I work with logic and rationality in real life, but I lost them when I enter with her. The experience is hard to explain until you have experienced it (Male 40)
Monetary Worth				
	Impulsive spending	impulsive	Monetary Worth	Some are impulsive, tipping amount goes way beyond their ability and affordability. For this, they can't help themselves to borrow and engage in unlawful activities. I am not like them, I have self-discipline (Female 22). In the long run, uncontrollable tipping is harmful to audience's rights, and the societal order. Live streaming is exciting to be part of, however, sensible tipping is required (Male 28) Husband tipped 670,000 RMB, the wife wanted the money back, what do you think? (Female 24) To show off/save face, impulsive tipping works (Male 19)

> *supporting them with virtual gifts. She is very nice to me; she sends me messages daily, and then I started to wait for her in the broadcasting room, which became my habit. she sings, she dances, she is happy, and I am happy, and we chat before I go to bed; I feel that someone is always there for me. Although I know this is based on gift-giving and tipping. It is fair because you support someone who cares about you.*
>
> (Female 27)

The virtual gifts range from simple digital stickers and emojis to more elaborate animations and custom-designed items with specific meanings to the giver and receiver, and these increase emotional engagement; the higher-value gifts are prominent on-screen effects ascending the giver above all, feeling like ownership of the live streamer for that moment. On top of public appreciation and gratitude, personalized private video messages follow initiating interaction between those two. *... shorten the distance between viewers and live streamers. In real life, if we like someone, we'd like to take him/her to a restaurant and are willing to spend time with him/her. With one live streamer for many viewers in the broadcasting room, an effective way to draw their attention is by tipping and giving gifts. Expressing encouragement and support, ultimately, is consumption-driven* (Female 32). *My friend was saying ...* "he is unhappy every day; thinking of his favorite live-streamer and having one or two moments a day with her makes him feel happy; it is like spending money in exchange for a sense of existence" (Male 23).

Emotions are associated with the flow experience in an interactive, engaging live-stream environment. The appreciation of virtual gifts and real-time chat impel viewers to the state of flow, where time ceases to exist and each moment is rewarding. "I was encouraged to be the number one in the room. At the end, I lost control. Initially, it was before bed, and then I started spending the night with it" (Male 26). The immediate feedback loop in live-stream commerce not only makes the experience enjoyable but also creates an atmosphere of a flow state. "My emotional connection influences time I spend in livestream viewership" (Female 23). This heightened flow state in the broadcast room creates a social proof effect, encouraging others to follow suit, a sense of urgency, and competition among viewers. *When I see others tipping, I feel compelled to join in to stand out and gain recognition from live-streamers (Male 40).* The dynamic and engaging live-stream environment ultimately drives higher sales for the advertised goods and increases viewer participation. Social proof leverages individuals' psychological tendency to conform to others' actions. *When I observe others tipping, it compels me to do the same to fit in with others* (Male 27). This phenomenon can amplify the perceived popularity and credibility of the content creator, further boosting trust and increasing the likelihood of additional tips and purchases.

Tipping often involves a complex interplay of social norms, personal beliefs and emotional responses. Psychological factors such as the desire to conform to societal expectations and the need to express gratitude can influence tipping behavior. Furthermore, consumers may engage in impulsive spending when tipping, driven by a spontaneous urge to reward in an effort to enhance their self-image. *Though some are impulsive tipping, the amount goes way beyond their ability and affordability. For this, they can't help themselves to borrow, and engage in unlawful activities. I am not like them; I have self-discipline* (Female 22).

"I think tipping impulsively incurs financial strain" (Female 23), particularly because they consistently tip more than they can afford. "They tip impulsively and experience a temporary sense of satisfaction and euphoria, feeling good but that does not last long" (Male 23). The impulsive tipping is followed by "feelings of regret or guilt they realize the financial impact the next morning" (Male 28). On the one hand, tipping provides a sense of satisfaction and social approval, reinforcing positive self-esteem and a feeling of generosity. "On the other hand, it can also lead to financial anxiety and regret when one realizes they have over overspent" (Male 23). Acknowledging top tippers can have a profound psychological impact on viewers. It creates a sense of belonging and validation, making viewers feel appreciated and valued. This recognition also fosters a deeper emotional connection between the streamer and their audience, encouraging continued support and engagement. Focusing heavily on top tippers can create an uneven playing field where only the wealthiest viewers receive attention. for example,

> Last night, I saw a dancer celebrating her birthday in the broadcasting room. She has received lots of gifts from viewers, e.g., rocketship, a racing car, etc., almost 30,000 yuan in total. The dancer is from Laos, but the live streamer is Chinese. 30,000RMB equals 2 years' income in Laos.
> (Female 32)

Conclusion

This study explored the meaning of money in tipping or token currency in donations and virtual gifts in live-stream commerce. We found that tipping currency influences user tipping or virtual gifts in live-stream commerce. Our results suggest that the emotional connection between live streamers and followers drives the purchase of virtual gifts, consistent with the findings of Lin et al. (2021). Direct interaction with live streamers in the broadcast room is elevated by others' presence, and a crowd effect exists where viewers knowingly or unknowingly compete with each other to gain streamers' attention and recognition. The elevation of emotional attachment is driven by a power that one may feel when they achieve the number 1 ranking among others in the room. This trophy is recognized and appreciated by the anchor. Streamers influence users' consumption motivation through live-streaming platforms, while immediate interaction with streamers stimulates viewers' enthusiasm (Wang & Wu, 2019). The positive emotions transmute to the mental state of flow when time ceases to exist, and followers lose control of their financial awareness. This is facilitated by the use of tokens or tipping currency, which is dissociated from real money and turns into 'monopoly money.' The loss of psychological ownership of money creates a fertile ground for impulsive spending. Results demonstrate that the existence of social competition empowers viewer's personal and social gratification and reinforces the continuation of participation in live-stream commerce platforms (Ma, 2021). The verbal and special effect intimacy creates a heightened emotional state for viewers to purchase virtual gifts (Wang & Wu, 2019). Viewers are intimidated when streamers call them husbands (wives) or brothers (sisters) and express the wish that more virtual gifts result in opportunities for privileged intimacy (Zhang, 2022).

While many studies have focused on the impact of social presence on live-streaming participation and consumption (Liu et al., 2020), this study looked at the core concept of the influence of tipping currency on purchasing virtual gifts. The live streamer–follower emotional connection affects the underlying psychological mechanism that drives the use of tipping currency; both enjoying the flow state and the viewer's need for excitement and recognition influence the impulsive purchase of virtual gifts.

References

Ahn, J., & Kwon, J. (2022). The role of trait and emotion in cruise customers' impulsive buying behavior: An empirical study. *Journal of Strategic Marketing*, *30*(3), 320–333.

Alexander, D., Boone, C., & Lynn, M. (2021). The effects of tip recommendations on customer tipping, satisfaction, repatronage, and spending. *Management Science*, *67*(1), 146–165.

Bajpal. (2021). *Countries Where Bitcoin Is Legal & Illegal (DISH, OTSK)*. Investopedia. https://www.investopedia.com/articles/forex/041515/countries-where-bitcoin-legal-illegal.asp

Boyatzis, R. E. (1998). *Transforming qualitative information: Thematic analysis and code development*. Sage.

Ceci, L. (2024, February 29). Subscription apps – Statistics & Facts [Review of Subscription apps – Statistics & Facts]. *Statis*ta. https://www.statista.com/topics/9684/subscription-apps/#topFacts

Chaudhry, A., Wang, Y., & Ouyang, E. (2024). Community gifting and recipients' engagement with peers and influencers: Evidence from natural experiments on Twitch. *Journal of Interactive Marketing*. https://doi.org/10.1177/10949968241257891

Chen, C. C., & Lin, Y. C. (2018). What drives live-stream usage intention? The perspectives of flow, entertainment, social interaction, and endorsement. *Telematics and Informatics*, *35*(1), 293–303.

Chevalier, S. (2024, April 5). *From China to the world* [Review of *From China to the world*]. Statista. https://www.statista.com/topics/8752/livestream-commerce/#topicOverview

Chiu, C. M., & Huang, H. Y. (2015). Examining the antecedents of user gratification and its effects on individuals' social network services usage: The moderating role of habit. *European Journal of Information Systems*, *24*(4), 411–430.

Claeys, G., & Demertzis, M. (2021). Digital currencies: What role in our financial system? In K. Thomas Liaw (Ed.), *The Routledge handbook of FinTech* (pp. 51–66). Routledge.

Csikszentmihalyi, M., & LeFevre, J. (1989). Optimal experience in work and leisure. *Journal of Personality and Social Psychology*, *6*, 815–822.

Feinberg, R. A. (1986). Credit cards as spending facilitating stimuli: A conditioning interpretation. *Journal of Consumer Research*, *13*(3), 348–356.

Hilvert-Bruce, Z., Neill, J. T., Sjöblom, M., & Hamari, J. (2018). Social motivations of live-streaming viewer engagement on Twitch. *Computers in Human Behavior*, *84*, 58–67.

Hou, F., Guan, Z., Li, B., & Chong, A. Y. L. (2020). Factors influencing people's continuous watching intention and consumption intention in live streaming: Evidence from China. *Internet Research*, *30*(1), 141–163.

Hunt, J. M., Chatterjee, A., Florsheim, R. A., & Kernan, J. B. (1990). Credit cards as spending-facilitating stimuli: A test and extension of Feinberg's conditioning hypothesis. *Psychological Reports*, *67*(1), 323–330.

Jhang-Li, J. H., & Liou, J. H. (2024). An analysis of operating strategy for a video live streaming platform: advertisement, advertorial, and donation. *Information Technology and Management*, *25*(1), 51–68.

Jia, A. L., Rao, Y., & Shen, S. (2021, May). Analyzing and predicting user donations in social live video streaming. In *2021 IEEE 24th International Conference on Computer Supported Cooperative Work in Design (CSCWD)* (pp. 1256–1261). IEEE.

Jingli, S. (2020, November 25). *Kuaishou acquires payment license amid booming e-commerce and livestreaming | KrASIA*. KrASIA. https://kr-asia.com/kuaishou-acquires-payment-license-amid-booming-e-commerce-and-livestreaming

Kaur, P., Dhir, A., Chen, S., Malibari, A., & Almotairi, M. (2020). Why do people purchase virtual goods? A uses and gratification (U&G) theory perspective. *Telematics and Informatics*, *53*, 101376.

Khan, J., & Belk, R. (2024). Money you could touch: Cash and psychological ownership. *Qualitative Market Research: An International Journal*, *27*(5), 820–840. https://doi.org/10.1108/QMR-04-2023-0049.

Khan, J., Belk, R. W., & Craig-Lees, M. (2015). Measuring consumer perceptions of payment mode. *Journal of Economic Psychology*, *47*, 34–49.

Koufaris, M. (2002). Applying the technology acceptance model and flow theory to online consumer behavior. *Information Systems Research*, *13*(2), 205–223.

Lee, D., & Wan, C. (2023). The impact of mukbang live streaming commerce on consumers' overconsumption behavior. *Journal of Interactive Marketing*, *58*(2–3), 198–221.

Lee, Y. C., Yen, C. H., Wang, D., & Fu, W. T. (2019, October). Understanding how digital gifting influences social interaction on live streams. In *Proceedings of the 21st International Conference on Human-Computer Interaction with Mobile Devices and Services* (pp. 1–10). Association for Computing Machinery, New York, United States.

Li, Y., & Guo, Y. (2021). Virtual gifting and danmaku: What motivates people to interact in game live streaming? *Telematics and Informatics*, *62*, 101624.

Li, Y., & Peng, Y. (2021). What drives gift-giving intention in live streaming? The perspectives of emotional attachment and flow experience. *International Journal of Human–Computer Interaction*, *37*(14), 1317–1329.

Li, Z., Liu, D., Zhang, J., Wang, P., & Guan, X. (2024). Live streaming selling strategies of online retailers with spillover effects. *Electronic Commerce Research and Applications*, *63*, 101330.

Lin, S. C., & Lee, Y. Y. (2024). Explaining the gift-giving intentions of live-streaming audiences through social presence: The perspective of interactive marketing. *Journal of Research in Interactive Marketing* , *18*(5), 945–969. https://doi.org/10.1108/JRIM-01-2024-0030

Lin, Y., Yao, D., & Chen, X. (2021). Happiness begets money: Emotion and engagement in live streaming. *Journal of Marketing Research*, *58*(3), 417–438.

Liu, Z., Yang, J., & Ling, L. (2020). Exploring the influence of live streaming in mobile commerce on adoption intention from a social presence perspective. *International Journal of Mobile Human Computer Interaction (IJMHCI)*, *12*(2), 53–71.

Long & A. C. Tefertiller. (2020). China's new mania for livestreaming: Gender differences in motives and uses of social livestreaming services. *International Journal of Human–Computer Interaction*, *36*(14), 1314–1324, 2020.

Lu, B., Wu, D., & Zhao, R. (2022). An investigation into factors affecting individuals' gifting intention in live streaming: A streamer–content perspective. *Journal of Electronic Business & Digital Economics*, *1*(1/2), 90–110.

Lynn, M., & Latane, B. (1984). The psychology of restaurant tipping. *Journal of Applied Social Psychology*, *14*(6), 549–561.

Ma, Y. (2021). To shop or not: Understanding Chinese consumers' live-stream shopping intentions from the perspectives of uses and gratifications, perceived network size, perceptions of digital celebrities, and shopping orientations. *Telematics and Informatics*, *59*, 101562.

McCall, M., & Belmont, H. J. (1996). Credit card insignia and restaurant tipping: Evidence for an associative link. *Journal of Applied Psychology*, *81*(5), 609.

Migiro, S. O., & Magangi, B. A. (2011). Mixed methods: A review of literature and the future of the new research paradigm. *African Journal of Business Management*, *5*(10), 3757–3764.

Ming, J., Jianqiu, Z., Bilal, M., Akram, U., & Fan, M. (2021). How social presence influences impulse buying behavior in live streaming commerce? The role of SOR theory. *International Journal of Web Information Systems*, *17*(4), 300–320.

Moro-Visconti, R., & Cesaretti, A. (2023). Cryptocurrencies and non-fungible tokens. In *Digital token valuation: Cryptocurrencies, NFTs, decentralized finance, and blockchains* (pp. 107–139). Springer Nature Switzerland.

Patton, M. Q. (1999). Enhancing the quality and credibility of qualitative analysis. *Health Services Research*, *34*(5 Pt 2), 1189.

Research Report World. (2024). *Global livestream e-commerce platform market – Industry reports. Researchreportsworld.com.* https://www.researchreportsworld.com/global-livestream-ecommerce-platform-market-28265863

Shimp, T. A., & Moody, M. P. (2000). In search of a theoretical explanation for the credit card effect. *Journal of Business Research*, *48*(1), 17–23.

Tyrväinen, O., & Karjaluoto, H. (2024). Willingness to pay for freemium services: Addressing the differences between monetization strategies. *International Journal of Information Management, 77*, 102787.

Wang, D., Lee, Y. C., & Fu, W. T. (2019). "I love the feeling of being on stage, but I become greedy" Exploring the impact of monetary incentives on live streamers' social interactions and streaming content. *Proceedings of the ACM on Human-Computer Interaction*, *3*(CSCW), 1–24.

Wang, M. (2022, August). The effect of flow experience on gifting in live streaming: A perspective of flow theory. In *Proceedings of the 5th International Conference on Information Science and Systems* (pp. 57–63).

Wang, X., & Wu, D. (2019). Understanding user engagement mechanisms on a live streaming platform. In F. H.Nah & K. Siau (Eds.), *HCI in Business, Government and Organizations. Information Systems and Analytics. HCII 2019. Lecture Notes in Computer Science* (Vol. 11589). Springer, Cham. https://doi.org/10.1007/978-3-030-22338-0_22

Wohn, D. Y., Freeman, G., & McLaughlin, C. (2018, April). Explaining viewers' emotional, instrumental, and financial support provision for live streamers. In R. Mandryk & M. Hancock (Eds.), *Proceedings of the 2018 CHI Conference on Human Factors in Computing Systems* (pp. 1–13). NY: Association for Computing Machinery.

Wongkitrungrueng, A., & Assarut, N. (2020). The role of live streaming in building consumer trust and engagement with social commerce sellers. *Journal of Business Research, 117*, 543–556.

Wu, T., Jiang, N., Kumar, T. B. J., & Chen, M. (2024). The role of cognitive factors in consumers' perceived value and subscription intention of video streaming platforms: A systematic literature review. *Cogent Business & Management, 11*(1), 2329247.

Xu, X., Wu, J. H., & Li, Q. (2020). What drives consumer shopping behavior in live streaming commerce? *Journal of Electronic Commerce Research, 21*(3), 144–167.

Xu, Y., Ye, Y., & Liu, Y. (2022). Understanding virtual gifting in live streaming by the theory of planned behavior. *Human Behavior and Emerging Technologies, 2022*(1), 8148077.

Yi, Q., Khan, J., Su, Y., Tong, J., & Zhao, S. (2023). Impulse buying tendency in live-stream commerce: The role of viewing frequency and anticipated emotions influencing scarcity-induced purchase decision. *Journal of Retailing and Consumer Services, 75*, 103534.

Yin, J., Huang, Y., & Ma, Z. (2023). Explore the feeling of presence and purchase intention in livestream shopping: A flow-based model. *Journal of Theoretical and Applied Electronic Commerce Research, 18*(1), 237–256.

Zhang, W. (2022). Understanding gift-giving in game live streaming on Douyu: An evaluation of PSR/social presence. *Frontiers in Psychology, 13*, 953484.

Zhao, L., Yalin, A., & West, E. (2023). E-commerce goes social: The rise of livestreaming as a hybrid promotional form. In *The Routledge companion to advertising and promotional culture* (pp. 347–359). Routledge.

Zhou, J., Zhou, J., Ding, Y., & Wang, H. (2019). The magic of danmaku: A social interaction perspective of gift sending on live streaming platforms. *Electronic Commerce Research and Applications, 34*, 100815.

Zhu, Z., Yang, Z., & Dai, Y. (2017). Understanding the gift-sending interaction on live-streaming video websites. In *Social Computing and Social Media. Human Behavior: 9th International Conference, SCSM 2017, Held as Part of HCI International 2017, Vancouver, BC, Canada, July 9–14, 2017, Proceedings, Part I 9* (pp. 274–285). Springer International Publishing.

9 Generation Z, Digital Currencies and Luxury Purchase

Jashim Khan, Russell Belk and Gary Rivers

Introduction

The second-largest market for luxury brands worldwide is China. The sector is expected to reach US dollars 65 billion by 2028 (Statista, 2023). The primary consumers of luxury goods are the growing middle class (Kapferer & Laurant, 2016). Generation Z values brands that elevate their status (Yeoman & McMahon-Beattie, 2018), and they have more discretionary income than their parent generation (Huang et al., 2024). This research focuses on Generation Z, their perception of digital currency and whether they intend to use it to purchase luxury brands. Generation Z is transforming the luxury sector by choosing affordable luxury items that align with their aspirations, such as status enhancement.

With the rise of big data and advanced technologies, digital currency is quickly gaining acceptance among Generation Z in the luxury market (Limna et al., 2022). The factors driving this trend include user-friendliness, usefulness, trust, security, risk and traceability (Phuong et al., 2022). This trend also reflects their willingness to use digital currency (Khan & Belk, 2024). Luxury brands are facing challenges from counterfeit and grey markets (Khan et al., 2020), and the blurring of the 'Made in' label is increasing the risk of counterfeit purchases (Choi, 2019; Hou et al., 2020). Generation Z prefers digital currency that can coexist with other digital payment systems, such as electronic financial transfers, online bill payments, direct debits and third-party payments (Khan & Belk, 2024). According to Rosário and Raimundo (2021), integrating digital currency provides practical alternatives for purchasing signature luxury brands due to its ease of use, speedy payments, privacy and anonymity and comfort (Schumacher, 2024). Given Generation Z's extensive access to digital information, which significantly influences their purchasing behavior, trust has become a highly valued asset for luxury brand purchases (Payal et al., 2024). Their level of trust likely influences their inclination to use digital money in payment methods and the risk of counterfeit brands. Buchori and Harwanu (2021) state that individuals who trust digital currency are also satisfied with premium luxury brands.

DOI: 10.4324/9781003425021-9

This chapter investigates the relationship between Generation Z's perceptions of user-friendliness, convenience of use and trust in digital currency usage intention for purchases of luxury brands. Our research explores the relationship between trust in digital currency usage intention and the risk of counterfeit purchases, given that digital currency offers security compared to cash and can be tracked online. In this study, we determine that the main factors influencing Generation Z's propensity to use digital currency to buy luxury brands are its ease of use, convenience and user-friendliness. Similarly, the presence of counterfeit brands in the market links the risk of purchasing them; thus, trust in digital currency manifests in their usage. This study offers practitioners insights into the purchasing behaviors of young Chinese consumers who have decided to carve out unique identities for themselves in the marketplace, with a focus on status-seeking luxury purchases (Wang & Qiao, 2020).

This chapter is organized as follows: literature review and conceptual development of the research question; next, we provide research methodology and, finally, results, discussion and conclusion.

Generation Z Consumers

The primary focus of this study is Generation Z's intention to use digital currency. The China Statistical Yearbook 2021 states that there are 239,473,147 young people in China between the ages of 15 and 29. The number of college students has increased, and their spending power has continued to expand with support from parents in the form of pocket money (Huang et al., 2024), contributing to Generation Z's fascination with luxury brand purchases. Generation Z makes up the largest share of customers of luxury brands (60%), according to the Chinese Academy of Social Sciences' Luxury Consumption in 2022. This study sets the context of luxury brand purchases using central bank digital currency.

Digital Currency

Digital currency is any currency used for transactions, saving, exchanging or spending using digital computer hardware systems, especially through Internet-enabled devices, and is referred to as digital currency, so-called e-money, digital money or money-like asset (Al-Laham et al., 2009, p. 340). Three types of digital currencies are virtual, cryptocurrency and digital currency issued by central banks (De Vauplane, 2024). Virtual currencies are unregulated digital currencies, and Central bank-issued digital currencies are regulated. At the same time, cryptocurrency uses cryptography to secure and verify transactions and manage and control the minting of crypto assets (Zatti & Barresi, 2024). Generally, digital files, stored-value cards and a dispersed network of databases on the Internet, like the centralized electronic database of an organization, are all examples of digital asset records (Cheng et al.,

2024). Research on the definition of digital currencies has been extensively studied in the literature (Gregoriou and Nian, 2015; Ali et al., 2014; Bordo et al., 2017; Keister & Sanches, 2021). The debate about digital currencies touches on potential risks and their potential benefits (Ali et al., 2014). Digital currency's lowest transaction costs are its main advantage (Nakamoto, 2008) since distributed ledger technology eliminates the need for a middleman. Customers oversee their digital currencies to and from anybody, at any time, and with no transaction restrictions and the absence of third-party clearing agencies or private banks (Gregoriou & Nian, 2015). Digital currency enables businesses to reduce transaction fees, interchange, statement and other transaction-related fees compared to third-party payment systems (Bijlsma et al., 2024). Credit payments have very little total cost with digital currency, which allows firms to pass those savings on to their customers. Furthermore, digital currency transactions are safe and irrevocable as opposed to third-party payment, which requires signatures and is susceptible to fraud or scams. Due to the low cost of transactions, businesses can accept micropayments, which makes them equally popular among customers and businesses. Digital currency that is password-protected remains in the hands of the customers (Ali et al., 2014). Because digital currency continues to exist digitally, security risks exist (Schumacher, 2024); for example, losing or forgetting credentials and their recovery can be challenging. Careless people may be more susceptible to theft, particularly from malware (Temara, 2024). Since digital currency is anonymous and easy to use, it has complete ledger data for every transaction, making data privacy questionable.

Technology Acceptance Model

The technology acceptance model (TAM) has undergone extensive testing, extension and generalization since Davis (1989) seminal work (Hess et al., 2014; Venkatesh & Davis, 2000; Venkatesh et al., 2003). Subjective norms, social influence and behavioral control were all part of the first stage (see Brown et al., 2010; Holden & Rada, 2011). Perceived utility and ease of use were incorporated in the second phase of TAM expansion (see Agarwal & Prasad, 1999; Stern et al., 2008). In the third research phase, boundary conditions were investigated on the impact of perceived usefulness and ease of use of TAM (Sun & Zhang, 2006; Venkatesh & Davis, 2000; Venkatesh et al., 2003). Gefen and Straub (1997) demonstrated the impact of gender on the TAM model, stating that women viewed the technology as more useful, while males reported the importance of ease of use. Gefen and Straub (2000) revealed that ease of use is dominant when an e-commerce platform is visited for informational purposes. However, usefulness is more important when a purchase is the motive to visit the e-commerce platform.

TAM model is applied in web-related technologies, including trust, privacy and risk (Thong et al., 2011). The expanded model has been successfully applied to user privacy and trust in mobile payment (Türker et al.,

2022; Yang et al., 2023), mobile phone usage (Venkatesh et al., 2012) and participation in social media sites (Lee et al., 2012). Perception of trust in technology and risk is associated (Pavlou, 2003).

Next, we discuss digital currency's perceived ease of use, usefulness and trust. Propose risk as a potential moderator in the relationship between perceived trust and usage of digital currency.

Perceived Ease of Use

According to Davis, perceived ease of use is "the degree to which a person believes that using a particular system would be free of effort" (Davis, 1989, p. 320). Hasan et al. (2024) suggest that perceived ease of use was the most critical factor in adopting mobile payment. Since digital currency is self-service, people would feel more at ease and likely to trial if they observed user-friendliness (Khan & Craig-Lees, 2009). This implies that learning how to use the digital currency app will not be too tough for the tech-savvy Generation Z. Ease of use will speed up the adoption of digital currency because they are accustomed to using platform-based third-party payment services like Alipay and WeChat and are aware of the payment environment. Perceived ease of use is linked to the user's efforts and motivation to learn and use payment apps. Seyal and Pijpers (2004) assert that perceived ease of use is a significant factor in predicting Internet and mobile phone usage. Consumers' familiarity with the Internet and smartphones positively influences digital currency usage (Ma et al., 2022). Generation Z, familiar with digital apps likely to use digital currency, alleviating the risk of buying counterfeit luxury brands (Surekha et al., 2024). Perceived ease of use is related to technology adaptation; the higher the perceived ease of use, the better it is in supporting users in continuing to use digital currency apps. Within luxury brand purchases, the risk of counterfeiting is associated with the trust users pay for digital currency apps (De Boissieu et al., 2021). This study examines perceived ease of use, as a critical factor influencing decisions to utilize digital currencies to acquire luxury products (Dimitrova, 2024). Therefore:

H1: There is a positive relationship between perceived ease of use and consumers' purchases of luxury brands using central bank digital currency.

Perceived Usefulness (PU)

Perceived usefulness is "the degree to which a person believes that using a particular system would enhance his or her job performance" (Davis, 1989, p. 320). In other words, usefulness is the degree to which a person thinks using digital currency to pay for luxury brands will improve the effectiveness and efficiency of payment processing (Yusuf et al., 2024). Lu et al. (2019) suggest that perceived usefulness requires the digital currency app to easily navigate between other payment apps, such as third-party platform-based payment. The navigation between payment apps derives the usefulness of digital currency when the accuracy, security, network speed, user-friendliness, user engagement and convenience are assured (Liao & Cheung, 2002) to enhance the quality of life. Davis (1989) demonstrated a positive relationship between perceived usefulness and usage behavior. Dimitrova (2024) suggests that perceived usefulness is directly and positively related to the intention to adopt a digital payment. Therefore, we hypothesize that:

H2: There is a positive relationship between perceived usefulness and consumers' purchases of luxury brands using central bank digital currency.

Perceived Trust

According to Marikyan and Papagiannidis (2021), perceived trust is when a user feels that the information they provide to a system during a transaction will be kept private and secure. Although people's trust in online transactions is declining (Gawron and Strzelecki, 2021), CBDCs are seen as trustworthy and secure since fiat currencies draw security from the central bank (Sankar, 2021). Trust in technology, such as e-commerce platforms, consistently demonstrated the relationship between perceived trust and adoption of that technology (Bijlsma et al., 2024). Studies by Saif Almuraqab (2019) and Mendoza-Tello et al. (2018) showed that people who place higher importance on trust are more likely to embrace digital currencies (Bijlsma et al., 2021). Trust often enables people to articulate their expectations for future behavior based on past experiences. Trust is a crucial component because the virtual environment is unstable and customers typically have no direct control (Ogunmola & Das, 2024). Perceived trust, according to Mayer et al. (1995), fosters confidence in successfully completing a transaction by lowering anxiety and uncertainty. When users feel at ease interacting with digital currency, they are more likely to gain confidence in it, and trust is an essential coping strategy for handling anxiety and uncertainty (Hoffman, 1999; Dimitrova, 2024). Similarly, customers' acceptance and contentment with using digital currency to purchase luxury products will suffer if perceived trust is diminished in the virtual currency with the possibility of purchasing counterfeit products. Therefore, we hypothesize that:

H2: A positive relationship exists between perceived trust and consumers' purchase of luxury brands using central bank digital currency.

Perceived Risk

An individual's intention is a deliberate and conscious plan to make efforts toward a particular action (Haider et al., 2024). The theory of planned

behavior posits that intention is the fundamental element that determines actual behavior (Ajzen, 1991). Empirical studies have provided evidence of a direct correlation between the behavioral intentions of individuals and their actual behavior (Khan et al., 2024; Hagger and Hamilton, 2024; Dimitrova et al., 2022). This study examines the intent of individuals to utilize digital currency for luxury brand purchases. In luxury brand purchase, risk plays a crucial role in influencing confidence in using digital money. Consumers express concerns about counterfeits when making luxury brand purchases. The existing literature indicates a relationship between perceived trust and digital currency usage. However, the likelihood of encountering counterfeit brands can influence this relationship between trust in digital currency and the intention to use it.

Perceived risk refers to an individual's personal assessment of the risk they face (Sohn, 2024). Within the context of luxury purchases, perceived risk is evident around the financial security of the payment method and the potential for acquiring a counterfeit brand. Baur and Dimpfl (2018) defined perceived risk as a limiting factor in the connection between individuals' intentions and their actual behavior in adopting digital currency. Specifically, when the perceived risk of counterfeiting is higher, the relationship between intentions to use digital currency becomes stronger. This is because digital currency leaves a digital trail and can be traced. For example,

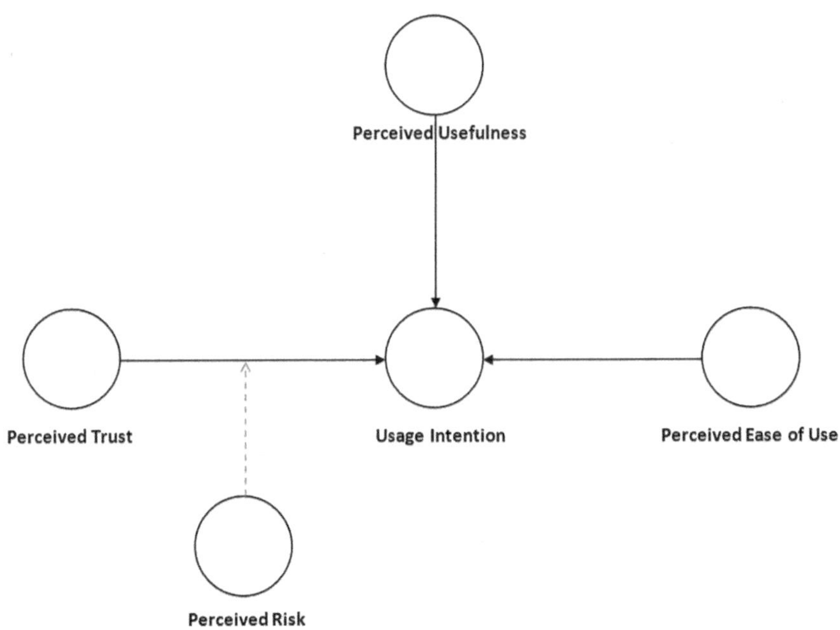

Figure 9.1 Research Model

vulnerable customers may easily be targeted by merchants because of the everyday monitoring of their financial behavior on the internet (Dimitrova et al., 2022) (Figure 9.1).

Methodology

Research Context

In 2022, China became the world's second-largest market for luxury consumption, with a growing middle class driving this trend (Statista, 2023). Despite the challenges of the COVID-19 pandemic, China saw 41% of the world's new luxury store openings in 2022 (Statista, 2023). The Chinese luxury market is projected to account for 25% of the global luxury market share, reaching ¥816 billion by 2025 (PWC, 2023). The pandemic has caused a shift in consumer behavior toward e-commerce, which represented 21% of sales in 2021, up from 13% in 2019. Live stream commerce and social media are also gaining importance as channels for luxury purchases (Statista, 2023). Furthermore, the younger demographic is playing an increasingly significant role in China's luxury market (Liu et al., 2019). Despite its growth, the industry continues to battle issues related to the grey market, copycats and counterfeit goods (Hou et al., 2020; Choi, 2019).

Survey Research

To investigate the research topic, we employed a survey research approach. We used existing scales from previous research in a self-administered questionnaire. The questionnaire included items for perceived usefulness, ease of use, intention to use based on (Davis, 1989; Venkatesh & Davis, 2000), perceived trust (Shahzad et al., 2018) and perceived risk (Pavlou, 2003). Participants rated questions on a five-point Likert scale from 'strongly disagree' to 'strongly agree.' Following McGorry's (2000) double translation method, the questionnaire was initially translated from English to Chinese and back-translated in a pilot study involving 31 undergraduate students. Data was collected in February 2024 using Wenjuanxing, a Chinese survey platform, resulting in 318 valid responses. The survey also inquired about participants' prior experiences in purchasing luxury brands using digital currencies. We utilized a non-probability criterion-based judgment sampling technique to recruit participants through social media platforms. 94.57% of the respondents were classified as Generation Z customers, as they were born between 1995 and 2009, and 53.14% were female (McCrindle, 2023). Of the participants, 58% had bachelor's degrees, while 32.29% and 9.71% had educational levels below a bachelor's and master's degree, respectively. Table 9.1 illustrates that 49.43% of participants reported a monthly discretionary income ranging from ¥3,000 to ¥6,000.

Participants Profile

Table 9.1 Participants Profile

Items		*Number*	*Proportion*	*Total*
Age	Male	164	46.86%	100%
	Female	186	53.14%	
Year of Birth	Before 1995	17	4.86%	
	1995–2009	331	94.57%	100%
	After 2009	2	0.57%	
Educational Level	Below undergraduate level	113	32.29%	
	Undergraduate	203	58%	
	Master's degree	34	9.71%	100%
	Doctor's degree	0	0%	
Average Monthly Disposable Income (RMB)	3,000 and less	53	15.14%	
	3,000–6,000	173	49.43%	
	6,000–9,000	72	20.57%	100%
	9,000–12,000	39	11.14%	
	Above 12,000	13	3.71%	

Data Analysis and Procedure

The Smart PLS software (Ringle et al., 2005) was utilized for data analysis and model validation in this study. Partial least square structural equation modeling (PLS-SEM) was employed to analyze quantitative data. The PLS technique effectively handles smaller sample sizes and non-normal data (Hair et al., 2014). The analytical procedure involves two stages: first specifying the measurement model and then assessing the structural model (Wong, 2013). The measurement model specification examines indicator loading, composite reliability, discriminant validity and convergent validity. The structural model assessment involves weighing path coefficients and testing their significance.

Measurements Model Assessment

Cronbach's alpha, composite reliability (CR) and rho_a indicate reliability, and in this study, the reliability of scale is satisfied. Convergent validity was deemed acceptable when the AVE was greater than 0.5 (See Table 9.2).

Validity: An assessment of discriminant validity evaluates the degree to which a construct is discriminated against others within the same model (Campbell & Fiske, 1959). According to Fornell and Larcker (1981), the construct's square root exceeded its correlation with any other construct, and the item loaded highest on the related construct (Table 9.3).

Structural Model

The pathways postulated in the research framework are included in the structural model. H1, H2, H3, H4 and H5 is supported (Figure 9.2).

Table 9.2 Convergent Validity

Measurement Items	λ	*VIF*	α	*rho_a*	*CR*	*AVE*
Perceived Usefulness			0.941	0.941	0.941	0.849
PU 1: Digital currency should enable me to purchase luxury brands without issues.	0.938	3.971				
PU 2: I find digital currency useful when purchasing luxury brands	0.889	3.969				
PU 3: Digital currency is more effective than other methods of payment.	0.870	3.550				
PU 4: Digital currency saves time and helps me to complete tasks more efficiently.	0.875	3.875				
Perceived Trust			0.948	0.949	0.948	0.828
PT 1: I believe that digital currency would act in my best interest.	0.906	4.598				
PT 2: I expect information about digital currency is sincere.	0.870	3.662				
PT 3: The digital currency is secured from cyber-attacks	0.827	3.239				
PT 4: I believe digital currency is backed by the Government to ensure security.	0.913	4.356				
PT 5: I believe that digital currency is a reliable and secure currency	0.912	3.612				
Usage Intention			0.935	0.935	0.935	0.837
UI 1: I intend to use digital currency to purchase luxury brands.	0.895	3.319				
UI 2: I intend to use digital currency regularly.	0.868	3.271				
UI 3: I will encourage others to use digital currency	0.896	3.851				
UI 4: I plan to use digital currency in the future	0.880	3.960				
Perceived Ease of Use			0.927	0.927	0.927	0.820
PEOU 1: I think that Digital currency is easy to understand.	0.885	3.347				

(*Continued*)

Table 9.2 (Continued)

Measurement Items	λ	*VIF*	α	*rho_a*	*CR*	*AVE*
PEOU 2: I believe that Digital currency is user-friendly and effortless.	0.836	3.070				
PEOU 3: It is easy to remember the functions of Digital currency	0.880	3.184				
PEOU 4: Overall, I think Digital currency is easy to use.	0.885	3.263				
Perceived Risk			0.862	0.905	0.914	0.781
PR 1: The decision to use a digital currency is risky	0.914	2.017				
PR 2: In general, I believe using digital currency over the Internet is risk	0.903	2.326				

Table 9.3 Discriminant Validity of Conceptual Model

Fornell–Larcker Criterion	*1*	*2*	*3*	*4*	*5*
1. Perceived ease of use	**0.91***				
2. Usage intention	0.67	**0.92***			
3. Perceived trust	0.72	0.75	**0.91***		
4. Perceived usefulness	0.68	0.71	0.70	**0.92***	
5. Perceived risk	0.20	0.15	0.20	0.12	**0.88***

Note: *the square root of the construct's AVE exceeded its correlation with any other construct and the item loaded highest on the related construct.

Perceived Ease of Use

The research findings show that young Chinese Generation Z buyers are influenced by the ease of use of digital currency when making luxury brand purchase decisions. This aligns with Kumpajaya and Dhewanto's (2015) study found that digital currencies are considered easy to use and that users are more likely to use them for transactions. This is also supported by Arvidsson (2014) found that ease of use influences Swedish consumers' intention to use mobile payment services. Previous studies demonstrate the importance of perceived ease of use as a determining factor of digital currency usage. Extant research also highlights the wide use of digital currencies for e-commerce transactions, citing advantages such as reduced transaction costs and simplifying the payment process for companies and customers. Our results confirm a positive association between the ease of

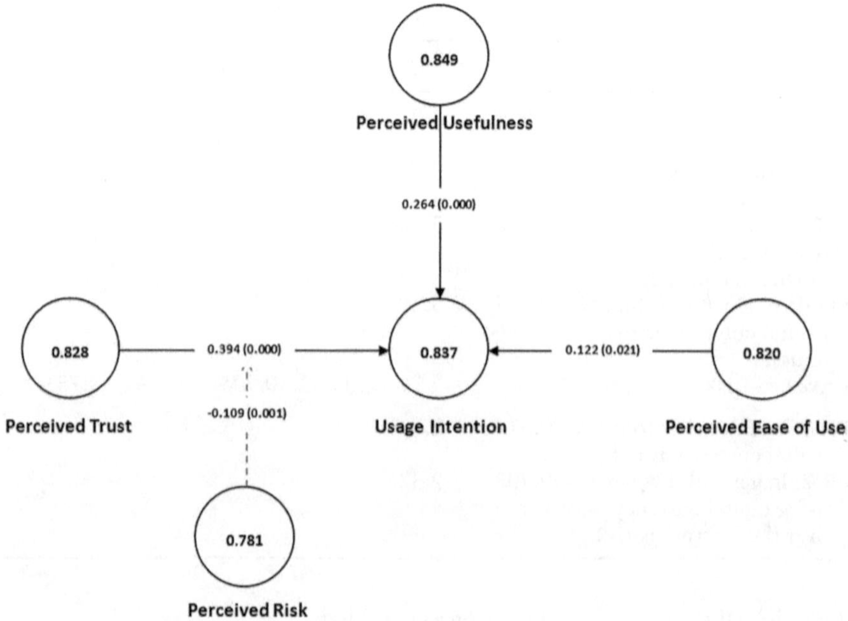

Figure 9.2 Path Coefficients Results

use of new technology and the intention to use it. Due to their familiarity with platform-based third-party mobile payment services, such as WeChat or Alipay, most Chinese Generation Z consumers find digital currency easy to understand. According to our study, Chinese Generation Z consumers use digital currencies to buy luxury brands because of perceived ease of use.

Perceived Usefulness

We have found that people view digital currency as a useful payment method for buying luxury brands. This aligns with Khelladi et al. (2024), who state that consumers are primarily looking for enjoyment in using new technology when purchasing digital luxury fashion brands. According to Wang et al. (2011), individuals are more likely to adopt new technology when they find it useful. Furthermore, Roussou et al. (2019) have shown that perceived usefulness positively affects adopting new technology. Our research supports the idea that digital currencies are useful for lessening transaction costs and saving time. Saif Almuraqab (2019) also found that perceived usefulness enhances efficiency and facilitates transactions. Based on our study, it is evident that the younger generation in China is open to utilizing digital currency technologies. Therefore, our findings emphasize that the perceived usefulness of digital currency plays a significant role in determining its suitability for purchasing luxury brands.

Perceived Trust

The findings indicate that trust in digital currency plays a role in influencing the use of digital currency to buy luxury brands, particularly among Chinese Generation Z consumers. However, businesses considering the adoption of digital currency may face challenges such as market regulations, risk, resistance to transition from third-party payment to digital currency, and concerns over security (Stark, 2013). Digital currencies face these challenges in the emerging digital economy (Stark, 2013). Individuals' perceptions of trust and risk associated with digital currency significantly influence the acceptance of digital currency in China, according to Shahzad et al. (2018). If consumers believe that using digital currencies for trading luxury items is more reliable and secure, they are more likely to use digital currencies for luxury purchases. To encourage the adoption of digital currency in China, the Chinese Central Bank is testing e-CN, aiming to make digital currencies more efficient and secure for international financial transactions. Our research suggests that consumers' trust perception is a key factor influencing their decision to use digital currencies for buying luxury items. If consumers view e-CNY as more trustworthy, a significant portion of luxury brand transactions could be driven by the use of digital currency.

Perceived Risk

Perceived risk is an individual's perception of both positive and negative outcomes (Rossmannek et al., 2024). Trust becomes crucial when dealing with risk (Pavlou, 2003). In Pavlou's (2003) study, trust was identified as a significant factor impacting perceived risk. Trust leads to a reduction in perceived risk, as evidenced by Featherman and Pavlou's (2003) studies. Baidoun and Salem (2024) suggested that the ease of use and perceived usefulness in online shopping impact perceived trust. Their study showed that perceived trust encourages shopping behavior, while perceived risk weakens this relationship. Perceived risk is an individual's anticipation of negative events while pursuing desirable results (Warkentin et al., 2002). It encompasses uncertainty about both behavior and the environment, such as the prevalence of counterfeit luxury brands in the market. The use of digital currency may reduce this risk and enhance trust in the payment mode. According to Pavlou (2003), in e-commerce, perceived risk reduces consumers' willingness to share information and engage in transactions. Studies also indicate that trust mitigates perceptions of risk (Dabbous et al., 2022). The literature on the technology acceptance model (TAM) (Schlosser et al., 2006) indicates that perceived risk influences how trust impacts intention. Our results suggest that perceived risk moderates the relationship between perceived trust and the intention to use digital currency in the context of luxury brand purchases.

Conclusion

This chapter investigates the relationship between Generation Z's perceptions of ease of use and usefulness of digital currency usage intention within the luxury brand purchase context. This study shows that the attributes of digital currency, such as ease of use and usefulness, influence trust in digital currency hence driving usage intention. The risk associated with counterfeit purchases encourages Generation Z to adopt digital currency, which offers security compared to cash and can be tracked online. From a theoretical implication standpoint, this study shows that perceived ease of use and usefulness drive the motives of Chinese Generation Z consumers to use digital currency. In contrast, perceived risk weakens trust in digital currency. The study also highlights the significance of Generation Z in adopting central bank digital currency. Our findings suggest that consumers' intention to buy luxury brands is influenced by perceived ease of use and usefulness of digital currency. The risk of counterfeit brands affecting Generation Z consumers' trust in digital currencies determines whether they use digital currencies to pay for luxury goods.

This study focused specifically on consumers from China and did not consider cross-cultural issues. Therefore, future studies should compare samples from different countries to gain a more comprehensive understanding. Additionally, the research concentrated on the ease of use, perceived risk and perceived usefulness to predict the usage intention of digital currency, revealing significant results. This suggests the need for further research to explore other factors that may predict customers' usage intention. As technology becomes more integrated into society, people's trust in digital currency will become increasingly important. Suppose government agencies want citizens to adopt digital currency. In that case, they need to pay attention to and improve citizens' perceptions of the trust in digital currency and mitigate risks associated with their usage.

References

Agarwal, R., & Prasad, J. (1999). Are individual differences germane to the acceptance of new information technologies? *Decision Sciences*, *30*(2), 361–391.

Ajzen, I. (1991). The theory of planned behavior. *Organizational Behavior and Human Decision Processes*, *50*(2), 179–211.

Ali, R., Barrdear, J., Clews, R., & Southgate, J. (2014). Innovations in payment technologies and the emergence of digital currencies. *Bank of England Quarterly Bulletin*, *54*(3), 262–275. Available at https://www.bankofengland.co.uk/-/media/boe/files/quarterly-bulletin/2014/innovations-in-payment-technologies-and-the-emergence-of-digital-currencies.pdf

Al-Laham, M., Al-Tarawneh, H., & Abdallat, N. (2009). Development of electronic money and its impact on the central bank role and monetary policy. *Issues in Informing Science and Information Technology*, *6*, 339–349.

Arvidsson, N. (2014). Consumer attitudes on mobile payment services – Results from a proof of concept test. *International Journal of Bank Marketing*, *32*(2), 150–170. https://doi.org/10.1108/ijbm-05-2013-0048

Baidoun, S. D., & Salem, M. Z. (2024). The moderating role of perceived trust and perceived value on online shopping behavioral intention of Palestinian millennials during COVID-19. *Competitiveness Review: An International Business Journal*, *34*(1), 125–143.

Baur, D. G., & Dimpfl, T. (2018). Excess volatility as an impediment for a digital currency. *Available at SSRN 2949754*.

Bijlsma, M., van der Cruijsen, C., Jonker, N., & Reijerink, J. (2021). *What triggers consumer adoption of CBDC?* De Nederlandsche Bank Working Paper No. 709, 1-33. http://dx.doi.org/10.2139/ssrn.3836440

Bijlsma, M., van der Cruijsen, C., Jonker, N., & Reijerink, J. (2024). What triggers consumer adoption of central bank digital currency? *Journal of Financial Services Research*, *65*(1), 1–40.

Bordo, M. D., & Levin, A. T. (2017). *Central bank digital currency and the future of monetary policy* (No. w23711). National Bureau of Economic Research.

Brown, S. A., Dennis, A. R., & Venkatesh, V. (2010). Predicting collaboration technology use: Integrating technology adoption and collaboration research. *Journal of Management Information Systems*, *27*(2), 9–54.

Buchori, A., & Harwani, Y. (2021). The effect of service quality and promotion on purchase intention mediated by trust (Case study: PT China Taiping Insurance Indonesia). *European Journal of Business and Management Research*, 6(2), 44–47. https://doi.org/10.24018/ejbmr.2021.6.2.764

Campbell, D. T., & Fiske, D. W. (1959). Convergent and discriminant validation by the multitrait-multimethod matrix. *Psychological Bulletin*, *56*(2), 81.

Cheng, Q., Gong, Y., Qin, Y., Ao, X., & Li, Z. (2024). Secure digital asset transactions: Integrating distributed ledger technology with safe AI mechanisms. *Academic Journal of Science and Technology*, *9*(3), 156–161.

Choi, T. M. (2019). Blockchain-technology-supported platforms for diamond authentication and certification in luxury supply chains. *Transportation Research Part E: Logistics and Transportation Review*, *128*, 17–29.

Dabbous, A., Merhej Sayegh, M., & Aoun Barakat, K. (2022). Understanding the adoption of cryptocurrencies for financial transactions within a high-risk context. *The Journal of Risk Finance*, *23*(4), 349–367.

Davis, F. D. (1989). Perceived usefulness, perceived ease of use, and user acceptance of information technology. *MIS Quarterly, 13*(3), 319–340. https://doi.org/10.2307/249008

Davis, F. D., Bagozzi, R. P., & Warshaw, P. R. (1989). User acceptance of computer technology: A comparison of two theoretical models. *Management Science*, *35*(8), 982–1003, https://doi.org/10.1287/mnsc.35.8.982

De Boissieu, E., Kondrateva, G., Baudier, P., & Ammi, C. (2021). The use of Blockchain in the luxury industry: Supply chains and the traceability of goods. *Journal of Enterprise Information Management*, *34*(5), 1318–1338.

De Vauplane, H. (2024). Chapter 7: Cryptocurrencies and central banks. In J. Madir (Ed.), *FinTech*. Edward Elgar Publishing. Retrieved Oct 25, 2024, from https://doi.org/10.4337/9781035314751.00017

Dimitrova, I. (2024). Barrier-breakers' influence on full-adoption of digital payment methods. *Internet Research*, *34*(7), 139–159.

Dimitrova, I., Öhman, P., & Yazdanfar, D. (2022). Barriers to bank customers' intention to fully adopt digital payment methods. *International Journal of Quality and Service Sciences*, *14*(5), 16–36.

Featherman, M. S., & Pavlou, P. A. (2003). Predicting e-services adoption: A perceived risk facets perspective. *International Journal of Human-Computer Studies, 59*(4), 451–474.

Fornell, C., & Larcker, D. F. (1981). Evaluating structural equation models with unobservable variables and measurement error. *Journal of Marketing Research, 18*(1), 39–50.

Gawron, M., & Strzelecki, A. (2021). Consumers' adoption and use of E-currencies in virtual markets in the context of an online game. *Journal of Theoretical and Applied Electronic Commerce Research, 16*(5), 1266–1279.

Gefen, D., & Straub, D. W. (1997). Gender differences in the perception and use of e-mail: An extension to the technology acceptance model. *MIS Quarterly*, 21(4), 389–400. https://doi.org/10.2307/249720

Gefen, D., & Straub, D. W. (2000). The relative importance of perceived ease of use in IS adoption: A study of e-commerce adoption. *Journal of the Association for Information Systems, 1*(1), 8.

Gregoriou, G. N., & Nian, L. P. (2015). Handbook of digital currency: Bitcoin, innovation, financial instruments, and big data. *The Journal of Wealth Management, 18*(2), 96.

Hagger, M. S., & Hamilton, K. (2024). Longitudinal tests of the theory of planned behaviour: A meta-analysis. *European Review of Social Psychology, 35*(1), 198–254.

Haider, C. M. R., Clifton, C., & Yin, M. (2024, March). Do crowdsourced fairness preferences correlate with risk perceptions? In Sigchi, S. (Ed.), *Proceedings of the 29th International Conference on Intelligent User Interfaces* (pp. 304–324).

Hair, J. F., Gabriel, M., & Patel, V. (2014). AMOS covariance-based structural equation modeling (CB-SEM): Guidelines on its application as a marketing research tool. *Brazilian Journal of Marketing, 13*(2), 44–55.

(2024). Determinants of behavioral intention to use digital payment among Indian youngsters. *Journal of Risk and Financial Management, 17*(2), 87.

Hess, T. J., McNab, A. L., & Basoglu, K. A. (2014). Reliability generalization of perceived ease of use, perceived usefulness, and behavioral intentions. *MIS Quarterly, 38*(1), 1–28.

Hoffman, D. L., Novak, T. P., & Peralta, M. (1999). Building consumer trust online. *Communications of the ACM*, *42*(4), 80–85.

Holden, H., & Rada, R. (2011). Understanding the influence of perceived usability and technology self-efficacy on teachers' technology acceptance. *Journal of Research on Technology in Education, 43*(4), 343–367.

Hou, P., Zhen, Z., & Pun, H. (2020). Combating copycatting in the luxury market with fighter brands. *Transportation Research Part E: Logistics and Transportation Review, 140*, 102009. https://doi.org/10.1016/j.tre.2020.102009

Huang, Y., Zhou, K., Yang, Y., & Xu, M. (2024). "Privileged adult": How relationship with parents influences adult's status consumption. *Family Relations,* 73(3), 1–19.

Kapferer, J. N., & Laurent, G. (2016). Where do consumers think luxury begins? A study of perceived minimum price for 21 luxury goods in 7 countries. *Journal of Business Research, 69*(1), 332–340.

Keister, T., & Sanches, D. (2021). Should central banks issue digital currency? *The Review of Economic Studies, 90*(1), 404–431.

Khan, J., & Belk, R. (2024). Money you could touch: Cash and psychological ownership. *Qualitative Market Research: An International Journal*, ahead-of-print. https://doi.org/10.1108/QMR-04-2023-0049

Khan, J., & Craig-Lees, M. (2009). 'Cashless' transactions: Perceptions of money in mobile payments. *International Business and Economic Review*, *1*(1), 23–32.

Khan, N., Acuti, D., Lemarie, L., & Viglia, G. (2024). The intention-behaviour gap in sustainable hospitality: A critical literature review. *International Journal of Contemporary Hospitality Management*, *36*(5), 1627–1646.

Khan, S., Fazili, A., & Bashir, I. (2020). Counterfeit luxury consumption: A review and research agenda. *Journal of Consumer behaviour-an International Research Review*, *20*(2), 337–367.

Khelladi, I., Lejealle, C., Rezaee Vessal, S., Castellano, S., & Graziano, D. (2024). Why do people buy virtual clothes? *Journal of Consumer Behaviour*, *23*(3), 1389–1405.

Kumpajaya, A., & Dhewanto, W. (2015). *The acceptance of bitcoin in Indonesia: Extending TAM with IDT*. https://download.garuda.kemdikbud.go.id/article.php?article=1529750&val=2218&title=The%20Acceptance%20of%20Bitcoin%20in%20Indonesia%20Using%20Technology%20Acceptance%20Model

Lee, W., Xiong, L., & Hu, C. (2012). The effect of Facebook users' arousal and valence on intention to go to the festival: Applying an extension of the technology acceptance model. *International Journal of Hospitality Management*, *31*(3), 819–827.

Liao, Z., & Cheung, M. T. (2002). Internet-based e-banking and consumer attitudes: An empirical study. *Information & Management*, *39*(4), 283–295.

Limna, P., Kraiwanit, T., & Siripipatthanakul, S. (2022). The growing trend of digital economy: A review article. *International Journal of Computing Sciences Research*, 6, 1–11, https://doi.org/10.25147/ijcsr.2017.001.1.106

Liu, S., Perry, P., & Gadzinski, G. (2019). The implications of digital marketing on WeChat for luxury fashion brands in China. *Journal of Brand Management*, *26*(4), 395–409.

Lu, D., Lai, I. K. W., & Liu, Y. (2019). The consumer acceptance of smart product-service systems in sharing economy: The effects of perceived interactivity and particularity. *Sustainability*, *11*(3), 928.

Ma, C., Jin, Z., Mei, Z., Zhou, F., She, X., Huang, J., & Liu, D. (2022). Internet of Things background: An empirical study on the payment intention of central bank digital currency design. *Mobile Information Systems,* 2022(1), 4846372.

Marikyan, M., & Papagiannidis, P. (2021). Unified theory of acceptance and use of technology. *TheoryHub Book*.

Mayer, R. C., Davis, J. H., & Schoorman, F. D. (1995). An integrative model of organizational trust. *Academy of Management Review*, *20*(3), 709–734.

McCrindle. (2023). *Years of birth*. https://generationz.com.au/articles/years-of-birth/

McGorry, S. Y. (2000). Measurement in a cross-cultural environment: survey translation issues. *Qualitative Market Research: An International Journal*, *3*(2), 74–81.

Mendoza-Tello, J. C., Mora, H., Pujol-López, F. A., & Lytras, M. D. (2018). Social commerce as a driver to enhance trust and intention to use cryptocurrencies for electronic payments. *IEEE Access*, 6, 50737–50751.

Ministry of Education of the People's Republic of China. (2021). *Education statistics for* 2021. https://www.moe.gov.cn/jyb_sjzl/moe_560/2021/

Nakamoto, S. (2008). *Bitcoin: A peer-to-peer electronic cash system*. https://bitcoin.org/bitcoin.pdf

Ogunmola, G. A., & Das, U. (2024). Analyzing consumer perceptions and adoption intentions of central bank digital currency: A case of the digital rupee. *Digital Policy, Regulation and Governance*, *26*(4), 450–471.

Pavlou, P. A. (2003). Consumer acceptance of electronic commerce: Integrating trust and risk with the technology acceptance model. *International Journal of Electronic Commerce*, *7*(3), 101–134.

Payal, R., Sharma, N., & Dwivedi, Y. K. (2024). Unlocking the impact of brand engagement in the metaverse on Real-World purchase intentions: Analyzing Pre-Adoption behavior in a futuristic technology platform. *Electronic Commerce Research and Applications*, *65*, 101381.

Phuong, N. T. H., Thuy, N. D., Giang, T. L., Han, B. T. N., Hieu, T. H., & Long, N. T. (2022). Determinants of intention to use Fintech payment services: Evidence from Vietnam generation Z. *International Journal of Business, Economics and Law*, *26*(1), 354–366.

PWC. (2023). *Luxury market insights in Mainland China and Hong Kong: "Reinventing customer value for sustainable growth"*. https://www.pwccn.com/zh/industries/retail-and-consumer/publications/china-hk-luxury-market-insights-feb2023.html

Ringle, C. M., Wende, S., & Will, A. (2005). SmartPLS 2.0 (Beta). *SmartPLS, Hamburg*. www.smartpls.de

Rosário, A., & Raimundo, R. (2021). Consumer marketing strategy and E-commerce in the last decade: A literature review. *Journal of Theoretical and Applied Electronic Commerce Research*, *16*(7), 3003–3024.

Rossmannek, O., David, N. A., Schramm-Klein, H., & Van der Borgh, M. (2024). Customer misbehavior and service providers' risk perception in the sharing economy. *Journal of Business Research*, *170*, 114340.

Roussou, L., Stiakakis, E., & Sifaleras, A. (2019). An empirical study on the commercial adoption of digital currencies. *Information Systems and e-Business Management*, *17*(2), 223–259. https://doi.org/10.1007/s10257-019-00426-7

Saif Almuraqab, N. A. (2019). Predicting determinants of the intention to use digital currency in the UAE: An empirical study. *The Electronic Journal of Information Systems in Developing Countries*, *86*(3), e12125, https://doi.org/10.1002/isd2.12125

Sankar, T. R. (2021, July 22). Central bank digital currency – Is this the future of money. *Reserve Bank of India*.

Schlosser, A. E., White, T. B., & Lloyd, S. M. (2006). Converting web site visitors into buyers: how web site investment increases consumer trusting beliefs and online purchase intentions. *Journal of Marketing*, *70*(2), 133–148.

Schumacher, L. V. (2024). Central bank digital currencies (CBDCs): Exploring characteristics, risks and benefits. In L. V. Schumacher (Ed.), *Decoding digital assets: Distinguishing the dream from the dystopia in stablecoins, tokenized deposits, and central bank digital currencies* (pp. 81–157). Palgrave Macmillan. https://doi.org/10.1007/978-3-031-54601-3_12

Seyal, A. H., & Pijpers, G. M. (2004). Senior government executives' use of the Internet: A Bruneian scenario. *Behaviour & Information Technology*, *23*, 197–210.

Shahzad, F., Xiu, G., Wang, J., & Shahbaz, M. (2018). An empirical investigation on the adoption of cryptocurrencies among the people of mainland China. *Technology in Society*, *55*, 33–40.

Sohn, S. (2024). Consumer perceived risk of using autonomous retail technology. *Journal of Business Research*, *171*, 114389.

Stark, B. (2013). Is the corporate world ready for bitcoin. *Risk Management*, *60*(7), 6–9.

Statista. (2023). *Luxury goods market in China – Statistics & facts*. https://Luxury goods market in China – Statistics & facts | Statista

Stern, B. B., Royne, M. B., Stafford, T. F., & Bienstock, C. C. (2008). Consumer acceptance of online auctions: An extension and revision of the TAM. *Psychology & Marketing*, *25*(7), 619–636.

Sun, H., & Zhang, P. (2006). The role of moderating factors in user technology acceptance. *International Journal of Human-Computer Studies*, *64*(2), 53–78.

Surekha, G., Sri, M. R., Abhishek, B., & Reddy, B. V. G. S. (2024, May). Identification of Counterfeit Goods by Implementing Blockchain Technology. In *2024 5th International Conference for Emerging Technology (INCET)* (pp. 1–6). IEEE.

Temara, S. (2024). The ransomware epidemic: Recent cybersecurity incidents demystified. *Asian Journal of Advanced Research and Reports*, *18*(3), 1–16.

Thong, J. Y., Venkatesh, V., Xu, X., Hong, S. J., & Tam, K. Y. (2011). Consumer acceptance of personal information and communication technology services. *IEEE Transactions on Engineering Management*, *58*(4), 613–625.

Türker, C., Altay, B. C., & Okumuş, A. (2022). Understanding user acceptance of QR code mobile payment systems in Turkey: An extended TAM. *Technological Forecasting and Social Change*, *184*, 121968.

Venkatesh, V., & Davis, F. D. (2000). A theoretical extension of the technology acceptance model: Four longitudinal field studies. *Management Science*, *46*(2), 186–204, https://doi.org/10.1287/mnsc.46.2.186.11926

Venkatesh, V., Morris, M. G., Davis, G. B., & Davis, F. D. (2003). User acceptance of information technology: Toward a unified view. *MIS Quarterly*, 27(3), 425–478. https://doi.org/10.2307/30036540

Venkatesh, V., Thong, J. Y., & Xu, X. (2012). Consumer acceptance and use of information technology: Extending the unified theory of acceptance and use of technology. *MIS Quarterly, 36*(1), 157–178. https://doi.org/10.2307/41410412

Wang, Y., Meister, D., & Wang, Y. (2011). Reexamining Relative Advantage and Perceived Usefulness: An Empirical Study. *International Journal of Information and Communication Technology Education*, 7(1), 46–59. https://doi.org/10.4018/jicte.2011010105

Wang, Y., & Qiao, F. (2020). The symbolic meaning of luxury-lite fashion brands among younger Chinese consumers. *Journal of Fashion Marketing and Management: An International Journal*, *24*(1), 83–98.

Warkentin, M., Gefen, D., Pavlou, P. A., & Rose, G. M. (2002). Encouraging citizen adoption of e-government by building trust. *Electronic Markets*, *12*(3), 157–162.

Wong, K. K. K. (2013). Partial least squares structural equation modeling (PLS-SEM) techniques using SmartPLS. *Marketing Bulletin*, *24*(1), 1–32.

Yang, C. C., Yang, S. Y., & Chang, Y. C. (2023). Predicting older adults' mobile payment adoption: An extended TAM model. *International Journal of Environmental Research and Public Health*, *20*(2), 1391.

Yeoman, I., & McMahon-Beattie, U. (2018). The future of luxury: Mega drivers, new faces and scenarios. *Journal of Revenue and Pricing Management*, *17*, 204–217.

Yusuf, M., Rahmiati, R., & Thamrin, T. (2024). The influence of perceived usefulness, perceived ease of use, perceived risk on behavioral intention for QRIS user. *Marketing Management Studies*, *4*(2), 100–118.

Zatti, F., & Barresi, R. G. (Eds.). (2024). *Digital assets and the law: Fiat money in the era of digital currency*. Taylor & Francis.

10 Generation Z and Irrational Exuberance

Spending in the Present, Speculating and Investing for the Future

Jashim Khan and Russell Belk

Introduction

Generation Z was born between 1997 and 2012 and is 11–27 years old in 2024 (Snelders et al., 1992, p. 71). They are the first 'digitally native' generation, characterized by their tendency to thrive in the present, spend and save (Langford, 2024). Generation Z's tendency to live in the present influences their spending habits. For example, Generation Z prioritizes experiences over material possessions, leading them to spend money on travel, concerts and other memorable activities (Hodžić, 2024). They are also more inclined toward impulse buying, driven by the desire for instant gratification and constant exposure to online shopping (Djafarova & Bowes, 2021). The 24/7 access to technology and social media allows them to instantly share their experiential moments with their peers (Watkins, 2009). Unlike previous generations, Generation Z's spending habits prioritize experiences over material possessions (Li et al., 2009). They are more inclined to spend money and put weight on travel, concerts and other memorable activities rather than saving money than their parents and grandparents; this shift can be attributed to their desire for instant gratification (Dasilva et al., 2023). They are also exposed to 24/7 online shopping opportunities and the ability to instantly share and experience moments with their peers through technology and social media (Mason et al., 2022). Additionally, growing up in a fast-paced and uncertain world has made them prioritize enjoying the present moment rather than worrying about the future (Gama Filho & Hopkins, 2018). However, this tendency toward instant gratification can negatively affect their financial stability. Generation Z's impulse buying and focus on immediate enjoyment can lead to overspending and a lack of savings (Gebeyehu & Mavridis, 2023). By prioritizing experiences and instant gratification, they build long-term economic security and their ability to save for the future or handle unexpected expenses (Koto, 2023). Compared to past generations, a paradox is that Generation Z prioritizes their spending by choosing value-for-money purchases, evident in the desire for light or little luxuries, in which Generation Z is the largest segment (Zuo et al., forthcoming). These patterns could

DOI: 10.4324/9781003425021-10

change given their age at this writing (teens and early 20s), but many seem well-entrenched.

Generation Z, the largest demographic group in the emerging middle class, drives demand for little luxury brands (von Wallpach et al., 2020); they are digitally connected, avid users of NFTs and third-party digital payments and potential digital currency users. They no longer view luxury as a distinctive and costly symbol of status, unlike their parents, who associated luxury with social standing (Yeoman & McMahon-Beattie, 2018). Generation Z prioritizes everyday luxuries and carefully evaluates the value of status-enhancing luxury items before purchasing. Generation Z was the largest segment that bought secondary-line luxury brands that befitted their 'living in the present' lifestyle. Secondary-line brands are considered a more affordable option, designated as a light luxury, and are produced by high-end firms as a distinct line with reduced prices compared to their trademark line, which shows their lifestyle and values (Feng, 2024).

Generation Z, characterized by their technological proficiency, digital connectivity and concern for personal and community well-being, prioritizes value for money and economic benefit (Khan & Rundle-Thiele, 2019). Prioritizing value for money significantly impacts their lifestyle. Generation Z is prudent in balancing financial advantage (value for money) and a hedonist lifestyle (Faschan et al., 2020) while believing in the present life. With their focus on value for money, Generation Z is more inclined toward purchasing secondary-line luxury brands that offer reduced prices than first-line brands. This shift has forced high-end firms to adapt and create more affordable options, known as light luxury, to cater to the preferences and spending habits of this digitally native generation. Light luxury refers to the luxury market segment offering more affordable options without compromising quality or style. This appeals to Generation Z because it allows them to experience the prestige and exclusivity of luxury brands while still being mindful of their money. By offering reduced prices, light luxury brands align with Generation Z's value-for-money mindset, enabling them to indulge in the present. The economic benefit serves one's self-financial interests, whereas the hedonist lifestyle optimizes the ability to derive pleasure from life by embracing the present moment (Lelkes, 2021). Ultimately, this gives Generation Z the best of both worlds: the ability to save money while also indulging in luxury. The essence of living in the present moment is based on mindful thinking—a customer-centric approach to economic sustainability (Mohammad et al., 2021; Sheth et al., 2011). However, Generation Z is pursuing value for money in their purchases and embracing digital money, often viewed while living under the illusion of overestimating the exuberance of money. Khan et al. (2012) draw the example that people tend to overestimate the amount of money they think they have rather than what they have in their accounts using debit cards. Overestimating wealth is also a money illusion (see Mishra et al., 2006). Digital money can lead to financial instability and irresponsible spending because of money illusion. Generation Z's reliance on digital transactions and the ease of making purchases can create a false sense of wealth, causing them to overspend and accumulate debt (Gebeyehu & Mavridis, 2023). Generation Z, equipped with digital money, may also be mindful of their financial situation and practice responsible money management to avoid falling into financial traps and jeopardizing their long-term economic well-being (Kusumawardhany, 2022).

The lifestyle perspective of living in the moment significantly influences the thoughts and behavior of Generation Z consumers (Zarra, 2017). This lifestyle perspective is driven by several factors such as the global consumer culture, the desire for immediate gratification and the influence of social media in promoting a 'YOLO' (you only live once) mentality (Jordan & Nuringsih, 2023). Social media plays a pivotal role in shaping the 'YOLO' mentality among young Generation Z consumers (Paramita et al., 2024). Through curated posts and influencers showcasing a glamorous and adventurous lifestyle, social media platforms create a sense of FOMO (fear of missing out), driving individuals to prioritize immediate experiences and live in the present moment (Zhang et al., 2024). This contrasts with the previous generation, prioritizing values such as harmony with nature, respecting order, interdependence, self-view, modesty and long-term orientation (Zhang, 1992). These principles foster a frugal and prudent attitude toward saving for the future (Garner, 2005). Influenced by social media and the 'YOLO' and 'FOMO' mentality, they seek immediate gratification. The shift in values reflects a growing emphasis on global consumer culture and a departure from the traditional principles of thrift and frugality. Social media pervades globally in one way or another. Young Chinese consumers' lifestyles have an additional ingredient that was influenced by China's rapid economic growth and globalization over the past two decades. These changes have led to shifts in consumer cultures and values, including an increase in consumption and self-gratification (Swanson, 1995; Wang & Qiao, 2020; Gentina & Tang, 2024). Advertising in mass media, with a focus on materialism and consumption culture, is believed to be the main driving factor behind lifestyle choices (Li et al., 2009). Secondly, affluent young Chinese consumers are given a larger amount of pocket money compared to what their parents received (Huang et al., 2024), who experienced or were aware of financial difficulties during their upbringing and developed a frugal mindset to avoid excessive self-gratification. Some specific lifestyle shifts among young consumers include a greater emphasis on luxury brands and status symbols, a desire for unique and personalized experiences, increased online shopping and e-commerce and a shift toward a more global consumer culture mindset (Pedro et al., 2024). These changes have resulted in a significant increase in consumer spending and a shift away from the traditional values of thrift and frugality. According to Yang et al. (2022), young consumers have been raised in a carefree environment and possess a greater ability to seize chances and make intelligent economic decisions that satisfy their immediate goals. This involves employing astute financial decision-making and giving priority to products that offer good value for the money spent (Hodžić, 2024). Young, smart consumer behavior is characterized by a focus on the present moment, motivation by a flexible and enjoyable lifestyle, and at the same time, consciousness about spending wisely. They prioritize light indulgences that provide maximum satisfaction while still being mindful of getting good value for their money. (Thompson, 2011; Von Wallpach et al., 2020). Young consumers' use of luxury goods in a hedonistic lifestyle is not driven by decadence and extravagance (See Soper, 1990). Instead, it is a reflective approach to life, focusing on deriving pleasure for oneself and others without causing harm to oneself or others (Onfray, 2015). According to the philosophy of joyful utilitarianism (as described by Burke, 2008), living in the moment refers to the "totality of the individual's views of their psychological future and past existing at a given point of present time" (see Lewin, 1951, p. 75). It is not harboring concerns or anxieties about the future; instead, it derives pleasure from each moment that embraces the present.

Generation Z's attitudes toward money, especially focusing on digital assets, could have long-term effects on Generation Z's financial stability and wealth accumulation by prioritizing financial experiences and digital possessions over financial assets, as these digital assets may not hold long-term value or provide a safety net in times of economic uncertainty (Lekshmi et al., 2024). Additionally, their emphasis on immediate gratification and pleasure-seeking may hinder their ability to save and invest for the future, potentially impacting their long-term financial goals and overall financial well-being. The prevalence of digital money has influenced Generation Z's attitudes toward saving by promoting a culture of immediate gratification and pleasure-seeking (Kulsum, 2024). With the ease and convenience of digital transactions, young consumers are more inclined to prioritize experiences and instant enjoyment over long-term financial goals, potentially undermining their ability to accumulate wealth and establish financial stability for the future. Understanding their focus on deriving maximum satisfaction from light indulgences while still seeking good value for their money allows businesses to tailor their products and marketing strategies to meet these specific needs. Additionally, their emphasis on digital assets and experiences suggests a shift away from traditional materialistic values, prompting companies to explore innovative ways to offer unique and memorable experiences that align with Generation Z's values (Oberoi & Puranik, 2024). Generation Z's consumer behavior demonstrates a preference for digital assets over cash. They prioritize experiential consumption and digital possessions that provide immediate gratification and pleasure rather than focusing on long-term financial goals and accumulating tangible wealth. This shift in consumer behavior poses challenges for industries and marketers, as they need to adapt their strategies to cater to Generation Z's desire for unique and memorable experiences that align with their values.

This chapter discusses embracing the present moment as a significant element of modern Generation Z's consumer behavior. They emphasize value for their money. Living in the present entails a hedonistic lifestyle. Consumer behaviors influenced by living in the present moment include impulse purchases, experiential spending (such as travel and entertainment), and a greater emphasis on the immediate gratification of products and services rather than long-term investments. The lifestyle requires a balance between the mindset of living in the present and the motivation to save for the future. This chapter offers valuable insights into Generation Z's consumption patterns, who have deliberately established their own consumer behavior identity, such as smart consumerism. Examples of how Generation Z practices smart consumerism include researching and comparing prices before making a purchase, seeking out discounts and deals, prioritizing quality over quantity and supporting sustainable and ethical brands. They are also more likely to engage with online reviews and recommendations from influencers or peers to make informed decisions. (Wang & Qiao, 2020). Embracing the present moment has both benefits and drawbacks. On the one hand, it allows Generation Z to derive maximum pleasure and satisfaction from their purchases, prioritizing their well-being and enjoyment. On the other hand, this focus on the present moment may lead to impulsive buying decisions and a lack of consideration for long-term financial planning and savings. However, prioritizing well-being and enjoyment in consumer behavior can also result in excessive spending and financial instability. In the pursuit of immediate gratification, Generation Z may overlook the importance of saving for future goals and emergencies, potentially leading to financial stress and limited opportunities for long-term financial growth. For an account of the particular irrational exuberance leading up to 2022, see Chandra and Belk (2022).

Embracing the Present

Living in the present entails a focused mindset on the present, shaped by external forces like economic, technological and social development. Economic development plays a significant role in shaping our mindset toward living in the present. It can create opportunities for financial stability and personal growth, allowing individuals to prioritize their immediate needs and desires. However, it can also lead to a constant pursuit of materialistic goals and pleasure-seeking, making it challenging to fully embrace the present moment.

Generation Z grew up with mobile payments and the ease of managing funds electronically (Xie, 2020). Social development also plays a crucial role in shaping our mindset toward living in the present. The rise of social media and constant connectivity has created a culture of comparison and FOMO, where individuals feel pressured to constantly be aware of what others are doing and achieve a certain level of social comparison (Fransiati et al., 2024). Living in the present may pressure to focus on the present, striving for a certain lifestyle or image and neglecting the future. One contributing factor is the ease of use of third-party digital payment and digital currencies, and the availability of funds as pocket money compared to the previous generation remains the driver of seizing the current moment to fully experience and savor life rather than postponing it for the future (Park, 2021). Money in digital form influences psychological ownership and spending (Khan & Belk, 2024) through affording living in the present. Psychological ownership refers to the feeling of possessing and having control over an object or experience (Krishna et al., 2024). In the context of digital assets, the ease of access and control over funds can enhance this sense of psychological ownership, making individuals more inclined to spend and enjoy their resources in the present moment (Khan & Belk, forthcoming). By having digital assets readily available, individuals may feel a stronger sense of ownership and agency, leading to a greater desire to seize the current moment and prioritize experiences over saving for the future (Kirk & Swain, 2018). Digital money lacks touchability, and perceptions of loss of funds are minimized with digital money (Khan & Belk, forthcoming). Because cash is tangible, digital money is easy to spend and the pain of paying is obscured (Khan, 2011).

Generation Z, who grew up knowing digital money, can consciously think about moments of joy and lack the conscious allotment of feeling the pain of paying (Raghubir & Srivastava, 2008). Compared to previous generations, Generation Z tends to prioritize immediate gratification and experiences over saving for the future. The ease of access and control over digital funds enhances their sense of psychological ownership and agency, leading them to prioritize the present moment and prioritize experiences over long-term savings. This results in a lack of worry about the possibility of not having the funds. The human mind naturally shifts between the past, present and future, which cognitive scientists call temporal junctures (Redshaw & Suddendorf, 2020). Building upon the works of Gazzaniga (2008) and Redshaw and Suddendorf (2020), we define living in the present as a mental state involving an individual's psychological past and future at a given time. Buddhists speak of pursuing enlightenment through transcendence, e.g., anatta, to achieve meaningfulness in life. The perspective of living in the present determines how we react to digital and cash assets. Digital assets are fluid, flowing within digitally connected devices, and remain half-full or half-empty as those numbers may not be fully realized since this money is numbers on screen. By contrast, cash is physical, and the feeling of money is memorable and allows rehearsal every time one spends (Soman, 2001). While digital assets may lack the tangible nature and emotional impact of cash, they offer a level of convenience and control that can enhance an individual's sense of ownership and agency. With digital money, the pain of paying is obscured, making it easier to spend and prioritize experiences in the present moment. However, this can also lead to a lack of conscious allotment and a diminished sense of the value of money. According to Thomala (2023), Generation Z prioritizes immediate gratification with money enjoying the moment and allocates less money toward savings, instead spending more on leisure activities and hobbies than earlier generations. This is because they have been raised in a stable economic environment, striving for a high standard of living (Jiang & Shan, 2018). Nevertheless, the purchasing decisions of young consumers are also influenced by traditional values, including frugal spending (Zhou & Nakamoto, 2001; Li et al., 2009; Jiang & Shan, 2018). The amalgamation of past values and living in the present results in smart consumerism, which is shaped by knowing the worth of money spent on purchases. In line with this reasoning, this research explores the role of digital money in influencing Generation Z's perception of living in the present. The influence of digital money on Generation Z's perception of living in the present is profound. Digital money offers convenience and control, allowing young consumers to prioritize experiences in the present moment. However, this ease of spending can lead to a diminished sense of the value of money and a tendency to prioritize immediate gratification over long-term savings. Despite this, Generation Z's purchasing decisions are still influenced by traditional values, resulting in a unique blend of smart consumerism that recognizes the worth of money spent on purchases (Figure 10.1).

The word map cloud shows the most frequent keyword voiced in public platforms is 'living in the present' in the TikTok platform. The word moment emphasizes its prominence and relevance in contemporary discourse. The most striking words are 'live' and 'present,' emphasizing the importance of experiencing life fully and embracing the moment. The words 'life,' 'day,' and 'time' suggest a sense of urgency, reinforcing that life is fleeting and every moment should be cherished. Positive words such as 'good,' 'well' and 'happy' suggest that living in the present is often associated with happiness and joy. In addition, the emphasis on 'now,' 'today' and 'tomorrow' suggests a preoccupation with the immediate and near future, which is consistent with the hedonistic desire for instant gratification.

Figure 10.1 Word Cloud 1

Digital Money and Its Value in Purchase

Recent research indicates that Generation Z exhibits lower patience when purchasing decisions than preceding generations. Because of their limited incomes, they prioritize rapid gratification and are very responsive to price fluctuations. However, prioritizing rapid gratification can lead to impulsive purchasing decisions and disregarding long-term consequences. Generation Z may be more susceptible to making choices based solely on immediate desires, which can result in financial instability and regret in the future. They need to develop patience and a balanced approach to decision-making to ensure their long-term financial well-being. Young customers rely on their parents' financial assistance and seek out reasonably priced luxury items and products that provide excellent value for their money. Impulsive purchasing decisions can lead to a cycle of debt and financial instability for Generation Z. By prioritizing immediate desires over long-term financial goals, they may find themselves accumulating credit card debt or falling behind on bills. This can have a negative impact on their credit scores and limit their ability to secure loans or make major purchases in the future. It can also lead to depression and feelings of helplessness.

The notion of 'value for money' is essential for young consumers, as it entails the prudent utilization of resources while reducing inefficiency and permitting a certain degree of indulgence. The concept of 'value for money' is crucial for young consumers as it encompasses not only the price they pay for a product or service but also the quality and utility they receive in return. Young customers are more likely to prioritize products that offer a balance between affordability and durability, ensuring that they get the most out of their limited resources. By making informed choices based on value for money, Generation Z can avoid impulsive purchases and make decisions that align with their long-term financial goals, ultimately promoting financial stability and responsible consumption. Research has indicated that this attribute significantly influences young consumers' purchase choices, especially in countries such as Hong Kong and the United States. Furthermore, luxury businesses must consider the symbolic/emotional value and utilitarian/economic value buyers desire in their products. Young consumers, particularly in emerging nations, prioritize getting good value for their money because they have less purchasing power. Cost-effectiveness evaluations can also impact the acquisition of high-end goods (Figure 10.2).

The words 'money' and 'value' highlight the central theme, emphasizing the importance of economic value and economic factors in people's lives. The words 'people' and 'life' suggest a broad social context, suggesting that discussions about money and value are integral to understanding human behavior and quality of life. In contrast, ancillary terms such as 'value,' 'make,' 'coin' and 'cent' suggest a focus on the tangible and measurable aspects of money, reflecting how individuals assess and accumulate wealth. Terms such as 'love,' 'feeling' and 'good' reflect emotional and qualitative dimensions,

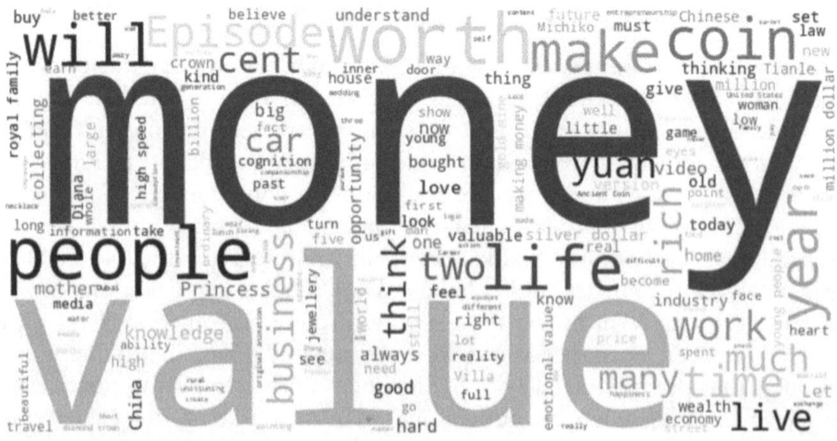

Figure 10.2 Word Cloud 2

suggesting that "money and value are not only about financial metrics but also about how they affect people's emotions and well-being." Words such as 'wealth' and 'future' also suggest an expectation that money is seen as a means of achieving goals, creating opportunities and securing a better future. This dovetails with broader savvy consumerism, where value for money and strategic financial decisions play a crucial role. However, work by Chandra and Belk (2024) suggests that Generation Z's interest in NFTs and cryptocurrencies is fueled more by a speculative desire to become rich rather than save for a comfortable retirement. As such the multiplied volatility of these digital assets (most NFTs are purchased and valued in digital currencies) is attractive rather than off-putting.

Hedonistic Lifestyle

Generation Z is confronted with substantial societal expectations to conform to the rapid development of contemporary culture. This rapid cultural development can create a sense of pressure and confusion for young people as they navigate their own identity formation. The constant exposure to new trends, technologies and social norms can make it challenging for them to develop a strong and authentic sense of self. As a result, they have placed higher importance on present-oriented life and instant gratification rather than considering potential long-term effects. Researchers have discovered that youthful consumers, compared to previous generations, prioritize present enjoyment and give less consideration to future consequences. Some specific societal expectations that contemporary youth face today include the pressure to succeed academically, the need to have a strong online presence on social media platforms and the expectation to conform to certain beauty standards. These expectations can contribute to the sense of pressure and confusion that young people experience as they try to navigate their identity formation. The hedonistic lifestyle prioritizes self-fulfillment, enjoyment of the present moment and engaging with others to avoid creating harm. In contrast to other approaches to self-fulfillment, such as pursuing long-term goals or prioritizing personal growth, the hedonistic lifestyle emphasizes immediate pleasure and avoiding negative consequences (Sandua, 2024). This can provide a temporary sense of gratification but may hinder long-term personal development and fulfillment (Ponsignon et al., 2024). Research (Chen, 2024; Fernandes & Oliveira, 2024) has indicated that young consumers, specifically, hold a favorable perception of this mentality, prioritizing enjoyment and being fully engaged in the present. However, as young consumers amass income, their indulgent impulses for consumption change toward tangible assets such as automobiles and residences, influenced by societal expectations and concerns about the future. Studies (Colombo et al., 2024; Scharbert et al., 2024) indicate that young customers who place a high value on experiencing the current moment are more inclined to actively search for products that can generate positive and joyful memories. However, prioritizing immediate pleasure over long-term goals can lead to a lack of discipline and delayed gratification. This can hinder personal growth and development, as well as limit opportunities for future success and fulfillment. Additionally, constantly seeking instant gratification can create a cycle of dependency and impulsivity, making it difficult to make thoughtful and informed decisions (Figure 10.3).

The word cloud on 'hedonism' reveals a complex and multifaceted perspective on the pursuit of pleasure and luxury. The central prominence of 'hedonism' itself suggests a primary concern with the concept. The most notable words such as 'discipline' and 'inspection' suggest a critical governmental attitude and reflect the scrutiny and control associated with the hedonistic

Figure 10.3 Word Cloud 3

behavior of officials. Terms such as 'people,' 'typical' and 'day' indicate the prevalence of hedonism in everyday life, suggesting that hedonistic desires are a universal human trait. Words such as 'luxury,' 'spirituality' and 'happiness' reflect hedonism's emotional and cultural dimensions, emphasizing its role in the pursuit of pleasure and luxury.

Conclusion

This study explored Generation Z's lifestyle, which focused on living in the present and the desire to get the most value for one's money, which influenced this connection. The study demonstrates that focusing on the present moment is related to a hedonist lifestyle, though Generation Z has an aspiration to obtain optimal value for one's money. The research indicates that younger consumers belonging to Generation Z have distinct views toward consuming compared to their parents. They demonstrate a predilection for adventures, a high living standard and a consciousness about money. While both living in the moment and a hedonist lifestyle value enjoyment and pleasure, living in the moment places a greater emphasis on mindfulness, presence and emotional awareness. It seeks to cultivate a balanced approach to experiencing life's pleasures while maintaining well-being. In contrast, hedonism tends to prioritize immediate gratification and sensory pleasures as the primary pursuit in life, sometimes at the expense of long-term fulfillment and consequences. Most importantly, the presence of value-for-money consciousness influences the interactions between living in the present and pursuing a hedonist lifestyle

References

Burke, T. P. (2008). Bentham, Jeremy (1748–1832). In Hamowy, R. (Ed.), *Nozick, Robert (1938–2002)*. SAGE Publications.

Chandra, Y., & Belk, R. (2022, October 3). Is that jpeg worth 70 million dollars? Value construction and perceptions of non-fungible tokens. *SSRN Electronic Journal*. https://doi.org/10.2139/ssrn.4830177

Chandra, Y., & Belk, R. (2024). Is That JPEG Worth 70 Million Dollars? Value Creation and Perceptions of Non-Fungible Tokens in a Bubble Economy. *SSRN Electronic Journal*. https://doi.org/10.2139/ssrn.4830177

Chen, W. (2024, July). Behavioral and psychological of the metamorphosis of hedonistic consumption in Asian cultures-with a focus on young consumers (Z generation). In *2024 9th International Conference on Social Sciences and Economic Development (ICSSED 2024)* (pp. 257–264). Atlantis Press.

Colombo, D., Pavani, J. B., Quoidbach, J., Baños, R. M., Folgado-Alufre, M., & Botella, C. (2024). Savouring the present to better recall the past. *Journal of Happiness Studies*, *25*(1), 20.

Dasilva, N. E., Hardanti, Y. R., & Harnoto, L. B. (2023). The phenomenon of the consumptive culture of Generation Z in Cilandak sub district in the perspective of behavioral Economics in the new normal order. In T. Handono Eko Prabowo (Ed.), *Shaping the sustainable future: Trends and insights in economics, business, management, and information technology* (p. 411). Sanata Dharma University.

Djafarova, E., & Bowes, T. (2021). 'Instagram made me buy it': Generation Z impulse purchases in fashion industry. *Journal of Retailing and Consumer Services, 59*, 102345.

Faschan, M., Chailan, C., & Huaman-Ramirez, R. (2020). Emerging adults' luxury fashion brand value perceptions: A cross-cultural comparison between Germany and China. *Journal of Global Fashion Marketing, 11*(3), 207–231.

Feng, S. (2024). *The transformation of luxury in post-consumerism* (Doctoral dissertation, Durham University).

Fernandes, T., & Oliveira, R. (2024). Brands as drivers of social media fatigue and its effects on users' disengagement: The perspective of young consumers. *Young Consumers, 25*(5), 625–644. https://doi.org/10.1108/YC-09-2023-1873

Fransiati, S., Aini, N. A., Ar-Rasyid, M. F., Safitri, S. A., & Septiani, R. (2024). Group guidance in helping to overcome the phenomenon offear of missingout in Generation Z. *BICC Proceedings, 2*, 187–191.

Gama Filho, J., & Hopkins, M. (2018). *Filling the void: Investigating the impact of the digital society on Generation Z's relationships*. Lund University (Dissertations) https://lup.lub.lu.se/luur/download?func=downloadFile&recordOId=8946277&fileOId=8946287

Garner, J. (2005). *The rise of the Chinese consumer: Theory and evidence*. John Wiley & Sons.

Gazzaniga, M. (2008). *Human: The science behind what makes us unique*. HarperCollinsPublishers (New Zealand) Limited.

Gebeyehu, F., & Mavridis, A. (2023). *Buy now, pay later: Assessing the financial and behavioral omplications for Gen-Z consumers in the USA*. In *Department of Industrial Economics at Blekinge Institute of Technology* [MBA Thesis]. Blekinge Institute of Technology. https://www.diva-portal.org/smash/get/diva2:1804246/FULLTEXT01.pdf

Gentina, E., & Tang, T. L. P. (2024). Youth materialism and consumer ethics: Do Gen Z adolescents' self-concepts (power and self-esteem) vary across cultures (China vs. France)? *Ethics & Behavior, 34*(2), 120–150.

Hodžić, A. (2024). *Impact of Generation Z values and attitudes on their consumer behavior* (Doctoral dissertation, [A. Hodžić]).

Huang, Y., Zhou, K., Yang, Y., & Xu, M. (2024). "Privileged adult": How relationship with parents influences adult's status consumption. *Family Relations, 73*(3), 1727–1745. https://doi.org/10.1111/fare.13005

Jiang, L., & Shan, J. (2018). Heterogeneity of luxury value perception: A generational comparison in China. *International Marketing Review, 35*(3), 458–474.

Jordan, A., & Nuringsih, K. (2023). Understanding financial behavior in Generation Z. *International Journal, 2535*, 2546.

Khan, J. (2011). *Cash or card: Consumer perceptions of payment modes*. Openrepository.aut.ac.nz. https://openrepository.aut.ac.nz/handle/10292/3937

Khan, J., & Belk, R. (forthcoming). Money you could touch: Cash and psychological ownership. *Qualitative Market Research an International Journal*. https://doi.org/10.1108/qmr-04-2023-0049

Khan, J., Belk, R., Craig-Lees, M., & Marshall, R. (2012). *Cash or Card: Perceptions of Payment Mode*. In *Australia New Zealand Marketing Academy Conference*, Adelaide, Australia.

Khan, J., & Rundle-Thiele, S. (2019). Factors explaining shared clothes consumption in China: Individual benefit or planet concern? *International Journal of Nonprofit and Voluntary Sector Marketing*, *24*(4), e1652.

Kirk, C. P., & Swain, S. D. (2018). Consumer psychological ownership of digital technology. In J. Peck & S. Shu (Eds.), *Psychological ownership and consumer behavior* (pp. 69–90). Springer. https://doi.org/10.1007/978-3-319-77158-8_5

Koto, M. (2023). Analysis of factors influencing digital financial literacy levels: A case study on Gen Y and Gen Z spending behavior. *International Journal Reglement & Society (IJRS)*, *4*(2), 110–119.

Krishna, A., Luangrath, A. W., & Peck, J. (2024). A review of touch research in consumer psychology. *Journal of Consumer Psychology*, *34*(2), 359–381.

Kusumawardhany, P. A. (2022). Frugal Lifestyle Trend Among Generation Z. In *Advances in economics, business and management research/advances in economics, business and management research* (pp. 331–338). https://doi.org/10.2991/978-94-6463-008-4_43

Kulsum, S. J. (2024). Analyzing the factors that influence Generation Z in making digital investments in the era of digitalization (case study: Universitas Terbuka students). *International Journal of Current Economics & Business Ventures*, *4*(2), 1–14.

Langford, B. (2024). *Intergenerational conflict and authentic youth experience: Adults denigrating young people*. Taylor & Francis.

Lekshmi, R. S., Jawaharrani, K., Vijayakanthan, S., Nirmala, G., Dheenadayalan, K., & Vasantha, S. (2024). Original research article digital assets for digital natives: Exploring familiarity and preference for cryptocurrency among millennials and Gen Z. *Journal of Autonomous Intelligence*, *7*(3), 1–6.

Lelkes, O. (2021). A flourishing life: Living well and doing well. In *Sustainable hedonism* (pp. 85–106). Bristol University Press. Retrieved Oct 25, 2024, from https://doi.org/10.51952/9781529218008.ch005

Lewin, K. (1951). *Field theory in social sciences*. Harper.

Li, D., Jiang, Y., An, S., Shen, Z., & Jin, W. (2009). The influence of money attitudes on young Chinese consumers' compulsive buying. *Young Consumers*, *10*(2), 98–109.

Mason, M. C., Zamparo, G., Marini, A., & Ameen, N. (2022). Glued to your phone? Generation Z's smartphone addiction and online compulsive buying. *Computers in Human Behavior*, *136*, 107404.

Mishra, H., Mishra, A., & Nayakankuppam, D. (2006). Money: A bias for the whole. *Journal of Consumer Research*, *32*(4), 541–549.

Mohammad, J., Quoquab, F., & Mohamed Sadom, N. Z. (2021). Mindful consumption of second-hand clothing: The role of eWOM, attitude and consumer engagement. *Journal of Fashion Marketing and Management: An International Journal*, *25*(3), 482–510.

Oberoi, S., & Puranik, M. (2024). Digital finance and the perspective of Gen-Z cohort: A review. *IPE Journal of Management*, *14*(1), 55–72.

Onfray, M. (2015). *A hedonist manifesto: The power to exist*. Columbia University Press.

Paramita, C., Supriyanto, C., & Putra, K. R. (2024). Comparative analysis of YOLOv5 and YOLOv8 cigarette detection in social media content. *Scientific Journal of Informatics*, *11*(2), 341–352.

Park, H. Y. (2021). How consumers spend and distribute money tainted by anger. *Journal of Distribution Science*, *19*(7), 51–59.

Pedro, Y., Friedmann, E., & Loureiro, S. M. C. (2024). High-end fashion as a social phenomenon: Exploring the perceptions of designers and consumers. *Journal of Retailing and Consumer Services*, *79*, 103877.

Ponsignon, F., Bauman, M., & Lunardo, R. (2024). Seeking relief or reward? A utilitarianhedonic journey perspective on escapism. *European Journal of Marketing*, *58*(6), 1543–1565. https://doi.org/10.1108/EJM-03-2022-0216

Raghubir, P., & Srivastava, J. (2008). Monopoly money: The effect of payment coupling and form on spending behavior. *Journal of Experimental Psychology: Applied*, *14*(3), 213.

Redshaw, J., & Suddendorf, T. (2020). Temporal junctures in the mind. *Trends in Cognitive Sciences*, *24*(1), 52–64.

Sandua, D. (2024). *The modern hedonist: Strategies for living fully*. Barnes & Nobles.

Scharbert, J., Utesch, K., Reiter, T., ter Horst, J., van Zalk, M., Back, M. D., & Rau, R. (2024). If you were happy and you know it, clap your hands! Testing the peak-end rule for retrospective judgments of well-being in everyday life. *European Journal of Personality*. https://doi.org/10.1177/08902070241235969.

Sheth, J. N., Sethia, N. K., & Srinivas, S. (2011). Mindful consumption: A customer-centric approach to sustainability. *Journal of the Academy of Marketing Science*, *39*, 21–39.

Soman, D. (2001). The mental accounting of sunk time costs: Why time is not like money. *Journal of Behavioral Decision Making*, *14*(3), 169–185.

Soper, K. (1990). *Troubled pleasures: writings on politics, gender and hedonism*. Verso.

Snelders, H. M. J. J., Hussein, G., Lea, S. E., & Webley, P. (1992). The polymorphous concept of money. *Journal of Economic Psychology*, *13*(1), 71–92.

Swanson, L. A. (1995). A longitudinal look at latitudinal influence on advertising in China. *International Journal of Advertising*, *14*(3), 277–294.

Thomala, L. (2023). *Luxury marketing in China*. https://www-statista-com.surrey.idm.oclc.org/topics/9835/luxury-marketing-in-china/#topicOverview

Thompson, M. (2011). Chinese hedonic values and the Chinese classical virtues: Managing the tension. *Journal of Management Development*, *30*(7/8), 709–723.

Von Wallpach, S., Hemetsberger, A., Thomsen, T. U., & Belk, R. W. (2020). Moments of luxury–A qualitative account of the experiential essence of luxury. *Journal of Business Research*, *116*, 491–502.

Wang, Y., & Qiao, F. (2020). The symbolic meaning of luxury-lite fashion brands among younger Chinese consumers. *Journal of Fashion Marketing and Management: An International Journal*, *24*(1), 83–98.

Watkins, S. C. (2009). *The young and the digital: What the migration to social-network sites, games, and anytime, anywhere media means for our future*. Beacon Press.

Xie, L. (2020). The growth, risks and benefits, and problems of payment apps (Doctoral dissertation). Wenzhou-Kean University, Zhejiang, P. R. China.

Yang, H., Cheng, J., Schaefer, A. D., & Kojo, S. (2022). Influencing factors of Chinese consumers' purchase intention towards sustainable luxury. *Asia Pacific Journal of Marketing and Logistics*, *36*(9), 2054–2067. https://doi.org/10.1108/APJML-03-2022-0198

Yeoman, I., & McMahon-Beattie, U. (2018). The future of luxury: Mega drivers, new faces and scenarios. *Journal of Revenue and Pricing Management*, *17*, 204–217.

Zarra, E. J. (2017). *Helping parents understand the minds and hearts of Generation Z*. Rowman & Littlefield.
Zhang, W., He, L., Chen, Y., & Gao, X. (2024). The relationship between Big Five personality traits and fear of missing out: A meta-analysis. *Personality and Individual Differences*, *230*, 112788.
Zhang, X. (1992). *Chinese children's evaluations of self and others: Self-enhancement or other-enhancement?* The University of Texas at Austin.
Zhou, Z., & Nakamoto, K. (2001). Price perceptions: A cross-national study between American and Chinese young consumers. *Advances in Consumer Research*, *28*(1), 161.
Zuo, N., Khan, J., & Zhao, M. (forthcoming). When East meets the West: Smart consumerism and western luxury brands.

11 Digital Currency Issues in the Metaverse

Jashim Khan, Russell Belk, Ansar Abbass and Khalid Mehmood

Introduction

Intimation of the real world in the metaverse is accomplished through a virtual world that, to varying degrees, mimics the real world (Aysan et al., 2024; Belk, 2024). Here, an individual communicates with others and performs real-life activities such as shopping, playing, meeting and driving. Expandability refers to possibilities in the metaverse that are not available in the physical world, particularly in imaginary tales, such as digital acting through a digital entity. On the other hand, immersive interaction in the metaverse outlines social communication via a digital entity (i.e., an avatar) instead of more veridical personas. This interaction is aimed at socialization to build a social profile, sharing thoughts through posts/comments and interacting with others in the metaverse.

The metaverse is not limited to these characteristics but enhances user experiences at the next level. For instance, people spend their cyber-life conducting business, making friends and playing for entertainment, parallel to real life. All these functions offer benefits to the physical person and, similarly, evoke security and privacy risks, such as a single physical person building their digital entity (i.e., avatar) with their personal information where risk is associated with leakage of personal information, data theft, unauthorized access, insecure design, eavesdropping, phishing. This data formation used in the metaverse for performing activities as in real life varies from consumer to consumer (see Figure 11.1). Notably, digital currency transactions are executed with personal data in the metaverse, which raises more concerns about security and privacy. Furthermore, the metaverse is less familiar in the current digital era due to its nascent advent, which causes problems that we have never experienced before. Therefore, it is challenging for scholars and practitioners to understand this metaverse of privacy and security issues. This chapter focuses on digital currencies, security and privacy concerns, which are essential for every meta-user for the smooth process of metaverse utilization.

DOI: 10.4324/9781003425021-11

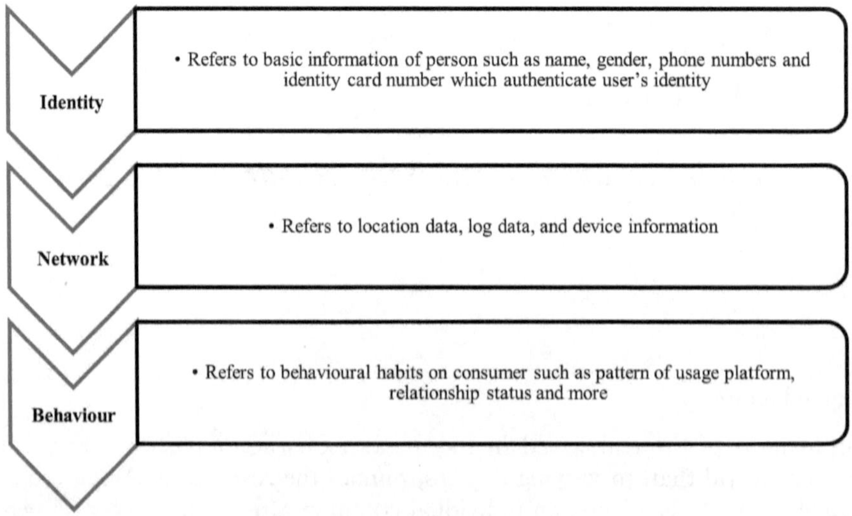

Figure 11.1 Personal Data Formation in the Metaverse

Understanding of Digital Currencies in the Metaverse

Digital currencies are considered digital assets, which rely on the technical design of the payment practice instead of issuers such as a country's central authority. Digital currencies offer value for peer-to-peer (P2P) payments verified without any third party, such as banks, credit card companies and governments (a central authority). These record-based mechanisms deal with payment transactions and ensure the availability of the balance using a 'blockchain.' Blockchains facilitate the metaverse transaction, preventing fraud, spurring the speed of transactions and reducing costs and verification procedures. Digital currencies perform transactions in the metaverse, as shown in Figure 11.2.

Next, we discuss the popular currencies in the Metaverse.

Non-fungible Tokens

NFTs (non-fungible tokens) are digital tokens based on blockchain technology with unique metadata that differentiate them from other tokens (Mazur & Polyzos, 2024). As their name suggests, NFTs are not fungible due to their uniqueness, while cryptocurrencies are fungible and can easily be exchanged and transferred. Elon Musk stated that NFTs are much more multifarious and have specific information (e.g., rare collectibles) (Barbosa, 2023). In retail transactions, NFTs validate the authenticity of goods in the metaverse. Individuals and companies can launch their NFTs using a blockchain (usually Ethereum). NFTs represent provable rights for scarce digital art, taking the world by storm. Artists worldwide find they can monetize their creative

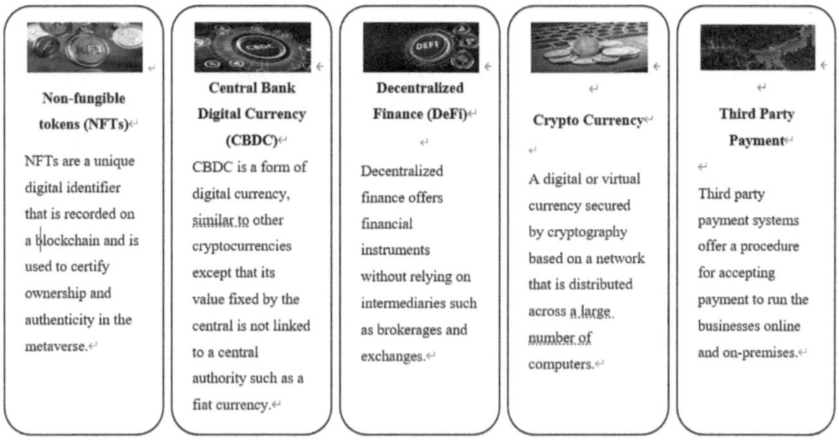

Figure 11.2 Digital Currencies in Metaverse

works at far better rates than in the real world by selling NFTs. By December 2021, collections like Cryptopunks and Bored Ape Yacht Club (BAYC—see Brouard, forthcoming) had become household names, while celebrity artists like Beeple sold some of their digital creations for more than $69 million, and the global market reached over $40 billion in sales.

NFTs are more than just digital jpegs; verticals like gaming, music and sports started integrating NFTs into their ecosystems, nurturing new projects like Axie Infinity. Altogether, 2021 cemented the digital primitive's demand for verifiable ownership, and despite a crash in early 2022, the NFT market continues to capture value. Undoubtedly, NFTs play a significant role in bringing blockchain to the mainstream. NFTs provide average internet users an easy entry point to the blockchain, even with high transaction fees (Mazur & Polyzos, 2024). Today, people around the globe have been minting their NFTs, representing art, photography, music, collectibles, in-game items and almost everything else. In short, the Web3 and metaverse platforms would not be where they are today without mainstream NFT adoption.

Central Bank Digital Currency

Money is a source of exchange; it facilitates transactions between sellers and buyers, securing an exchange agreement. Theoretically, central bank digital currency (CBDC) is a proxy for fiat currencies to complete business transactions. Three kinds of money are traditionally used in the market to deal with business transactions: banknotes, deposits and foreign currencies. If we compare it with banknotes, retail CBDC is expected to lower costs by substituting for printing money. Once it has developed, there is no need to replace it. Overall, CBDC is a beneficial replacement for printed money. It has legal protection and is easily carried around the globe. Furthermore, CBDC is a pure form of digital currency with liquidity security via a central authority. A liquidity account feature that is attractive to customers is offering the stability of banks during financial turmoil. However, CBDC creates issues with bank deposits in the short and long run. For example, rapid money transfers create a massive crisis in private banks because money is quickly moved to a central authority. Similarly, if the financial system is without private sector banks, the economy would face a lack of loans and rely on governments, which face challenges in growth with little financing for long-term investments. Aquilina et al. (2023) stated that CBDC is a part of decentralized finance (DeFi), a digital and distributed ledger-based finance system that a central bank issues. These concerns raise issues about the CBDC affecting bank deposits. A third substitute could occur against foreign currencies and is more essential for small developing countries. Developing countries rely on seigniorage for a component of their financial returns and utilize their local currency for their citizen betterment. This financial autonomy issue arose when Facebook announced the use of Libra in Asian countries. Governments in these regions expressed concerns about losing control over their monetary policies. They feared that widespread adoption of Libra could destabilize their local economies and undermine their financial sovereignty. Meanwhile, the Chinese government issued CBDC to prevent such an issue and set up this payment method in Asian countries. The CBDC overcomes the threat of financial autonomy and benefits the country's retail.

Decentralized Finance (DeFi)

Blockchain, considered a revolutionary technology, was introduced in 2008 as the engine for Bitcoin and has since led to the development of other blockchains like Ethereum, which powers most of decentralized Finance (Far et al., 2023). DeFi has been dubbed the 'FinTech revolution' and has spawned different applications like SocialFi (Guidi & Michienzi, 2022) and GameFi (Kiong, 2021). DeFi applications depend on smart contracts that create a decentralization mechanism and eliminate the central authority control at a low cost. Nevertheless, other essential elements remain the same, such as liquidity protocol vulnerabilities and its user-based nature for DeFi consumers. DeFi has numerous key features that distinguish it. One of the most well-known characteristics is that a bank account is not mandatory for using DeFi. The World Bank surveyed in January 2024 and reported that 1.5 billion people use DeFi without having a bank account.

Defi has following significant advantages in adopting blockchain technologies:

Controllability: The DeFi customer/consumer plays a role in financial transactions as a servicing party or the serviced party with no entry threshold. DeFi users control and monitor their digital assistants.

Transparency: DeFi protocol code is open source and runs on a public blockchain so that anyone can verify its security, interaction rules, transaction histories and network usage.

Censorship resistance: Censorship resistance refers to a network's features that prevent parties from altering or blocking data. Once data is added, it is virtually impossible to remove or alter it, making it permanent.

Programmability: DeFi includes typically smart contracts, which can be programmed and adjusted according to functional needs to align with different types of financial logic.

Composability: This is also called money Lego, meaning that the base-level DeFi protocols implemented by smart contracts can be leveraged by other DeFi projects to compose new DeFi applications. For example, DEX protocol UniSwap and DeFi lending protocol Compound can be leveraged by yield farm protocols to produce optimized yield by lending and swapping assets using these two protocols.

Interoperability: DeFi allows for the tokenization and exchange of the value of digital assets with fiat and physical assets. For example, the Synthetix project is a decentralized synthetic asset issuance protocol built on Ethereum. These synthetic assets are collateralized by the Synthetix Network Token (SNX), which, when locked in the contract, enables the issuance of synthetic assets (Synths). This pooled collateral model enables users to perform conversions between Synths directly with the smart contract, avoiding the need for counterparties.

Cryptocurrency

Cryptocurrency outlines the mechanism of digital payment supported by blockchain, which removes the physical cash from P2P transactions between the two parties anywhere on the globe. The national or fiat currency system is where a central authority, i.e., the government of a country, prints or issues the currency and controls it. However, cryptocurrency is not issued by governments and is not centrally controlled. A digital process produces cryptocurrencies through 'mining,' which refers to a dynamic process of crypto coin generation through using computers to solve complex mathematical problems. People can purchase these coins or a portion through physical cash and save them in their crypto account (called a wallet), which is entirely digital. The owners of cryptocurrency do not have any tangible assets; however, they have a record of digital units and use it as a means of payment. Cryptocurrency prices are affected by the demand and supply of other markets. Key features of cryptocurrency are security, irreversibility, permission and identity.

Cryptocurrencies are very secure: Cryptocurrencies are a safe source of payment. Every individual receives a specific code for a transaction, providing sufficient security to use cryptocurrency without fear.

Cryptocurrency transactions are irreversible: A big drawback of cryptocurrency is that it is used once and is not a refundable transaction. When performing a transaction, you need to verify before making a transaction while dealing with a crypto transaction.

There is no need for permission: Cryptocurrency transactions offer freedom of usage, meaning you do not need to get permission from anyone to install and use the software.

These currencies do not care about the specific location: Cryptocurrency dealings do not require any specific location where transactions will be performed. The consumer can use cryptocurrencies anywhere and anytime.

Cryptocurrencies are electronic assets that work without disclosing the customer's identity: Many consumers do not want to disclose their own identity while making a transaction; thus, cryptocurrencies can be used to hide identity and access benefits. However, because blockchains show the provenance of prior transactions, user accounts can be tracked.

Third-Party Payment

The metaverse is an emerging trend in the digital market, and its market value is predicted to reach $936.7 billion by 2030 (Grand View Research, 2024). However, how can we ensure payment transactions in the future? To resolve this question, many financial institutions are investing in the metaverse to deal with the financial necessities of metaverse consumers. Allied Bank Limited has opened its first brand in the metaverse to deal with financial transactions within a virtual environment. Digital currencies are also used to purchase digital assets in the metaverse. These extensions raise concern in the metaverse, one of the key elements in the metaverse business to make a secure, if not necessarily stable, means of payment.

The metaverse is still nascent, and payment systems have emerged in this new financial market. Different transaction methods are integrated with the metaverse, such as cryptocurrencies, and accepted overall within the metaverse. This process is completed with the help of blockchain, which is considered the foundation of value transfer and storage in the metaverse. Blockchain offers low-cost and high-security payment transactions, and cryptocurrency wallet payments are the primary method for metaverse transactions. However, traditional debit and credit card payment methods are also accepted in the metaverse. Some also allow participants to use PayPal, Google Pay and Apple Pay accounts. Nevertheless, in the metaverse, virtual currencies replace payment entirely.

Blockchain Concepts

The metaverse offers an economic system in which digital currencies used for transactions are facilitated by blockchain-enabled decentralized payment methods. Blockchain also helps the metaverse to build its infrastructure with various applications and data management tools. Digital revaluation has altered digital data in the real world and thus can be replicated in the virtual environment. The metaverse affixes the location where every individual is connected and seeks insight, information and data. Therefore, data management has become most critical in this new realm. Blockchain is most prominent in data management and protects against risks in the metaverse, which can include the Internet of Things (IoT), artificial intelligence and virtual reality (VR) and augmented reality (AR), empowering the metaverse. Blockchain is defined as:

> *Blockchains are distributed digital ledgers of cryptographically signed transactions grouped into blocks. Each block is cryptographically linked to the previous one (making it tamper-evident) after validation and undergoing a consensus decision. As new blocks are added, older blocks become more difficult to modify (creating tamper resistance). New blocks are replicated across copies of the ledger within the network, and any conflicts are resolved automatically using established rules.*
>
> (Narayanan et al., 2016)

Blockchains are database computing networks shared worldwide where each computer holds a copy of a ledger, which different protocols utilize to validate the information block. Thus, there is no chance of failure. Furthermore, blockchain has key characteristics such as a distributed digital ledger and a list of records. The central tenets of blockchain technology are P2P networks, consensus algorithms, smart contacts and public-key encryption. These technologies align together and work, enabling numerous applications in blockchain. The key components of blockchain are in Figure 11.3.

Smart Contracts refer to algorithmic functions installed through cryptocurrency transactions on the blockchain network. Nodes within the blockchain

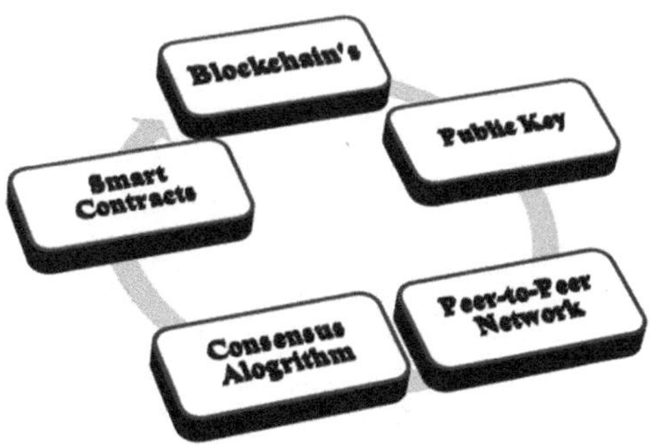

Figure 11.3 Blockchain Components in the Metaverse

network execute the smart contract; all nodes must derive the same results for the execution, which are recorded on the blockchain.

Public Key (Encryption) is also called asymmetric key encryption. As the name suggests, two asymmetric keys (i.e., two different keys) are used for public-key encryption. One key is used for the encryption process, and another key is used for the decryption process. Users can send or receive payments in Bitcoin through a P2P network, which is supported by its underlying blockchain protocol.

Consensus Algorithm, in its simplest definition, is an algorithm used by different distributed computers to agree on the state of the blockchain and archive the agreement without putting trust in any participating computers or the 'nodes' in the blockchain network. The carefully designed consensus algorithm must consider P2P networks' unreliable and asynchronous nature. A good consensus algorithm allows certain nodes to be in the faulty status, which means the nodes can be malicious or stop participating in the consensus process. Nevertheless, the blockchain network can still agree with many honest nodes. For example, Bitcoin's consensus algorithm proof of work (POW) leverages game theory and computation power to archive a reliable computation result in a trustless network environment that can tolerate up to 50% of attacks. Different blockchain networks, such as proof of stake, proof of elapsed time, proof of history and proof of replication, also use other consensus algorithms. The key idea of these consensus algorithms is to allow blockchain nodes to agree on the blockchain transactions and the ledger's state in a trustless and distributed manner without putting too many assumptions and constraints on the underlying network. The fundamental assumption of any consensus algorithm is that most of the network nodes are honest nodes, and, as such, the network can allow some 'bad apples' or malicious nodes in the network.

The consensus algorithm can be extended from the pure technical algorithm to social behavior in the blockchain ecosystem, which is called *social consensus*. A blockchain ecosystem comprises lifeless computer nodes and needs human participants, developers, investors, buyers, players, creators, wallet holders, exchange markets, government entities and regulators. The 'social consensus' refers to the agreements among individuals and organizations on the value of the blockchain network, the fairness of the blockchain-enabled token economy and the willingness to participate and contribute to the blockchain network. The social consensus is implied in the DAO (decentralized autonomous organization) structure to prompt the common interest and governance of the blockchain network. Both technical consensus and social consensus will play significant roles in metaverse applications. Because the 'social consensus' of DAO creates a new decentralized governance model, the DAO may replace corporations as the most popular organizational structure in the Metaverse.

P2P Networking: Although it is not a new concept and has existed long before the Bitcoin network existed, the P2P network is a departure from the traditional client/server architecture where there are separate computers to act as servers to serve different sets of computers as clients. In a P2P network, each computing node can be a server and a client. The peer node can discover a set of other peer nodes to communicate without any authentication or authorization. This can allow the information to flow freely and make the network more resilient to a potential system crash. In the blockchain, the peer node can broadcast the block, participate in consensus algorithms, validate each P2P transaction and get rewards for its contribution. The idea of a P2P network can be extended into the blockchain to advocate the idea that each individual or organization in the blockchain network has an equal voice and equal rights. Everyone's power can be somehow measured by their stake (from the proof of stake (POS) consensus algorithm's perspective) in the network or the electricity power they can use for the network (from the POW consensus algorithm's perspective). No individual is above any other if they all have an equal stake in the network.

Blockchain for Privacy and Security Concerns in the Metaverse

The metaverse has entered many leading industries enveloping digital interactive technologies, including finance and retail, where users participate in activities more or less like the physical world via their digital avatars. An avatar creation process requires information on behalf of a physical person and then mediates the activities in the metaverse. Since avatars are also tied to the blockchain rather than a single platform, theoretically, they are portable (interoperable) between metaverses. However, sharing personal information and data management in this virtual world raises concerns about privacy and security issues with the metaverse. Therefore, metaverse applications use blockchain technologies to protect and facilitate consumer data transactions and the purchasing/selling of digital brands in the metaverse. Scholars segregate privacy and security concerns in the metaverse into three strata: threats to communications networks, threats to metaverse end devices and threats to stored information and computing. Blockchain technologies are a prime source of protection against these threats in the metaverse. Focusing on metaverse privacy and security concerns, we elaborate measures based on blockchain technologies.

Metaverse end device threats come from users participating in meta-activities using wearable devices (e.g., AR/VR). In addition, the participants' data can also be accessed through other appliances like mobile devices and the IoT. Physical-world data is shifted into the virtual world through digital transformation. Considering the end device, this process can potentially attack data used in the metaverse.

Access control attack: This process offers a way to get access to the metaverse systems/devices through unauthorized methods, where the data is hacked using techniques such as phishing and used for illegal activities. This attack happens because people share personal credentials with friends and colleagues and data are appropriated and misused.

Malware attacks attach to multiple devices and can insert a malevolent third-party application whose operation runs with the user's data. A malware attack is conducted by sharing the attachment files via email and suggesting the respondent open the files. Thus, this attack can occur in the metaverse to get access to the intended device.

Digital footprint tracking: This attack happens when hackers identify the actual location and real identity of the digital identity in the metaverse and steal the record and behavior pattern on the devices.

Leakage of device data: The metaverse users fix their information in the device and use it for their tasks. This personal information is considered sensitive and has the potential for leakage threats such as device scams and data theft.

Firmware Vulnerabilities: Low device control has the potential to become a firmware threat, where multiple firmware insertions are entrenched into the device, causing security and privacy risks.

Distributed denial-of-service (DDoS) attack: The attack is related to IoT devices with limited resources, such as outage attacks, battery draining and sleep deprivation.

Tampering and injection threat: The metaverse offers an immersive experience where an individual uses their digital identity, i.e., avatar. Attacks on avatars, such as harassment, are possible. Other possibilities include fixing the wrong information behind the digital identity.

A single point of failure (SPOF) and third-party: Device management is centralized in the metaverse, where attack has potential through entire management. For example, sharing personal data from the central authority or their party is challenging.

Communication Network Threat

The metaverse is considered the next level of communication, where users communicate via their digital body, mirroring their physical bodily gestures and expressions with technologies. Therefore, it has the potential for a wide range of network-related threats. This section discusses the following threats.

Man in the middle and ever-dropping attack. This attack occurs when a middleman listens to metaverse users' communication between metaverse dialogue nodes. For example, a middleman inserts a device in the metaverse to record the communication between a metaverse application and a person and gets login credentials and other relative information.

The intrusion of the network. An intrusion into the network offers opportunities for the attacker to access the metaverse device, perform a phishing scam or spread malware.

Sybil's attack represents the many fake identities that manipulate the network and directly affect the metaverse reputation system.

Attack of Routing

This attack occurs when metaverse traffic is hijacked, stealing sensitive information and causing interruptions through route loops.

Privacy and security concerns and solutions in the metaverse. In the current digital era, the metaverse offers immersive social interaction via digital entities, i.e., avatars. This means the metaverse is a platform that facilitates social interaction and has a listed backbone. Therefore, it also suffers from network-related concerns, exposing privacy and security issues. Due to its nascent stage, we analyze the metaverse based on its four characteristics and raise concerns related to privacy and security with solutions in this chapter.

Security Issues and Solutions

Virtual interaction within the metaverse accepts the participants' input and allows hackers to inject viruses and attack data potentially. To guard against this intrusion, users need to validate all the information and input only adequate data with minimum privileges by applying cryptographic authentication protocols. This step enhances data confidentiality and reduces the chance of middleman attacks on the system. Algorithm authentication secures the integrity of transactions and monitors the system, which also prevents the attack. Attackers use JavaScript codes to enter the metaverse stores by requesting consumer links/websites. For this prevention, an algorithm proxy XXS is used to tackle such attempts. Furthermore, utilizing deep learning models with XXS increases the prevention of this attack in the metaverse.

Privacy Issues and Solutions

Privacy leakage is a prominent concern in every social network, even in a secure digital platform. Social network platforms ask users to create their profiles for interacting with the community on the platform. This profile consists of the user's personal information, where users share their life activities such as shopping and feelings. In simple terms, this profile represents the physical person and offers valuable insight to malicious parties to gather information from the profile. Prior literature suggests that unexpected individuals and platform facilitators, such as adversaries, can use social network data, which causes privacy leakage. For example, GAN (Generative Adversarial Networks) fabricate counterfeit audio, photos and videos based on the public and apply for various fraudulent activities. The prime methods to prevent the privacy issues of client data are L-diversity (which measures the diversity of sensitive values) and K-anonymity (which indicates the re-identifiability of its records), where algorithms facilitate the veil of the original information and detect fraud. Anti-GNN (graphic neural network) algorithms were launched to tackle such attacks for GNN threat prevention. Sometimes, due to platform inefficiency, data leakage incidents happen. For example, for prize competitions, anonymized information was leaked in the shape of prints by Netflix. To tackle these kinds of issues, the platform must ensure the proper mechanism for the privacy and security protection of the dataset.

Privacy and Security Issues to Immersive Interaction

The metaverse offers immersive interaction, where users enter the metaverse using headsets and wearable devices with huge data sharing. Data sending and receiving is part of sharing in the metaverse; however, hackers inject antagonistic serialized information and make it complex. This type of fraud is called de-serialization anxiety, which is considered one of the significant risks. For example, the Android system authorizes random code implementation in different apps, which creates a de-serialization vulnerability. The static scan analysis used detects de-serialization. Furthermore, the metaverse devices are embedded with information like location, fingerprints and facial scans. This sensitive information can potentially risk theft and leakage, critical factors in the immersive experience. To tackle this risk, users must use wearable devices based on quadratic residues to ensure authentication protocol. For example, authentication based on biometrics, voice, ID numbers and facial expressions are famous sign-on practices to prevent these issues.

Privacy and Security Concerns to Real World-building

Studies show that the metaverse is a virtual environment like the real world, where users participate in routine activities like real life. In the metaverse, every user tailors their profile setting to their interest, including hobbies and expertise, which formulate a virtual world with various applicants' profiles. This means that the metaverse combines various participants' data, which can interact with each other and perform real-life activities. However, a massive security and privacy risk is associated with users' information in the metaverse. Metaverse platforms introduce a mechanism such as an encryption paradigm to ensure the most appropriate privacy prevention.

Privacy and Security Concerns to Expandability

Dwivedi et al. (2022) explain that the metaverse has the potential to extend the physical world by employing more capabilities through AR and VR in the virtual world. For example, metaverse users interact through digital entities, shop and attend meetings in virtual rooms and even some medical practices are performed. These extensions of services and activities are accessed through different applications on desktops or other devices. Nevertheless, these functions occur with effective information communication from a physical person to a third party. As a result, it is prudent to secure and protect user information, which is used in all the functions discussed above. Thus, privacy and security concerns are tied to this transaction. For this prevention, cross-app tracking functions run to protect the redundant tracking channels in the structure of the metaverse. For example, Google and Apple introduced Android systems and iOS to prevent such issues. Conversely, metaverse devices are interlinked with other devices through Bluetooth. Detection algorithms and cross-app tracking are applied to prevent this scam.

Other Possible Security and Privacy Concerns

As discussed earlier, the metaverse is an extension of the real world in many ways. The metaverse economy is a pivotal factor that facilitates all metaverse activities based on the user's performance. Many brands and companies invest in the metaverse to conduct business and earn profits in the current digital market. As noted at the start if this chapter, metaverse investment achieved much intention through digital assets and digital brands and has become an essential part of the virtual economy in the current digital market, with an expected growth of $936.7 billion by 2030 (Grand View Research, 2024). Metaverse economies use digital currencies to run businesses such as NFT, cryptocurrency, DeFi and others based on blockchain technologies by certifying digital assets' identity. Physical currency is still used in the metaverse via third parties, which may mitigate credit fraud and privacy issues. Most users utilize digital currencies in their transactions in the metaverse based on blockchain technologies, avoiding the metaverse's central authority, which may cause potential privacy and security concerns.

As already discussed, the metaverse offers the creation of a digital entity of a physical person and performs all the transactions via their digital entity, i.e., avatar. An avatar is easily copied and captured in a phishing attack, where attackers steal sensitive information and utilize it for illegitimate aims. On the other hand, the creation of a copied avatar possibility is also available, where hackers build a copy of the avatar (i.e., fake replications) and use it for their purposes. However, this is only possible when they have the users' credentials.

In Summary, these are potential concerns in the metaverse:

Accountability of the metaverse platforms. Reporting, evaluating and inquiring about data exchange toward the outside or any centralized platforms. There are following four attributes defined as follows:

Traceability. This refers to the data collection, use and consent from the stakeholders of metaverse platforms, including data termination of consumption. This process is performed at the base of technical boundaries and prepares the future for data governance.

Auditability. Metaverse platforms are accountable to their participants when the users provide personal information to maintain their identity; the platform operators must ensure the security and privacy of every type of user's data, such as usage and sharing. Additionally, the choice of open access to user data is provided by the platforms where users want to share their information and audit by him/her publicly.

Accountability. Metaverse platforms and their management are accountable for protecting the user's data and privacy, offering various practices that showcase the platform's usage procedure. For example, third-party firms (e.g., brands and banks) must only use users' data for legitimate purposes and obtain prior consent.

Impartiality. Metaverse stakeholders, including firms and operators, are equally accountable for data protection and consumer privacy.

Data Protection

Data exchange is an essential part of any transaction held in the digital dominion and is always associated with various risks. Deterrence of data risks is a necessary part of metaverse operations, which must protect their client's information being processed, shared and used within the metaverse. There are following two measures used for data protection:

Privacy. Metaverse users use different tools to control the data management flow by the policies of the metaverse platforms. These policies are the platform jurisdictions where users control their data protection and experience. For example, personal identity, code or passwords and data of personal origin are in dexterity with the rights afforded to individuals through data privacy policies within their jurisdictions. The operators of the platforms are responsible for enforcing these practices to control privacy and security.

Dynamism. Metaverse platform operators provide users with ascendancy rules and enforce an individual's ability to grant, modify and revoke consent for data collection, use or sharing. In scenarios where consent modification and revocation are limited, such limits are communicated to users before the initial permission experience.

Individual Understanding

This section focuses on the ability of the users/individuals familiar with the metaverse platform to understand the purpose and uses of data and the choices available. It is a significant challenge in the metaverse because it is still nascent, and no one has experienced it before. The platforms must educate their consumers and clarify the data privacy and security measures and policies, which may reduce the challenges related to privacy and security on the metaverse platform. There are four ways to achieve individual understanding:

Transparency. Metaverse users have access to their information in due time and with ongoing purity on how an entity collects, shares and uses information transparently. This means platforms are responsible for maintaining and providing the sequence of data usage and its control. However, providing sufficient information to consumers about using their personal information on the platform is necessary.

Clarity. Metaverse users are enabled to understand how and why data is collected, shared and used. Consent choices are presented coherently and intelligibly. No dark-pattern behavior is permitted.

Consistency. Consent mechanisms (e.g., terminology, icons, structure) are presented to individuals in the same format across all user interactions in the data exchange.

Standardization. Consent choices are accessible to users across use cases and participants in a common, digestible format. Participants enable the necessary technology to read, interpret and implement consent choices received in the standard format. Operators enforce these standards.

This section addresses the tools metaverse users use to support how the data is collected, used and shared through a metaverse platform. There are following five attributes for individual control:

Interoperability refers to the individual capabilities of data, rights and permissions across the platforms.

Usability. Metaverse users can monitor how their data is used, shared and collected. Through the data exchange consent mechanisms, they are enabled to control the collection, use and sharing of personally identifiable data as well as de-identified data of personal origin.

Accessibility. Individuals can control how data is collected, used and shared through a simple consent mechanism interface available at relevant interaction points. Access should be available for all individuals, including minorities, those with disabilities and those of low socioeconomic status.

Adoptability. The governance approach for individuals' interactions with consent mechanisms should be implemented and managed by operators and participants in a metaverse platform.

Flexibility. Consent interfaces allow for easy modification to respond to the altered circumstances of operators, participants or individuals, as well as governance rules, regulatory policy or technology developments.

Conclusion

In this chapter, we have discussed the metaverse's emergence and its key characteristics, as well as personal data formation, digital currencies and privacy and security concerns. Additionally, the metaverse platform accountability, data protection and its understanding at the individual level as well as individual control. The metaverse is a virtual world where users enter via their digital identity, i.e., avatar, and enjoy real-life activities. Participation in metaverse activities occurs with information sharing, socialization and enjoyment. In early 2021, this concept got hype in the gaming and retail industry due to COVID-19 restrictions; people were restricted in their homes.

Still, it is in its early stages and many digital technologies have far to go in terms of user security and privacy.

The metaverse has revolutionized the industrial landscape and gained much significance in the finance, retail and gaming industries. People enter the metaverse for entertainment, shopping, trade and interacting with numerous objects. The key concept of the metaverse is an alternative world that offers surreal consumer experiences. Metaverse experience reduces the complexities, anxiety and tensions through escapism, tourism and shopping. Consequently, these transactions deal with personal data and sensitive information related to financial operations, i.e., currency transactions for trade. Due to these occurrences, privacy and security issues exist in the metaverse, which we have discussed in this chapter in detail, with possible solutions based on existing literature. This chapter also elaborates on the role of blockchain technologies in tackling privacy and security concerns in the metaverse. Finally, we have discussed possible issues in the metaverse causing privacy and security attacks. By summarizing the literature, we wish this chapter to understand better the security and privacy concerns and their possible solutions.

References

Aquilina, M., Frost, J., & Schrimpf, A. (2023). *Decentralizedfinance (DeFi): A functional approach*. CEPR Discussion Paper no. DP17810, Centre for Economic Policy Research (CEPR).

Aysan, A. F., Gozgor, G., & Nanaeva, Z. (2024). Technological perspectives of Metaverse for financial service providers. *Technological Forecasting and Social Change*, *202*, 123323.

Barbosa, V. (2023, December 27). Here's what Elon Musk thinks about NFTs. *Finbold*. https://finbold.com/heres-what-elon-musk-thinks-about-nfts/

Belk, R. (2024). The digital frontier as a liminal space. *Journal of Consumer Psychology*, *34*(1), 167–173.

Brouard, M. (forthcoming). Setting sail in a tokenized world: An exploration of the bored ape yacht club and co-created consumer experience. *International Journal of Research in Marketing*.

Dwivedi, Y. K., Hughes, L., Baabdullah, A. M., Ribeiro-Navarrete, S., Giannakis, M., Al-Debei, M. M., ... & Wamba, S. F. (2022). Metaverse beyond the hype: Multidisciplinary perspectives on emerging challenges, opportunities, and agenda for research, practice and policy. *International Journal of Information Management*, *66*, 102542.

Far, S. B., Rad, A. I., & Asaar, M. R. (2023). Blockchain and its derived technologies shape the future generation of digital businesses: A focus on decentralized finance and the Metaverse. *Data Science and Management*, *6*(3), 183–197.

Grand View Research. (2024). *Metaverse Market Size to Reach $936.6 Billion by 2030*. Retrieved October 25, 2024, from https://www.grandviewresearch.com/press-release/global-metaverse-market

Guidi, B., & Michienzi, A. (2022, Summer). SocialFi: Towards the new shape of social media. *ACM SIGWEB Newsletter*, *2022*, 1–8.

Kiong, L.V., 2021. *DeFi, NFT and GameFi made easy: A beginner's guide to understanding and investing in DeFi, NFT and GameFi projects*. Independently published.

Mazur, M., & Polyzos, E. (2024). Non-fungible tokens (NFTs). In *The Elgar companion to decentralized finance, digital assets, and Blockchain technologies* (pp. 280–297). Edward Elgar Publishing.

Narayanan, A., Bonneau, J., Felten, E., Miller, A., & Goldfeder, S. (2016). *Bitcoin and cryptocurrency technologies: A comprehensive introduction*. Princeton University Press.

12 Social Currency in the Metaverse

Jashim Khan and Russell Belk

The Metaverse

Compared to the first metaverse (Second Life, which started in 2003) this time the avatars are 3D and show us realistically as well as imitate our face and arm/hand movements. So they seem much more 'me' engaging in the virtual world. There is no universal definition of the metaverse, nor is it confined to platforms, e.g., Decentraland and Roblox. It is conceived as much broader and includes augmented reality (AR) and virtual reality (VR) applications in Web3 (Momtaz, 2022). Web3 is categorized by decentralization, transparency and ownership (Lai et al., 2023). It leverages blockchain technology to distribute data across a network of nodes, making it secure and giving its owners greater control over data and digital assets (Gadekallu et al., 2022). This unique aspect of Web3 is the fundamental idea for time-effort currency in the Metaverse.

Some observers (Belk et al., 2022; Cheng, 2024) broadly define the metaverse as a digital environment where the real world and VR are interconnected, creating a physical-digital experience (Braud et al., 2022; Khan et al., forthcoming)—a collective digitally shared space created by convergence-enhanced VR and the feelings of physical presence in the digital world (Hadi et al., 2024). It is commonly accepted that Neal Stephenson coined the term Metaverse in his 1992 science fiction novel Snow Crash (Lewis, 2008). In the book, Stephenson depicts the Metaverse as a VR based on the Internet (Stephenson, 2003). Current technologies contributing to the Metaverse's growth include VR headsets, which provide immersive experiences by simulating 3D environments and AR devices, which overlay digital information onto the physical world (Mystakidis, 2022). This interconnected experience involves shared spaces among users from different locations (Huang et al., 2023). Russell Belk (2024) contends that the metaverse offers a new realm for identity exploration and personal self-expression—the Metaverse allows participants to experiment with multiple identities of their digital selves. Belk et al. (2022) argue that the metaverse can foster unique forms of social interaction and community building, transcending geographical limitations in which money, possessions

DOI: 10.4324/9781003425021-12

and ownership-based consumption prevail. Interpersonal communication, digital goods and services exist digitally in this virtual space of metaverse commerce (Mogaji et al., 2023). Alsop (2024) predicts that the Metaverse will be worth $507.6 billion by 2030 (Alsop, 2024). Current metaverse platforms like Meta's Horizon Worlds allow users to engage with 3D avatars and interact in a digital environment (Ball, 2022). Other examples are gaming platforms such as Roblox, Axie Infinity and Fortnite, where players can socialize, build and explore together (Du et al., 2021)—additionally, VR platforms like Decentraland and Sandbox offer immersive experiences for social interaction and collaboration (Hennig-Thurau et al., 2023).

The metaverse potentially allows transporting digital assets across such platforms. In addition, virtual real estate is growing, with users buying, selling and leasing digital properties (Saiz, 2020). Within the Metaverse, businesses have opportunities to set up virtual storefronts and sell digital goods and services to a global audience without the limitations of their physical location (Ball, 2022). These operations are meant to be financial digital assets, necessitating new ways to account for transactions in the Metaverse (Wang et al., 2023).

In this speculative chapter, we sketch and ideal without speculating exactly what it will look like in the future with Central Bank Digital Currency. Time and effort are often quantified through mutually agreed-upon units, such as hours of work or specific tasks completed, and the amount of effort required is computed based on skill level, which is possible in the metaverse. It is a speculative concept where the value of a currency is tied to the amount of time and effort expended in digital asset creation or earning. The underlying idea is that that Blockchain technology with its decentralized digital ledger, ensures security, transparency and immutability. Together, this scenario potentially revolutionizes how we perceive and exchange digital assets. It is an instance of digital asset exchanges anchored in time and effort that will potentially creep into the Metaverse over time. Social media platforms use our digital content to market to businesses, and we help them achieve profitability and growth. As speculated, digital content creation in the metaverse enables creators to reward themselves by earning social currency.

Value-adding activities, such as blogs, webpages, social media profiles and other digital footprints (Mario Lavizzari et al., 2021) demand spending time and effort through which digital identity, reputations, collectibles and digital gifts derive meaning and value. These assets may be shared, exchanged/bartered and, in some cases, traded using financial digital assets—e.g., mobile-based payments to purchase accessories for avatars and parallel real-world accessories and clothing (Wang et al., 2023). Time and effort's future outlook in Metaverse commerce following avocational payment methods (activities taken up in addition to one's regular work on passion or interest) (Nordquist, 2021) are used to accumulate digital assets and value-added digital goods transacted or exchanged, resulting in automated recordkeeping as favors and gifts. This shift in payment methods means that people will be able to monetize their time and efforts by trading digital goods, such as virtual art, services or digital content. Additionally, this shift eliminates the need for manual recordkeeping, as transactions and exchanges are recorded automatically. Blockchain technology plays a crucial role in this automated recordkeeping by providing a decentralized and immutable ledger. Each transaction or exchange is securely recorded on the blockchain, ensuring transparency and preventing fraud. This not only enhances trust among participants but also streamlines the entire process of tracking digital asset exchanges. For instance, blockchain technology can be used to track the origins of a fungible digital asset and may be exchanged with CBDC.

We also envision avocational payment methods for digital assets as gifts, favors of digital assets that may not have direct financial implications, though they potentially and indirectly influence financial exchanges. An avocational payment method means to earn income through activities pursued primarily for pleasure rather than as a main occupation. This can include hobbies or side gigs that generate supplementary income. Examples might include freelance writing, crafting or teaching a musical instrument. These value-adding activities also potentially include digital content creation, sharing photos, mentoring, tutoring and profile presentations as well as collecting, exchanging, buying and selling in the Metaverse community (Mancuso et al., 2023). Social currency may be exchanged for CBDC to account for time and effort expended in immersive experiences for participants, enabling value-added avocational activities using augmented and VR technologies. For example, Gucci, Nike and McDonald's are among the companies that have invested their resources in meta-commerce (Silberstein, 2022; Meisenzahl, 2022).

These digital assets can be exchanged for virtual goods, services or real-world items or exchanged to CBDC. Popular digital assets, including virtual real estate and digital art, are traded and monetized using cryptocurrencies currently. However, there is speculation that people might prefer CBDC instead in the coming days. Digital goods like clothing and avatar accessories are successful examples of such virtual goods sold by Gucci (Joy et al., 2022). The digital assets include everything from virtual real estate to digital art and in-game items to unique avatars, skins or virtual experiences. These predictions are what Metaverse will become in the future, like Gucci Gardens is in Roblox, with the in-game currency of Robucks.

Next, we focus on the avocation payment method, in which time and effort could be the units of account, value measures and exchange media.

Avocational Payment

According to the Oxford Dictionary (2024), avocations are hobbies or leisure time pursuits that exist apart from or in addition to one's regular vocation. Taking Airbnb's reputation rating as a digital asset and as a prototype, a host with a high reputation rating attracts more bookings during peak seasons, leading to higher occupancy rates and, potentially, the ability to charge premium prices (Smartbnb, 2024). Guests are motivated to book with highly rated hosts because they equate a high reputation rating with reliability, quality and a positive experience. This trust in the host's reputation reduces the perceived risk of booking and increases the likelihood of a satisfying stay. Consequently, guests are often willing to pay higher prices for the assurance of a well-reviewed property. Satisfied guests leave positive reviews, accumulating a positive reputation for the host and a digital asset for the future. Avocational payment methods employ these reputation ratings to add value for services, collectibles traders or those exchanging virtual goods in Metaverse commerce (Dawson, 2022). These transactions are social and relational based on gifts and favors of the member community (Giobbi, 2022). Traditionally, the avocational payment method was not scalable because of challenges in determining the equitable value of exchange and transaction inequalities (Akkus et al., 2022). For example, Freecycle and Swap.com are successful examples of avocational payments (Luchs et al., 2011) that did not reach the global scale. Freecycle allows users to give away items they no longer need, while Swap.com enables users to trade clothing, toys and other household goods (Chapman et al., 2020). The issues of transaction inequalities might be easily overcome with time-effort-encoded CBDC that accounts for record-keeping facilitating digital assets transaction in the metaverse. Online gaming marketplaces are another example where players can exchange virtual items and in-game assets; though time is accounted for, efforts and skills are ignored due to the uniqueness of those digital collectibles.

Avocational payment in the Metaverse allows user to earn rewards for their hobbies and interests, such as virtual art creation, gaming or social interactions (Shen et al., 2021). In addition to rewarding pursuit of passions, these payments (tokens) provide contributors a sense of fulfillment and purpose. Thus, the avocation method in the Metaverse provides future opportunities (Henry & Shannon, 2023) in that contributors can use the tokens for future play. The avocational activities in the metaverse also foster community and social connections, enhancing each other's virtual experiences. Metaverses, for the most part, did not account for the fact that the in-game currencies and NFTs cannot easily be converted into real-world value, i.e., be converted into financial currency outside of the community (Huang et al., 2023). But platforms Decentraland and The Sandbox support avocational payment systems though the focus remains on financial digital assets, allowing users to earn tokens to participate in activities. In Decentraland, users can create and sell virtual real estate or digital art, while Sandbox encourages game development and virtual experiences. These platforms provide a robust ecosystem for contributors to monetize their hobbies and interests (Jeff, 2022). Examples of avocational payments in the metaverse also include freelance writing, where individuals get paid for contributing articles or blogs in their free time (Burrow, 2022).

The benefits of avocational payment methods also include encouraging sustainable practices in the Metaverse (Baral et al., 2024), which generate digital assets contributing to financial well-being. By rewarding individuals for participating in eco-friendly activities, these payment methods can drive more people to adopt green habits. This can lead to a collective reduction in carbon footprints and support the growth of environmentally conscious businesses. Additionally, avocational payment methods can incentivize local and community-based projects that promote sustainability.

The avocational payment method potentially provides an accessible way for individuals to exchange digital content or services (Gadekallu et al., 2022) with the time-effort currency of the account. For example, in a skill exchange, one hour of tutoring might not be equivalent to one hour of house cleaning. The involvement of blockchain and CBDC can account for time and effort, including skill level within the Metaverse community. Skills and efforts are computed based on the individual's skills and efforts and registered on a blockchain with each transaction. Time as a unit of exchange and account has been tried in the past; for example, the Time Banking UK initiative experimented but was unsuccessful in equating skills and efforts in payment methods, resulting in poor acceptance in the broader community (Seyfang, 2002). One potential problem in how participants traded skills and services in this time banking experiment was the lack of scalability for adoption by the public. Another big problem was in standardizing time and effort, given the subjective nature of different types of work (Verma et al., 2024). For instance, the perceived value of an hour of tutoring may not be equivalent to an hour of house cleaning for all participants, leading to disagreements. Variations in skill levels and the quality of work can further complicate the process, as not all contributions are seen as equally valuable (Del Moral & Pais, 2015).

Table 12.1 reviews significant tokens used in the Metaverse and shows that these organizations can differentiate their offerings by encoding time-effort and possibly converting to CBDC accounting for digital assets.

This chapter primarily focuses on digital assets, in which time and effort are units of account. Efforts can be quantified through metrics such as hours spent on a task, the complexity of the work performed and the level of expertise required. Decentraland and Illuvium utilize average session duration and time spent on tasks. These metrics assign value to contributions in digital asset creation. Time spent on digital content creation is related reputation rating. A high reputation rating enhances the visibility and credibility of a creator's work, thereby maximizing the return on the time invested in producing quality content. Reputation rating is also reflective of effort put in designing digital content indicating the quality and reliability, reflection of amount of effort and dedication put into creating digital content. The notion of time and effort currency draws on resource exchange theory. However, it is necessary to compare digital assets to financial digital assets in the Metaverse (see Table 12.1).

Table 12.1 Metaverse Currencies and Tokens

	Decentraland	*Sandbox*	*Axie Infinity*	*Illuvium*	*Horizon*	*Roblox*
Characteristics	- Focus on virtual real estate - Allows users to own assets and be controlled by them rather than a central authority	- Focus on user-generated content and decentralized governance. - Allows players to create, own and monetize their gaming experiences using blockchain technology	- Axie Infinity focuses specifically on a play-to-earn model - Allows players to earn cryptocurrency by breeding, battling and trading virtual creatures called Axies	- Focus on decentralized RPG game capturing and battling creatures known as Illuvials - Allows interaction with VR environment and other users, beyond gaming	- Focus on spatial audio technology and highly immersive VR environments - Collaborative tools specifically designed for professional and educational settings - Allows intuitive and responsive user interfaces, making virtual interactions feel more natura	- Focus on to create a singular, interconnected virtual world - Allows game creation system that allows users to create and share their own games and experiences using its proprietary game engine
Target audience	Users interested in digital land ownership	- Gaming enthusiasts, digital artists and virtual property investors	Younger, tech-savvy, gaming enthusiast aged between 18 and 35 years	Avid gamers and cryptocurrency enthusiasts and investors in decentralized finance (DeFi).	A broader demographic, aiming to connect existing social media users	Younger audiences who enjoy creating and playing games

(*Continued*)

Table 12.1 (Continued)

	Decentraland	*Sandbox*	*Axie Infinity*	*Illuvium*	*Horizon*	*Roblox*
User Engagement	- High engagement from a niche community passionate about virtual real estate and digital collectibles	- Daily Active Users - User Retention Rate - Session Duration	- Daily Active Users - User Retention Rate - Session Duration - Battles, breeding and transactions monitored	- Daily active users - Average session duration	- Leverages its integration with existing social media networks	- Millions of daily active users, reflecting its popularity and extensive library of games
Blockchain	Ethereum blockchain	Ethereum blockchain	Ethereum blockchain, Ronin sidechain	Ethereum blockchain	Sidechains and multiple, parallel blockchains	Does not currently use blockchain technology.
Token standard	ERC-721	ERC-721, ERC-1155	ERC-20	ERC-20	Own token standard	Own token Robux
Monetization	MANA (native token) and LAND (NFT)	SAND tokens to purchase digital assets and participate in (DAO)	SLP and AXS. SLP is used for breeding new Axies, while AXS serves as the governance token	ILV used to purchase in-game items and participate in governance.	Horizon Coins allow the purchase virtual goods and services within the platform	Robux to purchase various in-game items, avatars and experiences

Unit of Account

In economics, the unit of account for money is defined as a standard numerical monetary unit for measuring the market value of goods or services (Functions of Money, 2015). Money is divisible, countable and fungible (Tacanho, 2024). In the context Metaverse commerce with time and effort, using CBDC in a blockchain technology provides a mechanism to compute and compare the value of value-added activities and contributions in the Metaverse transactions for digital assets. In other words, it allows contributors to assess and exchange the time and efforts required in value-adding activities for digital goods, services, in a gift exchange manner (see Chapter 10) to collaborate in the Metaverse (Zhang et al., 2022). Blockchain technology ensures transparency and trust in a time and effort-based utilizing CBDC to convert digital assets to financial assets. By recording all transactions on a decentralized ledger, the blockchain provides an immutable and verifiable record of each user's contributions and exchanges (Gomez-Trujillo et al., 2021). Unlike traditional fiat currency, where value is often tied to tangible assets or trust in the issuing authority (Mărgulescu & Mărgulescu, 2021), time and effort currency in the metaverse is linked to participants' creative activities. This potentially creates a people-centric system where contributions such as creativity, collaboration and participation are the primary drivers of value tied to one's time, effort and possibilities of earning digital assets. It democratizes the value exchange, making it more accessible and equitable for all contributors. User engagement is measured through metrics such as time spent in digital creativity, level of participation in community events, the quality and impact of user-generated content and the frequency of interactions with other users. These metrics ideally entail a fair sense of equitable justice. Advanced algorithms analyze these metrics to assign a value to each user's contributions, ensuring that efforts and skills are accurately rewarded for creativity. Once a fair and equitable reward system exists within the metaverse network, engagement in digital asset creation will expand.

The motives for digital asset generation are encoded in one's time and efforts and paid as CBDC that can be used within the metaverse that is contemplated to include social networking virtual stocks, buying and selling services to exchange for digital assets. Users accumulate these digital assets based on their engagement metrics, which are periodically evaluated by the platform's algorithms employing artificial intelligence. Users can spend the digital assets to acquire goods and services and possibly reap benefit of converting their credits to CBDC, ultimately providing tangible benefits for the contributors' time and efforts. Machine learning processes these data to identify patterns and quantifies the value of digital assets in CBDC—accounting for contributors' consistency, quality and engagement levels. Users can track their token accumulation through a dedicated dashboard system within the Metaverse platform. This dashboard provides real-time updates on their current token balance, detailed breakdowns of how tokens were earned and insights into their engagement metrics.

This chapter details that time efforts are important in digital asset creation:

Time is a critical asset in human life, represented by wages and salaries to earn money, which are often set to accrue numbers of hours at work performing tasks that contribute to a firm's production. A country's gross domestic product is the accumulation of national production. Similarly, universities require credit hours and time spent within a course to earn degrees and certificates and for professors, assistants and adjuncts to earn a salary. Time remains a core element in human life. Apart from earning money, people also spend time caring for a dying loved one, doing community work to benefit people in society, voluntary work, as well time for themselves enjoying hobbies. Spending time without putting effort is problematic. For example, an artist may spend countless hours crafting art and painting and then then realizing the value of the artwork is not valued by others. A writer might not get published. And an actor, dancer or singer might not be hired based on their audition. The value of time is amplified by the immersive nature of the metaverse, where productivity and social exchange translate into digital assets, and potentially, those are converted to financial digital assets.

Effort in the metaverse converts into financial success to develop skills, earn a reputation and create creative content that potentially transfers to CBDC. The more a contributor is willing to put their efforts into digital content creation, the better their finished content and gains value of creativity within the metaverse community. While physical effort involves the expenditure of muscle power and stamina, mental effort demands focus and cognitive resources. Despite their different nature, both forms of effort can be equally exhausting. Similarly, we can classify efforts in terms of risk, for example, in high-risk situations where efforts come with the potential for greater rewards and carry a higher chance of failure. Low-risk efforts, on the other hand, tend to offer more predictable and stable outcomes. The contributor chooses how much effort they are willing to dedicate in digital content creation. This dedication can increase visibility and opportunities within the Metaverse community since more time spent on creative tasks indicates efforts invested in producing digital content. Contributors may have access to time stamps to unlock exclusive items to rate the reputation of the creative digital content.

Store of Value

We speculate that the growth of the metaverse and CBDC will be in tandem and cooperate with each other. These digital assets can be accumulated and traded, much like traditional currencies, thus providing a store of value for the user's time and effort invested in value-adding activities. Transactions are typically facilitated through blockchain technology, ensuring security and transparency. This creates a dynamic environment where the value of digital assets is tied to one's time and effort invested in the Metaverse. Scarcity plays a crucial role in determining the store of value of digital assets (Yi et al., 2023). While some assets are unique and limited in quantity, their rarity can drive up demand and, consequently, their market value. Yi et al. (2023) in their research on sales promotion in livestreaming suggest time and quantity scarcity are often artificially created by the streamers. This scarcity ensures that community members who invested time and effort into adding value potentially benefit from the increase in the value of digital assets. Roblox allows gamer members to create new games which are in high demand. The game showcases the time and effort of gamers and accounts for value for their creation.

Time is quantifiable and, in essence, serves as a store of value. For instance, in a time-effort-payment system in the Metaverse theoretically makes it possible to equate a graphic designer who might spend two hours creating a logo for a local bakery with the baker's time and effort so that both can be rewarded by digital assets, which they could use to have their taxes done by an accountant or possibly convert the assets into CBDC. This exchange uses time as a fixed measure and effort as a variable factor to equate the measure of value to settle the account with individuals in exchange. However, one potential challenge is ensuring the equitable valuation of different skills and services. Skills, experience and qualifications could mimic the rates in the offline market for time-effort in CBDC to be viable; for example, a novice may need to spend more time and effort to complete a task than an expert. Therefore, e.g., wage rates prevailing in offline businesses will likely require calibration.

The time-effort social currency concept reflects an inclusive environment where everyone can succeed based on their efforts and their time spent as well as the scarcity of what they produce—e.g., a unique piece of digital art or a special in-game tool, or by competing in challenges or contributing to community projects. However, disparities in access to technology and varying levels of skills could impede its adoption globally. Those accessible to the metaverse may benefit from meta-commerce economics. Those who cannot afford expensive digital assets can still accumulate wealth and status through their contributions of time and efforts to earn digital currencies, which reduces financial barriers and fosters a more equitable digital economy.

Medium of Exchange

Time-effort currency serves as a potential medium of exchange to acquire digital assets, access exclusive experiences or trade with other users. The system would incentivize active participation and collaboration in the Metaverse community. The currency is to be earned by participating in various activities, such as completing tasks, such as through creative tasks like designing virtual assets or organizing events. The more people spend time and effort creating and exchanging assets in the metaverse. Akin to earning points in a loyalty program or accumulating frequent flyer miles, more engagement means more rewards, more opportunities to earn digital assets and the potential to convert those to financial rewards. The underlying assumption is that the creation and exchange of digital assets within the metaverse potentially could redeem in real-life CBDC. The promise of rewards for efforts encourages users to continually invest their time and skills, enhancing activities in the metaverse, such as receiving tutoring by exchanging time currency with other community members, resulting in a vibrant trading platform.

Next, we delve into social resource theory to explore avocational payment methods in the Metaverse.

Social Resource Theory

Social resource theory posits that individuals have various resources, such as time, effort and social connections, to exchange in a social relationship (Foa & Foa, 2012). As conceived, these resources are incommensurate and cannot be exchanged. Though in digital environment, and with possibility of block chain technology, it is speculated that there is a possibility to exchange these resources as the digital footprint identifies some of these resources being offered. For example, log-in hours and real-time participation in events, tutoring, services within the platform. The key to social resources is understanding the types of resources people exchange in a social environment, such as emotional support, status, information, money, goods and services (Brinberg & Wood, 1983). Emotional support (Chiu et al., 2015) and affection to show off status, prestige and social standing (Maner, 2017) are prevalent in digital social platforms and documented in studies (Fiske, 2011). Information includes knowledge and advice that are shared to help others. Digital assets and services are resources exchanged to assist others. Social resource theory argues that a balance and fairness of these exchanges determine the quality and stability of the relationship (Sabatelli & Shehan, 1993). The balance and fairness suggested in balanced reciprocity in gift exchange by Sahlins (1972) are vital in resource exchanges as they encourage a give-and-take dynamic, ensuring that both parties benefit from the relationship. Sahlins (1972) identified three main types of reciprocity: generalized (altruistic), balanced (symmetrical) and negative (one-sided benefit). Of these three categories generalized and negative are not necessarily reciprocal. When people reciprocate symmetrically, they not only meet their own needs but also validate the contributions of others, reinforcing mutual respect and trust. This balanced exchange fosters long-term stability and satisfaction within the relationship, as both parties feel valued and appreciated. Consider a mentorship relationship where a senior employee provides career advice and guidance (information), and the student shows gratitude and extends favors to spread positive word of mouth for the professor. Social resource exchange, a shared sense of identity, understanding, norms, values, trust, cooperation and reciprocity among community members are the primary functions of an exchange relationship (Khan et al., 2021). The exchange of information, ideas and digital assets in time-effort currency is based on balanced reciprocity. Balanced reciprocity is expected when strangers work together to benefit each other.

In the Metaverse, digital assets can serve as such social resources. For instance, owning a rare digital asset could elevate one's status within the virtual community; on the other hand, the other may need financial gain—this creates a dynamic flow of giving and receiving favors and gifts that sustain the Metaverse community. These digital assets can create a sense of exclusivity and prestige, encouraging more active participation and fostering a culture of sharing and collaboration. Community members trade or gift assets to strengthen social bonds. For instance, individuals might invest time in social media to strengthen their social bonds or engage in face-to-face meetings to deepen personal connections. In the physical world, it is common for residents of a residential community to volunteer their time and energy to organize local events such as neighborhood cleanups or festivals. On the other hand, it is also common that negative reciprocity occurs. For example, free-riders benefit from the efforts of others without contributing equally, leading to resentment and unfairness with retaliatory actions, potentially erode trust and collaboration. Trust plays a crucial role in balanced reciprocity, ensuring that both parties feel secure in the exchange. When trust is established, individuals are more likely to engage in fair and equitable transactions, fostering long-term, mutually beneficial relationships. Reputation ratings help maintain accountability and encourage balanced reciprocity in the Metaverse community. Furthermore, overall civic participation and even knowing our neighbors appears to be declining globally (Putnam, 2001).

Social resource theory in the context of the Metaverse focuses on the exchange of digital gifts. These virtual gifts are exchanged with digital tokens or other digital assets of appreciation, which can foster relationships and build trust within the Metaverse community (see Chapter 10). Virtual gifts can influence one's social status within the Metaverse by serving as visible symbols of admiration and respect. Receiving valuable or rare digital tokens can elevate a person's standing within the community, indicating their importance and fostering a sense of prestige. Consequently, these exchanges enhance personal connections and the social structure in the Metaverse community. Akin to the physical world, virtual gifts can be instantly delivered without geographical barriers. They often come with unique attributes such as rarity, customization and the ability to be publicly displayed within the digital realm. Moreover, virtual gifts can be easily tracked and recorded, providing an ongoing digital footprint of social interactions and exchanges.

Favor

Social resource theory in which resources that enhance trust in relationships and balanced reciprocity within the Metaverse community may show favor and gift exchanges. The metaverse includes Avatars, which play a crucial role in building trust by providing consistent and recognizable representations of individuals. They allow users to express their identities and personalities, fostering a sense of familiarity and reliability. People can form deeper connections and enhance their social standing in the virtual world by interacting with their avatars. Thus, the balanced reciprocity involving avatars mimics the mutual exchange of favors as in the physical world. For instance, helping a fellow member to complete a challenging task or sharing valuable information can create a sense of not only indebtedness but also cooperation. These reciprocal interactions enhance individual relationships and are traded as non-rivalrous social resources, such as virtual gifts to build relationships. For example, users might attend virtual meetings or events and invest effort in creating and maintaining avatars for other members to enhance their social status. Time spent in such collaborative projects results in shared knowledge and skills that would be highlighted in a Metaverse dashboard. With a time and effort system, everyone gets the benefits apportioned according to their contribution. Building virtual social status can lead to increased influence and recognition within the community. The economic implications of time and effort currency in the Metaverse are profound. When one invests more time and effort, they can potentially monetize their virtual achievements through various channels, such as selling virtual goods, offering services or even consulting within the Metaverse as an expert, eventually if possible to CBDC.

A shared understanding of favors among the metaverse community would underpin avocational payments. For example, knowledge, information, music, videos, jokes, attire or performance are understood as time-effort tokens, which are agreed upon within the community. All these activities of favor require community members to spend time and effort adding value to digital content. Favors are exchanged in reputation-enhancing, mutually beneficial chores such as the return of comments, feedback, likes, dislikes, participation in polls and reflection, which are conducted at the expense of one's time and effort. Drawing on social resource theory (Foa & Foa, 2012 Törnblom & Kazemi, 2012), we see that resources embedded in social connections play important roles in the interaction between social structure and individuals (Lin, 1982). Lin suggests that resources can be material and symbolic goods, which are digital goods in this chapter that are accessed and used in social actions. In metaverse commerce, social resources are embedded in social networks and social ties among the community member eager to enhance their digital assets for their gain and contribute to the community. Lin (2019) draws an example from the physical world:

> A friend's car may be the one's social resource. They may borrow it for use and return it to a friend. They do not possess the car and access and use it only if the friend is willing to lend it.

The friend retains the ownership. For example, participating in a metaverse event or completing a series of challenges can earn users time-effort tokens. These tokens can access exclusive content, virtual goods or services within the metaverse. Online gaming demonstrates how digital services utilize the social resources of the community. For example, personalized avatars can be purchased where one spends their earned tokens on unique outfits, accessories and special effects to enhance their virtual presence and express their individuality. These social exchanges are based on helping each other in the form of a favor. Rupp (2003) draws an example: at Mr. Hoshino's house-building ceremony, his *true friends* gave a larger sum of money than his *superficial friends*. Similarly, close friends gave twice as much as just a friend. The part of a gift related to one's gratitude to the recipient may be hierarchy-driven, an ulterior motive influencing the giving. The pertinent actor that influenced the social relationship and the economic exchange in the case of Mr. Hoshino underlies that hierarchy and relationship strength influenced gratitude. Marcoux (2009, p. 671) presents an exception and disruption to the gift economy that "people use the market to free themselves from the straitjacket of social expectations—from the sense of indebtedness and emotional oppression—which constrains them in their reciprocity relations inside the gift economy."

The concept of balanced reciprocity, generally defined as the moral obligation to compensate someone for one's past behavior (Gouldner, 1960), is primarily a product of the social and economic sciences (e.g., Kolm, 2008; Kolm & Ythier, 2006), and it has also been extensively explored in consumer research, mainly through gift-giving. There is evidence that it also works in Metaverse commerce (Belk, 1976; Belk, 2010; Belk & Coon, 1993). Reciprocity in digital asset exchange in Metaverse follows the market principle documented in Marcoux's (2009) study, which is a mutual exchange of digital, often expecting a similar return. This concept ensures that all parties benefit fairly following Sahlins' balanced reciprocity, fostering trust and cooperation within the metaverse community. Time-effort currency following blockchain technology is crucial in facilitating digital asset exchange by providing a transparent and secure ledger for recording transactions and an example of balanced reciprocity. It ensures that all trades are immutable and verifiable, reducing fraud risk and enhancing participant trust. Similarly, smart contracts on a blockchain can automate and enforce the terms of exchanges, such as compensation for time and efforts contained in the CBDC exchanged, making the process more efficient and reliable. The metaverse-enabled social exchange echoes the avocational trade of time and effort as the currency of exchange.

Conclusion

Given the importance of time in human life, ideally digital assets revolve around spending time in value-added activities based on avocational passion and hobbies that may generate financial well-being for people who engage, which is not always the case point in current digital assets innovation. This chapter speculates the possibility of time-effort accounting for when valuing creative works using blockchain technology. We have discussed that time banking suffered an issue of scalability that lacked appeal. But in the 1970s, we did not have the method and technology to account for the efforts and skills in the payment mechanism of time banking. The time spent is associated with the effort and skills of the creative director but also produces meaningful experiences for others. We think time-effort banking is possible with blockchain development that ensures equitable and fair compensation for those who engage in digital asset creation.

This chapter has explored time and effort as potential basis for a digital currency in the metaverse and speculates that the metaverse will grow to its full potential, transcending people's lives. CBDC will also be adopted in the metaverse. Chapter 2 details the definition of financial and digital assets. Building on the characteristics of digital assets, we investigate the role of time and effort encoded in digital assets and the development of blockchain to implement time-effort algorithms to account for digital asset transactions.

The fundamental concepts of time-effort as social currency and the metaverse were sketched at the beginning of this chapter, along with the role of a new type of avocational payment method underpinning blockchain technology account for contributors' time-effort as a building block for fair and equitable transactions among members of the Metaverse community. Later in this chapter, we highlighted social resource theory for explaining the way resources are managed in the Metaverse; most importantly, the role of gift exchange and favors that drive the Metaverse community is fundamental to create digital assets that are essential to driving the Metaverse commerce in coming days.

Finally, the goal of this chapter is not to suggest technical improvements. Rather, we have showcased new opportunities and challenges for Metaverse commerce. Here, too, we have sketched out simple future research directions. How could non-financial digital assets be marketable in an avocational payment method? How is favor and gift exchange in the Metaverse accounted for using the time-effort concept? How do consumers perceive time-effort-based currency about other payment options, such as digital currency?

References

Akkus, H. T., Gursoy, S., Dogan, M., & Demir, A. B. (2022). Metaverse and metaverse cryptocurrencies (meta coins): Bubbles or future? *Journal of Economics Finance and Accounting*, *9*(1), 22–29.

Alsop, T. (2024, May 21). Metaverse market size worldwide 2022–2032 [Review of Metaverse market size worldwide 2022–2032]. *Statista*. https://www.statista.com/statistics/1295784/metaverse-market-size/

Avocational – Quick search results | Oxford English Dictionary. (2024). Oed.com. https://www.oed.com/search/dictionary/?scope=Entries&q=avocational

Ball, P. (2022). *The book of minds: How to understand ourselves and other beings, from animals to AI to aliens*. University of Chicago Press.
Baral, S. K., Goel, R., Singh, T., & Kumar, R. (Eds.). (2024). *Green metaverse for greener economies*. CRC Press.
Belk, R. (2010). Sharing. *Journal of Consumer Research*, *36*(5), 715–734.
Belk, R. (2024). The digital frontier as a liminal space. *Journal of Consumer Psychology*, *34*(1), 167–173.
Belk, R., Humayun, M., & Brouard, M. (2022). Money, possessions, and ownership in the Metaverse: NFTs, cryptocurrencies, Web3 and Wild Markets. *Journal of Business Research*, *153*, 198–205.
Belk, R. W. (1976). It's the thought that counts: A signed digraph analysis of gift-giving. *Journal of Consumer Research*, *3*(3), 155–162.
Belk, R. W., & Coon, G. S. (1993). Gift giving as agapic love: An alternative to the exchange paradigm based on dating experiences. *Journal of Consumer Research*, *20*(3), 393–417.
Braud, T., Fernández, C. B., & Hui, P. (2022, March). Scaling-up ar: University campus as a physical-digital metaverse. In *2022 IEEE Conference on Virtual Reality and 3D User Interfaces Abstracts and Workshops (VRW)* (pp. 169–175). IEEE.
Brinberg, D., & Wood, R. (1983). A resource exchange theory analysis of consumer behavior. *Journal of Consumer Research*, *10*(3), 330–338.
Burrows, G. (2022). *Your life in the metaverse: Everything you need to know about the virtual Internet of tomorrow*. Gideon Burrows.
Chapman, S., Hilton, A., Ward, A., Saull, D., & Gilstrap, C. (2020). Swap.com as a social style platform brand: Strategic use of social media brand communities. *Journal of the International Academy for Case Studies*, *26*(2), 1–9.
Cheng, S. (2024). *Web 3.0: Concept, content and context* (pp. 1–217). Springer.
Chiu, C. M., Huang, H. Y., Cheng, H. L., & Sun, P. C. (2015). Understanding online community citizenship behaviors through social support and social identity. *International Journal of Information Management*, *35*(4), 504–519.
Dawson, A. (2022). Data-driven consumer engagement, virtual immersive shopping experiences, and blockchain-based digital assets in the retail metaverse. *Journal of Self-Governance and Management Economics*, *10*(2), 52–66.
Del Moral, L., & Pais, I. (2015). Collaborative economy and the digitalization of timebanking: Opportunities and challenges. *Studi di Sociologia*, *53*(1), 3–21.
Du, Y., Grace, T. D., Jagannath, K., & Salen-Tekinbas, K. (2021). Connected play in virtual worlds: Communication and control mechanisms in virtual worlds for children and adolescents. *Multimodal Technologies and Interaction*, *5*(5), 27.
Fiske, S. T. (2011). *Envy up, scorn down: How status divides us*. Russell Sage Foundation.
Foa, E. B., & Foa, U. G. (2012). Resource Theory of Social Exchange. In: K. Törnblom & A. Kazemi (Eds.), *Handbook of social resource theory. Critical issues in social justice*. Springer. (pp. 15–32).
Functions of money. (2015, October 18). Web.archive.org. https://web.archive.org/web/20151018115939/https://www.boundless.com/business/textbooks/boundless-business-textbook/the-functions-of-money-and-banking-21/money-as-a-tool-123/functions-of-money-568-3194/
Gadekallu, T. R., Huynh-The, T., Wang, W., Yenduri, G., Ranaweera, P., Pham, Q. V., da Costa, D. B., & Liyanage, M. (2022). Blockchain for the metaverse: A review. *arXiv preprint arXiv:2203.09738*.

Giobbi, G. (2022). *Luxury brands in the new digital era: Metaverse, nft and gaming.* The Universidade Nova de Lisboa. http://hdl.handle.net/10362/148145

Gomez-Trujillo, A. M., Velez-Ocampo, J., & Gonzalez-Perez, M. A. (2021). Trust, transparency, and technology: Blockchain and its relevance in the context of the 2030 agenda. In S. H. Park, M. A. Gonzalez-Perez, & D. E., Floriani (Eds.), *The Palgrave handbook of corporate sustainability in the digital era* (pp. 561–580). Palgrave Macmillan. https://doi.org/10.1007/978-3-030-42412-1_28

Gouldner, A. W. (1960). The norm of reciprocity: A preliminary statement. *American Sociological Review*, *25*(2), 161–178.

Hadi, R., Melumad, S., & Park, E. S. (2024). The metaverse: A new digital frontier for consumer behavior. *Journal of Consumer Psychology*, *34*(1), 142–166.

Hennig-Thurau, T., Aliman, D. N., Herting, A. M., Cziehso, G. P., Linder, M., & Kübler, R. V. (2023). Social interactions in the metaverse: Framework, initial evidence, and research roadmap. *Journal of the Academy of Marketing Science*, *51*(4), 889–913.

Henry, C. D., & Shannon, L. (2023). *Virtual natives: How a new generation is revolutionizing the future of work, play, and culture.* John Wiley & Sons.

Huang, L., Gao, B., & Gao, M. (2023). The metaverse era: The fourth transformation in the age of Internet communication. In L. Huang, B. Gao, & M. Gao (Eds.), *Value realization in the phygital reality market: Consumption and service under conflation of the physical, digital, and virtual worlds* (pp. 99–123). Springer Nature Singapore.

Jeff, C. (2022). *Metaverse investing: The complete step-by-step guide on how to invest in NFT, virtual land, digital assests and metaverse cryptocurrency through the blockchain gaming. Discover the next big thing.* Clifford Jeff.

Joy, A., Zhu, Y., Peña, C., & Brouard, M. (2022). Digital future of luxury brands: Metaverse, digital fashion, and non-fungible tokens. *Strategic Change*, *31*(3), 337–343.

Khan, J., Abbas, A. & Tao, M. (forthcoming). Digital doppelgänger: Navigating consumer brand engagement in the metaverse.

Khan, S., Amin, M. B., Azar, A. T., & Aslam, S. (2021). Towards interoperable blockchains: A survey on the role of smart contracts in Blockchain interoperability. *IEEE Access*, *9*, 116672–116691.

Kolm, S. C. (2008). *Reciprocity: An economics of social relations.* Cambridge University Press.

Kolm, S. C., & Ythier, J. M. (Eds.). (2006). *Handbook of the economics of giving, altruism and reciprocity: Foundations.* Elsevier.

Oxford Dictionary. (2024). *Avocation.* [online] Available at: https://www.oxfordreference.com/display/10.1093/acref/9780199661350.001.0001/acref-9780199661350-e-419.

Lai, Y., Yang, J., Liu, M., Li, Y., & Li, S. (2023). Web3: Exploring decentralized technologies and applications for the future of empowerment and ownership. *Blockchains*, *1*(2), 111–131.

Lewis, J. (Ed.). (2008). *Tomorrow through the past: Neal Stephenson and the project of global modernization.* Cambridge Scholars Publishing.

Lin, N. (1982). Social resources and instrumental action. In Marsden, P. V., & Lin, N. (Eds.), *Social structure and network analysis* (pp. 131–145). Sage.

Lin, N. (2019). *Social resources theory. Encyclopedia.com.* https://www.encyclopedia.com/social-sciences/encyclopedias-almanacs-transcripts-and-maps/social-resources-theory

Luchs, M. G., Naylor, R. W., Rose, R. L., Catlin, J. R., Gau, R., Kapitan, S., ... & Simpson, B. (2011). Toward a sustainable marketplace: Expanding options and benefits for consumers. *Journal of Research for Consumers*, *1*(19), 1–12.

Mancuso, I., Petruzzelli, A. M., & Panniello, U. (2023). Digital business model innovation in metaverse: How to approach virtual economy opportunities. *Information Processing & Management*, *60*(5), 103457.

Maner, J. K. (2017). Dominance and prestige: A tale of two hierarchies. *Current Directions in Psychological Science*, *26*(6), 526–531.

Marcoux, J. S. (2009). Escaping the gift economy. *Journal of Consumer Research*, *36*(4), 671–685.

Mărgulescu, S., & Mărgulescu, E. (2021). Traditional cryptocurrencies and fiat-backed digital currencies. *Global Economic Observer*, *9*(1), 116–123.

Mario Lavizzari, M. G., Luzio, M. D., & Tommasino, C. (2021). The development of digital identity in the financial service industry: From an element that enables digital transactions to a new strategic asset for business. *Journal of Digital Banking*, 6(1), 57–65.

Meisenzahl, M. (2022). See inside the virtual worlds created by Wendy's, Chipotle, and McDonald's as the metaverse becomes the latest battleground for fast food. *Business Insider.*

Mogaji, E., Wirtz, J., Belk, R. W., & Dwivedi, Y. K. (2023). Immersive time (ImT): Conceptualizing time spent in the metaverse. *International Journal of Information Management*, 72, 102659.

Momtaz, P. P. (2022). Some very simple economics of web3 and the metaverse. *FinTech*, *1*(3), 225–234.

Mystakidis, S. (2022). Metaverse. *Encyclopedia*, *2*(1), 486–497.

Nordquist, R. (2021, February 16). *Avocation and vocation*. https://www.thoughtco.com/avocation-and-vocation-1689309

Putnam, R. (2001). *Bowling alone: The collapse and revival of American community*. Simon and Schuster.

Rupp, K. (2003). *Gift-giving in Japan: Cash, connections, cosmologies*. Stanford University Press.

Sabatelli, R. M., & Shehan, C. L. (1993). Exchange and resource theories. In P. Boss, W. J. Doherty, R. LaRossa, W. R. Schumm, S. K. Steinmetz (Eds.), *Sourcebook of family theories and methods*. Springer. https://doi.org/10.1007/978-0-387-85764-0_16

Sahlins, M. (1972). *Stone age economics*. Aldine Atheron Inc.

Saiz, A. (2020). Bricks, mortar, and proptech: The economics of IT in brokerage, space utilization and commercial real estate finance. *Journal of Property Investment & Finance*, *38*(4), 327–347.

Seyfang, G. (2002). Tackling social exclusion with community currencies: Learning from LETS to Time Banks. *International Journal of Community Currency Research*, *6*(1), 1–11.

Shen, B., Tan, W., Guo, J., Zhao, L., & Qin, P. (2021). How to promote user purchase in Metaverse? A systematic literature review on consumer behavior research and virtual commerce application design. *Applied Sciences*, *11*(23), 11087.

Silberstein, N. (2022). *Moving into the metaverse: Growing swath of brands test out virtual experiences*. Retrieved on Jun 30, 2022 from https://bit.ly/3c1aC0o

Smartbnb. (2024, April 30). *Airbnb superhost status: Benefits of becoming one*. Hospitable. https://hospitable.com/airbnb-superhost-status/

Stephenson, N. (2003). Snow crash. In *Google books*. Random House Worlds. https://books.google.com/books?id=RMd3GpIFxcUC&pg=PA45#v=onepage&q&f=false

Tacanho, M. (2024). Money demystified: Understanding why, how, and what it is. *Afrindependent Institute Paper* (02–EN).
Törnblom, K., & Kazemi, A. (2012). Some conceptual and theoretical issues in resource theory of social exchange. In K. Törnblom & A. Kazemi (Eds.), *Handbook of social resource theory: Theoretical extensions, empirical insights, and social applications* (pp. 33–64). Springer. https://doi.org/10.1007/978-1-4614-4175-5_3
Verma, A., Sridhar, S., Dar, K. F., & Asthana, M. K. (2024). Scope and challenges in the implementation of Time Bank in India: A qualitative study. *Discover Global Society*, 2(1), 14.
Wang, H., Ning, H., Lin, Y., Wang, W., Dhelim, S., Farha, F., ... & Daneshmand, M. (2023). A survey on the metaverse: The state-of-the-art, technologies, applications, and challenges. *IEEE Internet of Things Journal*, *10*(16), 14671–14688.
Yi, Q., Khan, J., Su, Y., Tong, J., & Zhao, S. (2023). Impulse buying tendency in live-stream commerce: The role of viewing frequency and anticipated emotions influencing scarcity-induced purchase decision. *Journal of Retailing and Consumer Services*, *75*, 103534.
Zhang, G., Wu, J., Jeon, G., Chen, Y., Wang, Y., & Tan, M. (2022). Towards understanding metaverse engagement via social patterns and reward mechanism: A case study of nova empire. *IEEE Transactions on Computational Social Systems*, *10*(5), 2165–2176.

Case Study One

Marshall Island's Sovereign Currency

Jashim Khan and Russell Belk

Introduction

The Marshall Islands is a small archipelago in the Pacific Ocean consisting of 1,000 islands, home to around 75,000 people (Kiste, 2024), and renowned for 67 nuclear tests between 1946 and 1958; the United States conducted 23 of these tests at Bikini Atoll, and 44 near Enewetak Atoll, but fallout spread throughout the Marshall Islands (Zak, 2015; Chavez-Dreyfuss, 2018). In 2018, its government passed infamous legislation initiating digital currency. The introduction of the Sovereign Currency Act allows for the creation and issuance of the sovereign (SOV), a blockchain-based new unit of account supported by the finance ministry. Among the countries promoting digital currency, the Republic of Marshall Islands launched the 'world's first national digital currency'—Sovereign Currency (SOV). First, we discuss background information, challenges, opportunities and outlook.

Background

From 2012 to 2022, the imports to the Marshall Islands increased slightly, followed by a continuous economic drop to half and then a stabilizing recovery. Three key periods of import are 2013 (US dollars 147 million), 2019 (US dollars 68 million) and 2022 (US dollars 94 million). From 2012 to 2022, exports experienced a sharp decline; in 2012, it was US dollars 106.79 million; in 2016, US dollars 36.05 million; and in 2019, US dollars 55 million. Last year, Marshall Island exported US dollars 43 million in goods (WTO, 2023). The decline in exports, over-reliance on imports and dependence on the United States aid make the economy vulnerable to export–import trade imbalance. The islands have few natural resources and their imports far exceed exports. According to the CIA, the value of exports in 2013 was approximately $53.7 million while estimated imports were $133.7 million. Agricultural products include coconuts, tomatoes, melons, taro, breadfruit, fruits, pigs and chickens. The industry is made up of the production of copra and craft items, tuna processing and tourism. The CIA Factbook (2024) estimates that the GDP in 2016 was an estimated $180 million, with a real

DOI: 10.4324/9781003425021-13

growth rate of 1.7% while the GDP per capita income was $3,300. Salary Explorer (2023) suggests that Marshall Islands citizens earn an average of around US dollars 2,260 (before tax) per month, which includes housing, transport and other benefits. Salaries range from US dollars 5,700 (the lowest average) to US dollars 10,100 and exhibit great income disparity among households and careers. An average person's living cost is approximately US dollars 1,079 (without rent) per month, and a family of four people's estimated monthly costs would be US dollars 3,622 (without rent). Living expenses in the Marshall Islands are 85.9% higher than in China, and housing rent is 80.7% higher than in China (Numbeo, 2023). Inflation in the Marshall Islands during the past 20 years has been severe. Compared to the previous year, the inflation rate dropped to –0.66 in 2020 and then rapidly went up to +2.6% in 2021. As predicted, it continued rising to about +6.16% in 2023, then declined to +2% in 2023 and maintained this number following 2024 (IMF, 2023). The purchasing power parity conversion factor refers to the number of units of a country's currency that could purchase the equivalent amounts of goods or services in the domestic market, such as the US dollar, which is referred to as LCU. In 2022, the purchasing power parity for the Marshall Islands was 0.9 LCU compared to the US dollar (Knoema, 2022b). Marshall Islands purchasing power parity fluctuated substantially in recent years, it increased between 2003 and 2022 and declined since 2022 (Knoema, 2022a,b). In the past ten years, Marshall Islands' GDP (Gross Domestic Product) has grown annually. In 2022, it reached US dollars 279,667,900 (World Bank, 2022a). The Marshall Islands have strong economic connections with the United States, and its national security and defense ability are managed by the United States.

The Marshall Islands' population was 60,397 on July 14, 2023. In the past ten years, the population has steadily increased year by year. The latest population is equivalent to approximately 0.00076% of the total population worldwide and ranks 207th in the list of countries and dependencies by population (World Bank, 2023). Seventy percent of the residents live in urban areas, and more than two-thirds live on the atolls of Majuro (capital) and Ebeye (Moody's Analytics, 2021). In 2017, the life expectancy of the Marshallese was 73.4, the birth rate was 24.4/1,000 population and the death rate was 4.2/1,000 population. The fertility rate was 3.03 children born per woman, ranking 54th worldwide (Kemp, 2023). The literacy rate in the Marshall Islands is high—more than 98% are considered to read and write. The literacy rate among men and women is equally distributed (Symbol Hunt, 2023).

The Republic of the Marshall Islands is inclusive of innovation and works hard to apply innovation to community empowerment. For instance, according to Marshall Islands' Innovation Work from 2020 to 2025, Pacific Pure Water, new processes incorporated using local products could benefit the economy (economic perspective), One Island One Product initiatives have been a source of investment and employment opportunities for the residents (social perspective), and Waan Aelõñ in Majel (WAM), which manufacturers traditional canoe offer training and employment for the communities, and ways to reduce carbon emissions. Other surveyed programs concerning environmental-friendly aims attach great significance to climate change, especially in dealing with rising sea levels. Government regulations, health and tradition protection are priority areas in the Marshall Islands' growth (United Nations Development Programme, 2020). At the beginning of 2023, there were 7,844 cellular mobile connections in the Marshall Islands (note that some people may have more than one mobile connection). This number shows that these mobile connections were equivalent to 18.8% of the total population of the Marshall Islands in January 2023 (Kemp, 2023). Overall, social media use in most areas has continued to grow, and the number of social media users at the start of 2023 has been more than 23,000 (Kemp, 2023). As a developing country, the Marshall Islands rely much on its fishing and service sectors, and its AI development and automation sectors are weak. Therefore, these perspectives will not be analyzed further.

The Marshall Islands' economic growth relies heavily on its natural resources, ranging from tourism to fisheries. However, the country's economic geography occasionally threatens its sustainable growth because of its characteristics such as extreme remoteness, small size, geographic dispersion, environmental fragility and other limited natural resources. Among the economic activities of three sectors (agriculture sector, industry sector and service sector), the service sector has the highest added value (accounts for 65.3% of GDP) while the lowest annual growth rate (–0.4%). The industry sector has the lowest percentage of added value in GDP (10.3%), and the agriculture sector has the highest annual growth of added value (+8.8%) (World Bank, 2022b).

Next, we delve into the banking sector entwined with the legal and economic frameworks.

The Marshall Islands' legal system includes a mixture of US and English common law, customary law and local statutes. Banks are the main source of loans for residents and firms in the Marshall Islands, and banking regulations are relatively comprehensive and modern (Republic of the Marshall Islands Judiciary, 2023). In 2020, the Banking Commissioner of the Marshall Islands enacted financial services providers licensing and fees regulation 2020 under the Banking Act of 1987. These regulations are targeted at prescribing the procedure for applying for Banks and Financial Services Providers licenses and other matters required to be prescribed under the Banking Act 1987.

The financial system comprises two commercial banks, insurance companies, money transfer agents and one pension and development fund. This excludes three main banks: The Bank of the Marshall Islands is a locally owned bank; the Bank of Guam is a branch of a foreign-owned bank; and the Marshall Islands Development Bank (MIDB) is the country's development bank. The two commercial banks are under the supervision of the Banking Commission, while there are calls to include the MIDB under the commission's oversight. This sector has two large money transfer operators (MoneyGram and Western Union), two insurance companies and a pension fund. Private sector credit and deposits exhibited similar trends from 2011 to 2017 (Asian Development Bank, 2018). According to the International Monetary Fund (2018), household debt reached 60% of total employee compensation. Such a figure burdens the financial system and threatens the banking system's stability. In 2017, the Marshall Islands cabinet authorized the Banking Commission to conduct guidelines for the MIDB (International Monetary Fund, 2018).

The domestic commercial bank was threatened with losing its correspondent bank relationship with the First Hawaiian Bank in 2015. This withdrawal would affect the economy, as the country would lose all connections with the US banking system, disrupt international payments and economic activity and weaken financial inclusion, especially for the outer islands. Until then, the US dollar was the legal tender. Given this backdrop in the financial sector, there are opportunities.

Opportunities and Incentives

In 2018, the Republic of Marshall Islands passed a Sovereign Currency Act, intending to release a new blockchain-based national digital currency known as the Marshallese SOV. According to an announcement, the Marshallese SOV purports to be the 'world's first national digital currency' as the coin will represent a SOV currency circulating along with the US dollar. In contrast to projects like the Bahamian Central Bank digital currency, known as Project Sand Dollar, the Marshallese SOV will not just represent the local fiat currency but rather an independent coin. Given that the service sector includes tourism and finance that dominate the economy, reliance on digital currency is convenient for tourists within the Marshall Islands. Additionally, easier transfers and shorter transaction times ensure foreign companies participate in trading in SOV digital currency; similarly, for local firms, it brings efficiency in transactions and reduction in operational costs. Given that Internet penetration and digital devices is a priority sector for country growth, supported by a very high literacy rate, digital currency seems a viable long-term strategy. A planned Digital Economic Zone was submitted to the Parliament in 2021 as a prospective step forward in maintaining and growing the digital economy.

Challenges

The Marshall Islands is a developing country, and its manufacturing industry is the weakest among all three industries, such as fisheries, tourism and financial services. Accordingly, the less advanced technology and poor infrastructure could not support the stability of the digital currency. For instance, frequent power and network outages have occurred within the Marshall

Islands and harmed the issuance and use of the SOV. The current laws and regulations are underway to support tacking anti-money laundering at par with digital currency. If internet security cannot be guaranteed, privacy and security issues could be concerns or worries for users.

Using digital currency is a creative attempt by the Marshall Islands. The government should solve the existing challenges to make the SOV work better for the Marshall Islands. For instance, it should enhance the legal system, especially for the digital currency. Sufficient supervision and regulation are necessary as well. Cyber security and digital infrastructure should be guaranteed through increased financial and technological investment. To achieve these goals, the government can work with more developed countries or international organizations such as the World Bank and Asian Development Bank to seek financial support and outsource technological assistance. Learning from the experience of other countries with a more mature use of digital currency would also be helpful.

References

Asian Development Bank. (2018). *Marshall Islands*. https://www.adb.org/sites/default/files/publication/529846/pacific-finance-sector-marshall-islands.pdf

Chavez-Dreyfuss, G. (2018, March 1). Marshall Islands to issue own sovereign cryptocurrency. *Reuters*.

IMF. (2023). *Marshall Islands: Inflation rate from 2008 to 2028 (compared to the previous year)*. Retrieved July 30, 2023, from https://www-statista-com.surrey.idm.oclc.org/statistics/731642/inflation-rate-in-marshall-islands/

International Monetary Fund. Research Dept. (2018). *World economic outlook, April 2018: Cyclical upswing, structural change*. International Monetary Fund.

Kemp, S. (2023). *Digital 2023: The Marshall Islands*. Retrieved July 30, 2023, from https://datareportal.com/reports/digital-2023-marshall-islands

Kiste, R. (2024). Marshall Islands | Map, Flag, History, & Facts. In the Editors of Encyclopædia Britannica (eds), *Encyclopædia Britannica*. https://www.britannica.com/place/Marshall-Islands Knoema. (2022a). *China - Purchasing power parity conversion factor for gross domestic product*. Retrieved July 30, 2023, https://knoema.com/atlas/China/topics/Economy/Inflation-and-Prices/Purchasing-power-parity

Knoema. (2022b). *Marshall Islands—purchasing power parity conversion factor for gross domestic product*. Retrieved July 14, 2023, https://knoema.com/atlas/Marshall-Islands/topics/Economy/Inflation-and-Prices/Purchasing-powerparity#:~:text=In%202021%2C%20purchasing%20power%20parity%20for%20Marshall%20Islands,at%201%20LCU%20per%20international%20dollars%20in%202021

Moody's Analytics. (2021). *Marshall Islands – Economic indicators*. Retrieved July 30, 2023, https://www.economy.com/marshall-islands/

Numbeo. (2023). *Cost of living in Marshall Islands*. Numbeo.com. https://www.numbeo.com/cost-of-living/country_result.jsp?country=Marshall+Islands

Republic of the Marshall Islands Judiciary. (2023). *Selected regulations*. Retrieved July 14, 2023, https://rmicourts.org/selected-regulations/

Salary Explorer. (2023). *Average salary in Marshall Islands 2023*. Retrieved July 30, 2023, https://www.salaryexplorer.com/average-salary-wage-comparison-marshall-islands-c134

Symbol Hunt. (2023). *National symbols of Marshall Islands*. Retrieved July 14, 2023, https://symbolhunt.com/marshall-islands/

United Nations Development Programme. (2020). *The Republic of the Marshall Islands innovation report & proposed innovation work plan 2020–2025*. Retrieved July 14, 2023, https://www.undp.org/pacific/publications/republic-marshall-islands-innovation-report-proposed-innovation-work-plan-2020-2025

World Bank. (2022a). *GDP (current US$) – Marshall Islands*. Retrieved July 14, 2023, https://data.worldbank.org/indicator/NY.GDP.MKTP.CD?locations=MH

World Bank. (2022b). *Latest available data*. Retrieved July 14, 2023, https://www.lloydsbanktrade.com/en/market-potential/marshall-islands/economy

World Bank. (2023). *Population, total – Marshall Islands*. Retrieved July 30, 2023, https://data.worldbank.org/indicator/SP.POP.TOTL?locations=MH

WTO. (2023). *Marshall Islands: Import of goods from 2012 to 2022 (in million U.S. dollars)*. Retrieved July 30, 2023, https://www-statista-com.surrey.idm.oclc.org/statistics/731687/import-of-goods-to-marshall-islands/

Case Study Two

China's e-CNY or Digital RMB

Jashim Khan and Russell Belk

Introduction

The COVID-19 pandemic accelerated the shift toward online shopping, with many consumers purchasing goods and services from e-commerce platforms and having them delivered to their homes (Gu et al., 2021). With COVID-19 in the distant past, China's economy is re-invigorated and stabilized, and more people have returned to physical shopping, driven by a desire for social and face-to-face interaction (Zhuoqiong, 2023). In response, retailers focus on creating seamless shopping experiences facilitated by digital environments (Zihan et al., 2024). COVID-19 indeed fueled China's e-commerce market, which is the largest globally, driven by a large consumer base with a high internet penetration rate and smartphone ownership becoming dominant (Piskorski, 2022). As a result of the sector's rapid growth, China's online retail sales exceeded 10 trillion yuan in 2020 (Fildes et al., 2019).

A significant contributor to the growth of e-commerce has been digital payment systems, such as platforms like Alipay and WeChat Pay, which dominated the market by making e-commerce seamlessly easy (Gu et al., 2021). The Chinese digital payment ecosystem is among the world's most advanced third-party platform-based payments, and Alipay, Jindong and WeChat Pay dominate. These platforms have revolutionized in-store payments, online shopping and bill settlement. With this phenomenal growth of third-party payment, the People's Bank of China (PBOC) engaged in innovation in alternative digital payment ecosystem to research and pilot the digital RMB (e-CNY), a digital currency designated by the central bank to further digitize cash transactions with centralized authority over the payment system.

Blockchain technology and artificial intelligence are set to drive further innovation in e-CYN, potentially redefining retail and wholesale global trade and cross-border payments. The widespread adoption of e-CYN significantly alters the dynamics of international trade by simplifying cross-border transactions and reducing reliance on reserve currencies worldwide (Kim et al., 2024). Digital currency enhances financial transparency and security, making tracking and verifying international payments easier (Jiang, 2024). Furthermore, e-CYN's integration to m-bridge (network of central banks) paves the

DOI: 10.4324/9781003425021-14

way for other countries to adopt similar technologies, potentially leading to a more interconnected and efficient global financial system (BIS, 2021). Government regulation plays a crucial role in adopting and insuring the success of e-CYN. The PBOC's oversight ensures that the digital currency operates within a secure and stable framework, mitigating risks such as fraud and cyberattacks (Wang et al., 2022). Additionally, clear regulatory guidelines will help build trust among users and international partners, facilitating smoother integration into the global financial system.

Background

Since adopting market-oriented reforms, China has had a very successful economy. Averaging more than 9.5% yearly, the gross domestic product (GDP) has grown since 1979 (Morrison, 2019). China grew into the world's second-largest economy (Katanich, 2024). Despite this, it is still a developing country with a GDP per capita of just over US dollars 1,000 in the 2000s. Growth policies in China must be viewed within the context of the country's transition economy and developing status. China has been transitioning from a centrally planned economy, which followed Soviet-style heavy industrialization, to a market economy for decades. Reforms were gradually implemented in China during this time. The result has been a gradual transformation of market forces into a managed economy, but it has not fundamentally transformed ownership into full private ownership. A partial liberalization strategy required the authorities to control the sale of goods to the regulated part of the market to allow firms to sell part of their products at market prices. While maintaining a degree of decentralization, China has experimented with market-oriented reforms without affecting the economy. Instead of following a predetermined reform program, this has allowed the authorities to adapt to changing circumstances (Jefferson et al., 2006).

Since the liberalization of its economy and rapid economic growth in the last 20 years, Chinese consumers have rapidly embraced digital technologies, affecting their behavior and expectations. In addition to the convenience, speed and variety offered by online platforms, consumers also seek authenticity, sensory experiences and social interaction offered by physical stores (Deloitte China, 2021). Consequently, live-streaming sales and virtual reality shopping experiences have been developed, as well as seamless integration between online browsing and offline purchasing (Yi et al., 2023).

With e-CYN, the Chinese Central Bank's digital currency, trade volume and value have steadily increased; in mid-2023, the e-CYN reached a significant milestone with 950 million transactions valued at 1.8 trillion yuan (US dollars 249.9 billion). In addition to its growing role in domestic transactions, e-CYN also shows potential for impact on international transactions, indicating a promising start for this pioneering digital currency. e-CYN is used within China and potentially internationally in transactions where it is accepted. Transactions are significant in both volume and value, as discussed above. Although the e-CYN had significant activity, it accounted for only

0.16% of China's money supply, indicating that despite its high velocity, it represents only a tiny percentage of China's money supply. A high e-CYN adoption rate indicates a significant penetration among both consumers and businesses. Furthermore, it demonstrates a broader acceptance of e-CYNs in China's financial ecosystem, including retail transactions and services. According to the People's Bank of China (PBOC), 260 million e-CYN wallets were used in January 2022, with $13.7 billion in transactions (87 billion yuan).

Market Factors

The e-CYN awareness rate is 18%, among China's population of 1,412.60 million in 2021. From 2022 to 2023, the e-CYN (e-CNY) grew by 1969%, indicating that e-CNY is well known to a significant segment of the population (National Bureau of Statistics of China, 2022). With the increased digital literacy in digital finance and the expansion of the infrastructure supporting e-CNY to cover more areas and use cases, this gap presents an enormous opportunity for growth for e-CNY, largely attributed to Chinese government's support for e-CNY. Government policies encouraging e-CNY's use may drive its rapid adoption, along with government initiatives to develop a digitized economy. It aligns with broader aims of enhancing financial inclusion, streamlining payment systems and expanding the yuan's international reach.

In addition to serving as a pioneering example of central bank digital currency (CBDC) initiatives globally, the e-CYN is at the forefront of China's push toward a more digitalized economy. E-CNY is designed to provide the public with a secure, efficient and convenient means of making payments digitally. This initiative demonstrates the government's commitment to innovation in the financial sector with its endorsement and proactive role. China's CBDC effort is among the most advanced (BIS, 2021). The Bank for International Settlements (BIS) has noted that CBDCs could improve payment efficiencies and financial inclusion globally.

Considering Alipay and WeChat Pay, the Chinese customer base is already familiar with digital payments. Customers value digital transactions' convenience, speed and security, indicating that digital payment culture is highly sophisticated. The McKinsey & Company report on China's digital payments landscape finds that Chinese consumers are much more open to adopting new financial technologies than consumers in many other countries, largely due to innovations in mobile payments (McKinsey & Company, 2020). Providing e-CNY meets or exceeds the standards set by existing services; this readiness lays a fertile ground for its adoption. Due to e-commerce's rapid adoption, online shopping accounts for a significant portion of total retail sales in China. In 2020, nearly three-quarters of China's Internet users engaged in online shopping, which shows how prevalent e-commerce is among the populace. Despite the popularity of online shopping, Chinese consumers still prefer offline retail experiences, especially when it comes to food and beverages, luxury goods and personal care (KPMG China, 2021).

Characteristics of e-CNY

- With the e-CYN, transactions are faster, more efficient and costs are lower than with traditional electronic payments. Small and medium-sized businesses (SMEs) and consumers in rural and underserved areas will benefit from this, promoting financial inclusion (PBOC, 2021a).
- In addition to its ease of use, the e-CYN can be accessed via a mobile app, which allows for both online and offline transactions. An accessible payment method that doesn't rely on bank accounts or physical cash is essential in countries with high mobile internet penetration levels (Zhou, 2021b).
- In several cities, the PBOC and local governments have launched pilot programs to promote the use of e-CNY through lotteries and red envelopes (*hong bao*). As a result of these initiatives, consumers can use e-CYN at participating retailers, demonstrating its practicality and encouraging broader adoption (Chorzempa, 2021).
- In addition to enhanced security features, controlled anonymity ensures compliance with anti-money laundering (AML) and counter-terrorism financing regulations. These features address consumers' privacy concerns and digital transactions are more trusted (Mu & Lee, 2020).
- Even with the incentives to use e-CNY, changing consumer behavior and encouraging widespread adoption remain challenges. If the benefits of switching seem marginal to consumers accustomed to Alipay and WeChat Pay, they may need more motivation to do so (Huang, 2021).
- A seamless integration with global financial systems is essential for the e-CNY to contribute significantly to international trade and finance. Other countries and international businesses, who may be wary of China's control over the digital currency, must be able to coordinate regulatory policies and accept the digital currency.
- Despite the PBOC's emphasis on 'controllable anonymity,' privacy concerns and the potential for government surveillance remain. Finding a balance between regulatory oversight and individual privacy rights will be crucial, especially when it comes to gaining trust among international users (Mu & Lee, 2020).

Opportunities

Among the Chinese e-commerce ecosystem's offerings are business-to-consumer (B2C) and consumer-to-consumer (C2C) shopping, as well as social commerce. Several major platforms serving diverse consumer needs exist, such as Alibaba's Taobao and Tmall, JD.com and Pinduoduo, which have pioneered innovations such as live-streaming sales and group buying (Zhang, L., 2021). AliPay and WeChat Pay dominate China's digital payment landscape, handling most of the country's mobile transactions. However, for e-CNY to gain traction, strategic partnerships or unique value propositions must be developed (South China Morning Post, 2021).

In addition, several countries are exploring or launching their own CBDC initiatives internationally. The Atlantic Council's CBDC tracker provides an overview of global CBDC projects, illustrating how the e-CNY is positioning itself both domestically and internationally. Underpinning the e-CNY is a two-tier system that ensures direct oversight by the People's Bank of China (PBOC) and public distribution through existing financial institutions. Using this system, retailers can make payments more efficiently and integrate digital currencies more seamlessly into existing payment systems.

In this system, the PBOC issues e-CNY to banks and financial institutions, which distribute it to consumers. With this method, e-CYN adoption can be enhanced without disrupting existing digital payment infrastructures (PBOC, 2021a). Digital wallets developed by the PBOC and commercial banks provide access to the e-CNY. In addition to supporting a range of transactions, these wallets also support offline payments, emphasizing the e-CNY's focus on accessibility and resilience. Smart contracts are included in the e-CNY, enabling transactions to be executed automatically based on predefined conditions. In order to facilitate programmable payments, this innovation could significantly affect transaction processes (South China Morning Post, 2021).

The e-CNY is more than just a digital currency. It serves as a platform for broader financial system innovation in China. In addition to addressing financial inclusion and reducing transaction costs, it may facilitate internationalization of the yuan.

E-CYN emphasizes 'controllable anonymity' to balance user privacy needs with compliance requirements for anti-money laundering (AML) and counter-terrorist financing (CTF) efforts (PBOC, 2021b). Based on China's proactive development and testing of the e-CNY, Chorzempa (2021) highlights China's position as a global leader in CBDC innovation. It is not only a demonstration of China's commitment to digital currency innovation, but it also has a significant impact on international standards and practices. In the future, other countries could use the e-CNY as a model when developing their CBDCs, further strengthening China's influence. The PBOC is exploring the application of e-CNY to cross-border payments. In addition to international collaborations and pilot programs, e-CYN will also be evaluated for international transactions, reducing the dependency on current international payment systems and challenging the dominance of currencies like the US dollar (Bank for International Settlements, 2021).

Challenges

E-CNY's offline transaction ability has been highlighted by the People's Bank of China (2021), which underscores its utility in improving liquidity. It is this feature that allows digital payments to be completed even in environments where internet connectivity is limited or unavailable, thus making them more reliable, faster and more efficient across a wide range of scenarios.

Emergency or remote areas require such resilience in payment systems to ensure continuity of economic activity.

According to Zhou (2021a), the e-CNY features 'controllable anonymity' to balance user privacy and regulatory requirements [said previously]. With this approach, the e-CNY offers a degree of privacy to users while monitoring and preventing illegal activities such as money laundering and terrorism financing. With these dual capabilities, CBDCs can address one of the major concerns about digital currencies, setting a standard for future CBDCs around the world. Huang (2020) examines the potential of the e-CNY to challenge the dominance of the US dollar through cross-border trade settlements in yuan. As a result, the yuan's global standing would be enhanced, and China and its trading partners would be less dependent on the dollar. Through the e-CYN, international trade could become more efficient, stable and direct, bypassing the complications and fees associated with the current dollar-dominated system.

As part of its ambition to expand its influence in international finance, the e-CNY infrastructure is designed for global interoperability. It has been noted by Chia and Ekberg (2021) that e-CNY is a currency that could be seamlessly incorporated into international payment systems, allowing its use to extend beyond Chinese borders. As a result of such expansion, China's economic ties with other nations would be strengthened, as well as allowing for the adoption of a digital currency as an alternative to the dollar in international trade and finance. The development of the e-CNY is seen by Li and Wang (2021) as a means for China to gain greater autonomy in international financial markets, potentially mitigating the impact of international financial sanctions. By providing an alternative to the current international payment systems, which are heavily influenced by Western countries, the e-CNY could offer China and its trading partners a way to conduct transactions that are less susceptible to external pressures, ensuring smoother trade and economic stability and independence. Compliance with anti-money laundering (AML) and counter-terrorist financing (CTF) regulations is essential for e-CNY [redundant]. E-CNY-related financial institutions must implement robust systems and processes to monitor transactions, report suspicious activity and maintain records to be able to comply with regulatory requirements (People's Bank of China, 2021).

Regulations protect the rights of consumers and their privacy. A key feature of the e-CYN is that it offers 'controllable anonymity [redundant],' but the PBOC requires that banks safeguard their users' data by ensuring privacy and security during transactions. In addition, the system provides regulatory access under specific conditions, which strikes a balance between privacy and the need for legal compliance and financial oversight (Zhou, 2021a).

The regulatory framework supports the interoperability of the e-CNY across China's existing financial and payment systems. e-CYN helps banks enhance their daily financial activities by developing innovative services around it (Subrahmanyam, 2023).

China's e-commerce market is fiercely competitive, with major players constantly innovating to capture and retain consumers. Alibaba and JD.com have long dominated the market, but newer platforms like Pingduoduo are rapidly gaining share by offering group buying options that offer significant discounts to lower-tier cities and rural areas (China Market Research Group, 2021). Amazon, one of the largest international e-commerce companies, has struggled to compete in this highly competitive environment (Reuters, 2021). E-commerce platforms in China have been regulated more strictly in recent years to protect consumers, protect their data and avoid monopolization. A sustainable and fair e-commerce ecosystem is the goal of these regulations, but they have created challenges for companies attempting to expand rapidly.

Future Outlook

- By integrating the e-CNY into everyday transactions and continuing pilot programs, we expect the e-CNY to expand its adoption across China in the near future. Currently, platforms such as Alipay and WeChat Pay dominate the digital payment market [redundant], so this expansion is likely to focus on more sectors and regions.
- With the e-CNY, cross-border transactions can be facilitated much more easily and foreign currencies can be eliminated from cross-border transactions. Depending on whether international regulatory bodies accept e-CNY for international transactions and if interoperable systems are developed, China may challenge the dominance of the US dollar in global trade.
- Blockchain and digital identity technologies could further enhance the e-CNY's features, including privacy protection, transaction efficiency and security. New avenues for its application beyond conventional payment systems could open up as it integrates with emerging technologies such as the Internet of Things (IoT) and smart contracts.
- It will become increasingly important to address regulatory, privacy and security challenges as adoption increases. It will be important for the Chinese government and the People's Bank of China (PBOC) to manage these issues carefully in order to maintain user trust and meet international standards.
- As other CBDCs emerge and cryptocurrency technologies advance, the e-CNY's competitive landscape could change. To remain competitive, China must continue to innovate and adapt, while offering users a compelling value proposition both domestically and internationally.
- It is predicted that widespread adoption of e-CNY will have profound social and economic impacts, including increased financial inclusion, changes in consumer behavior and changes in monetary policy. China's social contract can be transformed as a result of streamlining public services and social welfare distribution.

References

Bank for International Settlements (BIS). (2021). *Central bank digital currencies: Foundational principles and core features.* [online] Retrieved July 21, 2023, from https://www.bis.org/publ/othp33.htm

Chia, T. Y., & Ekberg, J. (2021). *The Digital Currency Battleground.* Www.oliverwyman.com; Oliver Wyman, LLC. Retrieved October 30, 2024, from https://www.oliverwyman.com/our-expertise/insights/2021/jun/the-digital-currency-battleground.html

China Market Research Group. (2021). *The battle for China's E-commerce market.* [online] Retrieved January 17, 2024, from https://www.cmrgroup.com

Chorzempa, M. (2021). *China's digital currency revolution: Understanding the e-CYN.* Peterson Institute for International Economics. https://www.piie.com/publications/working-papers/chinas-digital-currency-revolution-understanding-digital-yuan

Deloitte China. (2021). *A new era of digital consumer habits in China.* [online] Retrieved July 28, 2023, from https://www2.deloitte.com/cn/en.html

Fildes, R., Ma, S., & Kolassa, S. (2019). *Retail forecasting: research and practice,* MPRA Paper No. 89356). Munich Personal RePEc Archive. https://core.ac.uk/download/pdf/214008847.pdf

Garrick, H., Huang, Z., & Zhou, X. (2021). Digital currency and international trade: The challenge of global acceptance. *International Review of Financial Analysis, 74,* 101–112.

Gu, S., Ślusarczyk, B., Hajizada, S., Kovalyova, I., & Sakhbieva, A. (2021). Impact of the covid-19 pandemic on online consumer purchasing behavior. *Journal of Theoretical and Applied Electronic Commerce Research, 16*(6), 2263–2281.

Huang, Y. (2020). *Cracking the China conundrum: Why conventional economic wisdom is wrong.* Oxford University Press.

Huang, Y. (2021). China's digital currency: A leap into the future of money. *China Economic Journal, 14*(2), 123–137.

Jefferson, G. H., Huamao, B., Xiaojing, G., & Xiaoyun, Y. (2006). R&D performance in Chinese industry. *Economics of Innovation and New Technology, 15*(4–5), 345–366.

Jiang, J. (2024, February 9). Digital dollar: Privacy and transparency dilemma. *UC Law Journal*; Advance Online Publication. https://papers.ssrn.com/sol3/papers.cfm?abstract_id=4774186

Katanich, D. (2024, October 18). *China: World's second-largest economy sees growth slowing.* Euronews; Euronews.com. https://www.euronews.com/business/2024/10/18/china-worlds-second-largest-economy-sees-growth-slowing

Kim, S., Miksjuk, A., Suryakumar, N., Tuladhar, A., Velculescu, D., Wu, Y., Zuniga, J., & Hallmark, N. (2024). Digital money, cross-border payments, international reserves, and the global financial safety net: preliminary considerations. *International Monetary Fund* , *2024*(001), 1–19. https://www.imf.org/en/Publications/IMF-Notes/Issues/2024/01/04/Digital-Money-Cross-Border-Payments-International-Reserves-and-the-Global-Financial-Safety-538733

KPMG China. (2021). *Navigating the new normal of China's consumer market.* Retrieved July 28, 2023, from https://home.kpmg/cn/en/home/insights.html

Li, L., & Wang, J. (2021). The implications of digital RMB on the international monetary system. *China Finance Review International, 11*(3), 290–307.

McKinsey & Company. (2020). *China's E-commerce: The new retail.* [online] Retrieved March 28, 2014, from https://www.mckinsey.com/industries/retail/our-insights

Morrison, W. M. (2019). China's economic rise: History, trends, challenges, and implications for the United States. *Current Politics and Economics of Northern and Western Asia*, *28*(2/3), 189–242.

Mu, Y., & Lee, J., (2020). Digital currency: The future of payments. *Journal of Payment Systems & FinTech*, *1*(1), 1–15.

People's Bank of China (PBOC). (2021a). *e-CYN white paper.* Retrieved July 13, 2023, from http://www.pbc.gov.cn/en/3688110/3688172/4157443/4293696/2021071614584691871.pdf

People's Bank of China (PBOC). (2021b). *Introduction to China's digital currency electronic payment (DCEP).* [online] Retrieved March 29, 2024, from http://www.pbc.gov.cn/en/3935690/3935759/4749192/2022122913350138868.pdf

Reuters. (2021). *Amazon's exit from China and the competitive E-commerce landscape.* [online] Retrieved March 28, 2024, from https://www.reuters.com

South China Morning Post (SCMP). (2021). *China's e-CYN, explained.* Retrieved July 5, 2023, from https://www.scmp.com/economy/china-economy/article/3237317/whats-state-chinas-digital-yuan-2023

Statistical Communiqué of the People's Republic of China on the 2021 National Economic and Social Development. (2022). National Bureau of Statistics of China. Retrieved July 5, 2023, from https://www.stats.gov.cn/english/PressRelease/202202/t20220227_1827963.html

Wang, H. (2022). China's approach to central bank digital currency: Selectively reshaping international financial order? *University of Pannsylvania Asian Law Review*, *18*, 77.

Yi, Q., Khan, J., Su, Y., Tong, J., & Zhao, S. (2023). Impulse buying tendency in live-stream commerce: The role of viewing frequency and anticipated emotions influencing scarcity-induced purchase decision. *Journal of Retailing and Consumer Services*, *75*, 103534.

Zhang, D., & Freestone, D. (2021). *China's economic development and environmental protection.* Springer Nature.

Zenglein, M. J., & Holzmann, A. (2019). *Evolving made in China 2025: China's industrial policy in the quest for global tech leadership.* Mercator Institute for China Studies.

Zhou, X. (2021a). Data privacy in China's e-CYN. *Journal of International Banking Law and Regulation*, *36*(7), 275–284.

Zhou, X. (2021b). The e-CYN and financial technology innovation in China. *China Finance Review International*, *11*(3), 290–304.

Zihan, Y., Longgang, G., & Kunyu, L. (2024). The effectiveness of digitalisation usage on customer satisfaction amidst the COVID-19 outbreak and recovery phase. *Journal of Digitainability, Realism & Mastery (DREAM)*, *3*(03), 14–26. https://doi.org/10.56982/dream.v3i03.218.

Case Study Three

Japan's Digital Currency

Na Zuo, Jashim Khan and Russell Belk

Introduction

Japan is a chain of islands in East Asia, covering 377,915 km^2, home to around 124.4 million people. Japan is the fourth-largest economy in the world behind the United States, China and Germany ('Japan,' 2024). Japan is the first country that has achieved developed country status in Asia, and it is a founding member of G7 and an early member of the OECD ('Japan,' 2024). In conjunction with the Bank of Japan, the European Central Bank is pursuing project Stella, which explores the possibilities of Distributed Leger Technology (DLT) as a means of supporting financial market infrastructure, payments and securities settlements (CBDC tracker, 2024).

Background

Japan has adopted a mixed economic system which combines market economy and government intervention (Sakisaka, 1963). The country has a highly developed and technologically advanced market, characterized by strong consumer purchasing power and a well-established business environment.

Recent years have seen significant growth and diversification of Japan's international trade in terms of trade volume and value. Foreign trade in Japan reached 211.1 trillion yen in 2023, with electrical machinery being the most traded commodity at 34.55 trillion yen (Japan Foreign Trade Council, 2024b). Crude petroleum, natural gas, coal, semiconductors, medical products were the major import items, while major export items included motor vehicles, semiconductors, iron and steel products, parts of motor vehicles and semicon machinery (Japan Foreign Trade Council, 2024a). Japan's top two trading partners are China and the United States, which account for 38% of its exports. Even though Japan has a trade surplus with the United States, it has a trade deficit with Australia and China (Japan Foreign Trade, 2024b). Approximately 11.5 trillion yen of imports were made in 2023, compared with over 20 trillion yen in exports (Japan Foreign Trade Council, 2024a).

Japan has been experiencing modest growth in its GDP for the past couple of years, and this trend appears to continue despite inflation. It has been

DOI: 10.4324/9781003425021-15

challenging due to the global uncertainty, but Japan's economy has shown resilience mainly due to its strong export and domestic consumption (IMF, 2024a). Over the past decade, Japan's GDP per capita has experienced moderate fluctuations. Despite periods of growth, economic challenges such as aging populations and, until recently, deflation have also presented significant challenges.

In Japan, banking, insurance and securities companies are among the financial institutions that provide corporations and individuals with financial products and services. In Japan, the Financial Services Agency is the primary regulatory body for financial institutions (Statista Research Department, 2023). The Japanese banking industry is dominated by Mitsubishi UFJ Financial Group, Sumitomo Mitsui Financial Group and Mizuho Financial Group. Japan Post Bank is another major financial institution, a subsidiary of Japan Post Group, partially state owned, has over 20 thousand branches across the country and is one of the largest banks in Japan (Fukuyama et al., 2018).

The banking system in Japan operates under strict regulations and supervision to ensure stability and security. In 2020, Japan became the first country to regulate Cryptoassets (Arora, 2020). Being the primary regulatory body, FSA ensures compliance, security and consumer protection, these regulations play an important role in shaping the digital payment landscape. Digital payment services must comply with Payment Services Act and Anti-Money Laundering (AML) regulations, for example. Financial system integrity and trust are the primary objectives of the regulatory framework.

As of 2023, Japan had a total population of 124.62 million (IMF, 2024b), with an estimated literacy rate of over 99% (e-Stat, 2022). Due to low birth rates and an aging population, the overall population size is declining. Additionally, the demanding work culture and lack of support have discouraged young people from having children. Japan has the highest percentage of elderly population aged over 65 in the world. The issues with its population have also impacted the production significantly. However, Japan's unemployment rate is low, mainly due to the vacancies created by aging population leaving workplace (O'Neill, 2024).

The cost of living is very high in Japan, especially in big cities. Tokyo, the capital, ranked the second in terms of cost of living among Asia-Pacific megacities, following Seoul (Numbeo, 2023). In 2023 the average household spending was 20,140 yen per month on housing (Statistics Bureau of Japan, 2024a). However, a declining trend in the share of housing expenditures to disposable income for working households is observed, standing at 11.3% in 2022 (MLIT, 2024). The Consumer Price Index for housing in Japan has been steadily increasing, reaching 102.4 points in 2023, indicating a 2.4% increase since 2020 (e-Stat, 2024).

The Digital Payments sector in Japan is made up of Digital Commerce, Mobile PoS payments and Digital Remittances (Alda, 2024). In e-commerce segment, Japan has seen significant growth, both in value and volume. As a result of the country's strong digital infrastructure, widespread internet access and tech-savvy population, e-commerce has flourished. With a dominant business-to-business (B2B) market as well as a growing business-to-consumer (B2C) market and an emerging consumer-to-consumer (C2C) market, Japan is one of the world's largest e-commerce markets. In 2022, the B2B market size is 420 trillion Japanese yen in value, followed by 22.7 trillion Japanese yen for B2C and 2.4 trillion Japanese yen for C2C (Diep, 2023a). The growth of online shopping in Japan can be attributed to the increasing use of the Internet by consumers. The volume of online transactions has also steadily increased. A study indicates that 53% of Japanese households with two or more people purchased goods or services online in 2022 (Diep, 2023b). These transactions are largely driven by the purchase of consumer goods, including electronics, fashion and beauty products. Consumers in Japan have also become increasingly interested in booking travel and tickets, ordering food and engaging in online entertainment (Alda, 2024).

There is a wide variety of shopping types in Japan's e-commerce market. B2C transactions dominate the marketplace, but C2C platforms are present in significant numbers as well. Japan's C2C e-commerce market was valued at 2.2 trillion Japanese yen in 2021 (METI Japan, 2023). In recent years, the online market, which includes both products and services offered by consumers, has grown significantly, led by online auctions and flea market platforms. In Japan, popular C2C marketplaces include Rakuten and Yahoo Auctions. In recent years, social commerce has gained traction, where consumers purchase products directly through social media platforms. Social commerce revenues are forecasted to reach one trillion US dollars by 2028 (Chevalier, 2024).

The Japanese e-commerce market is highly competitive, with domestic and international players competing for market share. Nearly 50% of consumers in Japan named Amazon as their primary online shopping channel in a survey conducted in 2023 (Appliv Topics, 2023). There is a strong Amazon presence in the Japanese e-commerce market, offering consumers a wide range of products and services. Rakuten is the second most popular e-commerce platform, often referred to as the 'Amazon of Japan,' Rakuten operates an extensive e-commerce platform. As well as e-commerce, Rakuten offers financial services, such as banking and credit cards. Consumers can also find a wide variety of products and services on Yahoo Shopping (Appliv Topics, 2023).

A growing number of digital technologies are being adopted by consumers in Japan, and this has resulted in a change in consumer behavior (Diep, 2023b). Even though brick-and-mortar retail still holds significance for Japanese consumers, online commerce has gained significant popularity in recent years. Online shopping is convenient and offers a wide range of products, which have contributed to this shift (Planet, 2024). Further encouraging this trend is the integration of advanced payment systems and efficient delivery services. Digital payment platforms and services are widely adopted in Japan. Japanese consumers actively seek convenient, secure and user-friendly payment solutions due to the market's sophistication and innovation adoption (Statista Research Department, 2024). Consequently, businesses are increasingly focusing on their digital strategies to capture this growing market.

Recent years have seen a steady increase in the proportion of online commerce compared to traditional commerce. In 2020, approximately 10% of total retail sales in Japan were generated through e-commerce (JETRO, 2021).

In 2022, Japan has witnessed a 2.5% increase in electronic money transactions from the previous year, equivalent to 5.88 billion in value. This indicates that the value of e-money transactions reached the highest point in the past ten years (Bank of Japan, 2024a).

Studies show that in 30.8% of households in Japan, 1 family member was using electronic money in 2022. That year, an average of around 65% of the surveyed households had at least 1 member using e-money (Statistics Bureau of Japan, 2023). Vending machine and public transportation fees can now be paid with prepaid smart cards in Japan. Prepaid cards (Suica and Pasmo are the most common) are accepted at convenience stores, shops and restaurants. E-money terminals are becoming increasingly popular in Japan, offering cashless payment options (Nagata, 2021). By 2027, total transaction value is projected to increase by 14.89% annually, totaling US dollars 610.80bn (Statistics Bureau of Japan, 2024a,b).

Opportunities and Incentives

The government has recognized the importance of digital payment adoption for economic growth and has implemented initiatives to support its development. These include the introduction of cashless incentives and the establishment of a national QR code payment system.

The cashless incentive program was introduced in 2019. This program rewards consumers who use mobile payment apps or credit cards to pay by digital methods. The goal is to reduce physical currency usage by incentivizing consumers to switch to digital payments (Statista Research Department, 2024). The digital payment increased convenience for consumers and merchants, as transactions can be completed quickly and securely. In addition, businesses that adopt digital payment systems are eligible for tax breaks. Company salaries have been paid digitally since Spring of 2023, without the need for bank accounts. This system aims to address the challenges faced by foreign workers in Japan, stimulate growth and promote deregulation and expansion in the financial services market (World Economic Forum, 2023). It is anticipated that the widespread adoption of digital currency can stimulate innovation in financial services and fintech.

Businesses themselves often offer incentives to consumers to use digital currency. Customers who make payments online can take advantage of exclusive discounts, loyalty rewards and special promotions. Tax incentives and government support further encourage both individuals and businesses to transition to digital payment systems (Statista Research Department, 2024).

Challenges

Compared to other payment options, digital currency has increasingly gained a competitive advantage in Japan. Compared to cash transactions, cashless transactions offer benefits such as ease of use, speed and enhanced security (Nagata, 2021). A digital payment solution can also be seamlessly integrated with other services, such as loyalty programs, rewards and personalized offers. Japan has made good progress in digital payment, but there are still several challenges including its cash culture, lack of awareness, concerns about privacy and security (Statista Research Department, 2024):

First, Japanese culture still values cash over digital payments, despite their growing popularity. Consumers prefer physical currency because of its familiarity and perceived security, according to Statista (2023), Consumers' preferences for digital payments can be difficult to overcome and changing their behavior can be a challenge.

Secondly, lack of awareness. A 2024 survey revealed that 77.2% of Japanese consumers had never heard of central bank digital currency (CBDC) (Bank of Japan, 2024b). This low awareness contributes to the hesitancy in adopting digital currencies.

The usage of cryptocurrencies is low, reportedly 8.6% private investors in Japan, despite of its advanced technology infrastructure (Japan Securities Dealers Association, 2023). The adoption rate varies by age. Younger investors are more likely to use digital currencies compared to older investors. 17.1% of investors aged 20–39 years use digital currencies, compared to just 1.5% of those 70 and older (Japan Securities Dealers Association, 2023).

Thirdly, concerns about information security and potential leaks are prevalent among Japanese consumers (Statista Research Department, 2024). Gaining consumer trust requires ensuring digital transactions are secure. To foster wider adoption of digital payment methods, it is crucial to address concerns about data privacy, fraud prevention and secure payment systems. This apprehension extends to businesses, with 11.6% worried about information leaks and cyberattacks in e-commerce (JETRO, 2021).

Despite the growing availability of digital payment options in urban areas, there is still a need to improve accessibility and acceptance in rural areas. It is important to encourage small businesses and local merchants to adopt digital payment systems in order to improve consumer convenience (Statista Research Department, 2024).

Reference list

Alda, M. (2024). *Digital Remittances - Japan|Statista Market Forecast*. https://www.statista.com; Statista. https://www.statista.com/outlook/fmo/digital-payments/digital-remittances/japan

Appliv Topics. (2023, June 12). Most popular e-commerce marketplaces in Japan as of June 2023 [Graph]. *Statista*. Retrieved August 6, 2024, from https://www-statista-com.surrey.idm.oclc.org/statistics/1165994/japan-leading-e-commerce-sites/

Arora, G. (2020). Cryptoasset regulatory framework in Japan. *SSRN Electronic Journal*. https://doi.org/10.2139/ssrn.3720230

Bank of Japan. (2024a, February 29). Number of transactions with electronic money in Japan from 2014 to 2023 (in billions) [Graph]. *Statista*. Retrieved July 29, 2024, from https://www-statista-com.surrey.idm.oclc.org/statistics/1228464/japan-e-money-transaction-volume/

Bank of Japan. (2024b, April 12). Level of awareness of the term central bank digital currency (CBDC) in Japan as of March 2024 [Graph]. *Statista*. Retrieved July 30, 2024, from https://www-statista-com.surrey.idm.oclc.org/statistics/1270970/japan-awareness-central-bank-digital-currency/

CBDC tracker. (2024). *Digital Yen*. https://cbdctracker.org/currency/japan-digital_yen

Chevalier, S. (2024). *Social commerce – Statistics & facts*. https://www-statista-com.surrey.idm.oclc.org/topics/8757/social-commerce/#topicOverview

Diep, C. (2023a). *E-commerce in Japan – Statistic & facts*. https://www-statista-com.surrey.idm.oclc.org/topics/5262/e-commerce-in-japan/#topicOverview

Diep, C. (2023b). *Online shopping behavior in Japan – Statistics & facts*. https://www-statista-com.surrey.idm.oclc.org/topics/8134/digital-shopping-behavior-in-japan/

e-Stat (Japan). (2022, December 21). Enrollment rate in school education in Japan in academic year 2022, by institution type [Graph]. *Statista*. Retrieved August 6, 2024, from https://www-statista-com.surrey.idm.oclc.org/statistics/1189581/japan-attendance-rate-students-by-type-of-institution/

e-Stat (Japan). (2024, January 19). Consumer price index (CPI) of housing in Japan from 2014 to 2023 [Graph]. *Statista*. Retrieved July 29, 2024, from https://www-statista-com.surrey.idm.oclc.org/statistics/662253/japan-housing-consumer-price-index/

Fukuyama, H., Färe, R., & Weber, W. L. (2018). Valuing and ranking Japanese Banks: Application to Japan Post Bank and Mizuho Bank. *Journal of the Operational Research Society*, *69*(*12*), 2021–2033.

IMF. (2024a). Japan: Gross domestic product (GDP) in current prices from 1980 to 2023, with projections until 2029 (in billion U.S. dollars) [Graph]. *Statista*. Retrieved August 6, 2024, from https://www-statista-com.surrey.idm.oclc.org/statistics/263578/gross-domestic-product-gdp-of-japan/

IMF. (2024b). Japan: Total population from 2019 to 2029 (in millions) [Graph]. *Statista*. Retrieved August 6, 2024, from https://www-statista-com.surrey.idm.oclc.org/statistics/263746/total-population-in-japan/

Japan. (2024). In *Wikipedia*. https://en.wikipedia.org/wiki/Japan

Japan Foreign Trade Council. (2024a). *Foreign trade*. Japan Foreign Trade Council. https://my.ebook5.net/japan-foreign-trade-council/k6og3P/

Japan Foreign Trade Council. (2024b). Total value of foreign commodity trade in Japan from 2014 to 2023 (in trillion Japanese yen) [Graph]. *Statista*. Retrieved July 6, 2024, from https://www-statista-com.surrey.idm.oclc.org/statistics/1220746/japan-trade-value/

Japan Securities Dealers Association. (2023, December 1). Usage of cryptocurrencies among individual investors in Japan as of July 2023 [Graph]. *Statista*. Retrieved June 30, 2024, from https://www-statista-com.surrey.idm.oclc.org/statistics/1370380/japan-private-investors-virtual-currency-usage/

JETRO. (February 17, 2021). Leading challenges of selling over e-commerce platforms among businesses in Japan as of 2020 [Graph]. *Statista*. Retrieved June 30, 2024, from https://www-statista-com.surrey.idm.oclc.org/statistics/1244913/japan-challenges-e-commerce-business-sales/

METI (Japan). (2023, August 31). Consumer-to-consumer (C2C) e-commerce market size in Japan from fiscal year 2016 to 2022 (in billion Japanese yen) [Graph]. *Statista*. Retrieved July 6, 2024, from https://www-statista-com.surrey.idm.oclc.org/statistics/869749/japan-c2c-market-size/

MLIT (Japan). (2024, February 19). Monthly housing expenses as a share of the disposable income of working households in Japan from 2013 to 2022 [Graph]. *Statista*. Retrieved July 28, 2024, from https://www-statista-com.surrey.idm.oclc.org/statistics/1289461/japan-housing-expenses-share-disposable-income-working-households/

Nagata, K., (2021). *As e-money gains ground in Japan, so do local digital currencies*. https://www.japantimes.co.jp/news/2021/03/22/business/tech/local-digital-currencies/

Numbeo. (2023, April 18). Cost of living index score of selected megacities across the Asia-Pacific region in 2023 [Graph]. *Statista*. Retrieved June 30, 2024, from https://www-statista-com.surrey.idm.oclc.org/statistics/915112/asia-pacific-cost-of-living-index-in-megacities/

O'Neill, A. (2024). *Total population in Japan 2019–2029*. https://www-statista-com.surrey.idm.oclc.org/statistics/263746/total-population-in-japan/

Planet, Inc. (2024, April 15). Leading reasons for shopping online in Japan as of February 2024 [Graph]. *Statista*. Retrieved July 06, 2024, from https://www-statista-com.surrey.idm.oclc.org/statistics/696301/japan-reasons-to-shop-online/

Sakisaka, M. (1963). Economic planning in Japan. *The Developing Economies*, *1*(2), 202–217.

Statista. (2023). *Digital payments – Japan*. https://www.ide.go.jp/library/English/Publish/Periodicals/De/pdf/63_02_04.pdf

Statista Research Department. (2023). *Banking industry in Japan – Statistics & facts*. Banking Industry in Japan – Statistics & facts | Statista (oclc.org)

Statista Research Department. (2024). *Cashless payments in Japan – Statistics & facts*. https://www-statista-com.surrey.idm.oclc.org/topics/7754/cashless-payments-in-japan/#topicOverview

Statistics Bureau of Japan. (2023). *Electronic money usage penetration of households in Japan in 2022, by number of users*. https://www.statista.com/statistics/625072/japan-electronic-money-usage/

Statistics Bureau of Japan. (2024a). Annual average of monthly expenditure of households on housing in Japan from 2014 to 2023 (in 1,000 Japanese yen) [Graph]. *Statista*. Retrieved June 30, 2024, from https://www-statista-com.surrey.idm.oclc.org/statistics/1005518/yearly-average-of-monthly-household-housing-spending-japan/

Statistics Bureau of Japan. (2024b). Electronic money usage penetration of households in Japan in 2023, by number of users [Graph]. *Statista*. Retrieved June 29, 2024, from https://www-statista-com.surrey.idm.oclc.org/statistics/625072/japan-electronic-money-usage/

World Economic Forum. (2023). *How Japan is moving towards a cashless society with digital salary payments*. https://www.weforum.org/agenda/2022/09/japan-cashless-society-digital-salary-payment/

Index

Note: **Bold** page numbers refer to tables and *italic* page numbers refer to figures.

abstract value 3, 7
Accenture 74
access control attack 227–228
advertising 167, 168, 173, 206
Ahn, J. 172
Airbnb 21, 238
airplane token 131
Alibaba 264, 267
AliPay 9, 42, 51, 107, 116, 169, 170, 189, 196, 261, 263, 264, 267
Alsop, T. 237
altcoins 16
Amarullah, D. 108
Amazon 138, 267, 272
Amir, K. 113
Anderson, J. C. 117
Andreessen Horowitz 40
Android systems 231
Androulaki, E. 52
animated icons 168
anti-graphic neural network (GNN) algorithms 229
anti-money laundering (AML) 132, 264–266, 271
Apple 231
Apple Pay 224
Aquilina, M. 222
Aristotle 5, 90
artificial intelligence (AI) 225, 243, 261
Arvidsson, N. 195
Asian Development Bank 259
ASIC 38
asset-backed NFTs 17, 20
asymmetric key encryption 225, 226
Atari 41
Atlantic Council 45, 265
augmented reality (AR) 225, 230, 236
Ava Labs 40
Avalanche (AVAX) 34, 40
Avalanche Virtual Machine 40
average variance extracted (AVE) 94, 119, 153
avocational payment method 238–240, 248
Awareness, Interest, Desire and Action (AIDA) hierarchy 136
Axie Infinity 221, 237

Babylonian economies 4
back-based magnetic stripped card system 9
back translation 91
Baidoun, S. D. 197
Balaji 40
balanced reciprocity 246–249
Bank for International Settlements (BIS) 80, 82, 263
Bank for International Settlements (BIS) Innovation Hub 74, 76–82
Banking Act (1987) 257
Banking Commission 257–258
Banking Commissioner of the Marshall Islands 257
banking system 5–6, 8–9
bank-issued payment cards 8–9
banknotes 6, 221
Bank of China 49
Bank of England 6, 45, 78
Bank of Guam 257
Bank of Israel 74, 81
Bank of Japan 45
Bank of Thailand 45

Bank of the Marshall Islands 257
Banks and Financial Services Providers licenses 257
Banque de France 74, 76, 77
Bansal, H. S. 108
Barclays 8
Bardhi, F. 21
Bauer, R. A. 108
Baur, D. G. 191
behavioral inertia 112
behavioral loyalty 143–146, 148–151, 154–156
Beier, J. C. 22
Belk, R. 21, 83, 86, 88, 105, 107, 111, 170, 171, 212, 236
Belmont, H. J. 170
Berridge, K. C. 88
Bijlsma, M. 46
Bitcoin (BTC) 9, 10, 16, 17, 34–35, 39, 43, 51, 52, 54, 57, 105, 131, 132, 135, 139–140, 169
Bitcoin Magazine 35
Bitgold 16, 52, 56, 57
blind signature 52
blockchain 34, 35, 56, 57, 220, 224–227; asymmetric key encryption 226; consensus algorithm 226; definition 225; ledger system 9–10; P2P networking 226–227; technology 16–18, 25, 34, 41, 43, 52, 131, 134, 135, 137, 139, 236–238, 243, 250, 261
blockchain for Metaverse privacy and security 227–231; access control attack 227–228; attack of routing 229; communication network threat 228; device data leakage 228; device threats 227; digital footprint tracking 228; distributed denial-of-service attack 228; expandability 230–231; firmware vulnerabilities 228; immersive interaction 230; issues and solutions 229–230; malware attacks 228; real world-building 230; single point of failure and third-party 228; tampering and injection threat 228
Bluetooth 231
Boar, C. 106
Boden, J. 110
Bonnaire, C. 150
bootstrapping procedure 92, 153
Bored Apes Yacht Club (BAYC) tokens 131–133, 137, 221
Borget, Sebastien 41
brand equity 136
brand loyalty 148
Bretton Woods Agreement 8, 57
Bretton Woods system 6, 8
Britto, Arthur 37
Bronze Age 4
Buchori, A. 186
bullae 4
bullion economy 6
Burberry 134, 137
Burke, R. R. 89, 90
business-to-business (B2B) market 272
business-to-consumer (B2C) market 264, 272
Buterin, Vitalik 35

Cabanac, M. 88
Carapella, F. 10
Cardano (ADA) 34, 39
cash crops 7
cash disappearance 7
cashless incentive program 273
cashless payments 10, 273–274
cash notes 6
cash payment *vs.* digital money (non-cash payment) 83–87, 90
CBDC Tracker 45, 66–72, 265
C-chain 40
central bank digital currency (CBDC) 10, 16, 17, 25, 42–46, **47–48**, 84, 85, 105, 133, 190, 221–222, 238, 263, 265–267; advantages and risks 44; definition 86; development 73; distributed ledger technology in 43–44; e-CNY/digital RMB 45–46; projects 45, 74–82; *see also* money in CBDC
Central Bank of Luxembourg 77
Central Bank of Malaysia 79
Central Bank of Norway 74
centralization 46
CENTRE Consortium 37
Chandra, Y. 212
Chang, Y. P. 151, 152
Chemical Bank 8
Chen, C.-C. 151
Cheung, C. M. K. 149
Chia, T. Y. 266
Childers, T. L. 89
China: digital payment ecosystem 261; e-commerce ecosystem 264, 267; economy 262–263
China Statistical Yearbook 2021 187
China Telecom 49

China Unicom 49
Chinese Academy of Social Sciences' Luxury Consumption 187
Chinese Central Bank 197, 262
Chinese clay money *(ní qián)* 4
Chinese e-CNY *see* digital Ren Min Bi (RMB)
Chinese luxury brand market and consumption 186–198; convergent validity **194–195**; data analysis and procedure 193; discriminant validity **195**; of Generation Z consumers 187; measurements model assessment 193; path coefficients *196*; perceived ease of use 189, 195–196; perceived risk 190–192, 197; perceived trust 190, 197; perceived usefulness 189–190, 196; research context 192; research model *191*; structural model 193; survey research approach 192, **193**; technology acceptance model 188–189
chip-based card system 9
Chohan, R. 136
Chorzempa, M. 265
Chou, T. J. 151
CIA Factbook 255
Circle 37
Claeys, G. 169
classical economics 1, 2
clay tokens 4
Coinbase 35–41
coinmarketcap.com 139
Colicev, A. 135, 136
Collins, Reeve 36
commodification 21
commodity-backed representative money 7–8
commodity theory of money 1, 2
common method bias 93–94
communication network threat 228; intrusion 228; man in the middle and ever-dropping attack 228; Sybil's attack 228
composite reliability (CR) 94, 118, 153, 193
consensus algorithm 225, 226
consumer-to-consumer (C2C): market 272; shopping 264
content creators 166
controllable anonymity 264–266
convergent validity 94, 119, 153, 193
conversion economy 53
Corda 44, 79
cost–benefit analysis 116
Costes, J. M. 150
counterfeit brands 186, 187
counter-terrorist financing (CTF) 265, 266
Coutelle-Brillet, P. 112
covariance-based structural equation modeling (CB-SEM) approach 92
COVID-19 pandemic 9, 139, 192, 261
Craig-Lees, M. 84
credit cards 8, 9, 84, 91, 106, 169, 170
credit economy 5
Cronbach's alpha 94, 118, 153, 193
cross-app tracking functions 231
cross-border payments 16–17, 37, 42, 265
crypto assets 16, 17, 35, 132, 271
crypto coins 132, 223
cryptocurrency 15, 17, 20, 25, 34, 37, 42, 52, 84, 105, 130–140, 187, 212, 223–224, 274; Bitcoin 139–140; crash 10, 52, 54; emergence of 9–10; features of 223–224; NFTs 133–139; properties 131–133; tokenization, concept of 130–131
crypto funds 10, 139
cryptographic signatures 10
cryptography 20, 43, 130, 133, 140, 187
Cryptokick 134
CryptoKitties 41
Cryptopunks 221
Csikszentmihalyi, M. 88, 111, 147
Cuban, Mark 38
cultural identity 3
cuneiform 4
customer authentication system 109
cyberattacks 110, 262, 274
cyber threats 109

dApps 44
Dashing protocol 80
database technology 43
data immutability 43
data privacy 109, 188, 232, 274
data protection in Metaverse platform 232; dynamism 232; privacy 232
data safety 9
Davis, F. D. 188–190
DCash 75–76
DCash 2.0 75
debasement 7–8
debit cards 8, 9, 84, 106, 205
debt economy 4

Decentraland 40–41, 236, 237, 239, 240
decentralization, concept of 43, 51, 222
decentralized autonomous organization (DAO) structure 226
decentralized cryptocurrency networks 39
decentralized finance (DeFi) 17, 20, 35, 222–223; censorship resistance 223; composability 223; controllability 222; interoperability 223; programmability 223; transparency 223
Decentralized Finance Automated Market Makers (DeFi AMMs) 76
Delfabbro, P. H. 144
De Luna, I. R. 109
Demertzis, M. 169
denarius 7
de-serialization: anxiety 230; vulnerability 230
Desmond, W. H. 88
device data leakage 228
Dew, N. 111
Dhewanto, W. 195
Diamond, D. W. 53
Diem 42
digital assets 15–27, 209, 237, 238, 240, 243–247, 249; definitions 15–16; financial 16–17, **18–19**, 20; money with 25–27, *26*; non-financial 20–22, **23–24**; ownership 22, 25
digital avatars 227, 248, 249
digital cash 9, 51, 83
digital credit bonds 52
digital currency 7, 10; benefits and risks 188; definition 187; types 187
Digital Currency Research Institute 80
Digital Economic Zone 258
digital economy 45, 46, 54–56, 173, 197
digital euro 45, 75
digital footprint 237, 246, 247; tracking 228
digital game currencies 143–158, *149*; analyses 153; construct measurement 152, **152**; factor structure **152**, 153, **153**; flow state 147–150; gamer loyalty 148–151; impulse buying tendency 148, 150; limitations and future studies 158; managerial implications 157; microtransaction 146–147, 149–150; Qualtrix survey 151; research 145–146; sample profile 151; structural model fit index 153–154, **154**; theoretical implications 156–157
digital gaming tokens 247
digital gold 51–52, 54, 55, 57, 58
digitalization and money 46, 49, 56
digital marketing 50
digital natives 136
digital ownership 21–22; rights 21
digital Ren Min Bi (RMB) 10, 45–46, **47–48**, 49, 54–57, 82, 105, 116, 117, 121, 197, 261–267; challenges 265–267; characteristics of 264; future 267; market factors 263; opportunities 264–265
digital stickers 180
digital technology 46, 54
digital wallets 168, 170, 223, 265
Dimitrova, I. 110, 190
Dimpfl, T. 191
Di Muro, F. 89, 90
direct-to-creator model 168
discriminant validity 94, **94**, 119, 193
distributed denial-of-service (DDoS) attack 228
distributed ledger technology (DLT) 10, 15–17, 42–44, 74, 76, 121, 134, 188, 225, 243, 270
Dogecoin (DOGE) 38, 39
Dolce & Gabbana 134
double national currency model 55
double spending 44, 52
double translation procedure 91, 116
Douyin 166, 167, 173
Dowling, M. 135
Dwivedi, Y. K. 230
Dybvig, P. H. 53

Eastern Caribbean Central Bank 75
e-business model 54
eCash 1.0 82
eCash 2.0 82
e-cash system 52
Eckhardt, G. M. 21
eco-friendly activities 240
e-commerce 54, 192, 195, 197, 206, 261, 267
economic development 208
economic enthusiasts 155
economic perspective of money 1–2
effectance 86
ego-depletion effect 153
Ehrenberg, A. S. C. 148
Ekberg, J. 266

electronic banking 9
electronic-fiat currencies 8–10; bank-issued payment cards 8–9; cryptocurrencies 9–10; third-party mobile payments 9
electronic payments 8, 10, 46, 109
Elster, Jon 87
emojis 168, 180
emotional engagement 177, 180, 182
emotional value 112, 175, 211
emotions in decision-making 87–88
endorsements 168
equity theory 112
Erki, B. 87
e-thefts 110
Ether (ETH) 35
Ethereum 10, 17, 35, 37, 39–41, 43, 44, 80, 133, 223
Etzioni, A. 86
European Central Bank (ECB) 45, 75
European Investment Bank 77
Eurosystem 76
Eurozone 45, 75
ever-dropping attack 228
exploratory factor analysis 93
extended aggregated self 86

Faber, R. J. 156
Facebook 22, 42, 150, 222
factor loadings (FL) 94, 153
Featherman, M. S. 197
Federal Reserve Bank of New York 76
Federated Consensus mechanism 38
Feinberg, R. A. 91, 170
fiat currency 10, 17, 36, 44, 52, 54, 57, 58, 105, 121, 131, 139, 169, 190, 223; *see also* electronic-fiat currencies
fiat money 6–8
5G Internet network 54
financial crisis (2008) 9–10, 15, 52
financial digital assets 16–17, **18–19**, 20; asset-backed tokens 20; cryptocurrencies 17, 20; DeFi 20; NFTs 20; tokenized commercial real estate 20
financial identity 27, 224
FinTech revolution 222
FinTech services 113
firmware vulnerabilities 228
First Hawaiian Bank 258
five-point Likert scale 92, 117, 192
Fleming, R. 3
Flemming, J. 10
flow state 144–150, 153–158, 165, 171, 172, 181
flow theory 145, 147, 151, 171
FOMO (fear of missing out) 206, 208
Fornell, C. 94, 119, 153, 193
Fortnite 237
Freecycle 239
free-to-play mobile games 143–151, 154–156, 158
frugal spending 210
fungibility of money 84
fungible digital asset 138–139
fungible tokens 17, 166

Galoni, C. 83, 87
gambling: and addiction 147, 148; disorder 145
game enthusiasts 156
GameFi 222
gamer loyalty 148–151, 154–157
Gefen, D. 188
general equilibrium theory 2
Generation Z 88, 204–214; attitudes toward digital assets 207; consumers 136, 187, 198; digital money and its value 211–212, *212*; hedonistic lifestyle 205–208, 212–214, *213*; irrational exuberance 208; living in the present 208–210, *210*; saving and investment for future 207, 208; smart consumerism 208, 210; spending habits 204–205
Generative Adversarial Networks (GAN) 229
generative AI 137
Gerbing, D. W. 117
Gibson, J. J. 90
Giddens, A. 3
gold 1, 5, 6, 8, 51, 56, 57
gold coins 5, 7–8
gold standard 6, 8, 57
González-Benito, Ó. 85
goodness of fit (GOF) 95, 119, 153
Google 231
Google Pay 224
G-power tool 92, 116
Graeber, D. 4
Graziani, A. 7
Gresham's law 7
Gucci 137, 238
Gucci Gardens 238

Habermas, J. 3
hackers and hacking 52, 110, 227–231

Hair, J. F. 91, 153
Hamari, J. 144–147, 150, 154, 155
Haponiuk, M. 15
Harman's single-factor technique 93, 153
Harwanu, Y. 186
Hasan, S. Z. 113, 189
Havva, V. 15
Helix 41
Henseler, J. 94
Heterotrait-Monotrait (HTMT) 94
Hoffman, D. L. 144, 154, 156
Hofstetter, R. 136
Hölzl, E. 87
home and stimulation 86
Hong Kong Monetary Authority (HKMA) 79, 81, 82
Hoskinson, Charles 39
Hsiao, K.-L. 151
Hsieh, Y. 145, 151
Huang, L. 145, 151
Huang, Y. 266
Hulten, B. 89, 90
human–computer interaction 144
Hunt, J. M. 170

IBM 43
Illuvium 240
impulse buying 144–150, 154–157, 165, 170, 176, 182, 204, 208, 211
impulse spending 83, 171–172, 181, 182, 208
impulsivity 166, 172, 213
in-app store 169
individual understanding of Metaverse platform 232–233; accessibility 233; adoptability 233; clarity 233; consistency 233; flexibility 233; interoperability 233; standardization 233; transparency 232–233; usability 233
inertia 111
in-game advertising 143
in-game currency 238, 239
in-game virtual tools 143–151, 154–157
Ingham, G. 2, 3
instant gratification 204, 206–213
integrated tipping systems 170
International Monetary Fund (IMF) 106, 258
Internet Gaming Disorder (IGD) 145, 150
Internet of Things (IoT) 225, 267
intrinsic value 2, 7, 8, 51, 57, 58
iOS 231

Jackie Li 168
Jacoby, J. 148
Japan: banking system in 271; e-commerce in 271–273; economy in 270–271; electronic money and digital payment systems in 273–274; foreign trade in 270; population and cost of living in 271
Japan Post Bank 271
Japan Post Group 271
Japan's digital currency 270–274; challenges 274; opportunities and incentives 273
JavaScript codes 229
JD 166
JD.com 9, 264, 267
Jiang, L. A. 110
Jingdong Pay 9, 261
joyful utilitarianism 207
judgment sampling technique 92, 173

Kaal, W. A. 15, 16
Kahn, B. E. 148
Kamleitner, B. 87
K-anonymity 229
Kappa coefficient 116
Karjaluoto, H. 113
Kasser, T. 86
Kelly, S. 146, 155, 157
Keronen, L. 147
Khan, J. 83, 84, 88, 105, 107, 111, 144, 170, 171, 205
Khelladi, I. 196
Kiehl's 137
King, D. L. 144, 145
Klézl, V. 146, 155, 157
Knapp, G. F. 2; *State Theory of Money* 2
Kochergin, D. A. 16
Kock, N. 93
Kringelbach, M. L. 88
Krishna, A. 89, 90
Kuaishou 50, 166, 167, 169, 173
Kumpajaya, A. 195

labor division 4
LAND 40–41
Larcker, D. F. 94, 119, 153, 193
Larsen, Chris 38
Lavoie, R. V. 149
L-diversity 229
League of Legends 151, 152, 158

Lee, D. 171
Lego 223
Lehdonvirta, V. 144
lending services 6
Levin, D. 52
Li, J. 109
Li, L. 266
Liébana-Cabanillas, F. 91, 105
light luxury 205
likes and comments 26, 171, 174
Lin, H. 150
Lin, N. 248
Lin, W. R. 113, 154
Lin, Y. 171, 181
Linck, K 109
liquid consumption 21
liquidity 20, 52, 54, 76, 265
Litecoin 10, 16, 17
Liu, H. J. 150
live-stream commerce 192; Chinese 168; free-to-use model in 166, 167; tipping currency in *see* tipping currency in live-stream commerce; viewership 172; virtual gifts and donations in 165–169, 171–174, 176, 177, 180–182
live streamers 166, 171, 181
live-stream immersion 165
live streaming 165, 176; channels 166, 173; market 167; platforms 166, 167, 171, 173, 176, 181, 182; shopping 165, 171
living in the moment 206–208
Lloyds Bank 8
Long, N. T. 168
Louis Vuitton 134, 137
Luhmann, N. 3
luxury brands 186, 187; *see also* Chinese luxury brand market and consumption

Madrid, Arthur 41
Main, K. J. 149
malware attacks 228
MANA 40–41
Marcoux, J. S. 249
marginal utility theory 2
Marikyan, M. 190
market capitalization 17, 34
market ownership 25
Marshallese Sovereign Currency (SOV) 255–259; challenges 258–259; opportunities and incentives 258
Marshall Islands Development Bank (MIDB) 257–258
Maryaningsih, N. 42
Mauss, M. 3
Mayer, R. C. 190
McCaffrey, M. 147, 157
McCaleb, Jed 37
McCall, M. 170
McDonald 238
McGorry, S. Y. 91, 116
McKinsey & Company 263
meaning of money 2, 3, 25–27, 46, 49, 56, 57, 88, 130, 140, 166, 181
Meilich, Ariel 40
Mendoza-Tello, J. C. 190
Mesoamerica 4
metajacket 134
Meta's Horizon Worlds 237
Metaverse: currencies and tokens **241–242**; definition 236; in fashion industry 137; platforms 35, 41
Metaverse, digital currencies in 219–234, *221*; accountability 231, 232; auditability 231; blockchain concepts and components 224–227, *225*; blockchain for privacy and security concerns *see* blockchain for Metaverse privacy and security; central bank digital currency 221–222; copying avatar and phishing attack 231; cryptocurrency 223–224; data protection 232; decentralized finance 222–223; impartiality 232; individual understanding 232–233; non-fungible tokens 220–221; personal data formation *220*; third-party payment 224; traceability 231; *see also* social currency in Metaverse
Mexican peso 36
microtransactions 143–150, 154–158
military coinage slave complex 5
Mill, John Stuart 1–3
mining 16, 36, 38, 51, 223
Mitsubishi UFJ Financial Group 271
Mizuho Financial Group 271
mobile games 143, 145–147, 149–152, 154–158
mobile payment system 9, 109
Monetary Authority of Singapore 76, 79
monetary policies 10, 46, 52
monetary system 3, 7, 9

money, philosophy of 1–3; cultural perspective 3; economic perspective 1–2; sociological perspective 2–3
money in CBDC 46–58; consumption *56*, 57–58; content categories 54, *55*; data cleaning and analysis procedure 50–51; data collection 49–50; digital economy, finance and technology 54–56, *55*; instability of cryptocurrencies 52; methodology 46, 49; research context 49; stability *53*, 53–54; trustless transactions 51–52
money laundering 49, 52, 266
money origin and history 4–7; early period 4–5; Middle Ages 5–6; post-World War II 6–7
monopoly money 182
Moody, M. P. 170
Möser, M. 52
multicollinearity 93–94
multiple central bank digital currency (mCBDC) platform 81
Musk, Elon 38, 220
MXNT 36

Nah, F. F.-H. 144
Nakamoto, Satoshi 9, 10, 16, 57, 133, 139
near-field communication (NFC) 49
Netflix 230
netnography 46, 49
network effects 107, 112
Nickmercs 168
Nike 134, 238
Nike tokens 132
non-financial digital assets 16, 20–22, **23–24**, 25; definition 22
non-fungible assets 25
non-fungible tokens (NFTs) 16, 17, 20, 25, 35, 131–140, 212, 220–221; customer journey 137–138; in fashion industry 137; as financial asset 135; and fungible digital asset 138–139; in marketing 135–137
non-market ownership 25
non-probability criterion-based judgment sampling 91, 97, 192
non-probability criterion-based purposive sampling technique 151
Noseworthy, T. J. 83, 87, 89, 90
'Notary' stamps 44
Novak, T. P. 144, 154, 156

offline payments 49, 107
Öhman, P. 110
One Island One Product 256–257
online banking 9
online games 146, 147
online gaming 145, 151, 249; marketplaces 239
online shopping 89, 90, 197, 204, 206, 261, 263, 272
OpenSea 134
Ordano, Esteban 40
Ouroboros consensus mechanism 39

P2P networking 225–227
Pacific Pure Water 256
Pahl, J. 3
pain of paying 84, 88, 91, 154, 155, 209
Pakrou, M. 113
Palmeira, M. 146
Papagiannidis, P. 190
paper money 5–8, 130
Parson, T. 2, 3
Parsonian sociology of money 3
Partial Least Square Structural Equation Modeling (PLS-SEM) 117, 119, 193
Partior 79
Paschen, J. 136
Pavlou, P. A. 197
Payeco 169
payment networks security 9
Payment Services Act 271
PayPal 169, 224
P-chain 40
Peck, J. 85, 86, 89
peer-to-peer (P2P) payments 9, 17, 42, 43, 133, 220, 223
peer-to-peer technology 43
People's Bank of China (PBOC) 10, 45, 46, 105, 107, 261, 262, 264, 265, 267
perceived convenience 105, 106, 108, 110, 114–115, 120
perceived ease of use 105, 108, 188, 189, 195–196, 198, 209
perceived risk 105, 106, 108–109, 114, 120, 121, 190–192, 197, 198; types of 109
perceived security 105, 106, 109–110, 114, 120, 121
perceived trust 190, 197
perceived usefulness (PU) 189–190, 198
perceived utility 188
perceived value 105, 106, 111–115, 119–121

personal gratification 172, 177, 182
personal identification number 8
Pierce, Brock 36
Pijpers, G. M. 189
Pingduoduo 264, 267
Pixowl 41
Plato 5
pleasure of saving 84, 88
Pokimane 168
Polychain 40
Pomery, E. A. 116
Porter, S. 22
positive emotions 106, 108, 111, 113, 115, 120, 121, 148, 154, 155, 165, 171, 181–182; *vs.* negative emotions 87–88
privacy leakage 229–230
probability-based sampling techniques 97
Project Aurum 79–80
Project Cedar x/Ubin+ 76–77
Project Dunbar 79, 81
Project Helvetia 77–78
Project Icebreaker 74–75
Project Jura 74
Project Mandala 80–81
Project Mariana 76
Project mBridge 80
Project Polaris 78
Project Rosalind 78–79
Project Sand Dollar 258
Project Sela 81
Project Tourbillon 81–82
promissory notes 6
proof-of-history (PoH) 36, 37
proof-of-stake (PoS) verification method 17, 35–37, 39, 41, 43, 51, 227
proof of work (POW) consensus algorithm 39, 43, 51, 57, 226, 227
psychological ownership of CBDC 83–98; analyses 92; cash payment *vs.* digital money 83–87; conceptual model *98*; construct measurement 92; emotions 87–88, 97; multicollinearity and common method bias 93–94, **93–94**; path coefficients 95–96, **95–96**; payment method and spending behavior 90–91; post-hoc sample and effect size determination 97, 104; research with Chinese participants 91–92; sampling 92; social gratification 88–89, 96, 97; structural model 94–95; touchability 89–90, 96
public discourse 25, 49, 54, 58, 172, 174
public-key encryption *see* asymmetric key encryption
push–pull–mooring (PPM) and switching behavior 105–122, *113*; analysis 117; application of 108; in digital currency 107–108; inertia 111; intention and willingness 116, 119; measurements 117; measurements model assessment 118–119, **118–119**; perceived convenience 110, 114–115; perceived risk 108–109, 114; perceived security 109–110, 114; perceived value 111–115, 119, 120; positive emotions 111, 115; research method 116–117, **117**; structural model assessment 119–121, **120**
Python 25, 50, 174

Qian, Y. 42
QR code 9, 106, 107, 110, 273; based mobile payment 107
Qualcomm 36
qualitative mixed-method approach 172
quality value 112
Qualtrix 151
Quorum 44

Raghubir, P. 90, 91
Raimundo, R. 186
Rakuten 272
Raneri, P. C. 145
Redshaw, J. 209
reliability and validity 93–94, **94**, 118–119, **118–119**
representative money 1, 5; coinage concept of 5
Republic of Marshall Islands 255; banking sector and legal system in 257–258; economy in 256–257; export–import trade in 255; mobile connections in 257; population in 256
reputation rating system 21
Reserve Bank of Australia 79
retail central bank digital currencies 42–45
retail payment: costs 46; system 42, 43, 46
Rigby, C. S. 144
Ringle, C. M. 96
Ripple Labs 38

Ripple payment network 37, 38
Roblox 137, 236–238, 245
Rochberg-Halton, E. W. 86
Rosário, A. 186
Rousseau, D. M. 86
Roussou, L. 196
routing attack 229
Rupp, K. 249
Ryan, R. M. 86, 144
'Ryoshi' 39

Sahlins, M. 246, 249
Saif Almuraqab, N. A. 190, 196
Salem, M. Z. 197
Sandbox (SAND) 41, 237, 239
Sarstedt, M. 96
Schilling, L. 53
Schwartz, David 37
Scrypt 16
secondary-line brands 205
Second Life 137
Sekniqi, Kevin 40
self-gratification 206
self-identity 86
Seligman, M. E. 88, 111
Sellars, Craig 36
semi-fungible tokens 17
sensory perception 85, 87, 90
Seo, Y. 143
Serravalle, F. 148
Seuring, S. 53
Seyal, A. H. 189
Shahzad, F. 197
Sharma, E. 83
Shelstad, W. J. 145
Shiba Inu (SHIB) 38–40
Shibarium 39
Shiba-Swap 39
Shimp, T. A. 170
Shiue, Y. C. 150
Shperling, Z. 86
Shu, S. B. 86
silver 1, 5, 6, 51
silver coins 5, 7–8
SIM card-based e-CNY wallets 49
Simmel, G. 2
Simon, M. 111
Singh, S. 3
single point of failure (SPOF) and third-party 228
Singles Day 137
Sirer, Emin Gün 40
SIX 77
smart consumerism 208, 210
smart contracts 17, 35, 37, 39–41, 43, 44, 133, 222, 223, 225–226, 265, 267
smartphones 54
Smart PLS software 92, 117, 153, 193
Smith, Adam 1
Snoop Dogg 38
Snow Crash (Neal) 236
social agreement 1, 7, 8, 10
social consensus 226
social currency in Metaverse 236–250; avocational payment 238–240; unit of account for money 243–249
social development 208
SocialFi 222
social gratification 85, 88–89, 96, 112, 113, 172, 176, 177, 182
social media platforms 192, 206
social resource theory 246–248
social status and money 88–89
social value 112
Society for Worldwide Interbank Financial Telecommunications (SWIFT) 8, 9, 42, 51, 106
sociological perspective of money 2–3
Solana (SOL) 36–37
Solidity language 80
Soman, D. 87, 90, 91
Soutar, G. N. 112
South African Reserve Bank 79
Sovereign Currency Act (2018) 255, 258
Srivastava, J. 90, 91
stablecoins *see* Tether (USDT)
State Theory of Money (Knapp) 2
Stephenson, Neal 236; *Snow Crash* 236
Straub, D. W. 188
subscriptions 167, 168
Suddendorf, T. 209
Sumerian civilization 4–5
Sumitomo Mitsui Financial Group 271
Sun, C. T. 150, 154
Sveriges Riksbank 6, 74
Swap.com 239
Sweeney, J. C. 112
Swiss National Bank 74, 76, 77
switching costs 107, 112
Sybil's attack 228
synthetic assets (Synths) 223
Synthetix Network Token (SNX) 223
Synthetix project 223
Szabo, Nick 16, 57

tampering and injection threat 228
Tan, E. L. P. 147

Tang, C. 111
Taobao 137, 166, 264
technical consensus 226
technological development 208
technology acceptance model (TAM) 188–189, 197
Tefertiller, A. C. 168
temporal junctures 209
Tenenhaus, M. 95
Tether (USDT) 16–17, 34, 36, 42, 105
third-party mobile payment 9, 106, 110; services 113, 189, 195, 196
third-party payment 58, 121, 209, 224, 263; apps 54, 84, 92, 106, 110–113, 115–117, 120, 121, 171, 190, 261; systems 106, 107, 109, 188
Thomala, L. 209
3D avatars 236, 237
3D NFTs 41
TikTok platform 54, 56, 58, 210
time banking experiment 240
Time Banking UK 240
time efforts in digital asset creation 244; favor 247–249; medium of exchange 245–246; social resource theory 246–247; store of value 244–245
time-effort social currency *see* social currency in Metaverse
Ting, C.-C. 151
tipping coins 170
tipping currency in live-stream commerce 166, 169–182; data analysis 174; data collection 172–173; emotions 171, 177, 180; flow theory 171; impulse spending 171–172; in-depth interview 173, 176–177, **178–179**, 180–181; likes by classification of category *175*; personal and social gratification 172; public engagement *176*; semi-structured interview 173; tipping and payment method 165–167, 170–171, 175, 181; word-cloud representation *175*
tipping tokens 169
Tmall 137, 166, 264
tokenization 17, 27, 130–131, 140
tokenized commercial real estate 17, 20
tokens 130–131
Tokyo University 39
touchability 85, 89–90, 96, 209
Traczyk, J. 111
transaction costs 46, 105, 107, 110, 115, 121, 188, 195
transparency of payment methods 44, 84, 90, 91, 109
'trapezitai' (ancient bankers) 6
Trevino, L. K. 147
trustlessness 51
trustless transactions 52
Tsinghua University 80
Twitch 168

UniSwap 223
University of Edinburgh 39
USDC 34, 37
US dollars 6–8, 36, 37
user-friendliness 186, 187, 189, 190
US Security and Exchange Commission (US SEC) 38, 139

validators 38
value-added activities 237, 238, 243, 244, 249
value chain 56
value for money 112, 205, 211–212
value propositions 34
van Evers, E. 145
Van Niekerk, A. 15, 16
variance inflation factor (VIF) 93, **93**
Venus initiative 77
Vidal-Tomás, D. 135
videography 46, 49
virtual assets 15, 17
virtual currency 57, 168
virtual gifts and donations 165–169, 171–174, 176, 177, 180–182, 247, 248
virtual goods 21
virtual reality (VR) 225, 230, 236
virtual world 40, 41, 137, 219, 227, 230, 233, 236, 248
Vohs, K. D. 156

Waan Aelon in Majel (WAM) 257
Wan, C. 171
Wang, J. 145, 266
Wang, Y. 196
Wang, Z. 44
wash trading 132
Web 3 25, 133, 221, 236
Weber, M. 2, 7
Webster, J. 147
WeChat 42, 50, 51, 116, 169, 170, 173, 189, 196
WeChat Pay 9, 107, 261, 263, 264, 267
Weeda, D. 145
weekly grocery spending 92

Wehrli, A. 106
Wenjuanxing 192
wholesale CBDC (wCBDC) 44, 45, 74
Wisselbank 6
word-of-mouth promotion 167
World Bank 222, 259
World Economic Forum's white paper 45
world reserve currency 7, 8

X-chain 40
Xie, J. 113
Xinbang 50, 173
XRP 37–38
XRP Ledger (XRPL) 37, 38
Xu, X. 172
Xu, Z. 111

Yahoo Auctions 272
Yahoo Shopping 272
Yakovenko, Anatoly 36
Yang, H. 206
Yao, Y. 109
Yi, Q. 21, 170, 245
Yin, J. 172
Yin, Maofan 'Ted' 40
'YOLO' (you only live once) mentality 206
Yoo, J. M. 151
YouTube 168
Yuga 133
YY 166, 167, 169

Zaleskiewicz, T. 111
Zeithaml, V. A. 112
Zelizer, V. A. 2, 3
Zendle, D. 147
Zhang, P. 52
Zhao, X. 117, 121
Zhou, K. 83–85
Zhou, X. 266
Zhu, D. H. 151

FSC
www.fsc.org
MIX
Papier | Fördert gute Waldnutzung
FSC® C083411

Kolibri 360 GmbH
Ferdinand-Jühlke-Straße 7
99095 Erfurt, Deutschland
produktsicherheit@kolibri360.de